Revolutionary Generation

Conrad Edick Wright

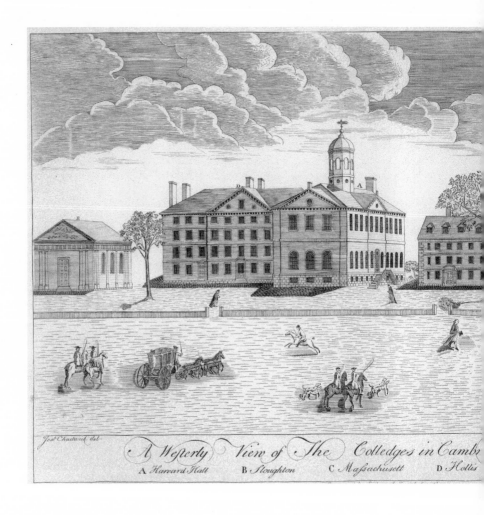

A Westerly View of The Colledges in Cambr
A *Harvard Hall*   B *Stoughton*   C *Massachusett*   D *Hollis*

REVOLUTIONARY GENERATION

Harvard Men and the Consequences of Independence

University of Massachusetts Press
Amherst and Boston

in association with
Massachusetts Historical Society
Boston

LC 2005007283
ISBN 1-55849-484-7

Designed by Dennis Anderson
Set in Monotype Bell by Binghamton Valley Composition
Printed and bound by The Maple-Vail Book Manufacturing Group

Library of Congress Cataloging-in-Publication Data

Wright, Conrad Edick.
Revolutionary generation : Harvard men and the consequences of independence /
Conrad Edick Wright.
    p. cm.
Includes bibliographical references and index.
ISBN 1-55849-484-7 (cloth : alk. paper)
1. Harvard University—Alumni and alumnae—Biography.
2. Harvard University—Alumni and alumnae—History.
3. United States—History—Revolution, 1775–1783—Social aspects.
4. United States—History—Revolution, 1775–1783—Influence.
5. United States—History—1783–1865—Biography.   I. Title.
LD2139.W75 2005
378.744'4—dc22

                    2005007283

British Library Cataloguing in Publication data are available.

This book is published with the support and cooperation of
the Massachusetts Historical Society.

For Mary

CONTENTS

ILLUSTRATIONS

ACKNOWLEDGMENTS

Revolutionary Generation: Harvard Men and the Consequences of Independence is in its own right the product of generations of work. John Langdon Sibley, at the time Harvard's librarian, began research for the series now known colloquially as *Sibley's Harvard Graduates* in the late 1850s, and without that magisterial work, now eighteen volumes long and still growing, this one would have been impossible. In 1985, when I took up my present position as editor of publications at the Massachusetts Historical Society, the series's publisher since 1933, the opportunity to follow in the footsteps of Sibley and his prolific successor, Clifford K. Shipton, was perhaps the job's greatest attraction. Since the publication of Sibley's first volume in 1873, it has grown to more than ten thousand pages of entries on nearly three thousand graduates, non-graduates, and honorary degree holders. We know more about the men who attended colonial Harvard College than we do about any other large group of American men, women, and children before the Revolution. I cannot overstate my debt to Sibley, Shipton, and all who assisted them.

Revolutionary Generation owes a particular debt to those involved with the final 213 pages of volume 17, Shipton's last, his entries on the class of 1771, and all of volume 18, entries for the classes of 1772 through 1774. Although my book repeats only occasional fragments of the prose of the individual entries, it depends heavily throughout on the research and judgments. I wrote about 100 of volume 18's 140 entries, but the work was in the best sense a collaboration. There are six names on the title page. Edward W. Hanson shared the writing with me, and we benefited from the assistance of four fine colleagues: Helen R. Kessler, Katheryn P. Viens, Donald J. S. Pattison, and Franklin A. Dorman. I owe thanks to all, especially to Ed Hanson, whose dedication to the project and deep knowledge of the sources relevant to the history of colonial New England prevented more mistakes than I like to admit. I am also grateful to the Society for permitting me to draw on my *Sibley* entries for this book.

Volume 18 acknowledges all the individuals and institutions whose efforts made it possible. I hope it will not seem churlish to repeat those thanks here only by referring to those remarks, which appear on pages xxxiii–xxxiv. As I did additional research for this book, many who helped on *Sibley* helped again, notably Harley Holden and Brian Sullivan of the Harvard University Archives and Ruth Quattlebaum of Phillips Academy, Andover. Patricia Cleary and Holly Heinzer shared some of their research discoveries with me, and I am grateful to each of them.

Colleagues, friends, and one relative helped by reading and commenting on parts or all of this book while it was still in manuscript. My special thanks go to John D. Burton, Ondine E. Le Blanc, Elisabeth Nichols, Mark A. Peterson, Laurel Thatcher Ulrich, and C. Conrad Wright. Classmate and novelist William Martin provided valuable advice and encouragement at important junctures in the project. Charles Capper directed me to writings on Ralph Waldo Emerson's "American Scholar" address, while Cathleene B. Hellier generously supplied information on dance in colonial America. At the Massachusetts Historical Society, friends and colleagues who provided assistance of various sorts include Anne Bentley, Anne Decker Cecere, Peter Drummey, Mary Fabiszewski, Carrie Foley, Nicholas Graham, Nancy Heywood, Brenda Lawson, Jennifer Shea, Jennifer Smith, and Celeste Walker. The members of my own department, Publication and Research Programs, helped in various ways, not least by covering for me during nine months of research leave over a span of approximately three years. Here my thanks go to Ondine Le Blanc, Erin Pipkin, Jean Powers, Seth Vose III, and Donald Yacovone. Kristin Lynch helped my work through her efforts to provide a clean copy of Stephen Peabody's journal. Seth Vose also promoted that effort through his transcription of the document.

The multipart research leave mentioned earlier, was a great boon to my work. Scholars not in teaching positions rarely benefit from sabbaticals, so I feel especially fortunate that the Massachusetts Historical Society provided me with one. Henry Lee, the president of the Society for many years, urged me to take time off, and when I seemed to be delaying the start of my leave, he pestered me to get on with it. The Society's Council voted me my time away, and one of its members, Bernard Bailyn, provided important encouragement that he may not remember. Louis Leonard Tucker, the Society's director from 1976 to 1997, was instrumental in developing a program of staff research leaves and in enabling the first of mine in 1997. William M. Fowler, Jr., the Society's present director, encouraged me to take the time I needed, resisted my attempts to defer my departure, and helped to cover for my absence while I was out. I am grateful to all.

A portion of chapter 2 has appeared in Laurel Thatcher Ulrich et al., eds., *Yards and Gates: Gender at Harvard and Radcliffe* (2004). This material reappears here by arrangement with that book's publisher, Palgrave Macmillan.

I am grateful to the following repositories for permission to quote materials in their collections: American Antiquarian Society; George J. Mitchell Department of Special Collections & Archives, Bowdoin College Library; Concord Free Public Library; Connecticut Historical Society; Dedham Historical Society; Fordham University Library; Harvard University Archives; Massachusetts Historical Society; New Hampshire Historical Society; Peabody Essex Museum; Phillips Academy, Andover; Rhode Island Historical Society; and Manuscripts and Archives Department, Yale University Library. I am indebted to the following repositories for permission to use images in their collections: Bowdoin College Art Museum; Concord Museum; Harvard University Archives; Harvard University Art Museums; Massachusetts Historical Society; Munson-Proctor-Williams Institute Museum of Art; Museum of Fine Arts, Boston; and Wheaton College. I am also grateful to James A. Henretta for permission to adapt a table of his to my own needs.

Finally, I owe thanks to my family: to C. Conrad and Elizabeth H. Wright for encouraging in their son a love of history and (in my father's case) for serving as a professional role model; to Abby and Betsy for understanding that their father needed to spend time on his book and for acceding in most instances without grumbling; and especially to Mary, my wife and partner in life for thirty years, whose support of all kinds I recognize inadequately through the dedication of this book.

Revolutionary Generation

INTRODUCTION

JONATHAN FRENCH was the first, born on January 30, 1740.[1] More than nineteen years later, on May 16, 1759, Sam Jennison came last.[2] Between French and Jennison there were 202 other boys, members of the Harvard College classes of 1771 through 1774, born over a span of nearly two decades.

This book traces the lives of the 204 members of these four Harvard classes, the last to graduate before the outbreak of the American Revolution. I call these men collectively Harvard's "revolutionary generation." My story takes them stage by stage through their lives, from birth and childhood through their college years to maturity, careers, marriage, and parenthood, then to old age and death.

What can the members of this "generation" have had in common? If more than nineteen years separated the youngest from the eldest, then surely their lives, their experiences, must have been wildly different.

In important respects they were. The subjects of this book entered college both as men and as boys. They came from wealthy families and from families of modest means, from countinghouses and from farmhouses. At the start of the war, some became loyalists, although many more were patriots. Some were in communion with the Church of England and a few were Universalists, although most adhered to one wing or another of the Congregationalist Standing Order which dominated colonial New England. They were the sons of doctors, lawyers, clergymen, teachers, sea captains, farmers, artisans, and merchants, and after school they followed an even wider choice of careers. In view of this diversity of backgrounds, beliefs, experiences, affiliations, and inclinations, what can they possibly have had in common with one another?

One might plausibly argue that the only attribute they all shared was that they attended the same college at about the same time. From varied backgrounds, perhaps they came to Cambridge for four years, studied subjects such as the classics, moral and natural philosophy, and oratory together, and then went their separate ways to adult lives and careers, leaving their college experiences far behind them.

If their common experiences were as limited as such an argument suggests, though, this book would never have been written. The two theses that underlie it are, first, that in most cases their lives exhibit a common structure, and second, that events during and shortly after college radically redirected the course of life for the boys and men of Harvard's revolutionary generation.

On one level, *Revolutionary Generation* is about growing up and growing old. The appendix to the book details an eight-stage social and psychological profile of the lives of most New England college men during the second half of the eighteenth century. This model underlies my depiction of Harvard's revolutionary generation. Readers with a systematic interest in human development may wish to turn first to this discussion before they encounter the collective biography at the heart of the book. For other readers, it suffices at the outset to say that I believe that most members of the classes of 1771 through 1774 followed a common course from birth to death. This path brought them from the complete dependence of infancy to adulthood, characterized by independence and responsibility for others, to the renewed dependence of old age.

On another level, though, the book is an account of the various ways in which a great event, the American Revolution, redirected many lives. Men who had entered college expecting to join a provincial elite discovered not long after graduation that, thanks to the war, the terms of the game had changed. At a peculiarly critical time for them, the members of the revolutionary generation faced a new set of challenges. In the final decades of the eighteenth century no less than at the start of the twenty-first, men in their late teens and early twenties had to make a series of important decisions: How will I earn my living? Where will I make my home? Whom will I marry? The answers to these three basic questions have been central to determining the shape of lives at many times and in many places. For men in the process of making such critical choices, the conflict had unavoidable consequences.

For timing mattered. As little as a year or two often made a great difference. Among college graduates, every year past commencement allowed more men to answer those three basic questions. Most men who had graduated in 1770 and before were already becoming settled in their adult lives when the war broke out. As for the boys and men who were still in college, members of the class of 1775 and subsequent years, they had not yet arrived at the point to decide these issues.

Do not conclude that the Revolution had the same consequences for every member of the generation. It did not. In general, for example, men who served in the military experienced more enduring effects from the war than those who did not, and loyalists, the losers, suffered more seriously for their views than those who won. After the conflict, though, it soon became apparent that to varying degrees it had affected everyone, civilians as well as veterans, winners as well as losers. New opportunities and new challenges awaited everyone, no matter what his wartime experience.

This book, then, tells how a small group of privileged young men adapted to the *novus ordo seclorum* of postrevolutionary America. And a new order of the ages it was for the members of these classes. No one was insulated against the events of the revolutionary years, and in many instances the consequences were profound.

Before the war, as Great Britain's imperial system began to feel the strains of mounting political tensions, provincial Harvard was a troubled place. Some of the school's difficulties were internal and others were external to it, but whatever their sources, the stresses of the day were a constant fact of life at prerevolutionary Harvard.

During the war, fully half the students bore arms at least briefly, and one-quarter put in extended military or naval duty. Those who did not serve nevertheless felt the effects of the conflict as friends and neighbors went off to war, inflation pervaded the American economy, rumors of enemy forces on the move brought fear to families and settlements loyal to either side, and actual combat destroyed civilian lives and property.

The war continued to shape events for the members of the college's revolutionary generation long after the guns fell silent. Many men who remained loyal to the crown found themselves thousands of miles from home, forced to invent new lives for themselves. Meanwhile, new responsibilities and new opportunities confronted the majority whose primary loyalties were to their community, state, and infant nation, not to a distant monarch. After wartime service as a civilian employee of the British army, for example, Thomas Aston Coffin set his course for the mother country, where he eventually became commissary general of Great Britain, the domestic chief supply officer for the British army.[3] At the same time, many of the subjects of this book played important roles in the creation of a new governmental order, and many more found that nationhood opened new career avenues. Fisher Ames, a four-term member of Congress;[4] John Trumbull, the nation's first college-educated painter and the preeminent artist of the Revolutionary War;[5] Tilly Merrick, who built and then lost a career in international commerce;[6] and Samuel Emery, the owner of a candle factory,[7] all followed callings that did not even exist in the American colonies when they attended college. Nothing in their experience as youths before college could have prepared Coffin, Ames, Trumbull, Merrick, Emery, or dozens of their schoolmates for the twists and turns of their adult lives.

It would be fatuous to assert that the members of the revolutionary generation were fully "representative" Americans of their era—any more than one could make the same claim for any other subset of society. At a time when college men were the exception, not the rule, former Harvard students benefited from advantages that most contemporaries could only envy. Before the Revolution, a college education opened doors into the professions, into polite society, into the highest circles of provincial power and wealth. Old school ties continued to assist young men on the make after the war, providing them with the best of opportunities.

And yet, for the most part, the responsibilities and opportunities that Harvard's revolutionary generation addressed after the war were not unique to college men, nor were the later life experiences of the subjects of this book. With the exception of the Congregational and Episcopal ministries, for example, none of the professions required a college education, although in many instances it was actively encouraged. Foreign trade was a possibility for any man with the required capital, contacts, and aptitude, no matter whether or not he had spent time struggling over the fine points of Greek grammar or the nature of the human mind's faculties. The frontier was open to anyone who had the wit, the courage, and the connections to exploit it, and college men monopolized none of these attributes.

In the late eighteenth century, there was nothing about a college education that inoculated the boys and men who received it against the events of their times. As long as we remember that a liberal education conferred some special advantages on those who were fortunate enough to acquire it, we can see on a personal level many of the consequences of the War for Independence. They are the subject of this book.

PROLOGUE

Alma Mater (September 8, 1836)

T HEY CAME by twos and threes at first, dim figures in the dark shadows
of a cloudy late summer morning dulled by the threat of rain. Soon,
their numbers grew. Now they were arriving by tens and twenties, dressed
in the male fashion of the day—black tailcoats, pantaloons of a light contrasting color, dark brimmed hats, canes. They had come from all quarters—
from Boston across the West Boston Bridge and through Cambridgeport,
from Lexington and Concord tracing the path British troops had taken in
the opposite direction on April 19, 1775, from Watertown past the man-
sions of old Tory Row, where Cambridge's loyalist elite had once lived. The
date was September 8, 1836, the day that Harvard University observed its
two hundredth anniversary.

The bicentennial procession returns to Harvard Yard from the meetinghouse of the First of
Parish, September 8, 1836. (*Harvard University, with the Procession of the Alumni from the
Church to the Pavillion, September 8, 1836,* by G. G. Smith. Engraving, 7.8 × 4.4 in. From
Josiah Quincy, *The History of Harvard University* [Cambridge, Mass., 1840], 1:frontispiece.)

Inside Harvard Yard, the trappings of celebration drove away the gloom of the weather. The undergraduates had adorned Harvard, University, and Dane halls with evergreen branches and garlands of flowers, and they had erected arches accented with floral chains and pine boughs over the Yard's three main entrances. More blossoms ornamented the college grounds. Behind gray granite University Hall, where there was a natural bowl, for $650 a committee of alumni had erected an enormous pavilion 150 feet long by 120 feet wide. Over its wooden frame they had stretched thousands of square yards of white sailcloth. At the pinnacle of this pagoda-like structure flew a huge white flag bearing the three books of the college's shield and in large capital letters on the opened pages its motto—VERITAS—truth. Inside, there were more blooms and evergreen boughs, arranged by the ladies of Cambridge under the direction of John W. Webster, a chemistry professor,[1] as well as tables to accommodate 1,500 diners.

By nine o'clock a chattering throng of men milled about in front of University Hall. Young graduates and old as well as other friends of the university, they gathered in clusters to exchange cheery greetings and reminiscences. Meanwhile, thirteen men carrying blank books passed from one knot to the next asking everyone for his signature.

At 9:45, twenty-seven-year-old Robert C. Winthrop, a graduate in the class of 1828 and the chief marshal of the day, began to organize the caravan that would transport the gathering a few hundred feet from the Yard to the new meetinghouse of the First Parish in Cambridge. Lean, aristocratic, born to command, Winthrop was a scion of the Massachusetts Bay Colony's first great family, a descendant of Governor John Winthrop. One day he would serve as the speaker of the United States House of Representatives. Undergraduates, a band, and assorted dignitaries took the first places in the double column. The main division, though, would be made up of alumni. Nearly seven hundred graduates had responded to the invitation to attend the festivities, about one-third of the college's living A.B.'s.

Winthrop began to call a roll of the classes. The earliest surviving graduate was former senator Paine Wingate, class of 1759, ninety-seven years old, of Stratham, New Hampshire. Wingate's health was too delicate to permit him to travel to Cambridge, however, so after a pause Winthrop resumed the roll with the class of 1763, the next with a living member. Still no one stepped forward, and Winthrop continued: "1764 . . . 1765 . . . 1766." In a few moments, he reached the classes that had graduated immediately before the outbreak of the American Revolution: "1771 . . . 1772 . . . 1773 . . . 1774." Finally, an alumnus shuffled forward. The stooped, frail frame was that of Samuel Emery. Eighty-five years old, Emery was one of only five living members of the class that had graduated sixty-two years before. He had traveled to Cambridge from Philadelphia, where he had resided for more than four decades.

After the classes of 1775 through 1836 had fallen into line by twos behind Emery, the procession set off for the meetinghouse of the First Parish. Erected only three years earlier after a division between the congregation's religious conservatives, who now gathered every Sunday in the Cambridge courthouse, and the liberals, or Unitarians, who worshiped here, the meetinghouse contained the community's largest auditorium. Harvard had contributed to the costs of construction in return for the right to use the building at commencement and on other festival occasions.

By the time the double column reached the sand-textured, carpenter Gothic façade of the wooden meetinghouse, the gallery, which wrapped around three sides of the auditorium, was already filled with the ladies of Cambridge and the surrounding towns. In the vanguard, the undergraduates divided to the right and left to allow their elders to pass between them. Soon, all 112 pews on the ground floor were occupied with dignitaries and aged graduates, perhaps five hundred of them, so the younger alumni and students stood, filling the center aisle, the two side aisles, the stage, and the stairways to the balcony.

Over the next three hours, Harvard honored its past. After a prayer (it lasted for seventeen minutes) by the Reverend Ezra Ripley of Concord, the senior clergyman in attendance, the meeting heard a professional choir sing the four verses of a new ode by Samuel Gilman. The Unitarian minister in Charleston, South Carolina, Gilman had written the piece, "Fair Harvard," for the anniversary under the pressure of time over thirteen frantic hours a day or two before. President Josiah Quincy took up most of the observance with an historical oration that lasted more than two hours. Then, after another prayer, the singing of the doxology, and a benediction, it was time to return two-by-two following a serpentine course to the pavilion for dinner. Once again, Winthrop called a roll of the classes. This time, when Emery stepped forward it was to a rolling thunder of applause.

Speech after speech, toast after toast filled the afternoon as the throng absorbed the happy glow of the occasion. "I never before dined with so large a company as I did that day," one young alumnus confided to his diary the next week, "and I never expect to again."[2]

When the dinner finally adjourned at eight o'clock after more than six hours, there was a final treat. The undergraduates had bathed the Yard in lights. On the façade of each hall its name was written in fiery lamps, along with its date of construction and a suitable inscription. Lanterns also decorated buildings outside the Yard, including the meetinghouse, whose tall Gothic windows glowed. On several of the heights outside the village, bonfires blazed. "It was brilliant, it was beautiful," one senior recalled.[3]

It had been a time for memories. A few days later, when Ezra Ripley's step-grandson found an opportunity to transcribe his reflections into his journal, his thoughts turned to the line of men who had wended their way to and from the meetinghouse. "Cambridge at any time is full of ghosts," Ralph Waldo Emerson wrote, "but on that day the anointed eye saw the crowd of spirits that mingled with the procession in the vacant spaces, year by year, as the classes proceeded; and then the far longer train of ghosts that followed the company, of the men that wore before us the college honors and the laurels of the state—the long, winding train reaching back into eternity."[4]

On such an occasion it was difficult not to compare the present with the past. How much had changed since Samuel Emery and his schoolmates, in knee breeches and buckled shoes, had crossed the Yard as students more than six decades before? And how different had the college, Cambridge, their world, their lives become from anything they could have imagined?[5]

1

FAMILY PRIDE

IT WAS a moving moment for Samuel Cooke, the birth of his first son, Samuel Jr., on March 29, 1752.[1] So affected was the new father, the pastor of the Congregational church in the Menotomy parish of Cambridge, that as he sat at the writing table in his handsome parsonage, he had to express how he felt.[2] An acrostic poem said it all:

> Save, Lord, this tender son of ours,
> A son whom thou didst give,
> May he not die in tender hours,
> Unto thy praise still live.
> Each day commended to thy care,
> Let him thy tender mercies share.
>
> Christ in his arms did infants take,
> Of saving grace did this partake.
> O earthly blessings needful shine,
> Keep from every hurtful snare,
> Ever guided by thy watchful care.[3]

It was a proud occasion—and one for apprehension, too. What would become of baby Samuel? What kind of person would he turn out to be? Would he have a long, productive life or would he die in infancy? Would he share his father's faith in God or would he abandon it? Would he be a leader of his community or a follower? Would he be tall or short, thin or fat, fair or dark, clever or stupid, kind or callous, honorable or contemptible?

Anxious parents at different times and in different places fret over the same concerns about a newborn son or daughter. Every infant's future, after all, is filled with possibilities, not certainties, an almost boundless range of options. There is no way to anticipate all of life's possibilities because there is no accurate way to predict the future. Ambitions are a different matter, though. They are the product of specific times and specific places, expressions of the hopes and dreams—the recognized opportunities—of a particular society and culture at a particular time.

Anxieties shaped the fears, but ambitions shaped the dreams of the parents of Samuel Cooke, Jr., and those of the other boys who eventually entered Harvard College as freshmen between 1767 and 1770—that is, as members of the the college's revolutionary generation. As the boys grew up, their parents envisioned the future for them, and the school was often an important part of the plan. Did it make sense to spend years preparing the boys for college? Everywhere they looked, there was evidence of the advantages of a liberal education. Some parents set their sights on Harvard College (or Cambridge College, as it was sometimes called) when their boys were still toddlers. In a few instances a college education did not seem feasible until a youth reached his twenties and became a young man. Whatever the case, the decision to prepare a son for college spoke volumes about a parent's hopes, dreams, and values.

For in New England in the mid-eighteenth century, higher learning had a specific social function. It prepared boys and young men for genteel leadership in a community in which most adult males had a rudimentary education but little more. Harvard and the other colleges of colonial New England were gateways to the region's upper reaches, places of status, respect, power, wealth, and refinement. Ambition ordinarily began at home. And its path often led through Harvard College.

IN ROXBURY, John Warren (Jack to his family and friends) was born in a cottage surrounded by more than fifty acres of fields and orchards, the son of a substantial yeoman and his wife.[4] John Eliot grew up among the urban artisans of Boston's North End calling his father's parsonage on the corner of Hanover and North Bennet streets home.[5] For John Trumbull, home was the finest house in rural Lebanon, Connecticut, a handsome two-story wooden Georgian structure encircled by lawns, kitchen gardens, and rolling acres of farmland.[6] Fisher Ames was born at the sign of the "Rising Sun" on High Street in Dedham in his family's tavern, a community landmark where neighbors and travelers gathered nightly in the great room, a low-beamed hall with sanded white oak floors and a massive hearth.[7]

The boys who were destined for Harvard's revolutionary generation came from a diversity of backgrounds. Born to parents who made a living in the field or the pulpit, in the workshop or the countinghouse, they were a testament to the allure of colonial Harvard for ambitious, talented students and their parents.

Who were the 204 members of Harvard's revolutionary generation? Most of the boys shared three important characteristics: local origins, family prominence, and age.

With very few exceptions they were, first of all, from New England's

Atlantic coast or not far inland. At an earlier time, particularly during the seventeenth century, when college-bound Americans had no practical alternative to Harvard without crossing the Atlantic, the school drew significantly from southern New England, the Middle Atlantic region, and the South, but no more. The establishment between 1693 and 1767 of eight other North American colleges—in Connecticut, western New Hampshire, Rhode Island, New York, New Jersey, Pennsylvania, and Virginia—had constricted the area from which Harvard ordinarily drew its student body. Only about three-fifths of the members of the college's classes of 1696 through 1699 came from Massachusetts or coastal New Hampshire; in the classes of 1771 through 1774, 98 percent called these areas home. Nearly 30 percent of the classes of 1696 through 1699 came from Connecticut; of the men of Harvard's revolutionary generation, only two came from that colony.[8] Only two members of the revolutionary generation, one from St. Eustatius in the Caribbean,[9] the other from Annapolis, Nova Scotia,[10] came from outside New England.[11]

In most cases, students from the classes of the early 1770s were also the sons of men of some (usually local) prominence. The ladder that Harvard extended into the upper levels of colonial society reached not from the lowest orders but from somewhere above the middle. Although only a few students came from the most elevated ranks of colonial society—sons of provincial leaders such as Trumbull, whose father, Jonathan, was the governor of Connecticut, and Eliot, whose sire, Andrew, the pastor of Boston's New North Church, was a member of both of Harvard's governing bodies, the Corporation and the Board of Overseers—most of the others could point with pride to their fathers' standing within their home communities.

The typical student was the son of a leading citizen of a mature agricultural or market town, often a farmer, artisan, or merchant who was also a deacon or a selectman, and a mother who performed the traditional tasks of the eighteenth-century homemaker: cooking, cleaning, spinning, sewing, gardening, child care, and running a household that might include servants and even slaves as well as blood relatives. Most often, the father had not attended college: fewer than one in four students had followed his father to Harvard.[12] Like Levi Lincoln of Hingham, whose father, Enoch, was a respected farmer and glazier as well as a selectman and representative to the General Court,[13] or Thomas Aston Coffin, whose father, William, was a successful Boston importer, most of the boys came from families of substance and local influence. Many times, a father who worked with his hands and had his neighbors' esteem looked to college to open up a more refined way of life for his son.[14]

Finally, despite considerable range from eldest to youngest, the great majority of the members of the classes of 1771 through 1774 were actually of about the same age. Most were born in the early or mid-1750s and entered college in their mid-teens. Of the 204 members of the revolutionary generation, 167 were teenagers at matriculation, and nearly two-thirds were between the ages of fourteen and seventeen.[15]

There were exceptions to the usual age pattern. Some students were no longer boys but men. They had begun other careers before turning to college. Many of these students had answered a late call to the ministry. Jonathan French was a sergeant at Castle William in Boston Harbor, where the military chaplains taught him enough Latin and Greek to qualify for admission.[16] Daniel Chaplin was living with his parents in Rowley, where he helped his father work the family farm before he entered Dummer Academy in his early twenties to prepare for college.[17] Joshua Armsby entered from Medfield, where he helped his parents work a small farm.[18] Fewer than one-seventh of the members of the revolutionary generation, however, thirty men, entered college after the age of nineteen.[19]

At the other extreme, only fifteen boys were younger than fourteen. The youngest of all were Sam Jennison and Fisher Ames, both members of the class of 1774. Sam was only eleven years, three months old, the son of a rural doctor, when he matriculated. Academically ready for college, he was nevertheless still a young boy in a teenagers' world, less than half the age of his year's oldest entering freshman. By the same token, Fisher, who entered at twelve years, four months, the son of a widowed mother, was as capable a student as the best of his classmates but not old enough to be included in their extracurricular activities. Too young to get into mischief with their classmates, both boys would have to wait a few years for social acceptance. In every other respect, though, their prospects could not have seemed brighter.

Most of the members of the revolutionary generation were similar to one another, however, in local origin, family background, and age. They came to Cambridge with common objectives: to refine God-given talents, make a comfortable living, and earn a respected place in polite society. Generations of students had followed the same course, often using the college as a stepping-stone from local esteem to provincial prominence, from a good income on the land or at a trade to a better one in a profession or in commerce.

THE PATH to Harvard began in infancy at home, then led to common school and either to grammar school or to private tutoring before it was time to decide whether or not to attend college.

Individual childhoods in colonial New England are ordinarily difficult to reconstruct in detail, fragmentary as the surviving evidence usually is. Crises and catastrophes dominate what little information survives about the early lives of the members of Harvard's revolutionary generation. John Trumbull, who wrote a book-length memoir in the early 1840s, left the most detailed account of his first years, but even he devoted only a few paragraphs to early childhood. Seizures at nine months threatened his survival, and at five years he permanently damaged the optic nerve in his left eye when he fell down a flight of stairs.[20]

For the great majority of boys who did not suffer such traumas, their unrecorded early lives must have followed the common pattern of the day. Child-raising practices in colonial New England were on the cusp of an important transformation at mid-century, and in the early 1750s young boys experienced a mélange of old ways and new. Restrictive swaddling began to go out of fashion, as did the use of confining cradles and walking stools that forced a young child to stand upright, sometimes for hours. In dress and in discipline, increased freedom replaced physical coercion, although parents still taught their children to defer to their elders.[21]

Most of the boys of Harvard's revolutionary generation, children of caring mothers and fathers, grew up in nurturing families. In order to prepare for the challenges of advanced education and adult life, in order to grow up strong and honest, a child needed to mature mentally, morally, and emotionally as well as physically. Like young roses, they required tender cultivation. Boys and girls were malleable in the hands of caring yet firm mothers and fathers intent on gaining the best for their children. In contrast to the harsh disciplinary methods of an earlier age, parental practices in the families of most of the boys probably tried to leaven authority with love and compassion.[22]

Education—religious and moral as well as secular—was every parent's duty, and in the middle of the eighteenth century, instruction began early at home, sometimes supplemented by a dame school run by a woman in the neighborhood. Conscientious parents improved even the youngest child's free moments with snatches of moral guidance and scriptural wisdom. Hornbooks and primers introduced young children beginning their lessons to letters and simple words before the age of six. Elementary readers, catechisms, and the Bible taught religious and moral tenets. "In Adam's fall, we sinned all," admonished the *New England Primer*.[23]

Every boy achieved two important mileposts at age six or seven. The first was called "breeching." Until that age, boys and girls wore very similar clothes, long robes that fell to the floor. Only the shape of the collar distinguished a boy's robe from one his sister might wear. Boys traded in their robes for breeches, shirt, waistcoat, and jacket when they were ready to

Thomas Aston Coffin, about age four, in 1758. This painting by John Singleton Copley, colonial Boston's most important portraitist, shows Coffin before breeching. (*Thomas Aston Coffin* [1758], by John Singleton Copley. Oil on canvas, 50 × 40 in. Munson-Williams-Proctor Institute, Museum of Art, Utica, N.Y., 58.1.)

begin to learn the role of adult males.[24] Common school, the second mile-post, began at about the same age.

For its time, eighteenth-century New England was an extraordinarily literate place, a society of readers and writers, although many of the region's residents still possessed relatively crude skills. The simplest measure of literacy is the ability to sign one's name, and circa 1760, four-fifths of the New England men who left wills to be probated signed them.[25] Common schools were the reason for literacy's wide reach.

Common schools—also known as English or petty schools—taught simple, basic skills. In Massachusetts, where these schools were almost universal, a law adopted in 1647 required every community of fifty or more families to "appoint one within their town to teach all such children as shall resort to him to write and read."[26] Although the act made no demands on the colony's residents actually to send their children to the schools it required most towns to provide, almost every boy and girl attended at least intermittently. When Fisher Ames took his first lessons at age six in the English school in Dedham, he must have had plenty of company.[27]

Reading was the most important subject in colonial New England's elementary schools, but writing and ciphering also received attention. One objective for each student was the ability to function in society. Because God's revelation was written in the Bible, a second goal of at least equal weight was to read His word in the scriptures. Young students took several years to advance from hornbooks to primers, syllabaries, spellers, grammar books, readers, catechisms, and the Bible. Meanwhile, texts such as *Arithmetick Vulgar and Decimal* by Isaac Greenwood, Harvard's Hollis Professor of Mathematics and Natural and Experimental Philosophy from 1727 to 1738, introduced rules for solving numerical problems as well as examples to work.[28]

By the standards of the eighteenth century, a common-school education was enough to achieve a working level of literacy and numeracy. Shopkeepers, tradesmen, farmers, and their spouses could get by with no more knowledge than such schools provided, and the spiritual needs of the day were also satisfied as long as a sincere believer could manage to read the Bible and perhaps a few other standard works of faith and inspiration. A girl's education typically ended with the completion of common school. But was a petty-school education enough to meet the goals of a talented and ambitious boy and his parents?

At the end of petty school, New England boys and their families faced a life decision. If they chose to conclude formal schooling at this point—and most of them did—the plow, the workman's bench, and the small retail shop each offered a worthwhile calling. Common-school graduates as young as nine or ten committed themselves to such livelihoods if they determined not to continue their formal education.

Boys who yearned for more in life, however, probably needed a college education. And before entering college they faced four or more years of grammar school, where they would acquire the classical prerequisites of higher learning. For many students it must have been a difficult decision. To make it wisely, they needed to understand what a liberal education could do for them.

ON THE EVE of the American Revolution there was nothing routine about attending college. According to one plausible estimate, at the outbreak of the war only 2,500 to 3,000 living Americans in a population of about 2.2 million—roughly one-tenth of 1 percent—had received any college education at all.[29] All of them were men—the first colleges did not begin to admit women until the 1830s[30]—and most of them had achieved a measure of local reputation and influence at the very least. College men were a select and honored group in the 1760s and 1770s, the sort of community leaders to whom neighbors were likely to turn for service as deacons, selectmen, town meeting moderators, and provincial legislators. For a family with high hopes for a talented young son, college was often an important way station.

Nowhere in the American colonies was the value of a liberal education more firmly established than in eastern Massachusetts. College men, a circle of intimates who guided the settlers along their chosen path, had provided much of the colony's leadership since the early seventeenth century. To be sure, college training was not the norm even here. Nevertheless, in the early 1760s, when many of the families of the boys who were to belong to Harvard's revolutionary generation were beginning to consider whether or not to pursue advanced learning, higher education had deeper roots in eastern Massachusetts than anywhere else in British North America.

The Puritan founders of the Massachusetts Bay Colony had believed from the outset that their community needed a college. When the colony's Great and General Court established Harvard in 1636, it was in order to ensure the Bible Commonwealth a learned clergy. The college was never exclusively a religious seminary, however, even at first, and by the middle of the eighteenth century, only a modest minority of its graduates went on to the ministry. In the 1760s and 1770s, no less than in the 1630s and 1640s, by preparing the best and the brightest of provincial society for community leadership, the college continued to serve an important public role.

Boys in their mid-teens before the Revolution were at a critical age whether or not they aspired to higher education. Most entering freshmen were about the same age as beginning craft apprentices, and if they followed traditional paths, they would probably end up on a farm or in one of the trades.[31] Instead of fitting themselves for careers as yeomen or printers or blacksmiths or tanners, though, beginning collegians were entering an apprenticeship of a different sort.[32]

If he did not already know the customary career paths open to Harvard men, all a student considering college had to do was to look around. He could predict his future through the lives of the college's alumni. Harvard counted more than one thousand living graduates in the 1760s, and a substantial majority of them were neighbors, residents of the same Massachusetts communities that provided most of the entering students in the late 1760s and early 1770s. Of the 1,133 living Harvard A.B.'s in mid-August 1767, when the members of the class of 1771 set off for Cambridge to begin their freshman year, about half lived in the eastern Massachusetts counties of Essex, Middlesex, and Suffolk, and another quarter lived elsewhere in the colony.[33] As a proportion of the population of these counties and of the province as a whole, their numbers were still modest—about half of 1 percent of the three eastern counties and about one-third of 1 percent of the province.[34] But the concentration of college men in the three eastern counties of Massachusetts was undoubtedly greater than in any other area of comparable size in British North America, and Harvard graduates held a prominence in the life of the Bay Colony far beyond what numbers alone might have dictated.

By almost any standard, Harvard men stood at the pinnacle of provincial Massachusetts society. Occupation, political power, wealth—whatever the measure, Harvard men had a disproportionate influence over the affairs of the colony.

In the 1760s Harvard graduates followed nearly a score of different careers. There were farmers and surveyors, soldiers and sea captains, merchants and government officials. But it was in the three learned professions of colonial Massachusetts—the ministry, the law, and medicine—that the college's standing was the most apparent and its sway the most nearly complete. In August 1767 more than half of Harvard's living graduates followed one of these three callings, and many of the tenth who were teachers were actually in the classroom only temporarily while they studied for one of the triumvirate of learned professions.[35] For reasons that had relatively little to do with curriculum, the liberal education that the college provided was a valuable (in some cases an almost indispensable) preparation for professional standing.

At the time, the three professions adhered to different educational standards. At the very least, a college education was an advantage, and in the case of the Congregational ministry, in all but a few atypical instances it was a practical requirement. In 1767 Massachusetts counted 291 ordained and settled Congregational ministers. All but 13 were college graduates—most of those who had not attended college served Indian congregations—and 215 (nearly three-quarters) had attended Harvard.[36]

Of the professions in colonial Massachusetts, the ministry had the closest ties to higher education and to Harvard.[37] The college dominated the colony's ministry, and in turn the ministers of Massachusetts dominated the college. Congregational clergymen served almost every town in the province—small, rural, and isolated settlements as well as urban places—and most of these men were Harvard graduates, a fine-meshed net of alumni stretching from one end of the colony to the other. So comprehensive was the web of ministers that almost every resident of Massachusetts must have known at least one college man, and most must have known at least one graduate of Harvard. By tradition rarely breached, the president of Harvard College was a clergyman, called from a successful ministry to administer the school and prepare the rising generation of community leaders. Some of the professors were also ordained. Moreover, most of the junior members of the faculty—called tutors—aspired to the ministry. Between the late 1760s and the mid-1770s, many of the tutors who taught the members of the college's revolutionary generation—for example, Joseph Willard and Isaac Smith—spent their Sundays in the pulpits of eastern Massachusetts, where they practiced their preaching and stood as candidates for permanent positions.[38]

Because it was possible to enter the law and medicine, both fields requiring apprenticeships with experienced practitioners, without a college education, Harvard did not exert the same overwhelming dominance in the province over these callings that it held over the ministry of Massachusetts. Nevertheless, on the eve of the American Revolution, the school's presence in each profession was formidable. In 1767 four of the five Superior Court judges in Massachusetts were alumni of the college, and eight years later, in 1775, of eighty-one lawyers in Massachusetts, fifty-nine were Harvard men.[39] Of twenty-two doctors active in Boston in 1767, ten were graduates of the college.[40]

Professional acceptance meant admission into a cosmopolitan community of brother practitioners. In private meetings, public gatherings, chance encounters, and regular correspondence, the members of each profession gossiped, advised one another, provided moral and emotional support at times of stress and crisis, and generally maintained a spirit of fraternity toward one another. Each of the professions was an exclusive club, and a young man who traveled in one of these circles knew that he had arrived socially as well as occupationally.[41]

Outside of the professions, the most promising occupational avenue to social prominence in provincial Massachusetts led through commerce.[42] Because a large proportion of merchants learned their business on the job without the benefit of college training, no one wondered at prominent traders who had not spent time in Cambridge.[43] Nevertheless, Harvard men had an important place in Boston's commercial community on the eve of the war. Of 438 merchants active in Boston in the 1760s and early 1770s, 62 (nearly one-seventh) were graduates of the college.[44]

Occupational prominence led readily to political influence in colonial Massachusetts. By custom, provincial ministers stayed aloof from public office, either elective or appointed. The same was not true of doctors and lawyers, however, to say nothing of leading merchants. Here the province found much of its civic elite. It follows that if Harvard men were leaders of Massachusetts's professional and commercial communities, then many of them must have been well placed to acquire political influence as well.

As long as Massachusetts was a crown colony, the British monarch and his ministers retained the right to bestow the governorship. For the most part, this meant that before the Revolution, the colony's chief executive was a British placeman, a supporter of the prime minister whose loyalty earned him a term in a lucrative and prestigious office. Since the governor's chair was filled in London as a reward for political services rendered, provincials were rarely in a position to compete for preference at the most elevated level. During the years leading up to the war, only one American, Thomas Hutchinson, a graduate of Harvard with the class of 1727, spent time in the governor's office.

Apart from the highest office in the colonial administration, though, the seats of civic power were often available to Americans. The higher the post in Massachusetts, in fact, the more likely it was that the occupant had graduated from Cambridge College. Each year the lower house of the colony's legislature nominated candidates for the upper house, the Provincial Council. In May 1767, of the twenty-eight men the lower body proposed, twelve were Harvard graduates.[45] The lower house itself was a preserve of Harvard men. Although the great majority of the members were not graduates of the college, the leadership of the house was disproportionately in their hands: at mid-century, more than half of the Harvard alumni in the house served in the leadership, but only about one-eighth of those who had not attended college.[46] College men were also more likely than others to hold the reins of local government. It was the rare town that filled all of its most important offices—such posts as selectman, town meeting moderator, and treasurer—with college men, but graduates were much more likely to take up high local responsibilities at a young age than non-graduates.[47]

Relative wealth complemented the disproportionate occupational prestige and political influence of the college's alumni during the decade before the start of the American Revolution. Not all graduates were wealthy, and the wealthy men of provincial Massachusetts were not all Harvard graduates. Nevertheless, the two groups intersected so substantially that it was impossible not to notice the conjunction.

More of the most affluent residents of Massachusetts lived in Boston than anywhere else, and it was here that the convergence of wealth and higher education was the most apparent. When the local tax assessors surveyed Boston in 1771, they documented how well off as a group the alumni were. Just over half the graduates whom they assessed fell within the top fifth of the town's taxpayers, including four of the seven wealthiest. Only about one-eighth of alumni taxpayers were listed in the bottom half of Boston's assessment rolls.[48]

By British standards, affluent and genteel provincials in the 1760s were distinctly minor notables, modest targets for aspiring boys. In his old age, John Adams, a 1755 graduate of the college, recalled to Thomas Jefferson that in his youth the height of ambition was to "be worth ten thousand pounds Sterling, ride in a Chariot, be Colonel of a Regiment of Militia and hold a seat in his Majesty's Council. No Mans imagination aspired to any thing higher beneath the Skies."[49] Massachusetts had no aristocracy, nor even anyone to compare with the great planters of the colonial South and the Caribbean, although by mid-century a few wealthy Bostonians were beginning to build impressive country estates in nearby communities such as Medford, Milton, and Cambridge. In England at the time country gentlemen might lead lives of leisure, but in New England higher education did not come with an independent income. With very few exceptions, prominent New Englanders had to work for their bread, not live off of inheritances. Outside the largest communities, even the most respected gentlemen—including college-educated ministers, lawyers, and doctors—very often worked a farm as well as practicing a profession. Nevertheless, Harvardians who earned or inherited places of influence in the region's social order could anticipate local respect and honor.

It would have been difficult to argue in the 1760s that higher education actually caused the prominence that so many Harvard men enjoyed, but it was not hard to recognize a correlation between the two. Even though a Harvard education did not guarantee a brilliant career, public influence, or affluence, no one who was capable enough to consider a college education could have failed to notice the relationship.

THE PROSPECT of occupational prominence, political power, and wealth might have been enough in itself to lure a full class of incoming freshmen to the college each August, but a Harvard education offered two further attractions: an opportunity to acquire the social graces, the skills that seemed to come naturally to a gentleman but actually required conscious cultivation, and entrée into the most fashionable drawing rooms of Boston, Massachusetts, and New England. Gentility implied higher education. As John Adams explained, when he used the word "gentleman" he meant not "the rich or the poor, the high-born or the low-born," but "all . . . who have received a liberal education."[50] Without the manners of a gentleman, no one could ascend to the highest levels of colonial society. To be sure, even a Harvard education was insufficient to provide every would-be gentleman with a refined manner suitable for polite society. Many of the college's Eliza Doolittles arrived at school too rough-hewn and insecure to advance to the very top of the social ladder, but even they could hope to rise a few rungs. Where better than at Harvard to acquire some polish?

When John Adams's great-grandson Henry, a graduate in the Harvard class of 1858, looked back on the education he received in Cambridge, he recognized the college as "a mild and liberal school, which sent young men into the world with all they needed to make respectable citizens, and something of what they wanted to make them useful ones." Harvard's governors "had given to the College a character of moderation, balance, judgment, restraint, what the French call *mesure*; excellent traits, which the College attained with singular success, so that its graduates could commonly be recognized by the stamp."[51] Nearly a century earlier, when the members of the revolutionary generation occupied the dormitory rooms in Massachusetts and Hollis halls where the men of the class of 1858 would live one day, Harvard was already charting the educational road that Henry Adams eventually traveled as an undergraduate.

The mildness and moderation of a Harvard education were no recommendation as far as Henry was concerned in the 1850s. He found the college intellectually arid. In the late 1760s, however, in the eyes of many candidates for admission and their families, these attributes were an attraction, perhaps the best reason to go to the effort and expense of a college education.

Since the late seventeenth century, Boston and its environs had been home to a small but growing community of influential men and women whose role models were England's rural gentry and urban mercantile establishment. One may conveniently date the emergence of this circle with the founding in 1686 of Boston's King's Chapel, the first Anglican church in Puritan Massachusetts, although genteel ambitions here were certainly never exclusively the province of adherents to the Church of England. In religion, aspiring members of eastern New England's gentry and mercantile orders were usually either Anglican or moderate Congregationalists of a variety often identified in the eighteenth century with Boston's Brattle Street Church.[52] In matters of fashion, they dressed and styled their hair according to the dictates of the best-informed purveyors of British taste, albeit often a year or two out of date. In architecture, they followed Georgian principles of restraint, moderation, and balance. Their furniture was Queen Anne and Chippendale, their cups and saucers were of porcelain, their manners came from instruction manuals such as John Locke's *Some Thoughts Concerning Education.*[53]

This way of life had not spread uniformly throughout New England in the years immediately proceeding the American Revolution. Although many clergymen, as isolated emissaries of culture in rural parishes across the region, practiced the polished arts that they had learned in college when they were not plowing their fields or milking their cows, for the most part gentle manners and mores were the domain of town life. In Boston, Newport, Salem, Newburyport, and Portsmouth, as well as in a handful of smaller ports and inland towns, there was a critical mass of men and women of taste; but throughout the rest of New England, even large, long-settled farming communities lacked a sufficient concentration of gentlemen and gentlewomen to sustain a proper circle of refinement. Before the war, most lawyers, doctors, merchants, and their families—who together with the clergy and their families constituted the majority of New England's gentlefolk—were urban as well as urbane.[54]

In their own eyes, and in the eyes of their contemporaries, too, genteel New Englanders were an order set apart from the rest of colonial society. Indeed, the manners they adopted, the styles they affected, the excesses they countenanced all served to draw a line between themselves and their less polished neighbors.

College in this context was a finishing school where, according to Benjamin Franklin, "for want of a suitable Genius" the students learned "little more than to carry themselves handsomely, and enter a Room genteely."[55] Very little in the curriculum of the colonial colleges was of immediate practical benefit. Most of the staples of the course of study (the classics, natural philosophy, moral philosophy, rhetoric, belles lettres) and the unofficial, elective subjects (notably French, etiquette, and dance) that many students pursued on their own time with private instructors for extra fees refined the mind and opened them to the wider world of learning, both humane and professional, but how much help were they in the day-to-day pursuits of tilling a field or drawing up a will or curing the croup? To men of parts, however, the cultivated community leaders who issued from Harvard and the other colonial colleges each commencement day, they were essential marks of gentility, ways to identify men of quality.

EVERY MORNING in the late 1760s except Sunday, through rain, snow, sleet, and heat, Eliphalet Pearson trudged between three and four miles along twisting country roads, past the barns and pastures of his neighbors, from his father's farm in Byfield to a small, two-room red-clapboard schoolhouse in the northeast corner of the parish, a precinct of the town of Newbury.[56] As he walked along, he reviewed his lessons to himself. Pearson was one of the most promising students at a new institution, Dummer Academy. The school, established only a few years earlier in 1763, had but one objective—to prepare boys for college.[57]

Tall and gangly, Eliphalet was a farmer's son. If he had been born a few years earlier than his June 1752 birthday, perhaps he would have followed his father's calling. Academically gifted, though, he had demonstrated his talents to those who knew him. Dummer Academy opened new possibilities for a promising boy such as Eliphalet, and he had seized them.

In his early teens, Pearson had faced an important decision and answered yes. Was it worth the cost—not only in tuition and fees but also in forgone earnings—to devote years to preparing for and attending college?[58]

Every family considering higher education for a son had to address the same four questions: Was he capable of the work? Was he sufficiently diligent to do it? Did he need a college education for the career he hoped to pursue? Could the family afford the sacrifice? Aptitude, industry, aspirations, family finances—they all contributed to the decision. There was no point in wasting the time and money of a scholar who could not or would not do the necessary work. Nor did it usually make sense to educate a candidate for college if his heart led him to the plow or the workbench. As for the cost, not only was there tuition to weigh, but also a family needed to be able to spare the labor of its teenage son.

If higher education was in a boy's future, then he had a choice of two paths leading from common school to college. Like Pearson, he could attend a secondary school—in many towns simply an extension of the common school and taught by the same master. In Roxbury, Massachusetts, in 1770, for example, the one-room schoolhouse the town's Latin School occupied sheltered eighty-seven pupils, of whom only nine were sufficiently advanced actually to be studying Latin.[59] Or there was the alternative to school—private tutoring, usually in the study of a nearby minister.

Surviving records are so fragmentary that there is no way to be certain which course most members of Harvard's revolutionary generation followed. It is clear, though, that both paths were well worn. Pearson's school, Dummer Academy, trained thirty-nine members (nearly one-fifth) of the classes of 1771 through 1774; Boston Latin School prepared another twenty-nine (almost one-seventh). Roxbury Latin School as well as the grammar schools in communities such as Ipswich, Salem, Portsmouth, Cambridge, and Lebanon, Connecticut, each added one or more boys. The larger institutions attracted students from a distance who boarded with nearby families as well as local boys, like Pearson, who could walk to class each day. Eliphalet's contemporaries at Dummer included boys from as far to the south as Boston and as far to the north as Greenland, New Hampshire, a neighbor of Portsmouth;[60] Winthrop Sargent, whose parents lived in Gloucester, more than twenty miles from Boston, stayed with a family in the metropolis when he attended Boston Latin School.[61] Meanwhile, Levi Lincoln read for college at home in Hingham with his minister and the town's schoolteacher; Fisher Ames studied with the Reverend Jason Haven of Dedham; "having thots of sending him to College if Incouragement appears," the Reverend David Hall of Sutton sent his son Joseph to study with an uncle;[62] and Sam Jennison, his brother William,[63] and his neighbor Timothy Jones[64] all studied with their minister, the Reverend Amariah Frost of the Second Parish in Mendon.[65]

Whichever path a student followed, with only minor variations the course of study was the same: Latin, augmented by a little Greek. At the Boston Latin School, which dedicated a total of seven years to the classics, each class sat by year on long wooden benches, or forms, and devoted most of its attention to Latin. Memorization filled most of every year, especially at first. Declensions, conjugations, vocabulary building, and grammar were the order of the day for the youngest classes, leavened by readings in Aesop's fables. Masters often expected their charges to memorize verbatim entire volumes of Latin grammar, such as Ezekiel Cheever's *Short Introduction to the Latin Tongue*. More of the same took up the following year. The third year in the classical curriculum brought Eutropius and more grammar as well as a Latin reader by John Clarke, a British disciple of John Locke. By the fourth year, Eutropius, Clarke, Caesar's *Commentaries*, and beginning efforts at composition filled the curriculum. Eventually, the upper three classes added Tully, Virgil, and enough Greek to attempt Xenophon and Homer.[66] Because the college did not question candidates for admission on mathematics, Boston Latin School saw no reason to teach the subject. It taught to the test. Instructors elsewhere who did teach mathematics followed the same pedagogical practices that the common schools employed: textbooks taught general rules, followed them up with examples, then provided problems to test a student's comprehension.[67] Nor was there any place in the Boston Latin School curriculum for such modern subjects as English, French, and the natural sciences.

In the end, the education a student received was only as good as his instructor. Several teachers in the 1760s developed such strong reputations that students traveled long distances to prepare for college with them. John Trumbull needed only to cross the town green from his house to a two-story brick school building in Lebanon, Connecticut, to study with one of the most highly regarded teachers, Nathan Tisdale, a 1749 graduate of Harvard, but some boys traveled to the small town from as far away as the Caribbean, drawn by the instructor's fame.[68] John "Old Gaffer" Lovell of the Harvard class of 1728 effectively trained generations of candidates for college in the Boston Latin School's one-story brick building at the same time that he terrorized them with his harsh discipline.[69] Sixty years after John Bradford, one of Lovell's best students, escaped Boston Latin School, he still awoke sometimes "in the middle of the night, with tears trickling down his cheeks, smarting under the castigation" of his teacher.[70] And then there was Samuel Moody, a graduate with the Harvard class of 1746, the first master of Dummer Academy. Kindly, scholarly, and a superb instructor, Moody took up teaching after he determined that he was too meek to preach twice each Sunday. For three years beginning in 1760, York, Maine, Moody's hometown, employed him to run the local school. In 1763, though, when the trustees of the new academy in Byfield sought a master, he was the unanimous choice. Each day, eccentrically clad in a long green flannel robe and a tasseled smoking cap, he taught the classics and exhorted his students to be clean and to exercise. Unlike Lovell, who was quick with the ferule, Moody never beat his boys. Encouragement brought better results than fear, he believed, and Moody's compassion won him the enduring affection of his students.[71]

BY THE TIME that college-bound boys were ready for Tisdale, Lovell, Moody, or some other instructor, they were also beginning to slip the chains that bound them closely to their parents. Once they reached their teens, they had to learn how to be independent. Boys and parents alike recognized that childhood was drawing to a close.

The changing relationship between parent and child was most obvious in cases when a boy had to leave home to prepare for college. Eliphalet Pearson might be able to walk between home and school every day, but Sammy Phillips, whose parents lived in Andover, had to board with a family in Byfield in order to attend Dummer Academy. Sammy was his parents' only surviving child, and a close connection held them together. It was not easy for Samuel Phillips, Sr., a merchant, and his wife, Elizabeth, to be apart from their son. They worried about his health and happiness, and at times Sammy also struggled with the separation.[72]

Sammy and his parents corresponded from time to time while he was at the academy, and a number of their letters have survived. The boy's notes to his parents bubble with news of events at school, reports on his health, and requests for pens, paper, a ribbon for his queue, and money.[73] When it was Samuel and Elizabeth Phillips's turn to write, their letters reflected the uncertainties of a father and mother who worried that their son was not quite ready to take care of himself. Sometimes their advice to him was practical: "Be Carefull of your Cloaths Dont wear them in the weat if you weat yr Linen it will take of the Gloss" and "Be carefull of your things But Especialy carefull of your time."[74] On other occasions their concerns were more spiritual: "Dont forgit to Give your self to God Every night before you Sleep" and "be all ways found in the Way of God if you are with God he will be with you But if you forsake him he will forsake you."[75] Before they knew it, their son would be a grown man. The days were getting short. They did not have much time left to prepare him for adulthood.

Even when a boy stayed at home before college, still in daily touch with his parents, these years could be difficult for everyone. Since in most cases a boy's father had not attended college, his son might be preparing for a cosmopolitan life of greater status than he himself had achieved. Contacts, polish, opportunities—weren't these among the most important reasons for attending college, after all? Eliphalet Pearson, who reimbursed his father years after graduation for the cost of his education, realized that his parents, who did without his help on their farm, had sacrificed so that he might advance himself.[76]

Whatever the specifics of an individual case, parents and sons recognized that before long, boys would become men, taking care of themselves, leading lives of their own. This was in no way a surprising discovery. New Englanders had always understood this fact of life. For as long as Englishmen had lived in the New England, many boys had left their parents in their early teens either to prepare for college or to learn a trade through an apprenticeship.[77] But the inevitability of this period of transition did not make it any easier either for a boy about to set out on his own or for his parents, who worried whether or not he could take care of himself.

After a few years with Tisdale, Lovell, Moody, or one of several dozen other teachers and ministers who regularly trained candidates for admission to college, it was time for another decision. There might be no reason to study the classics except to prepare for college and a profession, but not everyone who started along this path completed it. Of 122 boys who belonged to the four classes at the Boston Latin School that fed directly into the classes of Harvard's revolutionary generation, for example, only 35 went on to college.[78] For whatever reason, for the others higher education no longer beckoned.

For anyone who stayed the course, though, a bright future awaited, or so it seemed. It would be the fulfillment of a family's dreams.

Wouldn't it?

2

Cambridge College

Boys. They were everywhere. On the bed. By the doors to both small studies. Leaning against the faded, grimy whitewashed walls. In the deepening shadows at one corner of the room. In the soft, golden late afternoon sunlight that still streamed through a large window illuminating the center of the wide-planked wooden floor. Occupying almost every patch of space in the sparsely furnished room twenty feet square. Sammy Phillips—age fifteen, from Andover, tall, slender, and reserved—was there. So was stooped and slight David Tappan, also fifteen years of age, from Manchester.[1] And in the midst of the boys, there was Samuel Moody. The date was July 14, 1767. The place was the dormitory chamber of Stephen Peabody, a Harvard junior.[2]

Moody had prepared a bumper crop of candidates for the Harvard class of 1771, thirteen of them, Dummer Academy's largest contingent ever. Between school and college, though, there was a hurdle—the admissions examination. Harvard's "College Laws" specified the process and standards for entrance. Each candidate faced an examination in the classics by the president and at least two of the college's four tutors. Every boy had to be able to translate "the Greek and Latin authors in common use"—for example, Xenophon, the books of the New Testament, Tully, Virgil. He had to demonstrate his knowledge of grammar and his ability to write proper Latin. And he had to appear to be of good character.[3]

By custom, in mid-July at commencement time, when much of Massachusetts descended on Cambridge to enjoy the annual festivities that accompanied Harvard's graduation, New England's teachers brought in the boys they were offering for consideration. "Notice is hereby given to all who desire Admission into *Harvard College* this Year," intoned a newspaper announcement in late June, "that the President and Tutors have determined to attend the Business of Examination."[4] Thus Moody had herded his flock of students the forty miles from Byfield to Harvard Yard to meet with Edward Holyoke, the college's imposing but elderly and increasingly frail president, and whichever tutors happened to be available. Owing to the large number of candidates on July 14, the process had taken so long that during the afternoon Moody had turned to Peabody, a former student of his at Dummer Academy, for a place to stay the night with his boys before setting out for home the next day.

As formidable as the admissions requirements now sound, the entrance examination did not pose much of a challenge for Moody's candidates—or for anyone else who had received decent classical preparation. In the middle of the nineteenth century, Sidney Willard, a 1798 graduate, recalled his similar experience in the summer of 1794: "The amount of study ... required for preparation was very small. In Latin the Æneid of Virgil and Cicero's Select Orations were the complement, and in Greek the Greek Testament only was required. There was no examination in the grammars of these languages, except what arose from the passages translated. A few lines of English, consisting of forty or fifty words, were given to each, to be translated into Latin."[5]

Typically, the tutors put the applicants through their paces, then sent those they recommended for admission to the president for his pro forma stamp of approval. The prospect of a grilling by members of the college faculty was enough to intimidate nearly anyone. To "be weighed in the Scails" was a "fiery Tryal" as far as Sammy Phillips was concerned.[6] Nevertheless, the boys and their teachers knew the school's expectations in advance, and in most cases the outcome was foreordained. Harvard accepted all thirteen of Samuel Moody's candidates in 1767; between July 14 and July 20, the faculty examined fifty-eight students, of whom it immediately admitted forty-nine. Of the remaining nine, two were to return for reexamination after a few more weeks of review. The other seven had to wait and study for another year.[7] By the opening of school in mid-August, as more applicants received offers of admission, the class had grown to fifty-six. Eventually the number rose to sixty-four, Harvard's largest ever.[8]

As entering freshman, they were about to begin a new phase of life. For most of them, college marked their first time away from home and family. Mother Harvard would try her best to keep an eye on each young boy, but there were limits to this oversight. Not on their own quite yet, the boys of the revolutionary generation were nevertheless taking their first steps toward independence.

THE FRESHMEN who began their studies at Harvard College in August 1767 entered a community within a community.[9] The wider of the two was Cambridge, a town of 1,600 residents on the northern bank of the Charles River, a shade more than two miles west of the peninsula that Boston occupied. Cambridge had been settled in 1630 at the same time as Boston, and within half a dozen years it had become the educational center of the Massachusetts Bay Colony.

During the late 1630s, Cambridge had been a tiny cluster of perhaps fifty houses, most occupied by families who were at least part-time farmers, huddled on a flat, open meadow at the dogleg of the tract eight miles long allotted to the town.[10] By 1767, Cambridge's acreage had grown, then shrunken, as land had been added to the original grant then subtracted whenever new settlements had broken away from it to become townships in their own right.[11] In the late 1760s Cambridge retained its original village core, still complemented by some outlying agricultural districts.

Samuel Moody and his charges had traveled to Harvard from Byfield along a network of roads that passed through the farming and commercial towns of coastal Essex County, through the Middlesex County towns of Medford and Charlestown, and into Cambridge from the northeast. Other boys came from the northwest through Cambridge's Menotomy precinct, from western farming communities through Watertown, and from Boston and points south by the long bridge that spanned the Charles River, then across a causeway made of dirt, stone, and gravel through the flats along the northern riverbank to Wood Street, which led up a gentle incline a quarter of a mile past a couple of dozen small houses, shops, and taverns to the college.[12] Fisher Ames must have followed the last of these routes when he approached Harvard from Dedham to begin his freshman year in August 1770.[13]

Harvard College stood on the north side of Cambridge's main village. It was within a few yards of a boxy, spired meetinghouse, its façade of vertical planks painted white, and a lemon-yellow county courthouse with a big red front door and an octagonal cupola, the two buildings that shared the traditional center of town.[14] About half of Cambridge's population, perhaps eight hundred people in all, lived here in modest two- and three-story wooden structures. The other half resided in the outlying districts, most of them on farms, but several dozen of them in elegant country homes belonging to members of Boston's merchant elite.[15]

Over the course of a century and a third, the village had grown up beside Harvard. In the late 1760s the majority of its inhabitants lived along three long dirt roads that traveled up from the river roughly southwest to northeast and four shorter crossing roads. Tavern keepers, stable owners, carpenters, masons, glaziers (who replaced the windows the boys broke), tailors, and cobblers all had settled here to serve the needs of the college and its students.[16]

In fact, it was Harvard that made Cambridge different from a dozen or more other crossroads towns in Massachusetts. Braintree, Concord, Hingham, Taunton, Worcester, Springfield, and other communities all combined farms and markets; they were service centers for the surrounding towns, places to go to transact business. But none had Harvard. The college made Cambridge a special destination, a place to go to and stay for hours or days or weeks or months or years.

Harvard itself made up the smaller, inner community, the scholastic family the boys would come to know. At any given time in the late 1760s and early 1770s, the college numbered a little more than two hundred souls, including faculty members, administrators, resident graduates, undergraduates, and employees both full- and part-time.

The first sight of Harvard must have been impressive to most New Englanders.[17] Unlike the typical structures of rural New England—squat, irregular, and made of wood[18]—the college's principal buildings were tall, imposing Enlightenment statements about order: Georgian brick piles with white-painted wood trim aligned in two adjacent open quadrangles. The larger, southern square consisted of three edifices—Massachusetts Hall, Stoughton College, and Harvard Hall. Harvard Hall also served as one edge of the second quadrangle, together with Hollis Hall and Holden Chapel.

Massachusetts Hall, a dormitory constructed in 1720 and divided into two entries, rose four stories high. It accommodated between fifty and sixty students and other residents in thirty-two sleeping chambers, eight rooms to a floor, two undergraduates or one tutor to every occupied apartment. The other dormitories, Stoughton (finished in 1699) and Hollis (completed in 1763), followed a similar pattern, although Stoughton, which was much narrower than the other two, had half as many chambers.[19] In 1771–72 it housed just nineteen residents, while Massachusetts sheltered fifty-four and Hollis sixty-two.[20]

Harvard Hall was a bit taller at the ridgepole than the dormitories and was surmounted by a high cupola. Its two stories and basement held a chapel, the library, the dining hall, classrooms, and storage areas. When the college received two Egyptian mummies as a gift in 1769, they also found their way to Harvard Hall. Here a small connecting chamber on the second floor between the library, a grand hall divided into ten alcoves of books, and the Philosophy Room, a large science classroom with an expensive Oriental carpet and walls bearing pictures of the college's greatest benefactors, was set aside as a museum.[21] Harvard Hall was the third building of the same name; it had just been completed as a replacement for its predecessor, which a fire had destroyed in 1764.

At the northern edge of the college complex, Holden Chapel, a diminutive, elegant brick structure of a single story, bore the Holden family arms. These were beautifully carved and painted in a large white wooden baroque cartouche adorned with cherubs on a field of cornflower blue mounted above the entryway. Inside, in a hall lined lengthwise with several ranks of heavy oak pews facing each other across a central aisle, the college had held twice-daily religious services from 1742 until 1766, when it moved the exercises to the new chapel in Harvard Hall. In 1767 Holden Chapel had no regular function. It met occasional needs as they arose.[22]

Behind its five principal buildings Harvard had hidden other, more modest structures: a barn, shops for college workmen, a brick brewhouse, a pump, an outhouse.[23] Playing fields, meadows, and orchards adjoined them. So flat was the surrounding land, so low were the houses and barns of Cambridge, that from an upper window in Hollis across a broad, open plain on a fair day it was possible to see the clustered shops and residences of Boston and Charlestown more than two miles away.[24]

Senior members of the faculty and administration resided within a few steps of the college Yard. Closest of all were the president and two of the professors, who lived in a row along Braintree Street (now the portion of Massachusetts Avenue that extends toward Boston) on land that the college later acquired when it enlarged the Yard during the nineteenth century.[25]

In theory, Harvard was a rigidly hierarchical society, a relic of the medieval doctrine of the Great Chain of Being, although student fractiousness meant that the reality of the situation was otherwise. In fact, the members of the revolutionary generation experienced two very different Harvards.

The school's formal, adult façade masked an informal, adolescent culture. At the pinnacle of the formal structure was the president, the patriarch of this scholastic family. Then in descending order of honor and authority came the college's three professors, four tutors plus the librarian (who ranked with the tutors), a couple of degree holders serving Harvard as petty administrators, perhaps a dozen resident graduates who held the bachelor's degree and were preparing for the master's degree and the ministry, 170 or more undergraduates, and everyone else: cooks (at least some of whom were of African ancestry),[26] cleaning ladies, carpenters, masons, blacksmiths, and so on. Further status refinements differentiated the undergraduates. Each graduation year had priority over the succeeding ones, and a faculty ranking system (abandoned with the class of 1773 after an argument over placement with Sammy Phillips's disgruntled father) established an individual hierarchy within each class not of personal accomplishment but of family standing.[27] By placing the sons of public officeholders and clergymen at the head of the class and those of farmers and artisans at the foot, Harvard tried to mirror New England's social structure in each student list. Hierarchical considerations carried over into required forms of address: in college exercises undergraduates went by their surnames, recipients of the bachelor's degree added the honorific "Sir," and masters of arts merited "Mr."[28]

This remarkable watercolor, painted in 1796 or 1797 by William Jenks (A.B. 1797), portrays a view that was unchanged from the early 1770s, when members of the revolutionary generation occupied Hollis Hall. Jenks's papers at the Massachusetts Historical Society include a preliminary study for this painting. (*View from Hollis Window* [1796–1797], by William Jenks. Watercolor on paper, 6.12 × 5 in. Harvard University Archives.)

Both by tradition and by formal college law, respect and deference were the due of those at the top of the hierarchy. From a requirement that undergraduates doff their caps whenever the president or a member of one of Harvard's two governing boards was in the college Yard, to another regulation allowing any member of the faculty to draft a student to help him maintain order, to a set of sumptuary laws preventing undergraduates from wearing clothing that was elaborate beyond their station, the written statutes of the school established the authority of the boards, the president, the professors, and the tutors.[29]

Near the bottom of the ladder, in contrast, above only the hired help, the entering freshmen endured a probationary year of submission, subservi-

Edvardus Holyoke

Collegij Harvardini Cantabrigiæ Nov-anglorum Præses reverendus

Anno Ætat. 60. 1749.

The Reverend Edward Holyoke. This mezzotint shows Holyoke at his most imposing.
(*Rev. Edward Holyoke*, probably by Peter Pelham. Mezzotint. *The Holyoke Diaries, 1709–1856*,
ed. George Francis Dow [Salem, 1911], opp. p. 11.)

ence, and initiation before they could confirm their acceptance into the college community and assert their rights over the next incoming class. One evening each year, shortly after the start of the fall term, the sophomores instructed the freshmen to remain after chapel to learn the informal but long-standing codes, more than twenty of them, that also governed the college. "No freshman shall ware his hat in the College yeard except it rains, snows, or hails," the customs began. "No freshman shall intrude into his seniors Company." "No fresman [sic] shall talk saucily to his senior or speak to him with his hat on." Worst of all, the freshmen had to run errands for everyone above them in the college hierarchy. To avoid constant imposition, many first-year students took an individual senior as a patron and protector. In exchange for exclusive service, a freshman's senior would shield him from the demands of others.[30]

Unofficial though the freshman system was, the college government stood behind it. In the face of repeated criticism by the Board of Overseers, in 1773 the Corporation declined to regulate against "this long and ancient custom," promising only to see to it that no one but the members of the faculty enforced his orders with "Threats or Blows."[31] With the end of classes in July 1767, Stephen Peabody noted, the relieved first-year students "rejoic'd very much when their Freshmanship was up."[32]

The official rules and unofficial customs that governed colonial Harvard established an invisible line between it and its Cambridge neighbors, making it a society in its own right. Town and gown were not entirely isolated from each other. Cambridge furnished Harvard with most of the domestics and tradesmen who maintained its facilities and fed its students. The undergraduates patronized the shops and taverns of the village. And when Sunday came, the students went to church with the people of Cambridge. But the low wooden fence that enclosed the college grounds expressed the division between the wider and narrower communities. The freshman year was a boy's time of passage, of separation from his family, of entry into a hierarchical world set off from that of his childhood, his introduction to a new culture. When the college's tutors recommended a candidate to the president and Edward Holyoke signed his certificate of admission they were doing more than allowing the student to take a few courses. They were setting him apart from most other New Englanders. Once he joined the college community, he began a new existence.

THIS NEW LIFE was a never-ending commitment to personal improvement and social order. At the same time that many boys their age were undergoing an apprenticeship in a craft, Harvard students were novices of a different sort. Prerevolutionary Harvard had a clear and important civic role. It was to define and nurture provincial New England's elite. Much as modern medical schools teach their charges to think like doctors and law schools mold their students into lawyers, prerevolutionary Harvard transformed its students into refined and educated gentlemen. A diploma from the college was the surest entrée into polite society.

Harvard and the other colleges established in the American colonies before independence were not simply finishing schools, though, at least not in the sense in which later generations have used the term, implying an alternative to academic rigor. Instead, academic and social objectives complemented each other. Learning was a mark of a true gentleman. The nine American colleges—William and Mary, Yale, the College of New Jersey (Princeton), the College of Philadelphia (University of Pennsylvania), King's College (Columbia), Rhode Island College (Brown), Dartmouth, and Queen's College (Rutgers), in addition to Harvard—stood at the pinnacle of formal education in the colonies. At the same time, they provided an avenue into the honorable and genteel world of the upper reaches of colonial American society.

Not only was Harvard the oldest of these institutions; it was also the largest, the most prestigious, the most demanding. Long before the imperatives of academic tenure decisions brought research to the fore in many American institutions of higher education, creative scholarship had an important place within the Harvard faculty. Two of the college's three professors in the late 1760s were scholars of genuine distinction in their special fields. John Winthrop, a graduate in the class of 1732, became the Hollis Professor of Mathematics and Natural History in 1738 at the age of twenty-three. Winthrop's sophisticated astronomical observations earned him election as a fellow of the British Royal Society in 1766.[33] And Stephen Sewall, a 1761 graduate, named Hancock Professor of Hebrew and Other Oriental Languages only three years later at age thirty in 1764, was the author of an innovative instructional manual in Hebrew as well as other works on Latin, Greek, and Hebrew texts.[34] Only Edward Wigglesworth, Jr., a 1749 graduate and the son of the college's first Hollis Professor of Divinity, chosen his father's successor at thirty-three in 1765, failed to make a major scholarly contribution to his area of instruction. Wigglesworth was a dedicated teacher who defined his pedagogical role as lecturing to his students on the science of theology, not inculcating them in specific doctrines; his most important writing was not on the subject he taught but on political economy. In the tradition of Benjamin Franklin, who had addressed the topic in the early 1750s, Wigglesworth demonstrated in January 1775 that the population of the American colonies was growing so fast that within seven decades it would exceed that of the British Isles, thus moving the empire's center of gravity across the Atlantic.[35]

Professors at colonial Harvard devoted their classroom hours to lecturing. Public talks, for which they were paid with endowment income, were introductory and open to the entire student body. Private lectures, for which students in the upper classes paid them additional fees, provided advanced instruction.[36] For the most part, the professors stood apart from the daily affairs of the undergraduates, as removed from their concerns as it was possible to be in a small community.

The tutors, far less remote from the undergraduates than the professors, bore the brunt of the responsibility for day-to-day instruction through the recitations they led. They also oversaw the students' conduct and morals.

When the boys of the revolutionary generation began to arrive in Cambridge in the mid- to late 1760s, the school was nearing the end of an instructional review intended to improve the quality of a Harvard education. The college's tutors were at the heart of this transformation. Harvard's instructional reformation had two components. First, the college brought in new tutors. Then it changed its way of assigning them classroom responsibilities. Notwithstanding these innovations in the role of its junior instructors, the college struggled to maintain a balance between their places as teachers, concerned for the rigorous education of their students, and their responsibility in a school with strong connections to New England's Congregationalist Standing Order for the spiritual growth and cultural refinement of their charges.

Day to day, week to week, the tutors were the immediate agents of authority at prerevolutionary Harvard. By college law they had to be unmarried: "If any Tutor shall enter into the Marriage State, his Place shall be *ipso facto* void," the institution's statutes read.[37] Without family responsibilities, each tutor occupied a room in a dormitory, where he oversaw his obstreperous charges all day, every day, when school was in session.

In class, until 1767 each tutor conducted regular recitations in all the principal subjects of the college curriculum—Greek, Latin, logic (including ethics and metaphysics), and natural philosophy (mathematics and the sciences)—as well as offering less frequent instruction in supplements such as theology, geography, oratory, English composition, and belles lettres.[38] Memorization was the key to success in most subjects. Monday through Thursday each week the tutors drilled their students on the basic topics within the college curriculum. Friday and Saturday were given over to the supplementary areas, of which elocution was of the greatest interest and practical importance. The ability to speak articulately to an audience was indispensable in an aural society such as that of colonial New England,[39] and in 1756 Harvard began to require each student to declaim publicly.[40] In the late 1760s and early 1770s, as the political arena filled with talk of the imperial crisis, the students wrestled with the same issue in their elocution classes.[41]

At the end of the year, according to the traditional system, when a class advanced, so did the tutor, who remained with the same students as long as they stayed in school and he continued on the faculty. Forced to deal with each other every day for years, a class might come to loathe its tutor and vice versa. It was almost inevitable that a tutor, as a drillmaster and monitor, would come into conflict with many of the students he supervised. Under the best of circumstances, however, a permanent bond developed between the teacher and his pupils, and at graduation a grateful class ordinarily gave its tutor a commemorative silver bowl or flagon.[42]

It is hard to imagine making a career of such a demanding office; indeed, each tutor's appointment was for only three years, although the position might be renewed repeatedly for additional three-year terms. Most tutors were recent graduates, men in their mid-twenties—not much older than the majority of their students and often younger than a few of them—who served as instructors while they prepared themselves for the ministry.[43] Isaac Smith, for instance, a 1767 graduate, was twenty-four when the Corporation named him a tutor in April 1774. Beginning at the end of the seventeenth century, though, the college was blessed or cursed with a number of tutors who came and—it seemed—would never leave. Henry Flynt, a 1693 graduate, held the record for service. First appointed in 1699, he endured the adolescent pranks of undergraduates until 1754, when he was seventy-nine. Belcher Hancock, class of 1727, another long-serving tutor, left a week after commencement in July 1767 at the age of fifty-eight; he had spent a quarter of a century on the faculty.[44]

Hancock's resignation came a few months after the adoption of a new way to assign the tutors their responsibilities. The class of 1771 was the first to spend its entire collegiate career under the new system. As long as a tutor taught every subject, it made perfect sense to assign him to a specific college year, which he instructed in every branch of learning until he left or the class graduated. Near the close of 1766, however, apparently in an attempt to buttress the rigor of classroom instruction, the Corporation began to assign each tutor to a particular subject. Classes now met for recitation with the four instructors in turn, convening specially with their own tutor only for weekly sessions in theology, oratory, and belles lettres.[45]

The new policy weakened the emotional bonds between a class and its tutor, but it allowed the instructors to specialize. New appointments to the faculty might be made with an eye to the particular interests and aptitudes of the candidates for the position as well as to the specific vacancy to be filled. Every tutor who instructed the classes of Harvard's revolutionary generation was a recent graduate, and by the end of 1772 the last of the tutors appointed under the old plan had resigned.

The members of the revolutionary generation thus encountered a young and energetic corps of instructors when they arrived in Cambridge. In 1767–68, the average age of the four tutors was less than twenty-five. Each had graduated from Harvard within the past five years, and most in this Congregationalist enclave were at least considering a life in the ministry once the classroom tour was over.

The tutors would need all the energy they could muster. Their days began early, with morning prayers in the chapel at 6:00 A.M., and lasted until bedtime at 9:00 P.M. Breakfast was in the college commons. Each boy brought his own knife and fork; when he was done, he wiped his dirty utensils on the tablecloth. Recitations and lectures began at 8:00 A.M. and ran until the noon meal of beef and Indian pudding back in the commons. Then it was time for afternoon recreation, the evening meal (which the boys carried back to their rooms from the door of the college kitchen), and evening prayers. Harvard kept the undergraduates busy from early morning until bedtime and the tutors kept them under control.[46] At the same time the instructors sometimes carried extra administrative responsibilities designed to ensure the smooth operation of the college, for example, preparing the students' quarterly bills. And whenever a student violated one of the college's many laws, the tutors met with the rest of the faculty to consider the crime, determine guilt, and decide on a sentence.

For all the different kinds of responsibilities the tutors undertook, their primary duty was to teach. Faded recollections of the intellectual life of early Harvard, viewed through the prism of subsequent reforms and probably colored in some cases by Henry Adams's famously jaundiced memories of the college in the 1850s,[47] have sometimes led later writers to dismiss the school as little more than a boys' boarding academy, perhaps the equivalent of a modern prep school. John Trumbull recalled in his memoirs that when he entered midway through his junior year, home instruction and self-study had more than prepared him for the demands of the college classroom: "I soon found that I had no superior in Latin—that in Greek there were only two whom I had to fear as competitors."[48] Whatever the truth of this verdict, things looked different to contemporaries, especially those who lacked the advantages of extensive private tutoring and years of hindsight. "The last time I wrote you," one freshman commented to his father in 1767 during his first fall in school, "I was in such fear that I could hardly hold my pen, and now my studies are so severe I am obliged to write by candle light. We read Latin, Greek, Hebrew Geography and Logic, and are driven so close that we have as little comfort as a man who would run the gauntlet."[49] At least a few students wanted to do well, including one who remained at school over a vacation in 1773, "it being the Best Part of the time for Studying, when there is the Least noise."[50]

The college authorities sometimes referred to their students as "scholars," but the term carried none of its modern meanings connoting academic research. There was another purpose behind the memorization and drilling that occupied so many days of school. Boys attending the college in the late 1760s and early 1770s had "improvement,"[51] not the increase of knowledge, on their minds.

Self-cultivation took two forms: mental training and social refinement. Like a muscle, so the accepted theory went, the mind could be strengthened with exercise. Not every discipline challenged the mental faculties. "The study of history cannot be considered as a severe application of the mind," one member of the class of 1774 advised. But "the habit of thinking closely" that certain other disciplines such as mathematics and logic required could enhance the mental faculties.[52]

If some subjects were of at best limited use in strenuously training the mind, then there had to be a different reason for them to belong in the college's curriculum. Prerevolutionary Harvard was not a vocational school devoted to indoctrinating would-be doctors, lawyers, ministers, or merchants, so the reason was not pre-professional. Harvard undergraduates studied the classics, English literature, oratory, geography, and, for extra fees, French and dancing because every real gentleman needed to be acquainted with them.

There were good reasons to include a broad range of humanistic subjects in the curriculum. Why was so much time devoted to the classics? For the "very important purpose of improving . . . understanding, and cultivating . . . taste." As one alumnus told an incoming student: "The Roman and Grecian writers of established reputation will assist you in thinking, writing, and speaking well. In their works you will find the most liberal and elegant sentiments. Many of their productions may be considered as finished models of good sense, and good language."[53] Meanwhile, an acquaintance with the French language, it was said, introduced the student "to the politest people on earth."[54] The college licensed a local instructor, a Mr. Peter Curtis, to teach the undergraduates French, although it did not grant him a regular faculty appointment.

Curtis also taught dancing, a subject that included etiquette, though he offered this instruction in Boston without the formal approval of the college government. Almost every Monday and Thursday between 1771 and 1774, boys and girls from Boston's finest families, together with a representation of Harvard undergraduates, gathered at his school on Queen Street to learn how gentlemen and ladies carried themselves in polite society. From courtly forms of address to the steps of reels, cotillions, and gavottes, dancing masters such as Curtis taught their students the conventions of public intercourse in eighteenth-century Anglo-America's most refined circles. Of these, instruction in the minuet was perhaps the most important because of the risk the dance presented for public humiliation. In the most elevated social circles, every assembly began with a minuet. Each couple danced it alone in turn before the critical eyes of the rest of the company. A man who could not perform a creditable minuet, Harvard students knew, instantly and publicly revealed himself to be no gentleman.[55]

Four years of collegiate instruction in the classics, logic, natural philosophy, theology, oratory, English composition, belles lettres, French, and dance did not ordinarily produce creative scholars. Even after years of study, this learning was often superficial and ornamental.[56] If Harvard did not spawn many intellectuals of the first order, no one was particularly concerned. Harvard undergraduates were ambitious, but their aims had little to do with the life of the mind. The college's purpose was to provide provincial New England with a polished elite—with gentlemen. As long as there were no challenges to the traditional understanding of success, then the school served its objective well. No one gave even the possibility of an intelligentsia a thought.

BECOMING A gentleman could be an expensive proposition, although the full cost of college, including personal expenditures, varied widely depending on an individual student's means. Was it worth the cost? Tuition was £2 per year, a sum equal to slightly more than a month's wages for a common seaman in the late 1760s, but less than one week's income for the Reverend Andrew Eliot of Boston's New North Church.[57] In the colonial years, though, tuition was a secondary charge compared with other necessary fees: room, board, study rent, private lecture fees to the professors, quarterly payments to the college sweepers, as well as the expense of personal necessities such as clothing, books, grooming, and entertainment. By one calculation, tuition and lecture fees amounted to only about one-fifth of what a student paid Harvard in total, to say nothing of the additional personal expenses that college attendance also entailed.[58] It was possible to live frugally; George Morey, of the class of 1776, spent only about £14 on tuition, board, firewood, clothing, and sundries during his sophomore year, 1773–74. By contrast, for someone with the means, there were plenty of ways to spend money; Clement Weeks, from a much more affluent family than Morey's, went through more than £30 during his sophomore year, 1769–70.[59]

Thanks to Harvard's endowment, nearly twenty students received partial or full tuition scholarships each year. A dozen more boys waited on tables; eight others helped to monitor the college buildings and maintain the clock and fire engine. Much of this support went to the sons of ministers. Of the twenty-four boys in the classes of 1771 through 1774 whose fathers were clergymen, twenty-one received some kind of school aid. Most of the rest of the support went to students of modest circumstances. In the classes of 1771 and 1772, the last two to be arranged according to family status, only one student in the top half of the rank list whose father was not a minister received a college grant or job.[60]

The costs of college in time, effort, tuition, subsistence, and forgone earnings were worth shouldering only if the undergraduate years took unfinished boys (together with a few unpolished men) and turned them into gentlemen ready to join the provincial elite. If the college was doing its job well over the course of four years, then the students who entered, most of them in their mid-teens, would be shaped and refined by the time they graduated.

Growing up, which was the students' most important contribution to this process, required development in three different spheres: intellect, character, and maturity. For a young Harvard man to meet the common expectations of him he had to be at least an adequate scholar in the college's fields of instruction, a man of honor and principle, and a person of good carriage, independence, and judgment. That is to say, he had to be acceptable to the community's genteel leadership. What did it take to achieve these standards?

Academic expectations were both the easiest to define and the least important of these objectives. Every class included men such as John Eliot and Eliphalet Pearson, the students who competed for commencement honors, those who genuinely craved learning. But intellectual curiosity and classroom accomplishment, though gratifying to the faculty, were more than a professor or a tutor could reasonably require. After admission, not a single member of Harvard's revolutionary generation ever suffered because of scholarly incompetence. Instead, it was indifference to assignments that led to trouble. When Peter Heyliger, a senior, received a public punishment from the faculty in October 1771, his crimes were a combination of sabbath-breaking and an almost total neglect of the "Lectures of the Professors & Exercises with the Tutors."[61] There were never any sanctions against someone who merely did less, even substantially less, than his best work. More than two decades after college, looking back on an undistinguished academic career, James (Jemmy) Bowdoin regretted that he had taken the easy way out: "My own negligence for the first two years I was at college has occasioned me more uneasiness than all the other circumstances of my life."[62] Still, Bowdoin had met the college's lenient requirements. In the classroom, when all was said and done, a veneer of learning was enough; together with a modest show of diligence, it would suffice.

With respect to character, the standards were clear enough to anyone who paid attention to the implicit and explicit lessons of daily life. Honesty and reliability were the watchwords. Provincial society expected its leaders to be men of integrity, and the college's aspirations for its students were intended to ensure that they did credit both to the school and to themselves. The classroom offered one means to this end. Lectures and recitations on theology and moral philosophy afforded occasions to consider character systematically, and many of the authors both ancient and modern that the students read in their other courses touched on the nature of personal virtue. Students also learned by example from the men who taught them, teachers who had to be of unimpeachable probity and standing. As imperial political tensions rose in the 1760s and 1770s, moreover, public men on each side who stood up for their beliefs offered additional examples of honor in action, serving as role models for boys in the process of becoming young men.

Most of all, Harvard expected maturity from its graduates. Maturity was a compound of a number of different ingredients. It went without saying that the recipe included refinement and knowledge. But another component was even more vital: independence. Independence meant learning how to take care of oneself. There was a practical side to this process. College students attended to many of their own needs. They bought their own books, firewood, and clothes. They also learned how to behave as adults. Tentatively at first, they began to court.[63] Most of them also began to smoke; one member of the class of 1771 later contended that he was the only member of his college generation who did not use tobacco.[64] Above all, they experienced emotional growth and the development of new relationships with their parents. Sammy Phillips's mother recognized her son's increasing maturity by the form of address she used; "Samuel" had invariably taken the place of "Sammy" by his eighteenth birthday in 1770.[65]

Between the first day of college, when many of the freshmen, away from their families for the first time, must have struggled with homesickness, to the final day of senior year, when they said good-bye to the most intimate friends many would ever have, boys grew up as they learned to stand on their own. Being away from home was often difficult for the parents as well as for the boys. To reassure themselves and to shelter their sons from the harshest storms at first, the parents of many freshmen looked for surrogate Cambridge families with whom to place their boys for a year instead of leaving them on their own in a dormitory. "I esteem it a very great Favour to have my Son under your immediate Care at this time," Isaac Osgood wrote in 1768 to Professor Stephen Sewall, who had agreed to board his son Joshua, "as it is of the greatest Consequence to a Youth, that he set out Right at his Entrance upon a College Life."[66] Other anxious parents corresponded with their sons often, their letters filled with the earnest advice they would have spoken to them directly if they could: "Labour to maintain your Character, at College; Treat all Superiors with due respect; Shun all bad Company.... Keep good hours, go to [bed] in a good Season rise early."[67] And further: "Seek to God for Direction.... Remember to keep holy Sabbaths & that will be a means to keep you holy."[68] With each passing year, however, parental ties loosened as both the boys and their parents gradually recognized that a new stage of life was approaching.

Increasingly on their own but not yet quite independent adults, uneasy undergraduates also wrestled with their uncertainties. Surviving pages of a diary that Sam Phillips kept at age eighteen in 1770 reveal his anxieties. Phillips came from a strongly religious family, and throughout his college years he expressed his worries through fears for the health of his soul. Would he turn out to be the kind of Christian gentleman he aspired to be? When British soldiers killed five demonstrators in March, rather than a political reaction Phillips's response to the Boston Massacre was spiritual and personal. Life was fragile, as the fate of the victims attested, and not to be taken for granted: "This Day [a week ago] they made as much Dependance on Life and with as good Reasons [as] I did." Phillips's death might come as suddenly, "my Body rotting in the Grave before the Return of another such Day." It was up to Sam alone to ensure that he was ready for whatever life might bring him: "Let me turn about, with full Purpose of Heart to follow after Holiness." Over the course of the following months, Phillips repeatedly took his soul's temperature in order to assess whether or not he possessed "that Temper the Gospel requires."[69]

Refinement as well as faith was the mark of the Christian gentleman, and Sam knew that at the same time he tended to his soul, he also needed to learn to carry himself well. It was a sign of Phillips's growing independence that he stood up to his parents during his junior year when they resisted his efforts at personal refinement. Sam understood that if he wanted to make a place for himself among the finest families of New England, he needed to learn to dance. In Andover, something of a cultural backwater in the 1760s and 1770s, Phillips's parents did not appreciate the social necessity of an elegant line at an assembly. During the fall of his junior year, Sam asked his parents for permission to attend dancing classes. His father was not happy with this prospect: "My fears remain that it will Engross too much of your Mind and Time now, and will in Time be a great Temptation to Attend Balls and Assemblies, to lead you into Company and to be abroad at unseasonable hours, all which I do detest and Abhor as having the greater tendency to corrupt the morals of young people." But his son would not be deterred, and Samuel Sr. relented: "I shall not Object to your Attending one quarter of a year," he concluded, "the Tutors consent being first obtain."[70]

A responsible boy, Sam was well on the way to maturity by July 1771, when he graduated. His parents and friends could depend on him to exercise common sense and sound judgment. But not everyone followed the same course as Phillips. When a student fell short of expectations, it was important to correct him.

ON MAY 12, 1770, the president, professors, and tutors of the college voted to rusticate Winthrop Sargent, a senior two months shy of graduation. Short of expulsion, rustication was the college's most severe penalty. Fourteen of the 204 members of the classes of Harvard's revolutionary generation were rusticated at some point during their college careers.[71] Reprimands, fines, and degradation—reducing a student from his natural place in the class order to a lower position—served when transgressions were minor.[72] But Sargent—age seventeen, the son of a wealthy Gloucester merchant, and no gentleman—had become a pus-filled boil on the college's face, a wine-red stain on its good name. Nothing less than rustication—suspension for a year in an isolated town under the supervision of a trusted rural minister—would do. Someone who had been thus cast out could have no interaction with the college or its students until he had completed his sentence on pain of further punishment for himself and anyone whom he contacted. For a year, as far as the members of the college community were concerned, he was a non-person. And if the second most severe sanction were not enough, then there was always expulsion.

Sargent had run riot during the course of the spring. By the time the faculty voted to excise him from the body collegiate, it had compiled a lengthy bill of particulars. Toward the end of March, Sargent had entertained two prostitutes overnight in his dormitory room. On May 3 and again on May 8 he had taken a pistol outside and fired it wildly, endangering the citizens of Cambridge. When the faculty had called him in to discuss these actions, his response had been "insulting and Contemptuous." Sargent had then joined two schoolmates in assaulting Captain William Angier, a Cambridge resident who had reported Sargent's earlier misdeeds to the college authorities. All three boys had been "for a great while in their general Conduct, idle vicious, and disorderly persons disturbing of the peace of the College and of the town of Cambridge and a common Nuisance to both."[73]

Vandalism, petty theft, rowdiness, and consorting with prostitutes were recurring problems for the college authorities. In June 1771 a sophomore and a junior torched the college outhouse late one night after unsuccessfully attempting to force a cow into Holden Chapel. A year and a half later, after his readmission, one of the two was also apparently suspected of breaking into a student's chest and stealing a small sum of money. An affluent member of the class of 1773 even kept a prostitute for several weeks in a house near the college.[74]

Rustication was no less a public humiliation than confinement in a New England town's pillory had been during the seventeenth century. Harvard reserved the punishment for acts that violated the basic values of the college community. The boys who burned down the outhouse in 1771 received this sentence.[75] The president imposed the punishment while standing in the center aisle of the chapel before the entire community except the paid help.

Most boys accepted this punishment sullenly or angrily but without overt protest. Not Winthrop Sargent. He and his confederates "all exclaimed with a loud voice the Sentence is unjust and then threw themselves out of the Chapel."[76] Sargent would not be back for twelve months, when, after a humble public apology in the chapel before the community that had exiled him, he contritely took his place with the class of 1771, which had entered a year after he had.

Winthrop Sargent led a more tumultuous college life than most undergraduates, but the central lesson of his experience has broad application. Social realities rarely conform in all respects to social theory, and in fact the college was not the "deliberately, elaborately, smotheringly paternalistic" hierarchy to which its government aspired.[77] The boys who made up most of the college community had their own ideas about its objectives and values. Less visible than the formal hierarchy of the administration and the faculty was a second, more fluid and voluntary structure. Out of sight except when misconduct or rebellion brought it into view, there was an adolescent society, a boys' culture.[78]

Early each fall, at about the same time the sophomores instructed the freshmen in the college customs, the two classes observed a distinctly masculine ritual, a wrestling tournament that went on for several days. The sophomores, a year older and more experienced, usually prevailed, thus confirming their social dominance, but no matter what the outcome, one lesson for the newcomers in this particular custom was that there was room at Harvard for battlers as well as conformists.

After prayers one evening during the second week of classes, the sopho-mores would range the members of the two lowest classes in a large, ragged circle on the playing field behind Holden Chapel. In 1767 the first day of this wrestling tournament was Thursday, August 20. When everyone was in place, one of the sophomores swaggered to the center of the makeshift arena, challenged the newcomers' manhood, and dared them to send out their best. At first, there were dozens of matched jousts. Puny freshmen fought puny sophomores; burly members of each class tangled with each other. From his vantage point as a junior, Stephen Peabody could watch the proceedings with detachment: "There are some smart Fellows in the Freshman class," he concluded after a day of grappling. Eventually, after several more sessions of combat following evening prayers, only one boy remained standing. The winner was Daniel Tyler, a freshman,[79] who whipped two sophomores on the final evening: "& so," Peabody con-cluded, "the Freshman Class have concur'd [conquered] the Sophomores in Wrestling."[80]

Prerevolutionary Harvard was no meritocracy. College honors often went to the wealthy and well connected. Within the school, though, there was a space largely beyond the reach of the faculty for increasingly inde-pendent undergraduates to prove themselves no matter where they stood in the class list. Boys could pick their own friends and associates. Whenever they did, they established their own hierarchies—of insiders and outsiders, of students who had the respect of their peers and those who did not, of scholars and slackers, of leaders and followers.

Shortly after he returned to Harvard in August 1767, Stephen Peabody learned that his roommate—his "chum," to use the common term—from the previous year would not be living in college housing. Peabody would have to find a replacement or wait for the college to assign someone. Stu-dent culture began in the dormitories, where notwithstanding the most insistent efforts of the faculty, undergraduates like Peabody shaped their own lives.

Students had every reason to try to control dormitory assignments. An incompatible chum might mean a year of unhappiness. Each pair of room-mates shared an open sleeping chamber roughly twenty feet square with a fireplace against one wall, which they kept supplied with wood at their own expense. In two corners of the room were small closets with windows—a personal locked study for each boy. The study provided his only real pri-vacy. The rooms were sparsely furnished by the occupants, who invariably shared the only bed. In addition to the bed, the residents might each own a chest, some books and a bookcase, some cooking and tea utensils, a few chairs.[81]

To last the year, the boys who shared these quarters had to be friends. They had to trust each other. Thanks to a surviving list of room assignments from the late summer of 1771, it is possible to speculate on why many pairs of roommates chose to live together. Brothers always shared a room. Boys from the same hometown might also room with each other. Students with common career aspirations frequently shared a chamber. Politics sometimes brought boys together. When Stephen Peabody's chum opted not to live in a dormitory, Peabody asked to live with a fellow resident of Andover and graduate of Dummer Academy, incoming freshman Samuel Phillips.[82]

Dormitory life was not completely outside the control of the college authorities; during the fall of 1771, two tutors lived in Hollis, two resided in Massachusetts, and the librarian occupied Stoughton.[83] But short of constant monitoring, which was quite beyond the ability, if not the inclination, of the administration, the college had to rely on the goodwill and maturity of the majority of the students, especially the older ones, directing its efforts instead to checking the most serious threats to good order.

Over the course of an academic year, students came together in a variety of combinations, both unofficial and official. They sometimes organized to stage plays for one another; classical themes were popular.[84] Sports occupied some of the boys at all times of year; during the warmer months, in addition to wrestling, the students played at quoits and cricket, and they challenged one another to foot races across the college playing field. Fisher Ames liked to go hunting, and during the winter he sometimes traveled with friends a mile to Fresh Pond to skate.[85] As part of his freshman year of initiation in 1768, Clement Weeks chipped in to buy bats, balls, and other athletic equipment for the undergraduates.[86] Swimming in the river during hot weather in 1773 cost one freshman his life when he could not escape an undertow.[87] Stephen Peabody often liked to join in group sings in a dormitory room during the evening after prayers.[88] And toward the close of their senior year in 1772, Tom Coffin, Clement Weeks, and eight of their more stylish friends took a day off for an excursion to the ocean at Point Shirley in what is now the town of Winthrop.[89]

Formal student clubs and societies, almost all of them out of sight of non-members, also occupied the attention of many undergraduates. Prayer societies, about which the college administration certainly had no reservations, dated back to at least 1707. Most Saturday evenings in the late 1760s, a small group of undergraduates still met in a dormitory room for a "private meeting" to pray together.[90] Another group of undergraduates, concerned about a rash of profanity, gambling, and irreverence at the college, organized an association in 1767 for the suppression of vice.[91] And social clubs for promoting cultural interests and genteel conduct dated from at least as early as the formation in 1728 of the Philomusarian Club for discussion and poetry reading.[92]

In the early 1770s at least five clubs, four of them secret societies, were active at Harvard. Jack Warren, John Eliot, Tilly Merrick, and Eliphalet Pearson all belonged to the Speaking Club, of which Sam Phillips was the organizer.[93] Meanwhile, Fisher Ames and Samuel Emery were among the members of the Mercurian Society. A third association, the Clitonian Society, was very small; it may have had only four members. There was nothing insidious about the aims of any of these fraternities. The Speaking Club, the Mercurian Society (which merged with the Speaking Club eighteen months after establishment in September 1771), and the Clitonian Society all promoted oratory, discourse, and literature. "We the subscribers promise that we will obey all the Votes & Orders of the Speaking Club of Harvard College, & that we will not disclose any Secret relating to it, or even that there is such a one," declared the members of the largest of the secret societies. The Speaking Club met weekly in rented quarters, often in the home of Jonathan Hastings, the college steward, for debates and orations. As the political temperature in the American colonies started to rise in the early 1770s, current events were often on the clubs' agendas.[94]

Surviving membership rosters indicate that these clubs drew impartially from most sectors of the student population, with one exception: almost all the members lived in college housing, where upperclassmen predominated. In the fall of 1771, of the forty-nine club members in college whose names are known, forty-six lived in Harvard dormitories.[95]

Secrecy ensured the members' privacy from prying eyes, although it seems that most of the fraternities had no disorderly behavior to hide. In fact, far from engaging in insubordination, clubs with cultural objectives reinforced the college's classroom lessons. Jack Warren belonged to the only student organization that did have a reason to conceal its activities. The Spunke Club, made up of aspiring physicians, apparently plotted to rob graves to provide bodies for anatomical investigations.[96]

Only the Martimercurian Band, an undergraduate militia company with more than sixty members, established in 1769 or 1770, acted in the open. Wearing dashing uniforms of long blue coats faced in white, nankeen breeches, white stockings, black gaiters, and three-cornered hats, carrying muskets supplied by the province, the members of the company drilled in public under the command of Captain William Eustis, then passed around buckets of rum toddy.[97]

Away from home, in many cases for the first time, the students learned to rely on themselves and one another. Although grown-ups were around, they were less of a presence for these boys than in any previous situation they had encountered. Not yet completely independent of adult supervision, nevertheless they were beginning to strike out on their own.

IN FACT, collectively the undergraduates had more power over the affairs of the college than either they or the authorities acknowledged. In a college population of slightly more than 200 at any one time, the undergraduates numbered at least 170 and sometimes more than 190, or over 90 percent of the community. When the students believed that they had a grievance, they were so numerous that Harvard's administration had to pay attention to them.

During the late 1760s a series of student actions shook Harvard. In the spring of 1768 the most serious of these, a student strike, crippled the college.[98] At the root of the upheaval was concern among the tutors about the laxity of some students in class. By custom, pupils who had failed to prepare for recitation could excuse themselves by answering "nolo"—"I don't wish to"—when called upon to recite. To force the undergraduates to study, the tutors announced on March 21 that henceforth they would only accept excuses presented in advance. Only the seniors, whose college careers were nearly at an end, were exempt. The lower three classes revolted immediately. The new policy was "so ridiculous that it is really sickish," junior Stephen Peabody angrily entered in his diary.[99]

Tensions swelled between March 21 and April 4. Most of the underclassmen indignantly refused to comply with the new regulation, and at night the tutors had to dodge the brickbats that exploded through their windows. One tutor's room was ransacked, and another found his door slathered with manure. Rumors flew that a tutor had imprisoned a freshman for most of a day to try to compel him to inform on the ringleaders of the uprising.

The undergraduates' trump card was to quit school, leaving it a broken shell. On April 4, more than one hundred underclassmen resigned their rooms, and the seniors, who had tried to avoid becoming involved in the argument, petitioned President Holyoke for permission to transfer to the college in New Haven. The prospect for Harvard was a catastrophic reduction in the student body to only about forty.

By resigning their chambers and returning home, however, the students inadvertently sabotaged their own cause. No longer in regular contact with one another, they were prey to the maneuverings of the faculty, who gradually persuaded individual strikers to apologize, abandon their cause, and return to school. By early May, all but a few agitators had come back to Cambridge. One ringleader transferred to Rhode Island College rather than apologize for his role in the upheaval. By early July, though, the rest were back in class after offering humbling statements of repentance.[100]

Harvard had never seen anything like the disturbances of the 1760s. Student misbehavior was nothing new, but the concerted actions of angry undergraduates were a concern. It was hard to imagine what else might go wrong.

IN THE CONTEXT of the curriculum, student disturbances, and undergraduate organizing, it is not surprising that political turmoil came to Cambridge by the late 1760s. As Massachusetts Whigs mounted a boycott of luxury imports in response to the Townshend Acts in 1768, the majority of undergraduates went along readily, agreeing not to drink tea.[101] "The young gentlemen are . . . taken up with politics," a member of the Corporation wrote to an English correspondent the following year: "Their declamations and forensic disputes breathe the spirit of liberty. This has always been encouraged; but they have sometimes wrought themselves up to such a pitch of enthusiasm that it has been difficult for their tutors to keep them within due bounds."[102]

To be sure, Harvard students were not all of one mind as events, beginning with the Stamp Act Crisis, frayed the ties between the colonies and the mother country. Although the great majority of the students and all but two members of the faculty—both of them tutors—came to support American independence, a small but determined minority, which included Tom Coffin, took the other side.[103]

As the American resistance movement gained strength after the mid-1760s, what Harvard students were learning sensitized most of them to the cause's rhetoric. Most undergraduates discerned in their assignments warnings of threats to their independence as well as in what they read on their own. The college's classical curriculum included authors such as Plutarch, Demosthenes, and Plato, who taught republicanism, civic morality, and the virtues of liberty as well as the perils that might endanger it. Rhetorical exercises, which often drew on the orations of Cicero for their models, also instructed on the perils of public corruption and the need for constant vigilance against threats to subvert the common weal. Authors in the British Commonwealth tradition such as James Harrington and Algernon Sidney cautioned of the fragility of liberty in the face of conspiracy. And on their own, many students read authors such as John Trenchard and Thomas Gordon, who warned in *Cato's Letters* of the corruptions that imperiled the British political system. The modern-day implications of such writings were obvious to Americans who worried about systemic decay within the British political nation, and the result in Cambridge was a student body full of members on the lookout for surreptitious challenges to American rights and freedoms.[104]

Students who were ready to protest political developments had a substantial local record of resistance to college authorities on which to draw by the late 1760s. Beginning with the Bad Butter Rebellion, a protest against the food in the college commons in 1766, Harvard undergraduates developed a tradition of active responses against undesirable power centers. How many additional steps was it, after all, from organizing against local abuses by those in power, including tutors and the steward, to campaigning against the malfeasance of those who would misuse political power? And were students who were able to organize themselves into the clubs for cultivating self-improvement that became popular after 1770 any less able to associate for political purposes? A survey of the topics of presentations before the Speaking Club in the early 1770s reveals a strongly Whiggish cast to the themes of the members' discussions. As political tensions grew in the years before the American Revolution, as every provocation triggered disruptions, Harvard also became a college in turmoil, a community on the edge of an explosion.[105]

"IF ANY MAN wishes to be humbled and mortified, let him become President of Harvard College," Edward Holyoke declared on his deathbed in 1769.[106] By the end of his tenure, after more than thirty years in office, the frustrations of dealing with fractious students had finally become too much for the father of the college community. If Holyoke had known about the fate of his successor, however, he would have felt grateful to escape to his grave with his reputation intact. For all the problems due to student disobedience in the prerevolutionary years, the source of Harvard's greatest embarrassment was its twelfth president, Samuel Locke.

Edward Holyoke's death on June 1, 1769, left a void that was difficult to fill. Though elderly and tottering toward the end, the president was still a formidable presence. A capable scholar in a variety of disciplines, especially in the classics, at 235 pounds when healthy he was a dominating figure.[107] Generations of students had turned to him as the ultimate symbol of authority at the college. "His very look, as we well remember, commanded respect," recalled Professor Stephen Sewall in his funeral oration five days after the president's death.[108] It was hard to imagine anyone else in his place.

The search for a new president took half a year. In advance, no one could have guessed the surprising candidate it yielded, Samuel Locke, the short, stout, handsome, and thoroughly obscure minister of the Congregational

Church in Sherborn, Massachusetts.[109] Locke, who had graduated from the college in 1755, was only thirty-seven years old at his inauguration, the youngest man ever to hold Harvard's presidency, forty-two years younger than Holyoke had been at the time of his death. The new president had never served on the faculty in any capacity, although in between earning his two degrees he had spent some time in the late 1750s as the college butler—in effect, the manager of a convenience store for the students. Over slightly more than a decade between his ordination in November 1759 and his invitation to succeed Holyoke, he had come to the public's attention only once, in 1762, when he preached the annual sermon before the Ancient and Honorable Artillery Company in Boston.

As observers thought about Locke's selection, though, it began to make sense to some of them. John Adams, a classmate of Locke, was full of praise for the appointment, declaring that "no Man was better qualified."[110] And Andrew Eliot, a member of the Corporation, saw at least half a dozen arguments in Locke's favor: "He has fine talents, is a close thinker, had at College the character of a first rate scholar; he is possessed of an excellent spirit, has generous, catholic sentiments, is a friend to liberty." Locke was "universally acceptable so far as I have heard."[111]

The inauguration took place on March 21, 1770, in the meetinghouse of the First Parish. After a procession, which included the entire college community, the governing boards, Lieutenant Governor Thomas Hutchinson, the colony's House of Representatives, and a delegation of members of the clergy, the Reverend Nathaniel Appleton of Cambridge opened the festivities with a prayer. Hutchinson then addressed Locke in Latin before presenting him with the symbols of his new office, the college seal, keys, books, and charter, then seating him in the ceremonial president's chair. Locke replied to Hutchinson, also in Latin. A resident graduate delivered yet another Latin oration, Reverend Ebenezer Pemberton of Boston's New Brick Church offered a prayer, and the ceremony closed with a hymn. The company then returned in procession to Harvard Hall, where the college provided an entertainment. "The whole was conducted with Decency & Propriety," the faculty records noted with satisfaction.[112] All the same, that evening some of the undergraduates, still celebrating the events of the day, burned the college privy to the ground.[113]

Locke immediately set about to bring the college up to date. His most lasting legacy was the decision a few months later to abandon class ranking based on family dignity in favor of alphabetical order.[114] Personable and approachable to a degree that Holyoke had never been, he quickly began to win the favor of members of the governing boards, faculty, and students alike. The Corporation responded at the July 1773 commencement by awarding Locke an honorary doctorate. By now, though, Locke was already sowing the seeds of his own downfall.

Samuel Locke's wife, Mary, suffered from chronic ill health that may have made her sexually unavailable to him. Meanwhile, the president was unable to regulate his own human urges. When Mary's housekeeper became pregnant during the summer of 1773, President Locke tried to bribe her to disappear. She refused, and Locke, humiliated and under pressure from the Corporation, quietly resigned his office on December 1.[115]

What kind of moral leadership could an adulterer provide the young boys under his direction? Decency and propriety may have distinguished Locke's induction into office; nothing of the sort characterized his departure.

COMMENCEMENT ARRIVED four years, almost to the day for most boys, from their first heart-gripping interviews with the tutors and the president. The college years were over. It was time to celebrate and then to get on with life.

During the eighteenth century, Harvard commencement was the great summer festival in eastern Massachusetts. It was an excuse not only for the graduates and their families but also for men and women who had absolutely nothing to do with the college to drop their work for a day and carouse. When the college canceled commencement in 1774 in response to the growing political tensions of the day, the absence of the celebration was felt as much outside Harvard Yard as within it.

Graduation took place each year on the third Wednesday of July. In 1771 the third Wednesday came on July 17. Inside the Yard, and in the meeting-house of the First Parish, where the college conducted the formal morning and afternoon exercises, the atmosphere was decorous for the most part. To the north of the Yard, however, in instructive counterpoint to the mood at the college ceremonies, the ambience was anything but seemly. If the goal of college was to prepare young men for genteel and honorable lives, then the activities off the college grounds were an unmistakable reminder of another path.

The formal festivities in 1771 began with a procession. By 9:30 A.M. the faculty, the candidates for degrees, and other assorted dignitaries were gathered in the college's northern quadrangle to await the arrival of Thomas Hutchinson, who had recently been advanced to the governorship, with his entourage. The friends and families of the candidates were on hand, as were many of the local ministers and alumni. Almost everyone who had begun with the class was still here or on course to graduate at the next commencement. Of 204 boys in the classes of 1771 through 1774, 194, or more than 95 percent, graduated. None took longer than five years.

Once Hutchinson arrived, the procession could organize and set out for the meetinghouse of the First Parish, no more than 150 paces away. First came the candidates for the bachelor's degree walking two by two, wearing black academic gowns,[116] then the master's candidates, also in double columns and clad in black or dark blue. President Locke was next, unaccompanied. After the president marched the Corporation, the tutors, Governor Hutchinson, and the Provincial Council.

The members of the class of 1771, candidates for the first degree, performed during the morning exercises, offering addresses, dialogues, and disputations in Latin, Greek, Samaritan, and English. It was a high honor to be asked to speak at graduation, but the student commencement parts were also the most unpredictable and potentially controversial pieces on the program.[117] One irreverent speech in 1771, on "Quackery in all Professions," caused such hilarity at the expense of the dignity of the careers that many of the graduates planned to pursue that a Boston minister angrily published a pamphlet deploring "the satyrical drollery at Cambridge last Commencement Day."[118] In contrast, at commencement two years later in 1773, graduating seniors Eliphalet Pearson and Theodore Parsons caused such a sensation with their cogent and insightful forensic dispute on the morality of slavery that it was soon published by popular demand.[119]

During the afternoon, following a recess for dinner, the master's degree candidates took their turn, offering syllogistic disputes and an English oration. Commencement handouts, paid for by the graduates, listed the degree recipients and the "theses" or topics that the candidates for the second degree proposed to discuss. The political climate at Harvard in 1771 was apparent when the seniors took the job of printing their broadside away from Richard Draper, who had handled it for years, because he had close ties to the crown. Isaiah Thomas, whom they chose instead, was the most radical printer in Boston.[120] After the degrees were conferred, the ceremonies concluded with a Latin oration. According to the notice that the college placed in the Boston newspapers, "the whole was conducted with Elegance and Propriety much to the Credit of the College and to the Satisfaction of the Audience."[121] To ensure good order within its own community, the college regulated the commencement parties of the graduates and hired half a dozen local men to quell any disturbances.[122]

A more rowdy swirl of activities ebbed and flowed outside the Yard and the meetinghouse. Despite the gala atmosphere, the graduates and their families managed to remain under control. They had been preparing for the festival for weeks, laying in stores and securing rooms to entertain guests.[123] In the interval between the morning and afternoon exercises, Colonel John Murray celebrated the graduation of his son Daniel in 1771 with a lavish commencement spread attended by "A Large Company, the Governour, Councill and too many to Enumerate."[124] Other families and their friends repaired for refreshment to private homes or to the dormitory chambers of the new graduates. George Inman's graduation party at his family's Cambridge home in 1772 boasted a guest list of 347, of whom 210 dined at a single long table.[125] After an appropriate interlude, the college served dinner in the commons to many of the dignitaries, alumni, and new bachelors of arts.

Even at their most raucous, though, the parties of the graduates and their families were tame in comparison with what was going on to the north of the college grounds. Commencement was carnival time in eighteenth-century Cambridge, complete with jugglers, caged animals, paupers, pick-pockets, games of skill, and games of chance. In one corner, archers tested their marksmanship. In another, wrestlers pawed at each other. Fat dripping from grilling meats caused smoky cooking fires to leap and dance. If the college exercises attracted dignitaries, the parents of graduates, and alumni, the festivities outside the Yard drew a considerably less genteel audience of sailors, farm laborers, journeymen mechanics, apprentices.

There was nothing official—and certainly nothing formal—about what went on during commencement day in the tent city that emerged on Cambridge Common and neighboring fields shortly before graduation. Row upon row of large cream-colored tents appeared almost overnight, the work and property of opportunistic petty entrepreneurs. First came wooden frames, then enormous sheets of canvas sailcloth. If the owner intended to provide an opportunity for dancing, he also installed a floor of wide, rough planks. Each tent held tables and chairs as well as a crude counter to serve as a bar. For the rugged men and women who came to Cambridge each year to have fun, not to observe a collegiate rite of passage, commencement was a time for drinking, gambling, and cavorting.

Dusk came late to Cambridge in mid-July, well after 7:00 P.M. even in the years before the introduction of daylight saving time. The festivities were winding down. By sunset, many of the revelers, gentle folk and common folk alike, were beginning to wend their way home to Lynn or Dedham or Waltham. A happy glow settled over the town as the sun's last rays faded over the western horizon. For many of those who had spent the day in Cambridge, the night would be too short to sleep off the glow before the morrow came. And for the proud graduates, it was now time to think about the future.[126]

3

APPRENTICING FOR LIFE

KEEPING IN TOUCH. It was never a problem as long as classmates spent most of each year together in the familiar recitation halls and dormitory rooms of Harvard Yard. There were daily talks and walks, games and horseplay, meals and outings while school was in session, and there were opportunities to write to one another and visit during vacations, the prospect of renewing friendships when school resumed always beckoning. But commencement changed everything. Most of the new graduates scattered for home or other destinations, not certain when they would see one another again, and the small number who stayed on in Cambridge, no longer undergraduates, took on new roles and responsibilities.

Nathaniel Walker Appleton, a grandson of Cambridge's pastor, tried repeatedly to correspond with his friend and classmate Eliphalet Pearson over the months following commencement, but time and again his letters disappeared in transit. Still in Cambridge, where he held a postgraduate fellowship, Appleton attempted to reach Pearson, who was teaching school less than twenty miles away in Andover. "I had wrote you three or four Letters and received no Answers," Appleton scrawled in exasperation to Pearson in December 1773, five months after their graduation, "but . . . I concluded [they] had miscaried."[1]

Pearson and Appleton were each beginning a new stage of life. Their daily routines, their concerns, their associations were changing. They had memories in common—of classes and classmates, of successes and failures, of the opportunities and challenges of college—but never again would they share their lives day to day. It was time to get on with adult life now, time to make some decisions, time to find a niche within New England society, time to plan for a career and a family.

Some graduates made their decisions faster than others, but in general it took them three years or so to confirm a direction in life. Over the course of these years they fixed on a calling, trained for it, and began their life's work. They decided where to reside. A few, like Sam Phillips, simply returned home, where, for the moment at least, they could once again take up a place in their parents' household.[2] More often, though, on their own now, pursuing careers, they moved away from home, never to return except on visits. Although only a small minority married during this period, most began to court actively and to think seriously about what they wanted and needed in a wife. Many began to assume a role in public affairs. And at last they became adults. Most of them were in their late teens or early twenties when they graduated, not far beyond boyhood. After three years of preparing for their futures they were finally young men, ready for the challenges and responsibilities of adulthood.

In the tradition of Cambridge and Oxford, Harvard recognized the conclusion of this stage of life with a ceremony. After at least three years out in the world, Harvard A.B.'s might return to Cambridge and pay a fee for a second degree, the master of arts, which recognized not classroom achievements but preparation for adulthood. In the normal course of events, the college devoted the afternoon of commencement day to a final examination that no one ever failed, the orations and syllogistic disputes of the master's candidates. Each candidate for the second degree announced in advance a subject on which he was prepared to speak; in most instances the topic was related to the career he was entering. When the ceremony was over, the new masters of arts belonged to the world of genteel adults, certified as educated and refined young men.

AFTER SEVERAL years of college, was it too much to expect a young graduate to have a good idea of what he wanted to do with himself? The examples of earlier Harvard alumni illustrated the obvious career possibilities. Most graduates in recent decades had become ministers, doctors, lawyers, merchants, teachers, and farmers. The range of likely alternatives seemed apparent. Yet it was one thing to aspire to a calling and something else again actually to enter it. When they tried out a career, would-be doctors occasionally found medicine too gory; some potential lawyers grew to hate either the tedium or the contentiousness of life at the bar; neophyte merchants sometimes lost all their capital. Joshua Armsby, who had entered with the class of 1773 at twenty-seven in order to prepare for the ministry, discovered after graduation that he could not handle its demands. Stage fright struck the first time he attempted to preach before a congregation, and he gave up his dream in favor of farming.[3] The years following commencement were, consequently, a time for experimentation as each recent graduate looked for a comfortable occupational niche.

Young A.B.'s often floundered for a while, uncertain what course to follow. John Adams recognized the symptoms in Thomas Edwards, a recent graduate who was keeping school in Braintree in 1772: "Edwards is balancing in his Mind the several Professions, in order to choose one. Is at a Loss between Divinity and Law, but his Inclination is to the latter."[4] Fisher Ames, who entered college at twelve and completed it at sixteen, was still too young when he finished school to command the respect that professional careers required. Who would take him seriously in his mid-teens if he tried to preach a sermon or plead a cause or prescribe a cure? So precocious that he had impressed all his teachers at an early age with his gifts, Ames had to mark time teaching and farming until he grew into a persuasive professional bearing.[5] The lure of Cambridge sometimes held young graduates in thrall while they considered their options; Theodore Parsons remained there after his triumphant commencement disputation with Eliphalet Pearson in 1773 in order to consider, then reject, a life in the ministry. Parsons eventually decided in favor of medicine.[6]

Often, the best course of action was simply to take a few months or a year to consider the alternatives. One way to buy some time was to follow Ames's example and teach. Thanks to the education laws in provincial New England, which required all but the smallest towns to support a common school and large ones also to provide a grammar school,[7] in the 1770s the demand for young graduates in the classroom exceeded the supply. Very few college men set out to become schoolmasters—education was short on pay and prestige—but the opportunity to teach for a while attracted many uncertain bachelors of arts.

Nahum Cutler, who had been Eliphalet Pearson's undergraduate roommate, wrote in July 1774 to bring his old chum up to date on his affairs. A year after graduation Cutler suspected that he was destined for the pulpit, but for the moment he was still teaching school and considering his options. His classroom career had begun in York, Maine, but by the summer of 1774 he was the master of a school in Portsmouth, New Hampshire. Rowdy students and a constant headache made Nahum's circumstances nearly unbearable. He was ready for the end of this stage of life: "School keeping is not the thing. There is but very little to be got by it. It does not suit me— it is almost too much for my health. But I must be contented with it for the present. I wish I was able to study Divinity—or cou'd settle in some other agreeable useful business for life."[8]

At some point during the first three years after graduation, about one-quarter of the members of Harvard's revolutionary generation put in time as teachers. In many instances a classroom tour lasted only a few months. John Eliot taught briefly in Roxbury and Dedham in the early 1770s, Tilly Merrick in Concord after 1773, Sam Jennison in Westborough in 1774, and Fisher Ames at Dummer Academy between 1774 and 1777.[9] Once Clement

Weeks entered a New Hampshire classroom in 1772, he never left,[10] but as many other Harvardians found out, one of the great attractions of teaching was the possibility of combining it with preparation for another career.

Harvard had been established in the seventeenth century to prepare students for community leadership roles, particularly in the ministry, and in the 1770s one of its most important functions remained the education of candidates for the professions. "Young men who go to college should have before them the expectation of a learned profession," Jemmy Bowdoin observed some years after his class graduated.[11] In the daily life of colonial New England, the college's role was the constant replenishment of provincial leadership, both secular and ecclesiastical. Young Harvardians who followed the well-worn path into the professions took their places within a tradition-bound social order.

What was the difference between a profession and any other occupation? The learned professions were callings for gentlemen, not jobs or trades, each of which required of a practitioner the mastery of a common body of specialized knowledge. Before an aspiring doctor or lawyer was ready to practice, before a would-be clergyman was prepared to minister to a congregation, he needed to understand his profession's arcana. He also had to learn to carry himself as a professional. In the British Isles, where the professions had ancient heritages, each had developed an ascending hierarchy of status. Solicitors, attorneys, barristers; apothecaries, surgeons, doctors; deacons, priests, bishops: each had its professional station and function. Colonial New England's professions were not as differentiated as Great Britain's, although on the eve of the Revolution, Massachusetts lawyers were beginning to distinguish between attorneys, who handled routine matters, and barristers, or courtroom advocates, who presented themselves as a legal elite. Nonetheless, as a group, New England's professionals enjoyed much the same prestige and recognition among their neighbors that their British counterparts did at home.[12]

Add teaching to the three principal professions and almost half the members of the revolutionary generation spent the best part of their careers in such a calling. Since most teachers intended at the outset to train for a learned profession, most often the ministry, and since many others who ended up in a different field—government, commerce, agriculture—also began professional study before dropping by the wayside, at some point about half the young graduates worked toward a career either in the pulpit, in the surgery, or at the bar.

Independent reading carried many recent graduates at least part of the way to a professional career. When Fisher Ames was not occupied in the classroom in Roxbury or Byfield, he began to study the law by himself.[13] In

Andover, Eliphalet Pearson read on his own for the ministry.[14] During the first century of settlement, such self-study was adequate preparation for a professional career as far as most New Englanders were concerned. By the middle of the eighteenth century, though, standards had begun to rise as professionals worked earnestly to set themselves apart from legal petti-foggers, medical quacks, and self-anointed religious exhorters. New En-glanders increasingly expected of their professionals more supervised preparation.[15]

Before the days of professional schools, apprenticeships offered the most rigorous training for a calling, the preparation that best distinguished rec-ognized professionals from lay practitioners. Much as bakers and house-wrights, silversmiths and shoemakers instructed young apprentices in a craft, for a fee experienced ministers, doctors, and lawyers sometimes pre-pared candidates for their respective careers. In New England after mid-century, professional apprenticeships grew more and more formalized, and the demands on both student and master practitioner became increasingly codified.[16]

No matter what the career, professional apprenticeships had three objec-tives for the aspirant and two more for the calling itself. Every candidate had to acquire both theoretical knowledge and practical information at the same time that he entered the life of a professional community—a brother-hood. Meanwhile, each profession used apprenticeships to ensure the qual-ity of practitioners and to limit access to it.[17]

Training for the ministry through apprenticeships had its roots in late-sixteenth- and early-seventeenth-century England, where established Pu-ritan clergymen took on young men for a period of directed reading before ordination. Then, as in the 1770s, the focus was on the systematic study of theology.[18]

In a posthumous 1735 pamphlet, Samuel Willard, the late minister of Boston's Old South Church, outlined the common course of study. The Bible was its basis, "since all Theological Truths are commended to us in the Word of God." Candidates for the ministry needed to understand the scrip-tures in the original languages, a requirement that called for a background in grammar, rhetoric, and logic in addition to Hebrew and Greek. They also had to be able to probe the texts systematically for the "Theological Truths ... contained in the Word of God." After mastering the Bible, candidates needed to be "soundly principled in the Fundamentals of Theology," an objective they accomplished by reading the systematic inquiries of promi-nent writers such as John Calvin and William Ames. Reading on practical issues helped a minister to counsel his congregation, while polemical texts provided responses to the threat of heresies. Finally, works of inspiration combined with quiet meditation nurtured a candidate's own faith and piety.[19]

None of this study was beyond the reach of aspirants working on their own. In fact, many candidates for ordination read theology at home without direct supervision, during employment as a teacher or while in Cambridge on a college fellowship. A.B.'s who studied theology while in residence with an established minister as mentor or adviser, however, had at least two advantages over the others. Through reading and writing assignments and in discussion, experienced ministers such as Jason Haven, the pastor of Dedham's First Parish, who often supervised candidates, were able to draw meanings and doctrines out of Bible texts and theological treatises. Divinity students ordinarily worked with clergymen whose religious views accorded with their own, and their advisers helped them to support their beliefs through their analyses of controverted points. Mentors also served as role models. As ministers met the pastoral challenges of each day by preaching, counseling, and catechizing, the young men who studied with them were able to observe and learn. Much as a father teaches his son by example how to be a man, a mentor such as Haven taught his students how to carry themselves as members of the clergy.[20]

Of provincial New England's three professions, the ministry had the least codified apprenticeship and the broadest range of educational alternatives in the 1770s. There were never enough trained ministers to meet the demand in late provincial New England, so many congregations in search of an acceptable candidate were more concerned with his personal qualities—his learning, his manner, and his beliefs—than with how he came to acquire them. Nevertheless, in the end, the best way to learn how to be a minister was to begin to confront the calling's many challenges under a mentor's supervision.

Whether he read theology on his own or with a mentor, the typical candidate was prepared to be considered for vacant pulpits within a year.[21] The next step was to find a congregation somewhere to call him.

Medical students often remained apprentices longer than candidates for ordination read theology—anywhere from as few as one to as many as five years—but the objectives and the methods were much the same. A medical apprenticeship combined intensive reading of professional texts with practical experience and an informal education in medicine as a profession. At the end of his term of study, his mentor certified that the apprentice was ready to practice, a declaration that said as much about his professional bearing as his theoretical knowledge and technical skill.[22]

In Massachusetts in the early 1770s, a small number of doctors trained most of the medical students. Edward A. Holyoke of Salem, the son of

President Holyoke, was the busiest of the medical mentors. Others included James Lloyd, Boston's most active practitioner, who had introduced the latest obstetrical techniques to New England, and Joseph Warren, also of Boston, Jack Warren's elder brother. Holyoke, Lloyd, and Warren did not hold a monopoly on medical education, though, and many others occasionally took on students. In a few instances, medical students traveled abroad, usually to Edinburgh or London, for their training.[23]

Edward Barnard, who studied with Holyoke, experienced a typical medical apprenticeship. The product of a family of ministers, Edward determined to pass up the pulpit in favor of the surgery. In the fall of 1775, Barnard moved to Salem, where he lived with Holyoke's family in their handsome brick mansion on Essex Street for much of the next two years.[24] Edward Augustus Holyoke was short, pudgy, and physically unimpressive, but he was also a man of great spirit and professional reputation in Massachusetts. Within the town of Salem he was a leader, constantly active in the social and cultural life of his community. Holyoke's medical apprentices learned how to act their part at the same time that they learned a profession.[25]

By the 1770s a standard, progressive course of study was widely accepted, and Barnard must have followed it. Would-be doctors began by reading anatomy texts, to which they added both basic and current literature on other specialties, including internal medicine, surgery, obstetrics, and pharmacology. Side by side with their mentors, apprentices received patients, went on house calls, compounded medicines, and nursed the sick.[26] By 1776 Barnard needed his own set of instruments. Short of money to buy them, he borrowed £20 from a cousin. And from his mother he borrowed more than £12 to pay for inoculation against smallpox; Barnard spent the first three weeks of June quarantined in a hospital in western Massachusetts, subsisting on fresh pudding, skimmed milk, and roasted potatoes while he endured redness, swelling, diarrhea, weakness, and the eruption of as many as thirty pox. The completion of his medical studies in 1777 corresponded with the third anniversary of his graduation. Edward Barnard was ready to go out on his own.[27]

With some latitude for individual initiative and preferences, a standard core of legal readings was also developing by the 1760s. Aspiring lawyers who had graduated from college spent three years as apprentices in the offices of established attorneys, where they read legal treatises, volumes of statutes, and guides to professional practice while assisting their mentors and attending court sessions. Legal apprenticeships could be tedious—law students sometimes spent extended periods working as their mentors' scriveners, copying wills, deeds, and other documents—but a diligent student could take advantage of his clerkship to address some compelling legal, political, and philosophical issues.[28]

When Fisher Ames entered the office of William Tudor to read law in 1779, he had already started to ground himself in his profession's basic texts. Students typically began with works on the common law, including Edward Coke's *Commentaries upon Littleton* and William Blackstone's *Commentaries on the Laws of England.* Baron Samuel von Pufendorf's *On the Law of Nature and Nations* introduced the student to natural law, while treatises by Hugo Grotius and Emmerich von Vattel instructed in international law.[29] Books by Robert Richardson and Joseph Harrison provided practical advice on the operations of the court system.[30] Meanwhile, daily contact with Tudor, who was only eight years Ames's senior but was already an established and respected attorney, provided him lessons on how to carry himself as a member of the bar.

Because Ames had studied by himself before entering Tudor's office, in 1779 he petitioned the bar of Suffolk County, which required candidates for admission to work for three years in the office of an established practitioner, for credit for the work he had already done on his own. The bar ultimately acceded to Ames's petition, although it did so with reservations. Becoming an attorney required more than a theoretical knowledge of the law.[31]

Within a few years of graduation, Edward Barnard, Fisher Ames, and a host of other young Harvardians were ready to begin their life's work. Meanwhile, their professional communities were prepared to accept them. In some cases an examination preceded formal recognition. Prior to the ceremony, candidates for ordination had to demonstrate their doctrinal acceptability to a council of clergymen convened for the event.[32] In many Massachusetts counties candidates for the bar underwent an oral examination of their legal knowledge before admission.[33] In every instance, the process of preparation protected the calling itself.

By establishing and maintaining standards for practitioners, New England's three learned professions saw to it that they were not overrun by competitors. At the same time, they enhanced the dignity of their callings. By limiting the bar to trained lawyers, attorneys underscored the distinction between professional advocates and the self-taught pettifoggers who offered questionable legal advice in many backwater communities. Medical apprenticeships provided a way of drawing a line between doctors and quacks. And at a time of mounting religious controversy, the examination that preceded ordination provided a measure of assurance that clerical candidates were orthodox, capable, educated, and genteel.

In each case, the would-be practitioner was ready for admission into a brotherhood—in effect, a professional guild. It went without saying that it was in the interest of every member of this association to maintain its standards and its dignity. Professional men were also gentlemen in New England during the second half of the eighteenth century, as refined as they were adept as practitioners.

Once they had mastered a profession and secured the approval of established practitioners, ministers, doctors, and lawyers had to find a place to live. A would-be clergyman had to receive a call from a church that would ordain and install him as its settled minister.[34] In his professional preparation, as he supplied pulpits for one or a series of Sundays, a candidate received exposure. As his name circulated, churches with a vacancy invited him to preach on a trial basis. Sometimes several candidates would preach in turn before a church voted for its favorite.

Metropolitan churches in towns such as Boston, Salem, and Portsmouth had the most to offer a young minister both culturally and financially, so they usually had the pick of candidates for ordination. Most of the opportunities were elsewhere, however, with established country congregations looking for a new minister or in new towns on the frontier. Here a young minister might be his community's only college man, its only polished and genteel resident. Joseph Avery, born and raised in Dedham, understood how remote his new situation was when as a wedding gift his parishioners in Holden, Massachusetts, north of Worcester, gave him twenty huge slabs of spareribs from the game they had killed and slaughtered.[35] Of the revolutionary generation's twenty-seven ordained ministers, only two served urban congregations.[36]

As for doctors and lawyers, they could make their homes wherever they thought they could earn a good living. Prestige and income accompanied the establishment of a successful practice in a major town, but even the most talented young doctor found it a challenge to carve out a place for himself amidst urban competition. In 1773, writing on behalf of his brother Jack, Joseph Warren contacted Edward A. Holyoke to assess the prospects in Salem, where a leading physician had recently passed away: "[Jack] is now deliberating upon the Place of settling himself in. Marblehead was first in his Intentions but since the Death of Dr. Fairfield he has thought of Salem. No doubt some Person will step in upon this Vacancy as Salem is a large populous Town. I take the Liberty of requesting you to give your friendly Advice upon a Matter so Interesting to him and I believe your Opinion will determine him."[37]

Holyoke's response was sufficiently positive to encourage Jack to settle in Salem, but establishing a practice, even where there seemed to be an opening, was difficult and stressful. At the start of 1775, Jack found it a struggle simply to cover his bills, much less to save some money. "It is true

I have as good a share of business as I could reasonably expect for the time I have been here," he reported to his brother, "but I cannot collect more than money sufficient to defray the charges from clothing and other common expenses. I am not able to pay any thing towards my board or apothecaries' bill.... To enter the world under such circumstances is really discouraging."[38]

By the middle of the eighteenth century, many young doctors and lawyers were looking to settle in crossroads communities outside of Boston and Salem, for example, in Taunton or Braintree. There was less competition in rural market towns than in commercial centers, and the absence of trained professionals opened a niche for young practitioners.[39] Fisher Ames already knew when he began to read law that he wanted to practice in Dedham, his hometown.[40] Still, under even the best of conditions, most of these young men were not ready to settle down only three years after graduation. Even those who began immediately after commencement were barely completing their professional training when they and their classmates were ready to claim their master's degrees. Eventually, if recent patterns held true to form, they would settle in a variety of communities, perhaps half in New England's major seaports and the other half in smaller market towns such as Exeter, Worcester, and Haverhill.

Unlike ministers, doctors, and lawyers, merchants and others in business were not pursuing a profession. Commercial activities took many different forms. Harvard alumni in the late 1760s included foreign merchants, coastal traders, chandlers, braziers, distillers, small-town shopkeepers, land agents, shipbuilders, innkeepers, and ironworks owners. Such a varied group of specialists did not share a common body of knowledge beyond basic bookkeeping, and each occupation required its own network of contacts. Anyone with access to the necessary capital could set himself up in trade or in manufacturing, though certainly without any assurance of success.

Despite the absence of formal apprenticeship expectations, would-be merchants and manufacturers often worked for experienced mentors for a few years while they learned their business and attempted to establish themselves. Nathan Bond spent most of the five years between his graduation in 1772 and his first attempt in 1777 to trade on his own account as a clerk to Duncan Ingraham, a wealthy Tory merchant in Concord and the stepfather of Bond's close friend Tilly Merrick.[41] Bond's classmate Tom Coffin went to work for his father, a Boston provisioner.[42] In Portsmouth, James Sheafe benefited from his father's commercial experience.[43] As clerks to established merchants and manufacturers, men such as Bond, Coffin, and Sheafe learned how to make their way in the world as traders and manufacturers—how to buy and sell; how to make, use, and maintain contacts; how to read markets, set prices, and minimize risks.

In August 1771, slightly more than a month after his graduation, William Cheever found himself clerking for a merchant in Kittery, Maine. Cheever's family operated a warehouse in Boston, and their commercial contacts perhaps opened up an apprenticeship opportunity for him. "I'll give you an Account of how I spend my time here," he wrote his sister Elizabeth. "The first thing I do in the morning after washing is to go over to the Store ... & after staying there an Hour ... to breakfast & then to the Store again till dinner time, when that's over we set & chat [until] about three O'clock when to the Store again." Cheever passed almost every evening with visits: "We make a very sociable Company."[44]

The one common calling for which no one saw a need for a postgraduate apprenticeship was farming. Full-time agriculture did not attract many eighteenth-century graduates, although ministers, lawyers, doctors, and teachers who lived outside commercial centers often worked the land to augment their professional income. Farming was so much a part of the fabric of daily life in rural New England that almost everyone who took it up had been exposed to it from early childhood. Running a farm was a complicated and risky business, and those who worked the soil began to acquire what they needed to know to survive and thrive at a very young age. Among college graduates in the 1770s, full-time agriculture was almost always a second career for someone who had failed at a first or had a reason to maintain a discreetly low profile.

Whichever calling a member of the revolutionary generation followed, the events of the day conspired against him. Although the men of the class of 1771 had more than three years between their graduation and the outbreak of the Revolution, for the three succeeding classes time was progressively shorter. For the men of 1774, only nine months separated the end of their college course from the battles of Lexington and Concord. Career disruptions were an almost unavoidable consequence.

MINISTER, DOCTOR, lawyer, merchant, teacher, farmer. This list of occupations accounted for almost all of the members of the revolutionary generation during the first years after graduation, the years when young men found themselves and set a course for a lifetime. But among the members of the generation there were three noteworthy individual exceptions to the common pattern. By the time graduation day arrived, two students had left for Europe and a third was ready to do whatever he had to in order to follow them.

The common denominators for these boys were family wealth and high station, either already in hand or on offer. Many Harvard students depended on a college education to lift themselves into the upper ranks of local society, but not everyone needed such a boost. Jemmy Bowdoin was the only son of James Bowdoin II, one of the most affluent merchants in Boston and an active local politician. James Ivers was the son of a small-time Boston sugar refiner, also named James, but he was also the nephew of Barlow Trecothick, lord mayor of London in 1770, member of Parliament, representative at court for a number of American colonies, and a partner in a prosperous British mercantile firm.[45] John Trumbull's father, Jonathan, as we have already seen, was the governor of Connecticut and a successful trader. Each of the three young men could afford to set his own agenda.

When Jemmy Bowdoin left Cambridge for London during the winter of his senior year, early in 1771, the formal reason his father offered in requesting permission for his son to take a leave was his health. Jemmy had recently been involved in student mischief, though, and his father wanted him out of town before he could engage in any more. In England he would be far from college authorities and temptations. He might even gain in maturity from being abroad.[46]

During his first months in England, Bowdoin dabbled in the study of law at Christ Church, Oxford, but he showed the greatest enthusiasm for the alternative course of studies that he devised on his own after leaving Oxford in the fall of 1771. Bowdoin's new curriculum included riding, French, dancing, and fencing—necessary ornaments for a proper gentleman. He also made contacts for later use if he should go into trade. After sixteen months away, Bowdoin returned home in April 1772, but not for long.

This time it was Italy that called him. Together with Ward Nicholas Boylston, an affluent young dandy who had not bothered to attend college, Bowdoin returned to Europe in the fall of 1773. In Italy they visited sumptuously decorated cathedrals, storied natural wonders, and eye-opening archaeological excavations, and they marveled at the wealth and style of the aristocratic and commercial society of Naples and Rome. By the time Bowdoin finally returned to Massachusetts from his grand tour in December 1775, a great deal had changed at home.[47]

If James Bowdoin possessed wealth and station, James Ivers wanted it. An offer from Ivers's uncle Barlow Trecothick was too good to pass up.

By the time Ivers was an undergraduate, Barlow Trecothick had almost everything one might want. Born in Boston, Trecothick had married well, then settled in London sometime around 1750. The mercantile firm of Trecothick, Apthorp & Thomlinson flourished, and he soon become active

James Bowdoin III. Jemmy Bowdoin sat for this portrait during one of his two European excursions after leaving school, 1770–1775. (*Portrait of James Bowdoin III* [1770–1775], by an unknown artist. Oil on canvas, 30.25 × 25.5 in. Bowdoin College Museum of Art, Brunswick, Maine. Bequest of Mrs. Sarah Bowdoin Dearborn.)

in public affairs. In the early 1770s Barlow Trecothick lacked only one thing: an heir to carry on his name.

James Ivers was to be that heir. He came from a family of small retailers and manufacturers. Under normal circumstances, he might have expected to follow their lead, but now he had an opportunity for wealth and influence. All he had to do was to join his uncle in London and take his surname. Ivers left Harvard a few days before the start of his junior year, on August 10, 1771. When Uncle Barlow died at the age of fifty-six on May 28, 1775, his nephew, now James (Ivers) Trecothick, inherited a massive estate in Surrey that included a mansion and a farm of five thousand acres.[48]

John Trumbull returned home to Lebanon, Connecticut, after his graduation in 1773.[49] He took up teaching for several months that fall after his old instructor, Nathan Tisdale, collapsed with a stroke.[50] Trumbull also dabbled in trade. But his eyes were on nothing so conventional as a traditional career as a doctor, lawyer, minister, or merchant. Ever since childhood, art had fascinated him. He wanted to be a painter, and he yearned to go to Europe to study with the masters.

The American colonies had never seen a single college-educated painter when Trumbull returned to Lebanon from Cambridge. The best artists in provincial America were, like John Singleton Copley, talented craftsmen who had ended their formal education at some point before college.[51] Trumbull's goal, however, was a respectable life doing work that he loved. If he wanted to pursue such a calling, he would, in effect, have to invent his career. As time allowed, he studied engravings of European masterworks at home, and for the first time he tried his hand at composing and painting a classical scene. To please his father, who wondered how John would ever find a practical way to make use of his passion for art, he also drew two maps of land that Connecticut was contesting.[52]

Notwithstanding Governor Trumbull's reasonable attempts to force his son to follow a practical course, in the years following graduation John Trumbull expended most of his energies on his independent study of art. Like Jemmy Bowdoin and James Trecothick, he could afford to turn away from a traditional career thanks to his family's resources.

IT WAS THE rare alumnus who had not fixed on an occupation and begun to train for it within three years after graduation. Although the career paths of some were smoother and more direct than others', almost everyone had made up his mind about a calling by the time the members of his class began to qualify for their second degree. The search for a mate took longer. Eventually, nearly every Harvard man who lived to at least his mid-thirties found a wife, but most members of the revolutionary generation were still single on the third anniversary of their graduation.[53]

Although marriage involved the most personal of choices, arranged marriages were not unheard of in eighteenth-century New England. When Jemmy Bowdoin was fourteen, his father considered a match for him with the daughter of the governor of the island of Grenada.[54] If such thoughts ever actually led to a marriage, however, they were extremely uncommon. The customary path was a period of casual courting, when young men and women took stock of what their communities had to offer, followed by pairing off and more intense courtship. When they reached this stage, young couples understood that marriage was the end in view.[55]

New assumptions about the nature of the relationship of wife and husband had begun to shape marriage in provincial New England. Friendship and romantic love had not always been prerequisites. In the seventeenth century, if they developed at all, these sentiments often followed the wedding vows rather than preceding them.[56] By the 1770s, however, the common wisdom was that without love, a marriage was an empty form. Once everyone agreed to this view, the only people who could decide whether a marriage would work were the prospective bride and groom.[57]

Casual courting began during college, particularly for older students. Some undergraduates found companionship in Cambridge—Eliphalet Pearson's first wife was the daughter of President Holyoke[58]—and the college schedule was sufficiently flexible to permit occasional visits to Boston. Joseph Pearse Palmer, a member of the class of 1771, met Betsy Hunt, his future wife, on a blind date toward the end of his undergraduate years.[59] Betsy had expected to be fixed up with a classmate of Joseph's, and initially she was disappointed when Palmer appeared to squire her. But soon they were talking of books and periodicals—Betsy was reading the *Spectator*—and Palmer offered her the use of his personal collection of the latest publications. "We had a fine time and danced all day (Mr. Palmer was fine dancer)," Betsy later recalled, "and returned home in a thunder-storm in the evening."[60] Like Palmer, most students who made time for dancing classes must have used their training to socialize. College vacations could also be opportunities for rounds of visiting with neighbors at home and with the families of classmates.[61]

Before casual socializing could grow into a permanent relationship, however, a young couple had to develop a strong attachment, and—this was vitally important—the potential bridegroom had to demonstrate his career prospects. Even though the couple's parents did not arrange the match, both partners ordinarily sought family approval. Moreover, before the wedding itself, the groom had to be sufficiently secure in his work to be able to support his wife and the children they hoped to have.[62]

Consider John Shaw's courtship of Betsy Smith.[63] The son and grandson of ministers, Shaw aspired to the ministry himself. After he graduated in 1772, John went to Weymouth to live in the rambling, ancient parsonage of the Reverend William Smith, with whom he read theology.[64] Smith had three daughters. The two elder ones were already married and out of their parents' household. Mary had married Richard Cranch, a watchmaker, and Abigail had married John Adams, at the time of their wedding still a young lawyer in Braintree and Boston. Only the youngest daughter, Betsy, was still at home.

As Shaw prepared for the ministry, he and Betsy began to spend time together—so much so that Abigail Adams grew uneasy about the budding relationship. The reasons for her discomfort are not entirely clear. Perhaps she questioned Shaw's prospects, or possibly she favored another suitor. Whatever the case, she obviously did not approve of Shaw as a potential spouse for her younger sister, and she said so. Betsy denied that the friendship was serious. Eventually, in 1774, she drew up a "certificate" for Abigail to which she pasted Shaw's signature clipped from a letter and added her own: "We John Shaw, and Elizabeth Smith have no such Purpose in Our Hearts, as has been unjustly surmised."[65] Whether or not Betsy was serious in denying her feelings for Shaw, the two were wed three and a half years later, shortly after John was settled as the minister of the First Parish in Haverhill, in October 1777. William Smith, who must have approved of the match, or at least acquiesced to it, performed the ceremony.[66]

More than five years elapsed between Shaw's graduation in 1772 and his marriage. He knew Betsy for most of this time, and at least to the members of Betsy's family, the relationship appeared to be serious years before Shaw's ordination in Haverhill secured his prospects, permitting the couple to take the final step: marriage.

Like John Shaw, most members of the revolutionary generation were not quite ready for marriage by the time their classes qualified for the master's degree. Over the previous decade, young Harvardians had typically waited six or seven years after graduation to marry.[67] Only seventeen members of the revolutionary generation, one in twelve, married before their class qualified for the second degree. In more than half of these cases, there were special circumstances.

Abijah Richardson returned to Harvard with his classmates to start his junior year on August 12, 1772.[68] He had come from East Medway, where his father owned a farm. Two months later, on October 12, he abruptly left college. Richardson had tarried with Mercy Daniell, a sixteen-year-old neighbor from Medway, while he was home on vacation, and their casual courting had gone too far. Eighteenth-century parents usually allowed their children to entertain in private,[69] but when the Daniells left Mercy alone with Abijah, matters got out of hand. The third quarter of the eighteenth century was not a period of sexual restraint. Bundling, or sleeping fully clothed together in the house of a woman's parents, was common, and so was premarital intercourse. In some New England towns in the second half of the eighteenth century, more than two-fifths of the brides were pregnant on their wedding day, and Mercy Daniell was one of them.[70] Abijah Richardson left school to make an honest woman of Mercy, whom he wed on November 24. The following April 2 Mercy gave birth to a daughter, the first of the couple's ten children.[71]

Jonathan French had catching up to do. The oldest member of the class of 1771—thirty-one years of age at graduation—he had deferred starting a family while he had attended college. Men his age were already marrying and beginning families when French entered college as a freshman at twenty-seven. He had begun to court Abigail Richards of Weymouth while he was serving with the garrison at Castle William, but they had agreed not to commit to each other while he pursued his education. More mature than most of his classmates and certain of what he wanted to do with his life, French could accelerate the process of settling down. Ordained and installed by the South Parish of Andover in September 1772, he married Abigail the following August.[72]

Of the seventeen members of Harvard's revolutionary generation who married within three years of graduation, at least two had made their brides pregnant well before the wedding. Incomplete vital records and the chance of miscarriages and stillbirths leave open the possibility that several others may also have married under pressure. And seven of the seventeen had been twenty years old or more when they matriculated. Like French, many of them must have felt after graduation four years later that it was time to get on with their lives.[73]

Time pressures, however, did not squeeze most of the rest of the young graduates. Marriage and the responsibilities it entailed would come in time. There was no need to rush having a family. The day would arrive soon enough.

IN ANOTHER respect, though, the Harvardians were growing up earlier and earlier. As a political reckoning approached, they became increasingly caught up in the affairs of the day. A near-riot beneath the majestic

Copley portraits of King George III and Queen Charlotte in the college dining hall in early 1775 revealed the extent of tensions even among the undergraduates.

Until early 1775 college disorders were invariably parochial affairs, reactions to purely internal problems such as the abysmal quality of the food, which led to the Bad Butter Rebellion of 1766.[74] On March 1, 1775, however, the issue was tea, a powerful political symbol in Massachusetts after the Boston Tea Party of December 1773. In the ornate college commons in Harvard Hall that March morning, Whig and loyalist undergraduates nearly came to blows over the India tea that friends of the government had brought to breakfast. The college authorities were able to quell the disturbance before anyone damaged the room's elaborately carved woodwork, but not before emotions boiled over and someone broke a few pieces of crockery. Later that day, the faculty ordered the students not to bring tea to meals.[75]

The growing strains that divided undergraduates in early 1775 also affected the recent graduates of the college's revolutionary generation, forcing them to take sides. No previous generation of Harvard men had ever had to become so deeply involved in contentious political affairs at so early an age.

In more normal times, local government served as the avenue into public affairs for most men. New England town meetings were open to every voter. Young men began to participate in civic life when they joined their neighbors each year to choose community leaders and address local issues. The most responsible public offices—moderator, selectman, representative to the General Court—routinely went to established, mature men who had earned the respect of the town and could afford the time for these unpaid posts. But in most communities there were also many minor offices to fill— hog reeve, fence viewer, surveyor of highways—and younger men who successfully served public apprenticeships in these assignments qualified themselves for more substantial service later on.[76]

An important characteristic of the new politics, however, distinguished it from the parochial factional fighting of the past. As the Revolution approached, whichever side they took, many New Englanders found that they cared about real public issues as well as the usual partisan wrangling. Local quarrels over the placement of a schoolhouse or meetinghouse or the decisions of a tax assessor might be contentious, but they were rarely driven by ideology, and the factions that wrestled with one another were subject to reshuffling with the emergence of new problems.[77] As the imperial crisis pitted Whig against Tory, though, young men, including young Harvard graduates, had to stand up and be counted. The lines that began to harden in the late 1760s and early 1770s—the friends of the crown on one side, its opponents on the other—were not rigid or unchanging before 1775. In the end, some early critics of the administration were unwilling to break with the mother country, while some of its first apologists eventually determined that their strongest bonds were with their countrymen. If the final configuration of the battle lines did not emerge until the start of hostilities, the pressure to declare at least a preliminary allegiance squeezed more and more citizens.[78]

Across New England, the events that accelerated the march toward civil war—from the Stamp Act Crisis in the mid-1760s, to the Boston Massacre in 1770, to the Tea Party in 1773, to the imposition of the Intolerable Acts, which closed the harbors of Boston and Charlestown in 1774—divided the population and led each side to organize itself. The kernel of the loyalist faction was already apparent in the informal network of public officials, merchants, Anglicans, and others who considered themselves the friends of government. The Whig side was more numerous and more amorphous at first, but it too began to take shape gradually around such nuclei as the Sons of Liberty, the committees of correspondence, and local militia companies.

As young as they were, the recent graduates were leaders on neither side. They did not promote division, but many of them felt compelled by a combination of friendship, kinship, and conviction to take a stand.

The striking fact about the Tory members of Harvard's revolutionary generation in the years before the war is that their loyalism was almost invariably a family matter. It would be wrong to suggest that the men who stood with the crown did not believe in their cause or to claim that the conflict never split a Tory household, but it would be myopic to overlook the family allegiances and interests that bound them to the royal administration.[79] Ebenezer Boltwood, the son of a shopkeeper, returned home to Amherst after graduation in 1773 just in time to see an existing parochial quarrel take on ideological overtones and become caught up in the imperial crisis. At the start of the decade an insurgent group in Amherst had tried to divide the town for ecclesiastical purposes into two parishes. Boltwood's father, Solomon, was among the community leaders who vigorously resisted the initiative. This local division predicted the positions that many residents of the town assumed on imperial questions a few years later. Ebenezer, along with his father, his minister, and many other prominent members of the community, remained loyal to the crown, a position that became increasingly untenable after April 19, 1775.[80] Tom Coffin's extended family included loyalist uncles and cousins as well as his father and brothers.[81] In Worcester, meanwhile, William Chandler joined with a number of family members in signing an address in 1774 to protest rebel rioting

and the creation of the committees of correspondence.[82] The consequences
of family connections to the administration became apparent to Samuel
Murray of Rutland in August 1774, when he and his father, who had been
recently named a member of Governor Thomas Gage's Mandamus Council,
barely escaped a mob protesting the selection.[83]

On the other side, among the most common of defining moments was
the creation of a local company of Minutemen, pledged to muster at a
moment's notice in case of a confrontation with British troops. Too youthful
for political leadership, the members of the revolutionary generation were
the perfect age for military service. A few, including Joshua Bailey Osgood
of Haverhill, an ensign in an artillery company, served as officers in the
units their towns organized.[84] Whatever the rank, though, by the spring of
1775 dozens more were drilling regularly with their neighbors in anticipation of the coming struggle.

Many New Englanders, including some recent Harvard graduates, still
sat on the fence, waiting for developments before they committed themselves to one side or the other. As tempers rose, however, such irresolution
raised suspicions. In Concord, Nathan Bond hesitated before he took a
stand. "Brother Bond, it seems, has been in Limbo," a classmate wrote to
Jack Warren in 1775. "Whether he has regained the esteem of his countrymen, or came out the same heterogenious Quiddam he went in, I have not
been able to learn."[85] Pressures to take sides made it increasingly difficult
to be indecisive.

As the members of Harvard's revolutionary generation entered adulthood in the years after graduation, of course, they did so without the benefit
of foreknowledge. During the years before 1775, their tasks were the same
ones that generations of young New England men had undertaken at about
the same age: to settle on a calling, a place of residence, and a wife. At the
same time, most of them weaned themselves from their parental families as
they prepared to form nuclear units of their own. The common pattern was
well established. What reason was there to believe that larger developments might redirect the course of their lives?

ON JULY 31, 1775, Clement March, Clement Weeks, and Weeks's younger
brother, William, set out for Cambridge from their homes in Greenland,
New Hampshire, just west of Portsmouth. As the crow flies, Greenland and
Cambridge are fully fifty miles apart, and the twists and turns of provincial
country roads added many more miles to the trip, making it a journey of
more than a day. Three years had elapsed since the two older boys had
received their bachelor's degrees. Clement March, a son of Greenland's
most prominent resident (who was also the Weeks boys' grandfather, their

mother's father), had spent the years studying medicine in Portsmouth. Clement Weeks had passed the time teaching school in Greenland and serving as the town clerk.[86] Bill Weeks had just completed his senior year at Harvard.

Under normal circumstances, the three travelers would have enjoyed the pomp and ceremony, the celebrating and carousing of commencement two weeks earlier, but these were not normal times. Recent graduates usually looked forward to the chance to return to Cambridge to see old friends when they qualified for the master's degree. Ordinarily, almost the entire class returned for a reunion.[87] But the college, which had not held a public commencement in 1774, would not hold another one until 1781. The same day that March and the Weeks brothers set out, the college's Corporation met in Watertown to consider what to do about graduation during troubled times. "The Distress & Confusion" of the day made it "impracticable to hold a public Commencement or make the necessary preparation for conferring Degrees at the Stated Season," they decided, so instead Harvard would issue a general diploma that carried the names of everyone who had earned, and paid the fees for, either the first or the second degree.[88] Clement March, Clement Weeks, and Bill Weeks returned quietly to Cambridge to make some calls, conduct college business, and qualify for their several degrees.

March and the Weeks boys set out for Cambridge on a Monday. Between the time the trip required and the time it took to pay social calls and transact their errands, they were probably still busy making their rounds late Tuesday afternoon and possibly even early Wednesday morning. It had been a long time since Clement March and Clement Weeks had been to Cambridge, so they had friendships to renew. Bill Weeks must have had undergraduate bills to settle with the college as well as with Cambridge tradesmen, and then there were graduation fees to pay. According to a college official, each master's candidate had to pay five shillings and four-pence to be listed in the printed college catalogue, and there were additional charges for diplomas. "I gave him a Guinea & took no change back," Clement Weeks recorded in his diary.[89]

After they completed their calls, sometime on Wednesday, August 2, the three graduates set out for home, which they reached on the evening of August 3.[90] No doubt they had taken care of important personal business, but given the times, they had more significant worries. Owing to the events of the previous April 19, everyone did.

4

A TIME FOR CHOICES

I T WAS MIDDAY in Cambridge, a Wednesday in early spring before the
trees had filled with leaves, but all the doors in town were locked, the
windows were shuttered, and no one was on the streets. In the distance,
the high-pitched trill of fifes and the insistent tattoo of drums carried from
the south, softly at first, then louder and louder. The steady marching
cadence of a thousand pairs of heavy-soled black leather shoes shook the
earth with a growing thunder. Beside the advancing scarlet-coated column,
prancing horses confidently carried more than a dozen officers.

The date was April 19, 1775, and the troops were a force of British
regulars under the command of Lord Percy, sent from Boston to relieve the
retreating soldiers of Lieutenant Colonel Francis Smith, who had been
whipped earlier in the day at Concord. Percy's men had already covered
eight miles from Boston through Roxbury to reach Cambridge. When they
had arrived at the bridge across the Charles River a few hundred yards
south of the red brick buildings of the college a short time earlier, they had
discovered that someone had pulled up its planks to obstruct them—one
more in the series of delays that had plagued them since being called out in
the early morning. Then, when they reached Cambridge Common, immediately northwest of Harvard Yard, they encountered another problem.

The road they were taking forked at the Common. One branch went
west, the other northwest. Which way led to Lexington and Concord?
Nobody in the British line of march was certain, and in the empty village
no one was in sight to press for directions. The troops came to a halt and
waited in formation.

Finally, a young man appeared at the entrance to the college Yard. One
of the British officers hailed him and the figure indicated the way. The
column resumed its march.

The young man was tutor Isaac Smith, and whether or not he realized
it, he had just made a fateful choice. Smith's loyalty to the American cause
had long been suspect, and any lingering doubts his acquaintances may
have entertained about his allegiances were erased as soon as he sent Lord
Percy's force on its way.[1] Latter-day apologists have sometimes tried to

excuse Smith, explaining that honesty or innocence led him to give the redcoats the directions they needed, but his Cambridge neighbors knew him, and they were less charitable. They quickly concluded that he was simply showing his true colors. In a moment the town became too hot for him. Smith soon fled to Boston, and four weeks later he sailed for England to lie low until tempers cooled.[2]

Choices had consequences in April 1775. No one knew this better than Isaac Smith.

THE AMERICAN REVOLUTION lasted for more than eight long, bitter years, taking a heavy toll in lives, health, property, family ties, and friendships. Members of the Harvard classes of 1771 through 1774 were caught up in the conflict from its beginning to its end, although only a few men served under either the British or the American colors for its entire duration. From one individual to the next there were great differences in the nature and extent of participation. Young Harvard men were present at most of the important engagements in the North, and occasionally they made their way to other battlefields. They served in the infantry, the cavalry, and the artillery; on naval vessels and on privateers; as coastal guards and as prison guards; as doctors and as chaplains; as quartermasters and as paymasters; as aides-de-camp and as military lawyers; as civilian provisioners and as gunpowder manufacturers. Slightly more than half of the members of Harvard's revolutionary generation served with one side or the other—in the regular army, as militiamen, or at sea—for at least a few days. Roughly one-quarter served extended tours of duty lasting many months or years. Although a few spent a brief period of time in the ranks as enlisted men, most of those who served were officers—usually ensigns, lieutenants, and captains, occasionally majors, lieutenant colonels, and colonels. None of them died in combat, although two disappeared when their ships were lost at sea and five more suffered other service-related deaths.[3]

Whether or not he served in the military, however, almost every member of the college's revolutionary generation felt the effects of the war. It intruded on the customary path from young adulthood to maturity, the course that every previous generation of Harvard men had taken. Who could escape the social and economic disruptions—the shortages and inflation, the rumors and fears of imminent combat close at hand, the loss of friends and relatives—that were the unavoidable consequences of the Revolution?

And who could escape the pressure to choose a side? Individual situations were rarely as stark and immediate as the one that faced Isaac Smith on April 19, and somehow a few men did manage to keep their own counsel throughout the war, but they were a very small minority. Many others had to address the issue more than once as the competing military and political fortunes of the crown and the patriots waxed and waned over the course of eight years. The opposing loyalties of the day—motherland versus native land, identification as a royal subject versus identification as a citizen of Massachusetts or New Hampshire or Connecticut—tore at almost every heart and soul. For most young Harvard men, the war years were a time for choices.

On a day of wrenching decisions, each member of the revolutionary generation had to look inside himself to assess his own values, commitments, and ambitions. Which weighed more heavily: a comforting tradition of steadfast obedience to the crown or the apparent threat that political corruption was undermining a heritage of English liberties? Where did honor lie: in appointment to high positions of dignity and influence within the royal establishment or in courageously standing up against oppressive power? Where were the best opportunities: with the British and the known or with the Americans and the unknown? These were questions that almost every member of the generation faced. For most of them the war became a formative experience, a time of self-definition that shaped subsequent lives and outlooks in countless ways.

ALTHOUGH THE college generation's participation in the Revolution lasted from the beginning of the war to its end, it was at its highest point on the very first day of the struggle. Fully one in nine of its members had some kind of role in the engagement. As all eyes turned to two small New England towns and to the network of dirt roads that connected them to each other and to the rest of the world, Lexington and Concord attracted two dozen young Harvardians like iron filings to a magnet.

The evening before Isaac Smith took his stand with the king, another recent graduate made a similar fateful decision. Like Smith, Samuel Murray, now a medical student in Boston, was already widely identified with the crown. Murray had traveled the back roads of Middlesex County many times between the college and his parents' home in Rutland, Massachusetts, a small town in Worcester County west of Boston. The first British troops who marched to Lexington and Concord, those under the command of Francis Smith, had no better idea how to find their objective than Percy's men did many hours later, standing outside the college Yard. In preparing for the mission they had recognized the need for a guide. Murray was their man; as they made their way through Cambridge and its rural Menotomy precinct in the moonlit hours of the early morning of April 19, he led them past silent farmhouses, barns, orchards, and pastures, along miles of country roads.[4]

While Smith's troops were advancing on Lexington, Martin Herrick, a young doctor just completing his medical training, was doing his best to thwart his classmate Murray. Paul Revere, in the course of his ride that night to alert the Massachusetts countryside to the movements of the regulars, had the help of dozens of other messengers who picked up and carried his warnings from Boston into the interior of New England. Herrick was one of them. After college, he had taken his professional apprenticeship a few miles north of Cambridge in Medford, where he was visiting old friends on the evening of April 18 when Revere sped through town. Within moments of hearing the alarm, Herrick saddled his mount and raced to nearby Stoneham and Reading with the word.[5]

In more than a dozen New England towns, members of Harvard's revolutionary generation heard the alert that men such as Herrick spread, dropped whatever they were doing, fell in with their neighbors, and sped double-time in the direction of the shooting. From Northampton, where he was reading law, Levi Lincoln marched toward the action with the town's company of Minutemen.[6] Jacob Bacon, who had just begun to practice medicine eight or ten miles northwest of Boston in Woburn, formed up with his town's militia; he suffered a minor wound in an encounter later that day.[7] William Eustis, who was studying medicine in Boston with Joseph Warren, followed the skirmishing and ministered to some of the casualties.[8]

Not everyone who was present on April 19 served under the colors of one side or the other. In Lexington, Thomas Rice Willard, a civilian, observed the early morning shots on the town green that began the war; later he provided the American forces with a sympathetic eyewitness account.[9] At mid-morning, Tilly Merrick was in Concord visiting his mother and stepfather, Duncan Ingraham, the town's most uncompromising Tory, when a scarlet-coated horseman paid a call. Major John Pitcairn of the Royal Marines, the second-ranking officer in the British task force, had left the column of soldiers to offer his respects. Suddenly, firing broke out at the North Bridge. Pitcairn heard the volleys and spurred his horse in their direction.[10] In Menotomy, Sam Cooke saved his father's life. As the British troops fled Concord, they plundered and torched many of the houses, barns, and sheds they passed. Menotomy's parsonage lay along the regulars' line of flight. When they reached it, they broke the windows and shot into the house with small arms. Parson Cooke wanted to stand and fight, but Sam dragged his livid, sixty-six-year-old father out of harm's way to a chaise and off to safety.[11]

Samuel Murray was in confinement by now. As the regulars had broken and run for their lives, their guide had not been able to keep up with them. Captured by the American militia, Murray was transported to Worcester, where he remained under guard.[12]

By the end of the day, at least sixteen members of Harvard's revolutionary generation had stood up to the regulars, and one, Murray, had publicly pitched his lot in with the crown. For some it would be the most memorable day of their lives. People were in motion everywhere. Many young Harvardians were too far away from the scene of the fighting to reach the battle while it was still in progress, but they, too, were taking a stand. William Jennison was living in Mendon when the word of the action reached him. He and his town's militiamen were on the road to Boston by nightfall,[13] as were Levi Lincoln and the citizen soldiers of Northampton.[14] William Eustis and Thomas Welsh were busy tending the wounded.[15] Meanwhile, many of the generation's loyalists were fleeing to Boston and the apparent safety afforded by the presence of about twenty regiments of redcoats.

That evening, as more than one hundred British and American bodies lay stiff and cold, Massachusetts militiamen began to organize a siege around Boston.[16] For weeks to come, loyalists would continue to slip into town, and from Boston hundreds of patriots would surreptitiously flee in the other direction. The divisions were hardening rapidly. Eventually, twenty-eight members of the generation, one in seven, would side with the crown, at least for a time. Both figuratively and literally, the lines were being drawn.

WITHIN A few days, many of the militiamen who had answered the call on April 19 began to drift home, satisfied that they had done their duty. Some of the men and boys who saw service in April 1775 did not spend as much as another day under arms during the next eight years. Not long after the engagements, Levi Lincoln returned to Northampton to resume his legal studies.[17] William Hobart, a schoolteacher, recorded three days of service with the Weston militia before he hung up his musket.[18] Samuel Prentice, who happened to be visiting his parents in Cambridge from Weston, where he too was teaching school, formed up with his hometown militia, then submitted a bill for walking from Cambridge to Concord and back.[19] Encircling Boston, though, at various times over the course of the next eleven months, about thirty young Harvard men helped to mount the siege, while inside the town at least fourteen of their loyalist schoolmates looked out at the rebel guns.

Cambridge was now at the center of provincial military activities. On April 20 the council of war made up of the commanders of the assembled rebel units appointed the college steward, Jonathan Hastings, to the same post for the siege force, and when Artemas Ward took command of these men the same day, he established his headquarters in Hastings's house, where the Speaking Club had often met.[20] Less than two weeks later, on

May 1, the college suspended classes and the students vacated the dormitories, which the Massachusetts Provincial Congress immediately commandeered to serve as barracks.[21]

For the rest of 1775 and the early months of 1776, the troops around Boston and their hostages in the town cautiously attempted to wait each other out. The British made only one serious effort, at Breed's and Bunker hills in Charlestown on June 17, 1775, to break the siege, and even then they were reacting to an American initiative.

The redcoats confined to Boston were in a precarious situation. The town, on a hilly peninsula which jabbed at the harbor, and the protective shield of British naval vessels that guarded it lay within view of two unoccupied elevations, the Dorchester Heights to the south and the three hills of the Charlestown peninsula to the north. When about 1,200 rebel soldiers seized the Charlestown isthmus during the evening of June 16 and began to construct fortifications on Breed's Hill, the alarmed British commanders were roused from their lethargy. At first light on June 17, at about 4:00 A.M., lookouts aboard a British warship in Boston Harbor spotted the Americans' unfinished parapets and the vessel opened fire with broadsides from its cannons. Wherever the crown's troops were quartered around town the order went out to prepare for a landing in Charlestown and an assault on the incomplete American works. Under covering fire from five warships and two floating batteries, between 2,000 and 2,500 regulars and marines were ferried across the harbor in the early afternoon.[22]

From several miles to the south in Dorchester, where he was serving with a regiment of the Connecticut militia, John Trumbull could barely follow the action across the harbor on the hills of Charlestown. Trumbull had been inspecting a guardpost at daybreak when the first fusillade had startled him. Charlestown was too far from Dorchester to view the action easily with the naked eye, but as the British cannonade crescendoed and the first assault began at 3:00 P.M., he could hear the pounding. He could also discern smoke rising from the guns on either side and from the houses of Charlestown, which soon began to go up in flames as they came under a savage British barrage. With the aid of a telescope he could make out more detail, although it was not until evening that he learned the British had carried the day after three bloody charges had left a carpet of shattered bodies in scarlet tunics on the slope of Breed's Hill facing Boston.[23] The action had cost the regulars more than one thousand dead or wounded—more than 40 percent of their assault force, including Pitcairn, who had expired in the arms of his son. American casualties had amounted to about three hundred wounded or captured and another one hundred killed, among them Dr. Joseph Warren, who had died fighting as an infantryman on the parapets during the final charge.[24] It had been "a melancholy Scene of Fire and Slaughter," according to one 1771 graduate who witnessed the action from across the harbor in Boston.[25]

Through the stories that spread quickly after the British assault, in death Jack Warren's older brother Joseph took on an immortal glow. His courage in the face of repeated enemy charges earned him a place in the American pantheon of heroes. Joseph's stand at the crest of the hill epitomized American resistance to British oppression. In their dreams, if not in truth, most members of Harvard's revolutionary generation stood with Jack's brother, courageously ignoring the British bullets that threatened them moment to moment.

In the spring of 1775 there was no better way to make a name for oneself—no better way to earn the hero's mantle of honor—than through bravery in combat. Battle-tested soldiers were men of courage, coolness, strength, and character—that is, men of honor. How better to test one's mettle than by undergoing such a trial by fire? Or so it seemed.

In fact, most of the recent graduates who had been present at what is now called the Battle of Bunker Hill had actually served well behind the lines, including Jacob Bacon, William Eustis, and Thomas Welsh, all of them doctors, who had cared for the American wounded.[26] Martin Herrick, who had served in the line of battle despite his medical training, and his classmate George Inman, a volunteer with the king's troops, were apparently the only members of any of the four classes to take direct part in the engagement.[27] Benjamin Lovell, a loyalist seeking shelter in Boston, suffered the most humiliating experience of the day: assigned to supply a British battery of twelve-pounders with shot, Lovell inadvertently took it out of action by providing it with twenty-four-pound balls.[28]

Notwithstanding the carnage, the greatest British loss was not the casualties incurred but the opportunity wasted to break the American siege and possibly even snuff out the rebellion. By severing the route along the Charlestown isthmus, aggressive commanders might have cut off the fleeing Americans from the main body of rebel troops and launched a crushing attack on their headquarters in Cambridge two miles away; but shaken and badly bloodied, the British broke off contact.[29]

After June 17, life in British-held Boston assumed a wary and tense but predictable tone. Fresh provisions were in short supply because of the American land blockade, so the crown's troops, their loyalist dependents, and those residents of the town who had not yet fled had to rely on dried, smoked, salted, and pickled stores as well as whatever the British were able to bring in by sea from Ireland and the West Indies.[30] Smallpox and scurvy were increasing threats, and as the end of the year approached, a shortage of fuel meant that everyone within the menacing circle of American guns felt the penetrating New England cold. Discouraged by dreadful conditions, many loyalists, including Lovell, escaped Boston for England. Neither the besiegers nor the besieged attempted to take definitive action, although both sides probed ineffectually for openings. To support their cause, and probably to keep themselves occupied, a group of the crown's friends holed up in the town formed a militia company, the Loyal American Associators; at least three young graduates signed on.[31]

Outside the town looking in, not much more was happening. A few weeks after the Battle of Bunker Hill, Jack Warren, inspired by his brother Joseph's heroic death, volunteered for infantry service. Instead, he was assigned to medical duty.[32] The American army needed a doctor more than another junior infantry officer. "The Smallpox appoplexcy, consumption, scurvy, lunacy, coughs, catarrhs, dysentary, jaundice, avarice, wounds, bruises and putrifying sores are among us," one member of the generation wrote.[33] Toward the end of the summer of 1775, John Trumbull earned the recognition and favor of George Washington, who briefly made him one of his aides-de-camp, by stealthily slipping through the unharvested tall grass of a hillside pasture to a spot within sight of an important British guardpost. From this blind he was able to sketch the regulars' defenses at the end of the neck that connected Boston to the Roxbury mainland.[34]

A rumored British challenge in late February finally ended the sitzkrieg and compelled a decisive response by the American forces a few days later. When word began to circulate on February 27, 1776, that the British were planning to assault the Dorchester Heights, the American high command resolved to act. A farm behind the Heights belonging to the family of John Homans of the class of 1772 became their staging area.[35] After prefabricating movable fortifications, two thousand rebel infantrymen (Major John Trumbull among them), supplemented by at least twenty pieces of heavy artillery (some of them under the command of Captain Winthrop Sargent), took the promontory on the evening of March 4.[36] The American initiative posed a serious and immediate threat to the redcoats occupying Boston. The British commanders quickly organized an assault on the position under the leadership of Lord Percy. When a storm disrupted their plans, however, given time for reflection, they decided not to contest the American advantage and prepared to evacuate with any civilians who chose to accompany them.[37]

Not long after the British evacuation, Jack Warren visited Charlestown for the first time since the battle in which Joseph had perished. The town lay deserted and in ruins. The British cannonade had been so destructive that it was difficult to make sense of the houses that had once formed a small but active and vibrant port community. "Scarcely the vestiges of those beautiful Buildings remain," Jack observed, "to distinguish them from . . . mean cottages."[38]

After the battle the previous June, the British victors had heaped the corpses of the American dead in a common grave. "The Scene was inexpressibly solemn" to Jack, "when I considered that perhaps whilest . . . musing [about] the Objects around me [I] might be stand[ing] over the Remains of a dear Brother whose Blood had stained these hallowed Walks; With veneration did this inspire me how many endearing Scenes of fraternal Friendship now past and gone forever presented themselves to my view!" Warren eventually roused from his reveries, convinced that "the Blood of the innocent calls for vengeance on the guilty Heads of the vile Assassins."[39]

A FLEET composed of scores of small, fragile sailing vessels together with three men-of-war weighed anchor in Boston Harbor on March 17 and made its way a few miles south to Nantasket Roads to await a favoring wind. The flotilla was bound for Halifax, Nova Scotia, and safety. Aboard it were the entire British garrison of Boston and about a thousand loyalists.[40] Forced to uproot rapidly and secure whatever marginally adequate transportation was available after the long siege, the civilians had been able to pack just a few things. Not only were they fleeing the threat of the heavy guns overlooking Boston, but also, in most cases, they were leaving behind friends, relatives, possessions, and the only homeland they had ever known.

The loyalists at sea off the Massachusetts coast included six or seven recent graduates, most in the company of at least a few members of their families. Tom Coffin's father, William, a wealthy merchant, was among the refugees; Tom may well have been William's lone traveling companion.[41] Samuel Murray's brother Daniel, a lawyer, was undoubtedly aboard one of the vessels with his father and several siblings, as was William Chandler in the company of his father, two brothers, and a sister-in-law.[42] Once the wind finally turned in the proper direction, on March 27 the armada set its course to the northeast for Halifax, a small, muddy town of slightly more than three thousand residents near the midpoint of Nova Scotia's Atlantic coast.[43] The voyage was a short one, only six days.

In Halifax the refugees received an unsympathetic welcome. Far from reaching out their hands to assist their weary and suffering countrymen, some locals took advantage of a sudden increase in demand to extort unheard-of prices for food, clothing, and shelter. The cost of provisions doubled overnight, and rents multiplied by as much as sixfold as refugees and ordinary Haligonians bid against one another for the necessities of life.

"Thus Mankind prey upon each other," remarked the uncle of one young Harvard loyalist.[44]

"Nova Scarcity" provided the fugitives a brief and secure respite, but it had few other attractions. It certainly lacked many of the amenities that genteel Bostonians expected as a matter of course. Early April is often foggy and icy in the Canadian Maritimes, and without close connections to the people or the place, most of the loyalists chose not to stay there any longer than necessary. By the end of 1776, most of them had made their way from Halifax across the Atlantic to London or south to New York City.[45]

As THE TWO armies had faced each other across Boston Harbor between April 1775 and March 1776, most young Harvard men had chosen sides. Sometimes the decision was an obvious one. By the time Tom Coffin took his stand, two generations of his family had already used their imperial connections to make their way in the world. The Coffins were Anglicans, minor public officeholders, and merchants who traded regularly with English mercantile houses. It was natural for Tom to ally himself with the crown.[46] By the same token, Tom's schoolmates Samuel and Daniel Murray, who claimed kinship with the duke of Atholl, knew immediately where their interests and loyalties lay.[47] William Chandler, the son of perhaps the most prominent Tory in provincial Worcester, came from a family that was so entrenched politically before the Revolution that important town and county offices seemed to come its way by right.[48] For Coffin, the Murrays, and Chandler, the American Revolution threatened a way of life, and even how each one defined himself. The encirclement of Boston placed them emotionally as well as militarily under siege.

Even an obvious choice might be painful, however—in fact, occasionally too painful to carry out. Although the March family was even better connected politically in Portsmouth than the Coffins were in Boston, Clement March and his nephew Clement Weeks followed the lead of other relatives and broke with the crown.[49] New Hampshire and the rights of independent freeholders meant more to them than Britain and high office.

It took some men months to decide where they stood. As provincial Americans gradually gravitated toward rebellion, Joseph Haven, a New Hampshire minister, moved in concert. In June 1775 "reconciliation with the parent State" still seemed possible, even if American "rights and privileges are invaded . . . by those we looked upon as protectors." Haven signed New Hampshire's Association Test later that year, however, and when Rockingham organized a company of volunteers, he urged the troops to "remember that you are under the care of God."[50]

The anguish could be palpable when friends took opposite sides. Benjamin Loring was the son of a British naval officer who had "always eaten the king's bread and always intend[ed] to," so it is no surprise that Benjamin, a doctor, entered the king's service in 1775 as a surgeon's mate in the Royal Army.[51] Isaac Bangs nevertheless found Loring's choice difficult to accept. An infantry officer in the Continental Army, Bangs heard from a classmate in 1776 that "my old Friend Loring . . . is now a Surgeon to the Ministerial Butchers. This gives me great Trouble."[52]

Recent events seemed no less a threat to a way of life to many on the patriot side. It was the British ministry that had ignited the fires of resistance as far as many young Harvard men were concerned. John Trumbull's support of resistance to the crown was as predictable as Tom Coffin's opposition to it. Trumbull's native colony, Connecticut, was one of only two British mainland provinces that held the right to elect its own governor. In common only with the chief executive of Rhode Island, John's father, Jonathan, the sitting governor of Connecticut, owed his office to his constituents, not to the king or the ministry. The crown's attempt in 1685 to withdraw this right by combining Connecticut and neighboring colonies to form the Dominion of New England had produced the enduring legend of the Hartford Charter Oak, where opponents of the dominion initiative had hidden the colony's royal commission until the threat was ended. John consequently came to the imperial crisis of the 1770s with both a family investment in Connecticut's status quo of substantial self-government and his colony's heritage of resistance to royal intervention.

Many young Harvard men who did not draw on the same Connecticut tradition of partial governmental autonomy nevertheless believed deeply that a decade of attempts to circumscribe the provinces' political rights jeopardized every colonist's heritage of English liberties. "Hide yourselves like menial slaves in your master's kitchen," Jack Warren directed the British, "nor dare approach the happy asylum of once extinct liberty, for if ye dare, ye die."[53] Nevertheless, it was often difficult to come to terms with the implications of the lessons they drew from the events of the day. Tilly Merrick broke with his stepfather, Duncan Ingraham, and his mother's family by marriage when he enlisted in the Concord militia as a private in 1776.[54] Winthrop Sargent's father was a member of Gloucester's revolutionary Committee of Safety, but an uncle and a cousin were strong loyalists.[55] Merrick, Sargent, and scores of other members of the revolutionary generation found the threats they perceived to their political rights too serious to dismiss.

In the end, for many members of the revolutionary generation, personal determinations of honor drove them in one direction or the other. Honor was a calculus. A gentleman's proudest possession was his good name. It ensured his standing in society and undergirded his sense of self-respect. In order to maintain an unstained character, he had to follow the course of duty. This required an assessment of every situation. At the outbreak of the Revolution, where did duty call? Was it in support of the traditional order through fealty to the crown, or was it in the cause of independence? Whatever the final calculation, for many revolutionary Harvardians, as aspiring gentlemen, the course they followed revealed their assessment of honor's dictates.

THROUGHOUT THE spring, summer, and autumn of 1775, most of the members of the revolutionary generation who were in the service belonged to provincial militia regiments whose terms of service ended on December 31. When the new year dawned, about a dozen of them took up new commissions as officers in the Continental Army. Meanwhile, three of their schoolmates had already acquired regular commissions as infantry officers in the British army.[56]

Only a small fraction actually saw combat at the front between the beginning of 1776 and October 1781, when the surrender of Lord Cornwallis's army at Yorktown, Virginia, effectively brought the war to an end. Not many more than one in seven of the generation's members ever took the field of battle for either side, however briefly.

Two of the loyalists compiled particularly lengthy combat records. George Inman, who joined the British army on the day of the Battle of Bunker Hill, fought in North Carolina, South Carolina, New Jersey, and New York during the next seventeen months. Musket balls tore holes in his hat and his trousers in one skirmish on Long Island in late August 1776.[57] As the British forces pursued George Washington's army across New York and New Jersey toward the close of the year, Ensign Inman served with the regulars' Seventeenth Regiment. At Princeton in early January 1777, buckshot ripped through his crossbelt without injuring him. He also fought at Brandywine and Monmouth before being ordered to England in early 1780.[58] Inman's classmate John Lindall Borland saw action in 1776 in the Battle of Long Island as an ensign with the Twenty-second Regiment and in a series of lesser engagements over the next two years before a musket ball to his right shoulder in the battle for Newport, Rhode Island, on August 29, 1778, rendered him permanently unfit for combat. By October 1779, he was in England acting as a recruiter.[59]

On the American side, many of the young Harvard men who saw extended duty served as doctors, chaplains, or in other billets that were ordinarily out of the direct line of fire. Only about two dozen served at any time with the Continental Army in the infantry or the artillery, where the risks were the greatest. Only two, John Trumbull and Winthrop Sargent, had genuinely heroic careers as soldiers during the Revolution.

Military success came too early and too easily for Trumbull, who abandoned the army in a pout when he concluded in early 1777 that his honor had been sullied. Following his brief term in the late summer of 1775 as an aide-de-camp to George Washington, Trumbull had returned to the Connecticut militia, with which he had begun his service, this time as a major, the third-ranking officer in his regiment. He was still only nineteen years old. Early the next summer, after the successful conclusion of the Siege of Boston, General Horatio Gates, who was planning an invasion of Canada, invited Trumbull, now just twenty, to join him as his adjutant with the rank of colonel. During the summer and fall of 1776 at Albany, Ticonderoga, and Crown Point, Trumbull performed effectively in his new capacity, although the strength of the British forces the Americans were facing compelled them to call off their offensive.

As Trumbull served Gates, however, a cloud of political uncertainty began to envelop him. Gates named Trumbull his adjutant in June 1776, but weeks passed without word from Congress confirming the appointment. Congress had not yet approved Gates's own command, and until it did, some questioned whether or not the general held the authority to promote Trumbull. Finally, in February 1777, the legislature authorized Trumbull's new rank, but with a qualification. Trumbull had assumed his duties on June 28, 1776, but the effective date of rank in his congressional letter of appointment was September 12. By delaying his promotion, Congress placed two other colonels, both of them in Trumbull's view "more distinguished as jolly drinking companions than as intelligent officers," ahead of him in the army's order of seniority, which was determined by date of rank.[60]

Incensed at what he perceived to be an intolerable affront to his dignity, Trumbull angrily resigned his commission. Personal pride outweighed revolutionary ardor, at least for John Trumbull in the late winter of 1777. "A soldier's honor," he wrote to John Hancock, the president of the Continental Congress, "forbids the idea of giving up the least pretension to rank."[61] Trumbull later served briefly and heroically as a volunteer without rank in the unsuccessful attempt in August 1778 to liberate Newport, Rhode Island, from British occupation, but his military career was otherwise at an end. More than sixty years later, when Trumbull wrote his memoirs, the perceived slight still rankled him.[62]

During service that lasted several times longer than Trumbull's, Winthrop Sargent spent almost his entire term as an artillery captain. On one occasion he was court-martialed for being absent. In addition to the Siege of Boston, however, he also fought on Manhattan and at White Plains, Trenton, Brandywine, Germantown, and Monmouth, as well as enduring the long, cold, killing winter at Valley Forge in 1777–78. When Sargent mustered out on August 28, 1783, after more than seven and one-half years in the army, it was as a brevet major.[63]

Very few of Sargent's schoolmates served in combat billets as long as or longer than he did. Instead, most young graduates who served as infantry or artillery officers in the Continental Army remained under arms for at most a few years before yielding their places. Major Warham Parks, an infantry officer wounded at Saratoga in 1777, served three years, including the winter at Valley Forge, before resigning his commission.[64] William Jennison entered and left military service with the Continental Army and the marines on several occasions beginning in 1775 before deciding in 1780, after two incarcerations totaling five months as a prisoner of war, that he had done his share.[65] And then there was William's brother Sam, the most puzzling and disturbing of the military veterans in all the classes of the revolutionary generation. The youngest member of the class of 1774 by more than a year when he entered college in 1770 at eleven years of age, he was only seventeen on January 1, 1777, when he received a commission in the Continental Army. Sam served first as an ensign in the infantry with the Sixth Massachusetts Line—his engagements included the bloody Battle of Saratoga—and then took on the additional duty of quartermaster. Precisely what trauma he may have undergone during the thirty months before he left the service on July 11, 1779, it is now impossible to know. Warfare in the eighteenth century, like warfare before and since, was a brutal, shocking, emotionally transforming experience. What is certain is that this precocious student was never able to readjust successfully to the civilian world. He suffered psychological problems throughout the rest of his life.[66]

WHEN AN eighteenth-century infantry regiment drew itself up for battle, the officers stood with the men in harm's way. Thus the members of the revolutionary generation who served as commissioned officers in combat— men like Sam Jennison—faced the worst that their enemies had to offer. According to the drill manuals that the American militia and Continental Army employed, the place for the commanding officer, usually a colonel, was front and center in the position of greatest honor—and greatest danger. Behind him stood his second in command, a lieutenant colonel, ready to step into his place should he fall. Aligned with the lieutenant colonel, organized by units in long double ranks, were the companies of the command. Most of the men were privates and corporals, the rank and file carrying long-barreled muskets, but their own company-grade officers, captains and lieutenants carrying pistols and swords, gave them the order to fire, advance, or retreat from the first line. In the heat of the action there was no substitute for self-control, courage, and physical strength in an officer.[67]

Whether the command was to stand and fire, advance, or retreat, until a regiment came into close contact with the enemy, it worked as a unit following a choreographed pattern of movements, a military minuet that culminated in coordinated violence as devastating as any the eighteenth-century mind could imagine. Precise planning and repeated practice governed the evolutions, the maneuvers that transformed marching columns of men into ranks ready for combat. By the time the opposing forces stood ready for battle, only fifty to one hundred yards separated them. Muskets were still deadly at one hundred yards, but they were wildly inaccurate. The American soldiers were instructed to aim their weapons, but the British army did not even try; it relied on the power of a massed volley to blow a hole in its opposition.[68]

The immediate objective of pitched battles was to win the field of fray, putting the enemy to flight. Such engagements typically took place in pastures, not on parade grounds, and uneven terrain, including ridges, hillocks, and hollows, might help to determine the outcome. If there were time, as there was at Saratoga, one side or the other often constructed breastworks to shelter behind. In the noise and chaos of combat, one of the two sides eventually retreated, often running, stumbling, gasping for breath, splashing through streams and marshes, wading through tall grass, tripping over boulders and bushes, climbing fences, hiding in ravines. At the Battle of Kip's Bay on Long Island in September 1776, a British advance collapsed the American lines, putting hundreds of men to flight. Years later, an American private who had been there remembered retreating through fields, hiding from passing regulars under scrub brush in a bog, ducking a volley launched from a corn field, enduring heat and thirst, hopping a fence, and being soaked by a sudden rain shower before being rallied by officers to turn and take a stand.[69]

Such pitched battles were not the most common engagements, but they were probably the most memorable. More often, combat took the form of brief skirmishes involving foraging parties, scouting patrols, and other small detachments. After the Siege of Boston, young Harvard men on the American side fought in large engagements only occasionally. In the fall of 1777 twelve fought at Saratoga, where Sam Jennison's regiment made a violent assault against the British lines; eleven were at Monmouth in June 1778; and smaller numbers were at Long Island and Trenton in 1776, Princeton and Brandywine in 1777, and several lesser clashes.

By later standards, combat casualties were rarely high; during the entire war the American forces lost only around seven thousand men killed in action. At Saratoga the Continental Army lost about 110 men in three engagements between September 19 and October 7, 1777; at Monmouth on June 28, 1778, the 106 American deaths included 37 who succumbed to sunstroke.[70] And yet no one who had stared down death at such close quarters could forget the experience. Weeks or months of training helped; well-drilled soldiers knew where they should be in the order of battle. It was comforting to be certain.[71] Still, there was no way to prepare for the stomach-churning anticipation of battle, the black hatred as an opposing army took the field, the noise and confusion of an acrid, smoke-covered battlefield, the destructiveness of a scythe-like enemy volley, the shock of a friend's, death, the slaughter of combat involving thousands of well-armed men fighting hand-to-hand, the blood-curdling cries of the wounded.

The experience of battle was so terrifying that men often broke ranks and ran. Beginning in 1778, the Continental Army frequently placed a row of military policemen behind the rear line of infantry regiments in battle formation in order to fight the self-preserving desire of men in the front ranks to turn and hide.[72]

For those who survived to fight another day there were further perils. Forced marches, grinding fatigue, winter cold, inadequate clothing, a shortage of blankets, hunger, and camp fevers were the lot of the enlisted men of the Continental Army, and the officers closest to them—the ensigns, lieutenants, and captains of its infantry and artillery companies—shared these experiences. William Bradford, a lieutenant in the Eleventh Continental Infantry Regiment, wrote a friend from camp in Westchester County, New York, on what he believed to be the eve of battle, October 16, 1776. The American army had spent the summer in retreat, and constant British pressure had taken a toll: "The Enemy have landed upon Frog Point [Throg's Neck].... We have be[en] order'd to face them again, determined what Fatigue won't Kill the Enemy shall; We have but about 100 men in our Reg^t fit to be Carried into Action near 200 Sick, many we have lost in . . . two Engagements many by Sic[kness] that we are Amazingly Reduced, Our officers are likewise sickly, but thank God I have had but one Slight turn of the Flux [diarrhea] . . . and at present a touch of the Disintery."[73]

Israel Keith, would-be lawyer and aide-de-camp to General George Washington, wrote his brother Cyrus about the army's hardships: "I lay on the ground; some nights I got a little sleep and some none." By January 1777 the conditions were taking a toll on Keith: "I am sometimes ready to believe that we are in reality nothing but machines, serving to the pleasure or profit of some invisible Demons or Genii."[74] At Valley Forge, where the men in the ranks huddled in small log cabins, twelve to a hut, and lived on short rations, company-grade officers were less crowded but otherwise suffered the same adversity.[75] Throughout the war the common bond of the captains, lieutenants, and enlisted men of the Continental Army was the shared hardship they endured.

AS INMAN and Borland, Trumbull and Sargent, William Jennison and Sam Jennison were facing the perils of combat, five of their schoolmates were serving the crown as doctors and twenty-five more were tending to the American wounded.[76] A few others on each side had staff duties behind the lines. Another nine patriots had tours of duty as chaplains. The presence of artillery on revolutionary battlefields and the "Colds Fatigue, hunger, thirst, Dirt & Lice" of camp life meant that even noncombatants sometimes ran significant risks, but these were generally not of the same magnitude as those facing the men in the front ranks.[77] In compensation for the dangers and inconveniences that they did encounter, most noncombatants benefited professionally from their service. Wars can result in opportunities for the lucky and the ambitious, and during the Revolution no less than in later American conflicts, the best and the brightest often led from the rear.

If the grim cloud of modern warfare has a silver lining, it is the opportunity it has afforded for medical training and experimentation under profoundly adverse circumstances. Over the last century, military conflicts have provided many doctors with intensive professional experience. At the same time they facilitated the development of antibiotics, emergency medicine, and significant advances in psychiatry, to name only three ways in which they have sparked therapeutic innovations. In a similar fashion, the American Revolution was also a laboratory for American medicine. Because thousands of other soldiers were fighting, suffering, and dying, military doctors, including thirty members of Harvard's revolutionary generation, benefited from an important testing ground.

Medical skills are at a premium in times of war, and for young doctors barely at the end of their apprenticeships, military medicine in wartime was an opportunity born of repeated tragedy. Of the forty-two members of the revolutionary generation who became doctors after graduation, more than two-thirds served as surgeons or surgeon's mates on one side or the other for at least part of the war; four men served in the Continental Army and one with the British army with few or no breaks from 1776 to 1781, when the guns fell silent. No other identifiable community of men within the generation served as long or in such high proportions.[78]

Moreover, no other large group profited as much professionally from its service. Like a modern residency in a busy inner-city hospital, duty as a regimental or ship's surgeon or surgeon's mate during wartime afforded a young doctor the opportunity to see in a short period of time more examples of certain kinds of cases than he could expect to encounter in decades in a typical civilian practice. Combat traumas were only the most urgent of the injuries and illnesses that military doctors had to attend to during the Revolutionary War. In addition, army and navy doctors often treated conditions caused or exacerbated by poor camp or ship sanitation, bad nutrition, exposure, accident, and the psychological stresses resulting from the constant fear of impending danger. At Valley Forge, where Walter Hastings, a son of the college steward, served as surgeon with the Eighth Massachusetts Regiment of the Continental Army, soldiers had to make do with a soup consisting of bread, wheat, and sugar when they ran out of meat, and thousands of men lacked adequate clothes, shoes, and blankets.[79] Military service afforded a young doctor like Hastings an unparalleled chance to develop his professional skills.

A few doctors who had trained in the customary way in New England, as apprentices to senior practitioners, also received a second valuable opportunity for professional development—as medical officers in military hospitals. The military did not introduce hospitals to American medicine; there were hospitals in Philadelphia and New York before the war, and American physicians who were fortunate enough to take their training in Europe walked the wards in Edinburgh, London, and Paris. But for the small number of New England doctors who had direct contact with army hospitals after 1775, the experience was especially enlightening. There was nothing of the sort anywhere in New England, so for many doctors, military hospitals were a revelation.

Jack Warren benefited more than any of his schoolmates from such an experience. After the army rejected Warren's request in July 1775 to serve in the infantry, it assigned him to the general hospital it was organizing to attend to the army surrounding Boston. During the next eight years he served in hospitals in New York, Pennsylvania, New Jersey, and Massachusetts, usually as the institution's commander or surgeon general.[80] Military medicine was routinized, wholesale care, and Warren's introduction to the efficiencies of medical bureaucracy would continue to influence him throughout his career.

Soldiers charged with administrative responsibilities also had opportunities to profit professionally through experience from their service. On the American side, no one had ever seen anything quite like the Continental Army's massive, continuing demand for supplies. From regimental quartermasters in the field to the quartermaster general of the army, American officers, including several young graduates, had to solve logistical problems the magnitude of which no one they knew had ever had to address.[81] Meanwhile, Thomas Edwards, the Continental Army's deputy judge advocate general from 1780 to 1782 and judge advocate general from 1782 to 1783, had to deal with the legal problems of a battle-hardened army of nearly fourteen thousand men.[82]

For all the advantages that staff officers had over those on the line, they still had to share many of the hardships of the combat soldiers. The Continental Army fought a war of strategic retreats throughout much of the Revolution, and everyone shared the fatigue and fear of such campaigns. When the army abandoned Manhattan in 1776, Dr. William Eustis, accompanying General Henry Knox, was one of the last American soldiers to leave the island; Hessian mercenaries in close pursuit fired wild shots over his head as he evacuated.[83] Nor did rank confer immunity against many of the perils of camp life, including disease and sometimes cold and hunger.

On the British side, through their service behind the lines, Tom Coffin and James Putnam, Jr., scion of one of Worcester County's most prominent families, developed contacts in the British military establishment that when played correctly would benefit them the rest of their lives. Following the evacuation of Boston, by January 1777 Coffin had made his way to New York City. On Manhattan, he received a civilian appointment in the commissary department of the British army. After accompanying the army to Philadelphia, where it made its headquarters from mid-1777 to mid-1778, he returned with it to New York City. From then until 1783, he assisted Daniel Wier and Brook Watson, successive commissaries general for the British troops in North America, as they struggled to feed tens of thousands of soldiers and thousands more head of livestock. Meanwhile, as deputy barracks master general from March to November 1783, Putnam, who had made his way to New York City after the British evacuation of Boston, had to find housing for as many as 40,000 soldiers and 27,000 civilian refugees.[84]

Of the noncombatants who served with the military, only the chaplains did not reap an identifiable professional benefit. Service took them away from their homes and normal responsibilities, and for settled ministers it came at a high cost to families and congregations. None of the recent graduates who ministered to the spiritual needs of the American forces spent as much as a year with the soldiers, and for most the term of duty required only a few months away from home.

"I'm loth you shou'd think I neglect you," Tom Coffin wrote from New York City to his mother, Mary, in January 1777; Tom "embrace[d] every Opportunity of writing and shall continue to do so."[85] Long-term separations were among the most painful costs of the war. Separated from his mother and sisters since the evacuation of the Massachusetts capital on March 17, 1776, he did all he could to maintain contact with his family and friends. Letters became the best available remedy, as the Revolution often made it difficult for intimates to keep up with one another.

Letters from friends and relatives boosted spirits. Jack Warren's surviving wartime correspondence includes exchanges with several college contemporaries. Jonathan Norwood, an old friend from the Spunke Club, wrote about life in Maine in June 1775.[86] Isaac Bangs wrote in August to express his condolences on the death of Jack's brother Joseph and to resume a lapsed correspondence.[87] William Eustis dropped a line in June 1777 to announce his plans for a visit.[88] Meanwhile, Israel Keith worried about "the possibility of many of my letters never reaching" his college roommate Joseph Pearse Palmer. "I have wrote about seventeen sheets to you," he informed Palmer in November 1776. "If you have received enough to let you know I have not forgot you 'tis sufficient."[89]

Loyalists such as the Coffins were more likely than most others to experience the loneliness and anxieties of extended family separation, although they were common enough costs of partisanship on both sides. Many loyalist families split up for years as husbands, fathers, and sons, in fear for their freedom, and even their lives, fled New England with the redcoats in 1776, leaving their wives, daughters, and sisters behind to protect their property from patriot expropriations. The loyalist diaspora extended from Canada to the Caribbean, and from the southern colonies to the British Isles. In the late 1770s and early 1780s, while Tom was in New York and Philadelphia promoting the British war effort, his father, William, was on Long Island living with friends, his mother and sisters Polly and Nancy were in Massachusetts guarding the family assets, brothers Billy and Eben were with the British army, and a third brother, Frank, was in school in Twickenham, England, a short carriage ride from London. Whenever possible, letters flew back and forth as family members struggled to keep up with one another.[90]

Isolation, anxiety, uncertainty—these emotions plagued everyone who was away from his loved ones. Israel Keith and his mother both suffered from melancholy, in part because of their separation.[91] Winthrop Sargent with the American army, George Inman serving in a British regiment, Tilly Merrick conducting diplomatic and commercial business in the Netherlands, Isaac Smith in exile in England, and Tom Coffin on Manhattan all did whatever they could to keep up with family and friends. Through diligent efforts it was often possible to remain within a few weeks of the latest news. Between January 1777 and September 1783, Tom Coffin sent his mother about one hundred letters. He wrote about his health, his duties, and his social activities. When old friends passed through New York City, he duly reported on their well-being to his correspondents. Concerned for the comfort of his mother and sisters, Tom frequently sent them gifts, most often negotiable bills of exchange to underwrite their living costs but also cloth to make gowns and silver buckles for their shoes. When he heard from Frank in Twickenham, he quickly disseminated the news to his other correspondents, and Frank in turn received reports from Tom about goings-on at home. By mail, Tom was able to arrange for a commission in a British regiment for Frank, although he hesitated to inform his brother, who might have had other career plans in mind. And Tom wrote for information about family and friends. "Give me some Account," he urged his mother in May 1777, "of my Old Class Mates that remained behind."[92]

When there was no word, it was easy to imagine the worst. "It is now four Months since [I] have had a line from, or the satisfaction of hearing from you or the Family," Tom wrote his mother in October 1778, "and [I] can assure you [I] am not a little anxious about you."[93] Sometimes the word was grim: "It is with Pain and Grief I am now to communicate to you the Death of my dear Father," Coffin informed his mother in August 1779. William Coffin had collapsed and died suddenly in New York more than three years after he had last seen his wife and daughters in Boston. "He is now removed from the Troubles & Disappointments of this transitory Life, and we trust participating [in] Blessings beyond the reach of our Idea."[94]

As the months and years went by, Tom and his mother dreamed of their reunion. For Coffin to meet his mother and sisters in Boston, he would have to pass through enemy lines, an unlikely prospect as long as hostilities continued. "I wish when Leisure & Opportunity offer you wou'd favor me with a Line," Tom entreated in November 1777, "as nothing can afford me greater Pleasure (except a Meeting) than to hear frequently from you."[95] "There is nothing that can possibly happen in which I feel myself more interested," he added the following May, "or from which I can anticipate so much real satisfaction as again meeting you all."[96] Perhaps Mary, Polly, and Nancy might visit Tom in New York: "as I have not the least Prospect of coming to you," he wrote home in October 1778, "I most sincerely wish your State of Health and the Situation of the Family may be such as to enable you to come here."[97] Finally, in May 1781, Tom began to see an opening to come to Boston: perhaps it "would . . . be possible for me to obtain permission," he mused, "to pass three or four days, or a Week in Boston or near it."[98]

It was easier to dream about a visit than to pay one. "Nothing on Earth will afford me so much Pleasure as to be able to accomplish an interview with you," Tom wrote his mother early the following August.[99] "I am much obliged for your Anxiety to see me," he added near the end of the month. "I can assure you my Wishes for an Interview, are as earnest as yours."[100] Unfortunately, a combination of the demands of his position and the reluctance of American authorities to issue him a passport continually stymied his attempts to return to his family: "I was in hopes ere this to have enjoy'd the most ardent Wish of my Heart, that of embracing you.... [B]ut untoward accidents have put it out of my Power, and I now fear I shall not soon receive the Satisfaction."[101] It began to appear that in the course of his duties Tom might have to leave Manhattan for London before he could make it home.[102] And even though his trip to England was delayed repeatedly, obstacles continued to plague his efforts to travel to Boston. More than two years after Coffin first began to think that he might be able to visit his family, in the summer of 1783 he was still in New York, still petitioning for permission to come home.

ON OCTOBER 4, 1775, President Samuel Langdon, Locke's successor, called Harvard College into session in Concord, ending a hiatus that had begun on May 1. As long as American troops occupied the college grounds in Cambridge, Harvard would have to make use of expedients elsewhere if it were to resume operations. After considering several alternatives as temporary homes, the college authorities had determined on September 6 that the facilities in Concord came closest to meeting their needs. By October 10, a faculty tally showed that more than one hundred students had appeared to take up their studies, including twenty-five entering freshmen.[103]

Almost everyone in the college administration at the outbreak of the war favored the revolutionary cause, and for the next eight months Harvard willingly made do in Concord. The town, one of the most urban inland settlements in Massachusetts, was better equipped with large halls to use as classrooms than most of the region's other crossroads communities; an aging courthouse and an empty grammar school building both stood near the unornamented but roomy meetinghouse in Concord Center. There was space in residences near these three structures for a temporary library as well as for some of Professor Winthrop's scientific apparatus. Moreover, if the students were willing to tolerate more crowding in private homes than they would have faced in Cambridge, then there was enough room for everyone who was likely to matriculate. Isaac Smith was in England and not likely to return anytime soon, but in addition to the president, all three professors were present and lodged in private houses, as well as two tutors and the librarian. To fill in for Smith, Professor Sewall agreed to take responsibility for the freshman class for the time being. Concord was not

Cambridge, and sacrifices were necessary, but with cooperation and ingenuity it was possible to carry on.[104]

The two fundamental lessons that the college and civilian New England alike learned over the next eight years were that there was no escaping the military and economic consequences of the war but that it was nevertheless possible to persist. After March 1776, the main scene of military action moved to the south and west of New England, although as long as the British army and navy posed a threat, it was imprudent to relax, as the enemy reminded repeatedly. The British capture of Newport, Rhode Island, which the Royal Army held from December 1776 to December 1779, General John Burgoyne's attempt in the summer and fall of 1777 to sever New England from the other American states by using the Hudson River and Lake Champlain to join his British forces in Quebec with General William Howe's troops in New York City, a British incursion into Penobscot Bay in Maine in the summer of 1779, and a series of quick hit-and-run coastal raids over the course of several years all forced anxious New Englanders to remain on the alert. Meanwhile, labor shortages on New England's farms; the need to supply armies in the field with food, clothing, and munitions; and spiraling inflation in the late 1770s, which made it impossible to place any trust in the value of bills of currency, shook everyone who bought or sold provisions or who borrowed or loaned money—that is to say, almost everyone.

Under these circumstances, revolutionary Harvard struggled, especially financially. Tuition income, adjusted for inflation, fell as military service lured away many potential students. The classes of the revolutionary generation averaged about forty-nine graduates; those most seriously reduced by wartime pressures, 1778 through 1781, averaged fewer than twenty-nine, many of them not as capable as the students of the classes of 1771 through 1774.[105] Wartime inflation undermined many investments, making it difficult to manage the college's endowment. Even worse, the college's treasurer from 1773 to 1777, John Hancock, who never kept close track of the school's assets even before the outbreak of hostilities, took Harvard's books with him when he traveled to Philadelphia and the Continental Congress, then ignored repeated earnest requests to return the volumes. Without a vigilant business manager to oversee its finances, the college lost sight of both its credits and its debits. Provisions were also short, and from day to day there was no way to be certain whether there would be enough for everyone to eat. Nevertheless, apart from extended vacations in the summer of 1775 and the winter of 1777–78, the college remained in session in Concord until June 1776 and thereafter in Cambridge throughout the rest of the war.[106]

The domestic costs of the conflict affected everyone at home. Ministers on fixed salaries struggled to make ends meet as currency inflation devastated the value of the pounds, shillings, and pence they received in pay. Meanwhile, shortages developed for some necessities of life. When a French fleet put in at Boston in the fall of 1778, the town's resources were strained to feed the additional mouths, and prices skyrocketed. "The daily supplies which we are obliged to afford them," Abigail Adams wrote her husband, John, on September 29, "enhances the price of every article of life scarce before but now almost incredibley so."[107]

Despite the costs of war, supporters of the Revolution looked for ways to promote it at home no less than on the battlefield. In Andover, for example, where he was teaching school and reading for the ministry, Eliphalet Pearson joined with Sam Phillips, an old friend from as far back as their days together at Dummer Academy, to try to supply the army with needed munitions. The American troops were short of gunpowder, so Phillips, whose family was among the wealthiest in town, paid for the equipment to set up a powder mill. Neither man knew how to make explosives, but Pearson began to survey as many chemistry texts as he could find in search of an appropriate formula. Soon he was conducting experiments. Nearly ninety years later, one of Pearson's former students recalled arriving at school one morning only to discover that there would be no classes that day because all the desks and tables were covered with trays of saltpeter. Pearson's efforts were successful, and the mill that Phillips constructed supplied the American army for several years.[108]

Phillips and Pearson understood that there were many ways to advance the cause of the Revolution. Military valor brought honor in the face of physical risks, but battlefield heroics were not the only way to serve the cause. Public servants, diplomats, investors in privateers, and many others also helped the war effort.

As one consequence of the war, there fell vacant many public positions that mature, experienced local officeholders in towns across New England would ordinarily have held. For anyone ready to seize them, there were opportunities for the asking. In Worcester County, where almost all the men who had been lawyers before the war became loyalists, a legal vacuum developed when most of the attorneys fled to Boston in 1775. Once Levi Lincoln completed reading the law in Northampton and won admission to the bar in Hampshire County, he moved to Worcester. In the absence of much competition, he had no difficulty developing a practice. At the same time he took on public offices almost immediately. In December 1775, shortly after he arrived, he became clerk of the Worcester County courts; thirteen months later, in January 1777, he became judge of probate. In 1779 he also served as the moderator of the Worcester town meeting. At any other time it would have been inconceivable for someone so new to town and so young—Lincoln was only thirty years old in 1779—to have held such responsible offices, but not in the late 1770s, when talent, training, and availability sufficed.[109] Indeed, Dedham called on Fisher Ames at an even younger age. Ames was already developing a reputation as an articulate and persuasive orator in 1779 when his town chose him at age twenty-one to represent it at a convention in Concord to consider the state of the Massachusetts economy.[110]

While Lincoln and Ames were serving at home, Tilly Merrick and John Thaxter were in Europe. After enlisting in the Concord militia, Merrick received an appointment as a minor aide to John Adams in the Americans' diplomatic missions in Paris and Amsterdam.[111] Twice vessels on which Merrick was taking passage to Europe were captured and he was incarcerated.[112] Meanwhile, with Adams and his sons John Quincy and Charles, starting in the fall of 1779, Thaxter as a private secretary shared one of the great diplomatic adventures of the war. It began with a frightening late autumn crossing of the Atlantic. After landing at El Ferrol in Spain in December, the party traveled overland through the Pyrenees during the worst of winter to Paris and John Adams's diplomatic assignment, a journey of more than a month.[113]

Like Lincoln, Ames, Merrick, and Thaxter, dozens of other young Harvard men promoted the revolutionary cause without bearing arms against the British. Their contributions were not always entirely selfless; many revolutionary Americans did well by doing good. But in the last analysis, results were what counted; during a war they were more important than purity of motivation.

"HAD I FORESEEN every circumstance that has happen'd," Isaac Smith wrote home to his brother William in October 1775 after four months in England, "perhaps I sh'd not have left you." For all the troubles that friends of the Revolution faced between 1775 and 1783, life turned out to be much more difficult for most of the loyalists. Smith had left Massachusetts reluctantly in the spring of 1775—the college held his tutorship open until February 1776 in case he returned—and he was having trouble establishing himself in England. No one Smith had encountered since his arrival seemed very interested in the unrest in Boston, nor did anyone see a reason to come to the aid of displaced loyalists. Still, although he did not realize it, Smith was actually faring better than many others who would make their way to England in 1776 and later; by the fall of 1775 he was ministering to a small dissenting church in Sidmouth, Devon. He could get by, although the congregation was tiny and the salary was meager. Not everyone could claim as much.[114]

Outside the British military, there was little welcome for the revolutionary generation's loyalists between 1775 and 1783. Those who left New England could retain a modicum of self-respect and dignity, but like Smith they found that they were an afterthought in Canada and England. As for those who remained in New England, life was a trial. The pressures on them to change sides were intense.

If everyone who ended up in England had enjoyed the advantages of James (Ivers) Trecothick, no one would have had any reason for complaints. James had been living in style on his inherited estate in Surrey since the death of his uncle Barlow in 1775. A mansion with five thousand acres of farmland made him the most eligible of bachelors, and when he married in 1777, it was to the eldest daughter of a baronet.[115] In the absence of such an inheritance, though, gentility was almost out of reach.

For Samuel Sparhawk, who fled Boston for England shortly before the evacuation in March 1776, circumstances in London were straitened. Polite dinners with Thomas Hutchinson and Thomas Gage supported the image of a man of parts, but it was a pathetic pretense; Sparhawk was living on a modest pension. At most, the government provided him with £150 per annum, an amount it reduced to £80 in 1783.[116] Benjamin Lovell, who left Boston in August 1775 under a cloud of suspicion in British army circles after his bungling at the Battle of Bunker Hill, found a series of positions in London as a tutor, and then worked, ironically, as a clerk in the army's ordnance department before taking holy orders in the Church of England in 1784.[117] After the evacuation of Boston, Jonathan Simpson made his way to London, where his family suffered badly. In the spring of 1779 he received a commission from a London merchant to act as his agent in Savannah, which the British were occupying, and then in Charleston after its capture in 1780 by troops under Sir Henry Clinton.[118]

Except for a lucky few like Trecothick, faded gentility was the best for which American loyalists in England could hope. Even that was a better fate than most loyalists who remained in New England experienced.

The alternative to flight to the mother country was often an American exile. After April 19, 1775, it was almost impossible for neighbors to agree to disagree civilly over the imperial crisis. In New Hampshire, where in 1776 the revolutionary government forced all adult males to sign a loyalty test or face the consequences; in Massachusetts, where many loyalists were held under house arrest; and in Connecticut, where some loyalists were kidnaped and held as political prisoners, there was little patience with supporters of the crown.[119]

As long as the Royal Army maintained North American strongholds, one option for the loyalists was to take shelter within the British lines. Solomon Willard, who was "so unfortunate as to differ in Sentiment from his Countrymen," abandoned his New Hampshire home for the protection of the British forces on Long Island in 1777.[120] A second possibility was to attempt to disappear on the frontier; Daniel Rogers was trying to evade detection on the sparsely settled fringes of New Hampshire when the state's Committee of Safety arrested him "as a Person unfriendly to the Liberties of America."[121]

The most difficult option was to remain at home and attempt to carry on as if nothing had changed. John Eliot, who would have preferred to stay entirely out of politics, was shocked at the excesses he witnessed in Boston. At one town meeting in May 1777, speakers began to accuse prominent citizens of Toryism: "It got to be just as the affair of the witches of Salem,—every one naming his neighbor." To demonstrate his own good faith, Eliot eventually took a turn as chaplain to a regiment of infantrymen.[122] Ebenezer Boltwood endured house arrest in Amherst in August 1777 for demurring when asked, "Are you desirous to be independent of the Crown of Great Britain according to the Declaration of Congress passed in the Year 1776?" His loyalties tested, Boltwood decided that he had reached their limit. The following May, when Amherst needed to provide the Continental Army with nine men, he enlisted for eight months.[123] James Sheafe had to fight his way through an angry mob in front of the courthouse in Exeter, New Hampshire, in February 1777 to explain to the Committee of Safety why he had not signed the statewide loyalty oath. Despite posting a bond of £500 to ensure his good behavior, he was jailed briefly in Portsmouth the following May. Perhaps to rehabilitate himself, by the early 1780s he had bought a share in an American privateer.[124]

EVEN COMPLETE abstention from public affairs had its costs. It was not easy to resign from civic life. As Nathan Bond realized in Concord in 1776 and John Eliot learned the following year in Boston, community pressures made it very difficult not to choose a side. And there was no easy way to rescind an abstention. Men who chose to abdicate their public responsibilities permanently cast suspicion on themselves.

It is difficult to know how many members of the revolutionary generation consciously avoided coming out on one side or the other, but there were certainly a few. In New Hampshire, where the Association Test forced most men to take sides in 1776, Thomas Rindge Rogers did his best to avoid making a public choice by retiring from civic life after he refused to sign the pledge. The son of a member of New Hampshire's King's Council, the grandson of the colony's London agent, and a cousin of Governor John Wentworth, Rogers belonged to his province's inner circle. Under earlier circumstances he could have expected appointments to positions of honor and income. Instead, he settled permanently into a peaceful pastoral existence.[125]

Suspect in Portsmouth because of his family's provincial ties and his own refusal to come out in favor of the Revolution, Rogers moved fifteen miles west to Nottingham, a small agricultural town. Although he styled himself a gentleman and retained a small amount of real estate in Portsmouth, he made his living by farming. Apart from serving in 1792 on a town committee to establish school districts, he never accepted a responsible local or state office. Rogers had retired into the background where no one would notice him.[126]

ON SEPTEMBER 18, 1783, Tom Coffin, still in New York City, wrote a quick note to his mother in Boston. He was finally coming home for a visit.[127]

This would be no ordinary sojourn. Tom had not seen his mother in five years nor been home in seven.[128] What was more, it might be his last chance ever to do either. Except for the implementation of the Anglo-American treaty that concluded the Revolution, the war was over and Tom was among the losers. Before long, the British forces would have to evacuate New York City for Halifax, and he would go with them. Would he ever return to his native land? Would he ever see his mother and sisters again? There was no way to predict.

Five days after he sent his note, Tom set out for Boston with Ward Chipman, a 1770 graduate of the college who wanted to visit his family in Marblehead. Chipman had served the British army in 1777 as its deputy muster master general for North America before beginning the private practice of law in New York City in early 1778. New York had been good to Chip, who had made (and then quickly spent) £500 a year in his practice,[129] but he was widely identified with the British army he had served and with the loyalists who had been his clients, so he also planned to leave.

It took Tom and Chip nearly six days to travel from Manhattan to Boston. They rode in a phaeton, an open four-wheeled carriage, and many of the roads they encountered were so badly gullied from recent rains that their passage was frustratingly slow and arduous. At one point they broke one of the carriage's mainsprings, an accident that forced them to lay up for the night.[130]

Prudence dictated caution, so Coffin and Chipman were wary of letting people know who they were and what they were about. After all, how would the people of Connecticut and Massachusetts react to loyalists in their midst? Still, it was a more than pleasant journey. On a couple of occasions, Tom and Chip, fearing for their safety, hurried on from potentially threatening situations,[131] but for the most part strangers treated them cordially and old friends welcomed them.

At noon on their second day Tom and Chip shared a meal in Greenwich, Connecticut, with General Benjamin Lincoln, the Continental Congress's portly secretary of war, who was passing through on his way south from Boston to Philadelphia. Neither loyalist had met Lincoln before, but the meal was "very affable & polite," and Lincoln had "much conversation with Tom about old Boston Friends."[132] Later that afternoon in neighboring Stamford they called on John Lloyd, a merchant originally of Boston. Lloyd was already entertaining two visitors—his brothers Henry, a loyalist who had fled Boston with the departing British in 1776 but returned recently, and James, the Boston physician who had trained so many young doctors, including some of their classmates. The Revolution had divided the Lloyd clan—John had stood with the patriots, while James had sided with Henry and the crown, although he had not left Boston—but they were already making amends, making up for lost time.[133]

After Stamford, it was off to Fairfield, where Andrew Eliot, Jr., John Eliot's elder brother and a tutor during the travelers' college years, was the Congregationalist minister. Parson Eliot was away on a visit of his own to Boston, but his wife, Polly, a longtime friend, was at home, and she was overjoyed to see the two young men.[134]

The road then led to New Haven. Neither Tom nor Chip had ever visited the home of Yale College, but from the heights overlooking the town, Chipman found the setting both beautiful and surprisingly evocative:

> When we arrived at the top of the hill before you descend into the Town, the Landscape & prospect was really enchanting, the Spires, the College, the buildings, the River, the highly cultivated Fields & Orchards bending under the weight of fruit, the marshes cover'd with large Stacks of the finest salt hay, the rough hills & Forests the boundaries of the view on one side, the Sound & Long Island on the other—all together formed so variegated & pleasant a Scene most beautifully illumin'd by a western Sun, as I never before beheld. As we descended the hill & entered the town of New Haven, I was struck with the strong resemblance it bore to the entrance in to the town of Cambridge in Massachusetts Bay.

After Coffin and Chipman stopped for a break at a tavern adjoining the campus, there was time to tour the town and the school. A student saw the gentlemen taking in the sights and offered to show them the college library.

When Yale's president, Ezra Stiles, learned of the visitors, he came out to greet them and to see to it that their needs were met.[135]

As with each passing day Coffin and Chipman drew closer to their destination, their sense of anticipation grew, but so did their apprehensions. The nearer they came to Boston, the more they feared that they would encounter someone who knew them—that is, someone who knew of and despised their loyalism.

By the afternoon of Friday, September 25, Coffin and Chipman had reached the outskirts of Boston. As Chipman composed his diary a few days later, he could "barely relate the general facts. The agitations of my mind were too various to pourtray." Coffin and Chipman had sped through Sudbury, Weston, Waltham, and Watertown, eager to achieve their objective. In Watertown, though, "we began to have a thousand ridiculous (as they since prove) fears & alarms." It was after 7:00 P.M. when they crossed into Cambridge and about 8:00 P.M. when they reached the Blue Anchor Tavern, not far from Harvard Yard. Everything they found in the town was very much as they remembered, and they had to struggle with their anger at what had transpired in recent years. Many of the houses they passed had once belonged to loyalist friends but had since been confiscated by the patriots.[136]

At the Blue Anchor the travelers decided that they needed fresh horses.[137] Afraid of being recognized, they went to the tavern's rear entrance and called for Ebenezer Bradish, the proprietor. While Bradish was taking care of their request, Tom and Chip decided to visit old haunts. It was dark by now, and they felt confident that they would not be recognized. They went "round the College & thro' the town. Every thing appeared natural & familiar." After taking a drink with the college blacksmith, who was glad to see them, it was time to leave.[138]

By 10:00 they reached Mrs. Coffin's front door. Tom left Chip to fasten the horses. He "burst into the door in his *helter skelter slam bang* way, & was seated by the fire in a few minutes quite at home lolling in his sisters' laps. A more joyous meeting cannot be described; never was one more so."[139]

Tom's and Chip's fears about their reception were groundless. They spent the next day visiting old friends in Boston before Chipman set off to see his own family in Marblehead. They encountered Lieutenant Governor Thomas Cushing in the street, and he greeted them cordially, as did the Reverend Samuel Cooper, the fiery patriot who ministered to Boston's Brattle Street Church.[140]

Too soon, it was time to return to New York City. Coffin and Chipman left Boston for Providence early in the morning of Thursday, October 2. "We, of course, came away in a very *penseroso* stile, which continued the whole day," Chipman recalled, "Tom & I scarce speaking to each other the whole way to Providence."[141] From Providence, the travelers made their way to Newport and thence to New York by packet. They arrived on Manhattan on Monday, October 6.

It was a memorable trip, and for all they knew their recollections of it might have to last them a lifetime. Years before, they had made certain choices. Siding with the crown had seemed appropriate, sensible, honorable in 1775, but at the time they could hardly have guessed the cost of this decision. Their trip brought home to them the price they were paying. Despite the cordiality of the greetings they had received, each feared that as a loyalist he was still persona non grata to most New Englanders. The land of their birth no longer had a place for them, they feared. Moreover, they had made commitments of their own to the crown. The real cost of the choices Coffin and Chipman were now paying for was the familiar faces, the familiar scenes they might never see again.

5

Revolutionary Changes

I t was not yet harvest season when Sam Jennison returned home. Half-way through 1779 the war was entering its fifth year and showing no signs of ending, but Sam had had enough. Still only twenty, after more than thirty months in uniform he had done his share. It was time to get on with his life, but how would he try to make his way in the world?

Textiles. They might be the answer. Cotton factories were already changing the face of England. The mills were the latest important economic development there, and it did not take any great insight to figure out that they might become at least as significant in North America. There was a problem, however. The technology required to build and operate a cotton mill was so advanced that everyone who possessed it guarded it tenaciously as proprietary knowledge. Jennison had no means to break the information monopoly, but he had another way to profit from the textile revolution. Maybe he could take up a niche on the margins of the industry.

Fifteen miles west of Mendon, Massachusetts, where Sam had grown up, he set up a cloth-printing shop in Oxford. Using an oil-based dye, he began to stamp decorative patterns on calico and linen. Cloth printing was not new—the technology was European, and Philadelphians had used it for decades—but it was not common in New England.

Two years later Jennison announced that he was closing his shop and leaving Oxford.[1] More than two centuries afterward there is no way to be certain what went wrong. Perhaps Sam's costs were too high to compete with imported products or his quality was inferior or his designs were not in fashion or he was unable to procure a reliable supply of cloth to imprint. Whatever the case, his scheme had failed.

Sam decided to try something else. He was only in his early twenties, after all, he had the best of educations, and he needed to find a calling. Maybe he had a future in one of the learned professions. Jennison determined to become an attorney. While he was still attempting to make a go of cloth printing, he began to read law. The Worcester County bar, continuing to suffer from the vacuum the Tory exodus had created half a dozen years before, quickly admitted him to practice.[2]

Meanwhile, Sam's family responsibilities started to increase. On December 25, 1781, he married Sally Fiske, whose father, Nathan, was the Congregationalist minister in Brookfield, a town on the county's western border. By 1785 Sam and Sally had two children. Two more would come later.[3]

Failure continued to dog Sam, however, no matter what he did. Jennison's life at the bar was no more satisfactory than his manufacturing career. Professionally, he was in the wrong place at the wrong time. It was hard to make a living as a lawyer in central Massachusetts in the mid-1780s. Eighteenth-century attorneys spent much of their time collecting delinquent debts, but the same economic stresses and rural rage with creditors that would soon lead to Shays's Rebellion, a violent debtors' protest, made it extremely difficult to pressure borrowers to pay up. Lawyers who tried won no friends.

Scarred by his lack of success, Sam departed without his family sometime around 1786 for Thomaston, a rugged, growing settlement of nearly eight hundred souls at the end of an inlet along Maine's jagged coast about sixty miles as the crow flies northeast of Portland. In a deed he now described himself as a "yeoman"—a farmer. At times he also taught school in the area's recently established towns.[4]

Sam continued to maintain contact with his family. Since he and Sally conceived at least one—probably two—of their four children after his move, he must have visited her from time to time. He was in Oxford in 1790 when he wrote to a college acquaintance "begging charitable relief," but he was back in Thomaston again the next year.[5]

Eventually, Jennison's wife and children, unable to support themselves, had to return to her father's household in Brookfield, where they lived until Nathan Fiske's death in 1799. Pressured by relatives to terminate her marriage to a man who had effectively deserted her, Sally Jennison finally obtained a divorce.[6]

Sam Jennison had made a mess of his life. He had tried to ride the wave of the day's most advanced technology—no luck. He had entered a venerable learned profession—without success. He had tested himself in the borderlands of postrevolutionary Maine—and barely scraped by. He had married, and then with his wife he had brought four children into the world—but before long he left his family. A promising youth had turned into a shattered adulthood.

None of Sam's classmates failed as spectacularly as he did, although in time some certainly came to see themselves as inadequate. In important respects, however, the trajectory of Sam's life resembled that of many of his Harvard contemporaries. The Revolution interrupted their development at a critical time, the years when college boys ordinarily established them-

selves as adults. Some served in the military and others did not, but whichever was the case, once they put the war behind them, they made every
effort to compensate for lost time. They soon discovered that change was
sweeping across postwar New England. Like Jennison, some of them
sought the main chance in emerging areas of the economy. In the late
eighteenth century, commerce, the frontier, and the first appearances of
industry offered exciting opportunities to men with the skills and the luck
to exploit them. Many more young Harvardians were attracted to the traditional learned professions. Eventually, most of Sam's schoolmates found a
calling and a place to live, sometimes after several tries, and they began a
family. If only his own efforts had been as well rewarded.

HISTORIANS HAVE puzzled for generations over the social and economic
consequences of the American Revolution.[7] More recently, students of various American conflicts have also begun to investigate the psychological
cost of warfare.[8] The experiences of Harvard's revolutionary generation
offer some useful insights into the first of these issues and some suggestive
evidence concerning the second.

In important respects, the continuing effects of the war seemed negligible at first. In the early and mid-1780s, civilians and veterans alike attempted as quickly as possible to take up the lives they had once known.
They tried to treat the war as no more than a temporary interruption as
they sought to return to the paths they had charted before its outbreak.
Content with the goals they had set for themselves at the end of college,
they now tried to realize them. Over time, however, the conflict's lasting
consequences became increasingly apparent. There was no way to evade
the war's permanent effects. The members of the revolutionary generation
had prepared themselves for their parents' world, a way of life that was
quickly passing. The arc of personal independence intersected with the arc
of national independence, opening up a new range of life options for former
provincial students with obsolescent ambitions. The detour had definitively
set them onto a new course.

For Sam Jennison and his schoolmates the task at hand between the mid-
1770s and the late 1780s, simply stated, was to put their lives back together.
Before the Revolution, many had thought they had known what they
wanted to make of themselves—what careers they would follow, where they
would reside, in some cases even whom they would marry. Perhaps the war
had disrupted their first attempts to establish themselves among New England's leading citizens, but they were all well educated and most were well
connected. They still had a head start on life. To be sure, some of the
veterans came home with lingering or permanent disabilities. Winthrop

Sargent's health was broken by the time he was mustered out in 1783; before he could get on with building his future he had to recover his strength.[9] There is reason to believe that Sam Jennison may have brought emotional demons home with him from the war, and there is quite good cause to conclude that one of Sam's classmates, Benjamin Brown Plaisted, the scion of a wealthy Salem family, suffered a permanent psychological collapse while on garrison duty in the army. Plaisted mysteriously left the service in early 1777 after serving for four apparently uneventful months as an officer in an artillery regiment, and a little more than a year later the selectmen of Boston declared him *non compos mentis*.[10] Nevertheless, as soon as they felt secure from the threat of war, most members of Harvard's revolutionary generation were ready put the pieces of their disrupted lives back together.

Although the War for Independence lasted formally until the signing of the Treaty of Paris on September 3, 1783, informally each member of Harvard's revolutionary generation decided for himself when to declare it at an end. Almost all of those in the Continental Army were officers, as were all of those in the British army, and they were thus free to resign their commissions whenever they had had enough without waiting for the end of a stated term of enlistment. As for the civilian members of the generation, although some of the war's political and economic consequences were unavoidable, in most respects these men were nevertheless at liberty to shape their own lives.

Sam Jennison's personal conflict concluded, at least officially, on July 11, 1779, when he resigned his commission in the Continental Army and started for home.[11] For Fisher Ames it is hard to know when the war began for him, let alone when it ended. Ames's service—about two weeks of local militia duty—took place in the spring of 1778 while he was reading law in Dedham and helping run the family tavern.[12] Winthrop Sargent's war did not come to a close until after the formal end of hostilities in the fall of 1783.[13] Eliphalet Pearson briefly took time out from his career as an educator to work with Sam Phillips on a powder mill, but before long he was back in front of his young students.[14]

Sooner or later every young Harvard man decided that his own individual war was at an end. It was time to get on with life.

Of the 204 members of Harvard's revolutionary generation, a combination of illness and accidents had carried away 8 by April 19, 1775, when the guns began to thunder. Over the course of the next eight years, 23 more died, including the 7 men who lost their lives while under arms. Thus, by the autumn of 1783, 173 men, slightly more than five-sixths of the original number, were left. Of these, about 80, or somewhat fewer than half, underwent only the personal and economic disruptions that almost every American experienced during these years—inflation, losses to privateers and foragers, the absence and death of relatives and friends, fear of enemy attack, and so on. The remainder—more than 90—experienced more substantial war-related dislocations to their lives.

In a few cases, these disconnections were fortuitous. The war years could be a boon. They brought some men unanticipated opportunities to profit financially, professionally, or politically. For the rest, however, they were a struggle, a time of loss and deprivation, of putting one's life on hold for many months at the least, and in some cases for years. These men had to wait for their opportunities until the end of hostilities.

IT SHOULD not be surprising that the men who stayed home, spending little or no time in the service, were the least likely to suffer major dislocations. Officers in the Continental Army, by contrast, often passed years in the military away from loved ones, giving little thought to their careers and reluctant to commit to marriage when their prospects were uncertain. Most loyalists left their homes and careers unsure whether they would ever again see the familiar sights and hear the familiar sounds of New England. But for scores of men who went on with their lives without committing themselves either to extended service in the Continental Army or to the cause of the crown, the war was more a disruption than a dislocation.

As long as New England was the seat of the revolutionary conflict, property loss and damage were the most serious threats to the majority of civilians. Between April 19, 1775, and the British evacuation of Boston on March 17, 1776, they faced the predations of foraging troops and the destruction of battle.[15] When British salvos set Charlestown ablaze on June 19, 1775, the family of John Alford Mason lost its handsome mansion. Mason, the son of a Suffolk County official, was without a permanent home until 1786, when his father bought a new family residence in Cambridge about two blocks from the college Yard.[16] Onesiphorus Tileston, a housewright's son, similarly had to abandon his Boston home in favor of a place in Dorchester when the American siege began.[17]

Once the military focus of the war moved south after March 1776, however, the threat to most New England civilians became more indirect. There was never a time when they could afford to forget the possibility that British forces might carry the war back north, but as long as the redcoats' main armies remained in Canada, the middle Atlantic, and the South, it was economic disruption that particularly tested young Harvard men trying to establish themselves. The extent of this challenge varied from calling to calling.

As a group, the generation's ministers had among the easiest experiences. While many of their classmates were caught up in imperial affairs, most of the clergymen concentrated on their calling and their families. In the case of some ministers it is impossible to tell from a life and career outline that there was a war in progress after April 1775. Because almost none of them took up arms and fewer than half of them even served as chaplains, none for more than ten months, very few ever placed themselves in harm's way. Only two, Nathan Morey and Benjamin Muzzy, both 1774 graduates, lost their lives in the service. Morey read for the ministry after graduation, but he died aboard a British prison ship after the privateer on which he was serving as the ship's doctor was captured.[18] Muzzey was lost when the privateer on which he was acting as chaplain disappeared without a trace.[19]

The experiences of Daniel Chaplin and John Eliot were more typical among the clergy. After graduation in 1772, Chaplin read theology and began to supply pulpits. During the late winter of 1775, the political turmoil of the times created an opportunity for him. Samuel Dana, the minister of the Congregational church in Groton, had resisted the surging tide of revolution. That March, when Dana began to preach submission to the crown, his people rose up against him. At the same time that British regulars were preparing to march on Lexington and Concord, his congregation cast him out of the Groton pulpit, creating the opening that Chaplin filled by the start of 1778.[20] Settled in a desirable situation, Chaplin was ready for family responsibilities. He married Jane Prescott, the eldest child of a Groton family, in 1779. The following year, she gave birth to the first of their eight children.[21]

Despite intermittent service over the course of nearly ten months as an army chaplain in Boston in 1777 and 1778, John Eliot never had to put himself out seriously because of the war—or, indeed, even to leave town for military duty. When his regiment prepared to depart its Boston garrison in February 1778 and go into action, Eliot resigned his chaplaincy and turned his eyes toward the most important focus of his attention during the years following graduation: finding a suitable pulpit.[22]

Eliot's military duty had actually been a brief interlude in what was otherwise the normal sequence of events for a would-be minister in mid- or late-eighteenth-century New England.[23] After college he read theology, in his case while in residence in Cambridge, where he might benefit from the guidance of the Harvard faculty. By the summer of 1775 he was in Dover, New Hampshire, where Jeremy Belknap, the town's settled pastor, a decade Eliot's senior and the husband of one of John's cousins, oversaw his first sermons.[24] During the coming months Eliot supplied many other pulpits

John Eliot, 1779. Eliot never cared for this painting; perhaps he found its obvious romantic influences off-putting. (*John Eliot* [1779], by Samuel King. Oil on canvas, 46.3 × 41.2 cm. Massachusetts Historical Society.)

for varying periods of time. At one point in 1776, he actually considered the offer of an Anglican parish under the British ensign in Halifax, Nova Scotia, but then rejected it when his friends and family expressed their strong disapproval. In the fall of 1777, John was in Fairfield, Connecticut, practicing his preaching from the pulpit of his brother Andrew Jr.[25] Other engagements took him to Littleton, twenty-five miles northwest of Boston, and Salem, fifteen miles to the north. Politics aside—and in view of his flirtation with the people of Halifax, politics do not seem to have affected

Eliot seriously—John's search in the late 1770s for an appropriate pulpit was not very different from the experiences of hundreds of Harvard men from previous generations who had aspired to the ministry.

Eliot's quest finally ended in 1778. When his father, Andrew Sr., died on September 13, the pulpit of Boston's New North Church fell vacant. At the time, John was supplying Boston's New South Church, a more affluent, refined, and desirable congregation than the one his father had served. New South seemed almost ready to call him, but unhappily the course of duty was clear.[26] John was ordained and installed in his father's place on November 3, 1779.[27] After nearly five years at New North without a wife, he took a mate on September 10, 1784, when he married Ann Treadwell of Portsmouth.[28]

In a period of stress and anxiety, no minister had a carefree time of it, and because their salaries were ordinarily for fixed, agreed-upon sums, many clergymen found that rampant revolutionary-era inflation ate away rapidly at their income. Neither Chaplin nor Eliot escaped the temporary intrusion of the war. Nevertheless, the challenges they faced were modest and manageable. Circumstances were much the same for the revolutionary generation's teachers.

In Andover, Massachusetts, it was difficult for a teacher to ignore the conflict, but it remained possible to make accommodations to it. The end of Eliphalet Pearson's direct participation in the war through the powder mill he and Sam Phillips erected allowed the two friends to take up a new initiative: the establishment of a private classical academy for boys. Pearson had intended to offer himself for ordination, but a debilitating fever, which permanently weakened his eyes, convinced him that he lacked the stamina for the parish ministry. Phillips Academy, Andover, was the result of Pearson's search for a new calling. Eliphalet and Sam planned the school together, the Phillips family underwrote its initial costs, and Pearson served as its first preceptor, a position he held from 1778 to 1786.

In all this, the war's effects were real but secondary. Eliphalet was in Cambridge on a fellowship in the spring of 1775 when the shooting started. Along with the rest of the Harvard community, he fled to safety. When he chose Andover as his destination, he returned to the place where he had taught, a town heavily influenced by the wealthy Phillips family. The Revolution thus facilitated the collaboration of Eliphalet with his old friend Sam. Its immediate consequences for the school, however, were negligible.[29]

Wartime dislocation made certain callings more difficult to enter, at a cost that was both professional and personal. Jonathan Williams, the son of the crown's customs inspector in Boston, faced more serious problems than either would-be ministers such as Chaplin and Eliot or a practicing schoolmaster such as Pearson. In the mid-1770s Williams had to decide whether under the present circumstances his career plans made any sense. At the close of his senior year he determined to read for the law. John Adams took him on as a student, and he entered Adams's office in September 1772. As Adams became increasingly involved in the politics of the day, though, he had less and less time for his clerks. Williams studied the customary professional texts with Adams until October 1774, when he left for Worcester, where he hoped that James Putnam, Sr., might be able to afford him more attention. The next year he was still in Putnam's office when Worcester County emptied of its Tory attorneys. For some young law students the loyalist exodus heralded opportunity. Levi Lincoln saw a legal vacuum in Worcester County and rushed in to fill it as soon as he had completed his training in Northampton; before long he was building a successful practice and entering into public service as the county clerk of courts. More cautious than Lincoln, Williams worried that imperial disturbances might soon make it impossible to practice law. The province closed its courts in response to the crown's Massachusetts Government Act in 1774; they did not begin to reopen anywhere within the jurisdiction until 1776, and not until 1780 in western counties. Williams gave up his aspirations for the bar. Instead, he turned to a career in commerce.[30]

Trade, it turned out, was not an especially easy option either, as John Tracy knew too well. The son of a wealthy Newburyport merchant, Tracy took the path of least resistance after college when he entered his father's line of work. Operating out of his hometown, John, his brother Nathaniel, and a friend had established a mercantile firm in 1774. Their plan was to deal in European goods, but the outbreak of the war made their ventures imprudently risky. They dissolved their partnership, and John began to trade on his own in "choice Malaga wine, by the quarter Cask, Lemmons by the Box, Cocoa, and a few cases of Gin."[31] After 1775 John and Nathaniel concentrated increasingly on privateering until 1780.[32]

For civilian members of the revolutionary generation, the war made it more difficult to establish themselves in life than it would have been at a time of peace. Yet if the war was an obstacle for them, it was one they could eventually circumvent. For their schoolmates who served extended terms in the service, though, the Revolution's demands were much more substantial.

MANY VETERANS of more recent American wars have struggled to reenter the civilian world at the end of their service. It would be reasonable to assume that some of the soldiers of the Revolutionary War encountered the same physical and psychological challenges that have made it so difficult for many returning servicemen ever since the Civil War to come home, but the evidence for this conclusion is fragmentary at best. Apart from Winthrop Sargent, Benjamin Brown Plaisted, and Sam Jennison, it is impossible to identify confidently a member of the revolutionary generation who suffered any of the persistent physical and mental disabilities that have plagued so many more recent veterans, such as night sweats, alcoholism, and flashbacks. If other young Harvard men experienced similar symptoms and disabilities, persuasive evidence of their trials has now disappeared.[33]

For some of Harvard's young veterans it was relatively easy to take up their lives again after protracted periods of service. Physicians—for example, Jack Warren and William Eustis—had spent years facing much worse medical and surgical challenges than they were likely to encounter regularly in civilian practice, and the men who had fought in the front lines came home highly honored as conquering heroes. The war had cost New England many of its medical men, doctors who had sided with the crown. In Boston, between 1775 and 1776, twelve of twenty-one active physicians departed town, leaving a void that returning army doctors could fill. From the day he came home to Boston in 1777 to assume command of a military hospital, Warren became a leading force in the town's depleted medical community.[34] Meanwhile, opportunities such as those that Sam Jennison tried out were open to everyone else. Yet because of the length of time away from home in stressful situations, if for no other reason, extended terms of military duty had to affect the men who served.

The professional and business opportunities that a new nation offered anyone who was willing to take a risk on the unknown made it possible for many veterans of the revolutionary generation to test a variety of callings before selecting one. It was equally the case, though, that some of them had difficulty making up their minds and settling down. Like Sam Jennison, veterans such as Winthrop Sargent, Daniel Parker, and Jacob Welsh spent years looking for the main chance without fixing on it.

When Sargent returned home it was to a ruined family. Unlucky in privateering, the Sargents were struggling to support themselves. Winthrop offered his services as a mercenary to the prince of Orange and attempted to secure a diplomatic posting before taking a share in the Ohio Company, a venture to sell tracts of land in the Northwest Territory, and receiving an appointment in 1786 to survey the wilderness. After becoming the Ohio Company's secretary, in 1788 he moved to Marietta. Although he relocated several times, frontier communities remained his home for the rest of his life.[35]

Daniel Parker, the son of a Boston goldsmith, spent twenty-one months as an artillery officer before resigning on October 1, 1778.[36] He married the following year and attempted to set himself up in Boston in the early 1780s as a trader and auctioneer.[37] A decade later he was in Philadelphia acting first as a government clerk and then as a broker. When one of his brothers became insolvent in 1792, though, the debts pulled Daniel down, too. Daniel filed for bankruptcy, and by 1793 he disappeared completely from view.[38]

Jacob Welsh's service in the infantry and the artillery ended with his resignation in November 1778.[39] Not long thereafter Welsh, the son of a jeweler, was in England, where he tried and failed to smuggle textile machinery out of the country. By the early 1780s he was living in Lunenburg, Massachusetts, and speculating in real estate. Land speculation—probably in combination with farming—kept Jacob occupied but not satisfied. By the early 1790s, plans to build the nation's capital on the Potomac led him to propose himself unsuccessfully to supervise the work under the direction of Pierre L'Enfant.[40]

Although Jennison, Sargent, Parker, and Welsh were still searching in the mid-1780s for something to do for a living, for the most part their classmates had established stable civilian lives by the end of 1785. Thirty-eight members of Harvard's revolutionary generation served in either the Continental Army or Marines during the Revolution. Thirty-four of them were still alive at the close of 1785. Of these veterans, by December of that year all but seven had settled into the career they would follow for the next decade, and most resided where they would stay for the rest of their lives, generally somewhere in eastern Massachusetts.

Not everyone was happy with his choices. The roller coaster that was the American economy continued to make some occupations—notably commerce and the law—difficult to enter safely until near the end of the decade. Samuel Tenney and John Sprague, both 1772 graduates and both doctors, quickly grew dissatisfied with medicine and drifted in the direction of other callings without ever completely giving up their practice as physicians.[41] Meanwhile, John Hastings, the youngest son of the college steward, settled on a farm in Woburn, where he became a respected resident, but his finances eventually grew shaky, and for several years at the end of the century he tried unsuccessfully to reestablish himself in Maine.[42] Still, for all but a handful of veterans, within a couple of years of the end of the war, their life's outline was becoming clear.

For the generation's loyalists, things were turning out nothing like what they had anticipated. Twenty-six of them were still alive in 1783, and they were scattered from England to Canada to the Caribbean and throughout the former colonies. As they were growing up, Brinley Sylvester Oliver (the youngest son of Lieutenant Governor Andrew Oliver of Massachusetts), Thomas Flucker (whose father, Thomas, was royal secretary of the province), and Samuel Hirst Sparhawk (a grandson of Sir William Pepperrell) had every reason to assume that in keeping with the ways of their day, they would rise to their colony's most eminent stations. Yet where were they in 1783? Oliver was serving as a purser—in effect, a seagoing business agent—aboard the *Camelon*, a small sixteen-gun sloop in the Royal Navy. Flucker was a captain in the British army recently returned to England from Barbados. And Sparhawk, struggling to get by on a small crown pension, was in the process of acquiring a British army commission.[43]

Of the twenty-eight men who had begun the war as loyalists, only two were still angling to acquire the high power and position that so recently had seemed theirs by birthright. Their very different stories are instructive. James Sheafe had made an about-face in the mid- or late 1770s. After his humiliating and frightening confrontation with an angry crowd of patriots outside the courthouse in Exeter, New Hampshire, in 1776, he had reconsidered his allegiances. By the early 1780s, he was solidifying his finances and his place in Portsmouth's mercantile community in anticipation of reviving his public career. Tom Coffin, by contrast, was now fully committed to the crown. After visiting his family in the fall of 1783, he repaired to Halifax and then to London. Well regarded within the British military establishment after his wartime service, he was ready for high office as commissary and controller when one of his patrons, Sir Guy Carleton, became governor-general and commander in chief of British North America in 1786. By the mid-1780s, Tom had set out on a career that would bring him back to Boston and Cambridge for only a few brief visits.[44]

In the early 1780s, American loyalists faced two starkly different options: the crown or the confederation, Great Britain or America. It was certainly possible to do very well no matter which choice one took. Coffin and Sheafe were living proof. The reality of the situation, however, was that these were the exceptions, not the rule. For the most part, no matter where they threw in their lot, by the early 1780s the loyalists were outsiders looking in. Typically they lacked the contacts in Britain to stand anywhere but on the margins of polite society, and if they returned home to New England, they faced the difficult task of persuading disbelieving neighbors to trust them.

Consider the situation of Isaac Smith, the tutor who directed the lost British relief column on April 19, 1775. Smith was as frustrated as the majority of his former loyalist students. After fleeing Boston, he made his way to England, where the best opportunity he could find was the pulpit of the small Presbyterian chapel in Sidmouth, Devon. Separated from his family, severely limited in his prospects, Smith wrote to his mother, probably in 1780, lamenting his isolation and worrying about his future: "What scenes in life providence is reserving me, I know not. The distance at which I am . . . from you & the rest of my nearest connections in this world,—the narrowness of my present circumstances,—the uncertainty of my future situation,— . . . and the difficulty at least, if not the impossibility, of guessing . . . when this unhappy contest, in which we are engaged, will end, all together concur to fill me with anxiety and grief."[45] When, if ever, would Smith be able to return home?

Almost without exception, Harvard's loyalist sons suffered for their politics. If their allegiance to the crown were overriding, then they gave up their property, their friends, their homeland, and sometimes their families. If they chose to remain at home, then they compromised their honor and their political beliefs. Often they also jeopardized any possibility of a significant career in public life.

In the early 1780s, as the members of Harvard's revolutionary generation tried to find postwar places for themselves, eleven of the twenty-six surviving loyalists swallowed their pride, came home, and tried to set themselves up in the United States. Doctors, merchants, farmers, and ministers, all but Sheafe settled for life in the shadows, out of sight of the public. Meanwhile, former tutor Isaac Smith returned to Massachusetts in 1784 and to Harvard, which appointed him librarian, in 1787. In 1791 he succeeded Samuel Moody as master of Dummer Academy.[46] As for the fifteen loyalists who remained with the empire living in either England, Canada, or the Caribbean, the best they could hope for was an inheritance, military patronage—four held commissions in the British army as lieutenants or captains, three others served the army or navy as civilian provisioners—or a minor church living.

The generation's loyalist members were getting by, but with a few exceptions life was not at all what they had expected.

BY THE END of 1785, a little more than two years after the formal end of the War for Independence, most members of Harvard's revolutionary generation had charted the courses they would follow for the rest of their lives. In many instances, except in the case of the loyalists, these paths initially must have resembled the lives they had imagined for themselves as boys when they determined to prepare for college. Their homes, their jobs, and their family situations were generally similar to those of Harvard men a few years older than they were. In the summer of 1767, three-quarters of all living Harvard men were residing in Massachusetts, nearly half in Boston or the surrounding counties of eastern Massachusetts.[47] The proportion of members of the revolutionary generation who lived in the area at the close of 1785 was slightly lower—only about two-thirds lived anywhere in

Massachusetts[48]—but the commonwealth was still by far the most common home for members of the generation. The favored occupations among Harvard men in 1767 remained the popular professions in 1785, although the relative proportions had shifted slightly. In 1767, five-sixths of all living Harvard men were in the ministry, business, education, medicine, and the law.[49] At the end of 1785, fewer than four-fifths of the members of the revolutionary generation were pursuing the same five callings,[50] but these still far outpaced all of the alternatives. Although some members of the generation had still not found a wife, nearly seven in ten had married by the end of 1785,[51] a figure only about 4 percent below what it had been twenty-five years earlier for the classes of 1746 through 1749 when they had been at a comparable point in their lives at the close of December 1760.[52] Eventually they would sire almost as many children per man as the members of the classes that graduated a quarter-century before them.[53]

And yet with hindsight it is also possible to find the first signs of significant changes in the family and career paths that Harvard men would set out on after the Revolution. Despite many similarities, there were also differences between the life structure of the members of the revolutionary generation and that of the members of earlier Harvard classes, variations that were direct consequences of the conflict. Compared with their predecessors twenty-five years before them, the men of the revolutionary generation had substantially different levels of enthusiasm for certain professional paths. Three in ten of the members of the classes of 1746 through 1749 were in the ministry in December 1760; only 16 percent of the members of the classes of 1771 through 1774 were in December 1785. Nearly three in ten members of the earlier classes were following business careers in December 1760; fewer than one-quarter of the members of the revolutionary generation were in December 1785. In contrast, members of the revolutionary generation had entered the law and education in slightly higher proportions than the earlier classes had, as well as callings that no one in the earlier cohort had taken up: the military, art, and the sea. Possibly as an indication that Harvard men were becoming so adventuresome in their careers that they have escaped mention in traditional sources, no record apparently survives of the occupation of one in ten.[54]

When the Revolution detained young Harvard men from fixing on their callings, it also postponed life's next customary phases, settling down and beginning a family. Men whose fathers, uncles, and older brothers had found homes for themselves and married in their mid-twenties were being delayed in taking these same steps for years. For the men who had directly preceded the revolutionary generation at Harvard, five to seven years had usually elapsed between graduation and marriage. As a group, even the members of the class of 1770 had usually managed to find a mate before the war intervened.[55] Beginning with the class of 1771, though, the Revolution threw up obstacles that prevented them from starting families. For the better part of a year in 1775 and 1776, many men who in more placid times would have passed their evenings in courting had found themselves either besieging Boston or stationed within the embattled and uncertain town looking out. Thereafter dozens of men—particularly loyalists and officers in the Continental Army—had been too caught up in the affairs of the day to marry. It took the members of the class of 1771 about three years longer to wed than it had taken the class of 1770, and it took four or five years longer for the typical member of the class of 1772, about ten years.[56]

Men who served in the Continental Army experienced still greater delays. On average, they required nearly four more years to get married than was typical for Harvard men in the classes of 1761 through 1770.[57] Of the thirty-eight members of the generation who served in the Continental Army or Marines, half a dozen were at least thirty-nine when they first married; when confirmed bachelor William Eustis finally married at fifty-seven in 1810, he had already had at least two full careers, having practiced medicine and then served in government as a congressman and as secretary of war. By the time the average veteran saw his first child born, he was over thirty years old and ten years out of college.[58]

Loyalist sons of Harvard also had difficulty settling down. On average, more than ten years passed between commencement and first marriage, half again as many as for members of the classes of 1761 through 1770. The median number of elapsed years for these men—nine—was nearly twice the median of five years for the men of the classes of 1761 through 1770. Even more startling, seven of the loyalists—one-quarter—never married at all.[59] Tom Coffin was one of these lifelong bachelors, although he fathered five illegitimate children by at least three different women. The typical loyalist member of the revolutionary generation was thirty-one when his first child was born more than a decade after commencement.[60]

Although most of the members of the generation had come home to settle, finding places for themselves somewhere in New England, a growing proportion was moving away from the region. At the end of 1760, when the classes of 1746 through 1749 were the same distance from their college years as the classes of 1771 through 1774 were at the close of 1785, only two of their members lived outside the region, one of whom was a native North Carolinian who had returned home after graduation.[61] In contrast, of the members of the classes of the revolutionary generation, at least twenty-three—one in seven of those still alive—resided outside the New England states at the close of 1785.[62]

For the men who had sacrificed the most for their cause, on whichever side, the continuing consequences of the war remained the most severe. The Revolution had left a permanent imprint on their lives.

In the end, most young Harvardians would not return to lives completely untouched by the conflict. The aftereffects were too great and too varied. If the Revolution had left society unmarked, then they might have returned to the paths they had set for themselves at the close of college. In important ways, however, the war was transformative, and as its results became apparent, it grew increasingly clear that many lives would change as well.[63]

When it came time to settle down or choose a calling, the consequences of the Revolution often controlled the available choices. John Thaxter, who spent nearly six years in government service, first as a congressional clerk and then as John Adams's secretary during negotiations with European powers on the Continent during the late 1770s and early 1780s, felt constricted in his options when he came home to Massachusetts near the end of 1783. After his graduation in 1774, Thaxter, the son of a leading citizen of Hingham, had read law with Adams, and with his mentor's endorsement the Suffolk County bar had admitted him in 1777. By the time Thaxter returned to Massachusetts, however, he was worried that there might be no room for him to set up a profitable practice in Boston or elsewhere in the county. While he was serving his country, others had been able to establish themselves. "Suffolk Bar is crowded already," Thaxter fretted during the summer of 1783 as he prepared to return home, "& there are numbers yet to come in, who are now preparing. What is to become of me, I know not. I believe, if I dont turn Farmer, I shall push into some one of the back Counties." It was fortunate that John was still "single (thank God)."[64] At least he had some time to find himself a promising situation.

The most intriguing opportunity for John turned out to be in Haverhill, a community of perhaps 2,800 in northern Essex County along the New Hampshire border.[65] The Adamses had established a family outpost in Haverhill, where John Adams's brother-in-law John Shaw was the minister, and Thaxter took advantage of these connections. Stores and sheds lined the Haverhill bank of the Merrimack River, evidence of the active commerce of this country town.[66] Thaxter settled there in 1784, and in 1787 he married Elizabeth Duncan, the daughter of a prominent local merchant and, as far as John Quincy Adams was concerned, "the greatest beauty in Haverhill."[67]

There were other apparent opportunities on northern New England's leading edge of settlement. Before the Revolution, apart from southern New Hampshire and coastal Maine, where generations of pioneers and farmers had lived, northern New England was almost empty of white settlers. On the eve of the war only about a thousand colonial families lived anywhere in what would later become Vermont, and western Maine as well as western New Hampshire along the Connecticut River valley were just beginning to witness their first significant European incursions.[68] At the end of the conflict, though, settlers poured into the north country, a tide unleashed by wartime triumphs. Small land grants to soldiers and much larger ones to well-connected politicians and speculators encouraged settlement in regions that had seemed too remote from civilization before the Revolution. So long as British troops in Canada and their Indian allies did not contest the land that New Englanders were beginning to occupy, then the long winters and short growing seasons of inland Maine, northern New Hampshire, and virtually all of Vermont were worth enduring in exchange for the large farms and virgin forests of the back country.

Joshua Bailey Osgood, who was born and raised in Haverhill, left his home town before John Thaxter arrived, thinking that the timber country of Maine's interior afforded him his best prospects. Osgood's marriage in 1780 to Elizabeth Brown brought him to the district's frontier. Although Elizabeth was also a native of Haverhill, her father owned a large tract of land along the Saco River, which he had received in recognition of distinguished service during the Seven Years' War. The Browns moved to Fryeburg in 1768, and after the wedding Osgood joined them. Here in the rolling hill country of western Maine, Joshua worked with his father-in-law in the lumber business, while at the same time he attempted to bring refinement to the frontier. At his death in 1791, Osgood left an estate that included silverware, jewelry, fine furnishings, and a library filled with works that every gentleman ought to know—books by leading authors of the European Enlightenment such as Locke and Burlamaqui.[69]

The backwoods of Maine also offered Jemmy Bowdoin an opportunity to increase the family fortune, although he never left eastern Massachusetts to do so. In the aftermath of the war, Bowdoin's father, Governor James Bowdoin, took advantage of his political connections to acquire vast stretches of unsettled Maine land. As pioneers moved north, pushing the line of settlement ahead of them, many rented or purchased tracts from the Bowdoins, who employed land agents to oversee these holdings. Others simply squatted on the family's estate, hoping that by possessing a share of it, they might wrest its title from the speculator who held the legal claim. After Governor Bowdoin's death in 1790, Jemmy became a hard-nosed businessman in defense of his claims, and as his property filled in, through sales and rent he successfully cultivated his financial legacy.[70]

At the same time that the revolutionary outcome unlocked New England's frontier, it also provided new commercial opportunities. Tilly Merrick, who spent much of the war in the Netherlands, where he was affiliated with the trading house of a step-brother, began to cast around for a promising situation in the early 1780s. As long as the American colonies remained attached to the mother country, they were governed by Great Britain's Navigation Acts, which required them to ship most commodities through a British port. The revolutionary settlement unburdened American merchants of this requirement, however, and Merrick was first in line to take advantage of the new commercial climate.

While still in Amsterdam, Tilly attempted to assess the opportunities that each American port offered an ambitious young merchant. At first, Merrick and his business partner, a man named Isaac Course, planned to settle in Baltimore, where they judged that Maryland wheat and Virginia tobacco might fuel their efforts. At the last minute, though, they determined that Charleston, the principal entrepôt for South Carolina rice and indigo, promised them their best chance to become wealthy. It was a fortunate decision, as Course soon learned that trade was "greatly Stagnated to the northward Occasioned by the Large Quantities of goods that have been pour'd in from every Quarter in expectation of a ready sale which they are disappointed in."[71] Tilly and Isaac established their trading house in the summer of 1783, and the firm of Merrick & Course remained in business for the next fourteen years. An uncertain commercial climate subjected the partners to periodic crises, but at its peak the house did so well that Tilly was able to buy a plantation and the slaves to work it.[72]

Ambitious merchants now followed their dreams around the world. In 1791 Robert Williams set sail for the East Indies on a voyage that almost cost him his life. When his vessel, the *Commerce*, ran aground off the Arabian coast on the evening of July 10, 1792, he nearly drowned as he struggled ashore. Natives stripped Williams and the other shipwreck victims of their clothes and left them to die. Eleven naked survivors set off without provisions for Muscat, hundreds of miles distant, but for five of them, including Williams, the journey was too much. He fell by the wayside, and his companions covered him with brambles to camouflage him from predators. Before it was too late, an Arab traveler happened upon him and carried him to Muscat, from which he took passage home.[73]

Meanwhile, Sam Emery was following a different course. After attempting to establish himself as a merchant in Boston in the early 1790s, he moved to Philadelphia. Sam tried his hand at many businesses in his new hometown. As a commission merchant he served as Nathan Bond's agent in 1794. He was also a trader and a ship's broker.[74]

For men whose interests drew them in the direction of public service, the revolutionary settlement also offered interesting opportunities. Perez Morton, who saw brief and unhazardous military service as the aide-de-camp to a militia general, took advantage of the exodus of Tory officehold-ers by securing an appointment at twenty-seven in 1779 as the county attorney for Suffolk, the first in a series of offices that culminated with his selection in 1811 as attorney general of Massachusetts.[75]

A few members of the revolutionary generation even found their postwar opportunities at Harvard. The war was a seriously disruptive influence on the college. After the school yielded its dormitories to the American troops besieging Boston in May 1775, it took the rest of the decade to restabilize itself. Harvard's sojourn in Concord lasted only until the summer of 1776, but when the school returned to Cambridge, it found its buildings damaged, its finances askew, and its student body reduced in size. American troops had lived twenty to a room, not two to a chamber, in Massachusetts, Hollis, and Stoughton halls, and the buildings had suffered hard use as a result.[76]

Amid wartime hardships, the administration of President Samuel Lang-don grew dispirited and discredited. Langdon resigned, to no one's regret, in 1780. His energetic successor, Joseph Willard, inaugurated in 1781, had taught almost every member of the revolutionary generation during his six-year tenure as a tutor, 1766–72. Gradually, some of the generation's more accomplished students began to find their way onto Willard's faculty. In 1786 Eliphalet Pearson left Andover for Harvard, where he succeeded Stephen Sewall as the Hancock Professor of Hebrew and Other Oriental Languages. David Tappan, who had been one of Samuel Moody's flock applying for admission in July 1767, replaced Edward Wigglesworth as the Hollis Professor of Divinity in 1792. Most important of all, Willard made Jack Warren the first professor of anatomy and surgery in 1782; in 1791 his title became Hersey Professor of Anatomy and Surgery. Warren's ap-pointment marked the beginning of what eventually became the Harvard Medical School. Jack with two other professors of medicine formed Har-vard's first professional-school faculty.[77] Revitalized through the efforts of Willard, Warren, and others, Harvard began to seize new opportunities at the same time that its alumni were reaching for them.

For the rest of their lives, patriot members of the revolutionary genera-tion would think of their wartime achievements with pride. As early as 1776, Perez Morton, the speaker of the day at the reinterment of the re-mains of Joseph Warren, recognized the patriot's permanent contribution to society. "You fell in the Cause of Virtue and Mankind," Morton praised the departed hero's spirit. "The *Name and Virtues of* WARREN shall remain immortal."[78] Joseph's brother Jack was no less certain of the generation's indelible claim to honor when he delivered Boston's first Fourth of July address in 1783: "The generations yet unborn shall read with rapture the distinguished page, whereon in capitals shall stand recorded the important transaction of that day and celebrate to the latest ages of this republic the anniversary of that resolution . . . which gave the rights of sovereignty and independence to these United States."[79] By 1806, when Joseph Avery addressed an Independence Day audience of his neighbors in Holden, he could look back "with peculiar pleasure, and sentiments of the highest esteem" at the "band of patriots and heroes, who in the cabinet and field of battle, were the instruments, the blessed instruments, of our preservation from the horrors of vassalage."[80]

For the members of the revolutionary generation, whether the War for Independence foreclosed prospects or opened them, it controlled their opportunities and dominated their memories. For the rest of their days, the Revolution would shape the lives of the men who had lived through it.

SAM JENNISON'S war ended officially on July 11, 1779, although in a sense perhaps it did not end until his death in 1826. John Trumbull's war concluded formally when he resigned his commission in early 1777 at age twenty, and informally after his brief period as a volunteer at the Battle of Newport in 1778; but there is no doubt that his experiences stayed with him for the rest of his days, shaping the adult that he became. If Sam Jennison lost his way in the years following the war, John Trumbull found his, setting out on a new path, one that the Revolution had influenced and even made possible in important respects.

Like Jennison, Trumbull determined in the late 1770s to make a life for himself. More than Sam, though—indeed, perhaps more than any of his college contemporaries—Trumbull was ambitious and knew what he wanted to do. He was driven to succeed, and in his accomplishments he stood in sharp contrast to Jennison.

John returned from the army to his father's home in Lebanon, Connecticut, at the end of the winter of 1777 with a plan in mind. No college-educated American—and precious few others—had ever devoted his life to art, a calling for craftsmen in colonial America, not gentlemen. But great paintings had moved Trumbull since his childhood, and he had aspired to become an artist for almost as long as he could remember. Master artists created works of deep beauty and inspiration. No less important, they made a name for themselves. The finest European painters secured immortality through their works. Trumbull would not be stopped by anything, not even the prospect of having to persuade others that the studio was as suitable a place for a man of refinement as the minister's study, the attorney's office, the merchant's countinghouse, or the physician's surgery. Even if he had to invent a profession in order to pursue it, John was determined to devote his life to art.

Trumbull remained in Lebanon only long enough to settle on his next move. He could resume his drawing at home, of course, but he knew that he needed an environment that was culturally richer and more inspiring if he were to grow as a painter. After a brief stay with his parents, he moved to Boston sometime in 1777.

The capital of Massachusetts was an improvement culturally over Lebanon, but it still fell far short of the artistic hive that Trumbull craved. Before the Revolution, John Singleton Copley had been the town's most influential portraitist. On his way to college in 1772, Trumbull had met Copley, introduced to the artist by his eldest brother, Joseph, and the memory of that brief encounter had stayed with John. There were no painters of stature left in Boston in the late 1770s, however, no role models, nobody to instruct and inspire Trumbull. Copley had departed for London in 1774 and no one had taken his place.[81]

On arriving in Boston, Trumbull rented the best studio in town. John Smibert, a Scotsman and the first noteworthy limner to make the town his home, had put up the room on Queen Street near what would later become Scollay Square, then eventually Government Center. Smibert had died in 1751, but the studio still held reminders of his presence. Trumbull found copies of works by Van Dyke, Poussin, and Raphael, and he proceeded to use them to tutor himself.[82] He also fell in with a circle of ambitious young Harvard graduates who were not letting the war prevent them from getting on with their lives. William Eustis was a member of this set, as were Rufus King, Christopher Gore, Royall Tyler, Thomas Dawes, and Aaron Dexter.[83] As part of his course of self-instruction, Trumbull took the likenesses of many of these friends.[84]

By the autumn of 1779, Trumbull began to recognize that he had accomplished all he could in America. His work showed promise, but by any elevated standard his figures were still stiff and unconvincing. If he were to develop as an artist, if he were to achieve the enduring recognition for which he longed, he needed the instruction of a master. No one in North America would do. John had to make his way to Europe.[85] After consulting with Sir John Temple, who was married to Jemmy Bowdoin's sister and had contacts in the highest circles on both sides of the Atlantic, Trumbull concluded that since he was now a noncombatant, he could safely travel to England. Temple knew Benjamin West, the Pennsylvania native who lived

John Trumbull, self-portrait. Trumbull painted this picture in Boston in 1777 at the same time that he painted many of his college friends. It is an example of his work before he began to study in London with Benjamin West. Photograph © 2004 Museum of Fine Arts, Boston. (*John Trumbull* [1777], self-portrait. Oil on canvas, 30.25 × 24.1.2 in. Museum of Fine Arts, Boston. Bequest of George Nixon Black. 29.791.)

in London, where he was the official history painter to the king, and he promised John an introduction.[86] To finance the journey, a group of wealthy patrons appointed Trumbull their continental agent in a transatlantic trading venture.

John's first European port of call was Nantes, France, where he landed about five weeks out of New London, Connecticut, in June 1780.[87] The commercial undertaking that had financed Trumbull's Atlantic crossing required him to try to establish himself in trade in France. It did not take him long, however, to conclude that owing to the war, the continuing risks of international commerce were still too great to bear. Without regrets, Trumbull quickly packed for London.

Was there something odd about a former rebel colonel, a son of the governor of a colony in revolt, studying art in the capital of the empire while the war in which he had fought so recently was still in progress? At first, no one publicly questioned Trumbull's motives. He was too much the gentleman for anyone to voice reservations. Introductions to Benjamin West from Temple and from Benjamin Franklin, who had known the painter in Philadelphia years earlier, provided John entrée into the artist's studio, and his own evident talent persuaded the master to take him on as a pupil.

West had become a magnet for aspiring American artists—Gilbert Stuart of Rhode Island was Trumbull's contemporary and friend in London— but his connections at court were anything but provincial. As West's student, Trumbull soon had access to the most refined circles of British society and culture.

John could feel himself growing as an artist under Benjamin West's mature eye, but before long, gentleman or no, suspicions about his intentions began to emerge. Three months after John entered West's studio, Continental troops hanged Major John André, convicted of collaborating with Benedict Arnold on a plan to betray to the British the strategically valuable American fortifications at West Point along the Hudson River. Distrustful American loyalists residing in England, angered at André's execution and outraged by Trumbull's freedom of movement in London, demanded retaliation. John was the obvious target.

Was John an American spy cleverly disguised as an art student? If he was, no convincing evidence for his undercover activities has ever come to light. More likely he was what he claimed to be, a gentleman artist. In the wake of André's execution, though, it was easy to conjure up darker reasons for his presence in London. Under loyalist pressure, the British authorities took Trumbull into custody. He remained incarcerated for seven months before West, Copley, and other friends secured his release and he was able to return home to Connecticut.[88]

Trumbull's apprenticeship had been interrupted, but not for long. Unlike Sam Jennison, John had decided what he wanted to do with his life. Trumbull's course was set. In the face of extraordinary obstacles he had confirmed both his commitment to a life in art and his talent for it. Nevertheless, he was still raw and unformed as a painter. Nothing but further training under the supervision of a master such as West would do to turn him into the artist he dreamed of becoming. Determined to make a success of himself as a painter, he looked for a chance to return to his calling.

Before long he had the opportunity he needed. By February 1783 he was back in France, once again in international trade as the continental agent of a Connecticut merchant, this time his brother David. Once diplomacy brought the war to a close in September, after a brief visit home to Lebanon, Trumbull was ready to return to West's studio. His old mentor greeted him warmly, and soon he was back in a routine: "I rise at 5 or 6 & write or study Anatomy until breakfast which is at 8," John wrote home, "go then to Mr. West's, where I remain the whole day except for an interval of an hour or 2. for dinner."[89] This regimen quickly produced results: "The progress I have made is such as surprises me," he wrote his father. "Mr. West and some other Artists of Eminence have complimented [me] with saying that they never knew so great a progress made in so short a time."[90] As important as Trumbull's technical advances, though, was the development of new ideas about the paintings he would execute.

In the minds of eighteenth-century connoisseurs, history painting was the pinnacle of the art. Masterworks on subjects taken from the classics and the Bible, and more recently West's own paintings of contemporary British military engagements, built on the accomplishments of the portraitist by incorporating drama and scale. As the only trained artist who had served in the Continental Army, Trumbull recognized both an opportunity and an obligation to document the conflict.[91] He had experienced at firsthand one of the most stirring events in modern history; his mission now was to commemorate the determination, the virtue, the self-sacrifice of the patriots who had created a new nation. By 1785 he had resolved that the American Revolution would become the dominant subject of his work.

It was a daring decision. No other American artist had ever earned an adequate income except as a portraitist. There was no way to know whether the American public would support an artist who worked in any other tradition, even one who painted heroic and inspiring scenes of the Revolution. Moreover, in following West's lead by choosing a modern subject, he was taking what was still a very new course even in London.

And yet it was the obvious path for him to follow. Other life determinations, including the decision to marry, would have to wait. John Trumbull now had a calling. For better and for worse, the Revolution had shaped the lives of the artist and of the other members of his generation. It was their common reference point, an experience they all shared.

The Revolution had ruined the lives of some of Trumbull's contemporaries. Its gravitational pull had spun them off into unexpected and uncontrollable courses. For John and many members of his generation, though, it provided life's central meaning. For almost every member of the revolutionary generation, the war's aftermath, which created important and unexpected changes in the nature of American society, sent them off in directions that no one had anticipated.

6

THE AGE OF RESPONSIBILITY

I T TAKES decades for a boy to grow from childhood to full maturity. In eighteenth-century New England his path to manhood culminated with the gradual transition to a new stage of life during his thirties. Aging meant physiological changes—joints creaked, eyesight weakened, hairlines receded, waistlines expanded—but these were superficial symptoms of the advancing years compared with more fundamental social developments. More than other factors, interpersonal relationships defined life's new phase, which typically lasted until a man reached his late fifties or early sixties.

We now call this season of life middle age. Although the term was not in use in the late eighteenth century, most of the qualities we mean by it today were also common then within this extended swath of adulthood. The same relationships with family, friends, neighbors, and others that characterize the phase today also did so then. A middle-aged man took care of those around him. Before this stage of life, the age of responsibility, most men had only themselves to take care of; during it, however, almost all of them were family men with all the obligations of such a status. The age of responsibility was, moreover, a time when the most ambitious men tried to realize their highest aspirations—to set themselves apart from the crowd as men of consequence in their community, state, and nation. Before middle age, most men were followers, not leaders, supporting players, not principals; during it, however, some of them became mentors to aspiring young professionals and merchants, overseers of important private institutions such as Harvard College, and officers of the towns and churches of New England.[1] Once someone had proven himself as a husband and a father, as a local officeholder, as a respected doctor or lawyer or minister, as a breadwinner, as a person of ability and character, then his neighbors might even entrust him with one of the important provincial or statewide roles that were the lot of a select group of mature and responsible men.[2]

For the members of Harvard's revolutionary generation, middle age coincided with unprecedented changes in American life, ones that transformed the composition of the nation's leadership. For many of the generation's members, the consequences of this postrevolutionary development were immediate and profound. To be sure, as long as a man was content with domestic and neighborhood successes, he might live out his days as if the Revolution had never shaken American society. If he wanted more, however, if he coveted a leading role on a brighter stage, then he had to reckon with some of the Revolution's most enduring consequences. National independence had required Americans to take care of themselves to an extent that had never been the case before the war. In commerce, in civic life, in education, in cultural affairs, new leaders emerged in response to the challenge. By the late 1700s there were more opportunities to assume leadership than ever before. At the same time, though, there were also more candidates for recognition and honor than ever, and many of these went to men who had never passed through the gates of Harvard Yard.

Leaders never form the majority of any group, not even one as select as the membership of the Harvard classes of the revolutionary generation. There are never enough openings for everyone who craves recognition and influence, and the late eighteenth century was no exception. The more power and eminence a position conferred, the more men coveted it, leaving most of them disappointed. Still, as civic pillars or as husbands, as leaders in the professions or as fathers, most members of Harvard's revolutionary generation met their responsibilities to those around them.

FROM TIME to time at the turn of the nineteenth century, the residents of the small Middlesex County town of Lincoln were treated to a curious sight: their minister, Charles Stearns, out for a drive while one of his sons stood beside him in his chaise. Stearns, a man of middling height, had grown so stout that there was not enough room in the buggy for both of them to sit.[3] Physical aging affected everyone at midlife, although Stearns's case was extreme.

Wrinkles, bags, sags, and creaks were every man's experience at midlife. With the passage of time, John Eliot acquired an ample stomach; overweight and a sedentary lifestyle eventually undermined his health, leading him to an early grave.[4] Israel Keith and Zedekiah Sanger were developing puffy jowls by the time each man had his portrait painted, probably in his forties or fifties.[5] As long as fashion encouraged refined men to wear wigs, it was possible to hide one of aging's most common cosmetic consequences— hair loss. Wigs covered receding hairlines and spreading bald spots. Powdered and pomaded, they also cloaked the gradual transformation of dark hair to gray or white. Hairpieces were going out of fashion by the end of the century,[6] however, and surviving portraits of many members of the generation show the toll taken by the passage of time on their locks. Jack Warren's hairline rose only a bit at midlife, but Laban Wheaton's scalp was increasingly exposed, and Tilly Merrick had developed a shiny dome by his late fifties.[7]

Chronic conditions were at the root of many other signs of aging. A "slow nervous fever" permanently injured Eliphalet Pearson's eyes when he was still in his twenties, leading him to fear that he could never study enough to meet the demands of life in the parish ministry.[8] He had to console himself with a career as a Harvard professor.

Fisher Ames and Jemmy Bowdoin suffered among the most serious chronic illnesses. A pulmonary condition, probably consumption, or tuberculosis, forced Ames to curtail his activities by 1795, when he was thirty-seven. With the passing years, the progressive effects of the disease increasingly constrained him, leaving him housebound if not bedridden for extended periods.[9] Bowdoin's problem was a case of asthma that he developed while still in college. Possibly because his health limited him, he never achieved the success that a Bowdoin might reasonably consider his by rights.[10]

There was no way to retard the physical consequences of aging. Every man met and dealt with them. Midlife also brought a new set of social expectations, however, both at home and in public. For most members of the revolutionary generation, the responsibilities of middle age were much more welcome than the toll the passage of time was taking on their bodies.

AT HOME, life for these men had come full circle by the mid-1780s. Around thirty, for the most part, at the close of the war, the men of Harvard's revolutionary generation began to assume the same family burdens that their fathers and grandfathers had borne at a like age. And their first responsibilities were to their wives and children.

If anything seems remarkable about the family life of the members of Harvard's revolutionary generation it is its extraordinary stability. Life could be very risky before the day of antibiotics and anesthetics—infections were a threat to everyone, and every woman knew the mortal dangers of childbirth—but for most of the men of that generation, the family obligations they undertook when they married and began to father children were theirs without a break for decades.

Perhaps elsewhere life was short, brutish, and mean, but for the majority of Harvard's revolutionary generation it was not. Their marriages endured, and for most of them one wife was the full quota. Notwithstanding Sam Jennison's experience, divorce was nearly unheard of in postrevolutionary New England, and a Harvard man who wed in his late twenties or early thirties probably lived with his wife for the next quarter of a century or so. Only about one member of the college generation in six married more than once; approximately one man in five became a widower before the age of sixty. Many of those who lost a young wife and remarried had long and stable second marriages: Eliphalet Pearson's first marriage, to Priscilla Holyoke, lasted only two years until her early death following childbirth; his second, to Sarah Bromfield (Sally to her friends), endured for more than forty.[11] Only five men, scarcely more than 2 percent of the revolutionary generation, married more than twice.[12]

In most instances marriage produced children, and the responsibility for raising young sons and daughters often lasted for decades. Parenthood seemed to be almost a permanent condition, an inevitable consequence of middle age, one from which there was no exit short of death. A man who fathered his first child in his early thirties and eventually sired perhaps a half a dozen of them, a not uncommon experience for members of Harvard's revolutionary generation, could expect to reach his fifties, or even his sixties, before his youngest son or daughter grew old enough to be independent. Levi Lincoln, a father for the first time at thirty-three, still had a child under sixteen thirty-five years later when he was sixty-eight.[13] One member in four of the college's revolutionary generation—more than two-fifths of those known to have had children—had at least one son or daughter under sixteen at the time of his death.[14]

When Fisher Ames married Frances Worthington in 1792 at the age of thirty-four, he committed himself for the rest of his life to her and to the family they established together. Over the time that remained to them as a couple—nearly sixteen years, until Fisher's early death at the age of fifty in July 1808—they had seven children, the first during the year following their marriage, the last during the year before his death.[15] Despite substantial professional, civic, and political obligations, from this point forward his family had the first call on his time, attention, energy, and emotions. Relatives and close friends grew accustomed to periodic reports about his children's latest accomplishments, and when Fisher was worried about them, he shared his concerns with his regular correspondents. "There has been scarlet fever in one family two miles distant," he wrote a close acquaintance in 1804. "It gives me cold chills of terror. Thank god my little ones yet escape the pest."[16]

Until young sons and daughters were old enough to provide for themselves—to settle on a calling (in the case of the boys), to find a husband or a wife—fathers such as Fisher were responsible for nurturing them spiritually, morally, intellectually, and physically.[17] Fathers have "a great charge upon them," Sam Phillips instructed his eighteen-year-old son John in 1795. "They are cloathed with high authority—at the same time many & important duties are required of them."[18] Henry Pearson, who was often in trouble as a student, nevertheless looked to his father, Eliphalet, as a role model. When Henry followed Eliphalet's example and matriculated at Harvard, it pleased the boy that he was "describing an arc of the same circle which has been completed by a Father before."[19] And when a father's children were ready to leave home, it was his duty to provide them with a start in life—a dowry for the daughters, an education, either vocational or liberal, as well as some capital for the sons. In 1800, when Jack Warren sent his eldest child, John Collins Warren, to Europe for the latest in medical training, he was ready to spend dearly for his son's education. A degree from the University of Edinburgh cost "a considerable sum of money," but not too much for Jack, who was willing to accept the expense, he told his son, "because I think it would be some advantage to you."[20]

In late January 1808, less than half a year before Fisher Ames's death, he and Frances sent their eldest child, Worthington, away to school at Deerfield Academy. Worthington was fourteen and it was time for him to prepare for college. "I must send him from home," Fisher had once declared, "where he will learn that discipline of temper and those habits of application to his studies that he cannot get at home."[21] The academy was many days' ride from the Ames family residence in Dedham, but distance did not mitigate Fisher's paternal obligations. He played the role of father through letters to the boy that were filled in turn with affection and instruction. Ames freely admitted his love for Worthington: "Your mother and I felt our hearts pound at the sight of your first letter. It seems as if, by your being no longer under our immediate and daily care, our affection for you had augmented." Whenever he could, Fisher encouraged his eldest to do his best: "Resolve to cultivate your mind and to guard your conduct from vice and folly, and when you grow up others will view you in some measure with our eyes." As an evidence of his love, Ames gently corrected his son whenever necessary: "I like your letters, though they are too careless in spelling." "O may kind heaven grant you health," Fisher added. "Remember what I say so often, avoid excess in everything, and degree of *vicious* indulgence is excess."[22] In case of divine inattention, Ames even asked a friend to report on Worthington's deportment, "whether a pert impudent thing a dunce or what & Conceal that *I* ask the information."[23]

Ames had decided on college for Worthington by the time he sent him to Deerfield, but like their own fathers, the members of the revolutionary generation had to ask themselves whether a liberal education made intellectual and practical sense for a son. Usually the answer was no. Forty-six members of the revolutionary generation were sons of Harvard fathers, but only thirty-four sent at least one of their own boys to the school, and only a few others sent one or more sons to college elsewhere.[24]

The duties of marriage and fatherhood were always substantial; occasionally their weight was crushing. John Eliot's wife, Ann, struggled through several periods of disabling mental illness, leaving him alone responsible both for her and for their six young children—three daughters and three sons.[25] And despite Henry Pearson's admiration for his father, he caused Eliphalet repeated disappointments. At various junctures in Henry's undergraduate career, college authorities caught him playing cards, swearing, neglecting his studies, and leaving his dormitory without permission. Henry also spent to excess. Eliphalet minced no words in telling his son of his "grief . . . as your character has developed, more pride, passion, and selfishness, with less prudence, discretion, & gratitude." With respect to college charges, Eliphalet provided a comparative, itemized tally: "My total of first year's expenses $54.72," he concluded, "yours $245.01. Mark the difference, and learn prudence."[26]

A father's duties, his anxieties, were never completely forgotten, no matter the age of his child. When Edward Barnard's son became a mariner at twenty-one, Edward kept a constant lookout for the boy during each voyage and prayed that "the Almighty preserve him & return him to us in safety in his own due time."[27] When John Phillips reached the same age, his father, Sam, observed the occasion with a shower of advice. On the eve of John's birthday, Sam summarized a lifetime's worth of wisdom to his son: "Tomorrow will compleat 21 years of your life. As at that period, youth are generally considered as released from that Parental authority which they are the subjects of before, it may not be improper to offer some hints & give you some advice dictated by the feeling of a Parent, whose affection gives rise to much anxiety for your welfare." Sam devoted the "last counsel you will ever receive while in a legal sense in a State of minority" to the importance of regular prayer and an annual assessment of personal behavior. "If on such a review you do not find cause for . . . humiliations," Sam asked, "will there not be reason to fear you have not been sufficiently thorough in the examination?"[28]

It was hard to let go when a son or daughter grew up and just as easy to seem intrusive. Eliphalet Pearson's eldest daughter, Mary, and her fiancé, Ephraim Abbott, had courted for nearly five years, and both were already on the "wrong side of 30" in October 1812 as they thought about marriage, but her father still urged them to delay and "wait for decency." Under parental pressure, they postponed their wedding until January 1814, when Mary was nearly thirty-two. She appreciated her father's concern for her, but would he ever allow her to grow up?[29]

For all the burdens and challenges of marriage and fatherhood, nothing about them was new or unanticipated. As family men, the members of the revolutionary generation followed the same path as their fathers and grand-fathers. More than any other aspect of adulthood, family life for the members of Harvard's revolutionary generation at middle age was comfortable, familiar, and consistent with what they had experienced as children.

THE MEMBERS of the generation came of age professionally at about the same time that they assumed full family responsibilities. As mentors on the model of the men with whom they had studied, they became leaders in their fields, commanding the respect of colleagues, friends, and neighbors. As teachers and institutional organizers, moreover, after the war a few of them were responsible for extremely important professional developments.

Through mentoring, both formal and informal, men who had reached an age to be listened to shared their experience with younger men, each striving to make a place for himself in society. Mentoring provided opportunities to serve a student, a neighborhood, a community, a profession. When a mentor and his protégé hit it off, for the older man it could be deeply satisfying to help a promising youth chart his career.

Growing from youth to adulthood themselves in the early 1770s, Harvard men just out of college had turned to elders such as Edward A. Holyoke, John Adams, and Jason Haven to help prepare for careers in medicine, law, and the ministry. As would-be professionals they had honored their mentors for the lessons they had imparted and the examples they had set. In fact, such relationships often became emotional as well as professional when respect and affection developed between master and disciple. By the 1780s and 1790s it was the revolutionary generation's turn to share the secrets of the professions and other callings with younger men.

When Stephen Moody, a 1790 graduate of Harvard College, entered the Worcester law office of Levi Lincoln, Esq., sometime around 1791, Levi was in his early forties.[30] An attorney since the mid-1770s, Lincoln could draw on a decade and a half of experience at the bar as he prepared Moody for his calling. For the opportunity to learn the legal craft at his side he charged apprentices £70 for three years of instruction.[31] The Reverend David Osgood, also in his early forties, had served as the minister of the Congregational church in Medford for about fifteen years when Nathaniel Thayer, a 1789 graduate, came to read theology with him after commencement.[32] Meanwhile, Dr. John Barnard Swett was in his mid-thirties, a physician for well over a decade, when Moses Little, a 1787 Harvard graduate, came to Newburyport to read medicine with him.[33]

Once Lincoln, Osgood, and Swett began to take on students, each staked a claim for himself to a position of stature within his own professional community. By common consent, to be a suitable mentor a man had to be a capable, highly regarded practitioner, well established in his calling. When Stephen Moody decided to work with Levi Lincoln, through his choice he expressed his respect for his adviser's knowledge, judgment, and experience.

Until well into the nineteenth century, most New England lawyers, ministers, and physicians as well as merchants learned their vocations as young Harvard men had in the early 1770s through traditional apprenticeships with experienced practitioners. Novices read time-tested texts, learned traditional procedures under a mentor's watchful eye, and made a place for themselves within a professional community. Mentors and students both benefited from the arrangement.

Even before the members of the revolutionary generation reached the normal age to take on clerks or students, however, a new and formal development emerged in one professional field: medicine. Students who entered a formal program looked to it for career advancement. Its instructors had similar ends in view; teaching placed them at the center of their vocation. A new professional school—Harvard Medical School—needed faculty, and not long after 1780, a few ambitious doctors led by a member of the college's revolutionary generation, Jack Warren, seized this opportunity for early recognition and career advancement. As faculty mentors they assumed professional responsibility for dozens of young men, including most of the leading practitioners of the next generation.

New England came late to formal professional education. Medicine was the first of the three traditional professions to offer systematic instruction, but until the early 1780s, New Englanders had to go far from home if they wanted exposure to the latest in medical pedagogy. Throughout the eighteenth century, the Scottish universities, especially Edinburgh, offered the most advanced training for doctors. The hospitals of Paris and London also attracted students intent on walking the wards to learn the latest medical developments. In North America, after 1765 Philadelphia drew students to the medical school of the College of Philadelphia, now the University of Pennsylvania. Three years later, in 1768, King's College, now Columbia University, established a medical school in New York City.[34]

In New England, by the late 1760s physicians had already begun to consider the example of doctors in Philadelphia and New York.[35] When Dr. Ezekiel Hersey of Hingham died in 1770, he left Harvard £1,000 to endow a professorship of anatomy and physic.[36] By the early 1780s, Boston doctors who boasted advanced training or experience were beginning to offer lecture series in medical specialties. Members of Harvard's revolutionary generation took the lead, sometimes to the frustration of jealous colleagues.

Jack Warren was the first Boston doctor to offer public medical lectures;

John Warren. (*John Warren* [1783], by an unknown artist. Engraving. Edward Warren, *The Life of John Warren, M.D.* [Boston, 1874], frontispiece.)

drawing on his intensive study of anatomy, Warren gave two series of talks on the subject, in 1780 and in 1781.[37] By 1782, when President Joseph Willard took the initiative in the establishment of the Harvard Medical School, Jack was widely regarded as one of Boston's most skilled and ambitious physicians. Dr. John Clarke, a 1772 graduate and the scion of one of Boston's most prominent medical families, followed Jack's lead, offering a series of lectures on childbirth later in the decade when he returned from London, where he had studied obstetrics.[38] The new medical school's first three faculty members—Warren, the professor of anatomy and surgery; Benjamin Waterhouse, who taught the theory and practice of physic; and Aaron Dexter, a 1776 graduate of the college who was responsible for materia medica—quickly became New England's leading physician-mentors.[39] Between 1783, when the school offered its first instruction, and

Warren's death at sixty-one on April 14, 1815, eighty men completed the course and earned the degree of M.D.[40]

Corporation reports in the early years of Harvard Medical School outlined the institution's pedagogical objectives: instruction in anatomy and surgery, the theory and practice of medicine, and materia medica.[41] For the members of its faculty, the medical school offered a different benefit: immediate professional standing. Although they were still relatively young—Warren was only twenty-nine in 1782—their professorships quickly conferred dignity on them that might otherwise have taken them years to earn. In effect, Warren's appointment accelerated his professional middle age.

The status and emoluments of professorships did not go unnoticed by envious professional colleagues. Years after the founding of the medical school, Dr. Ephraim Eliot, John Eliot's younger brother and an apothecary, recalled a conversation in the early 1780s with Dr. Isaac Rand, Jr., of Boston. Rand, a decade Warren's senior and Ephraim Eliot's own mentor, viewed the school as a threat, its faculty as scheming interlopers:

> One night Dr. Rand returned home from one of his professional meetings and addressed himself to me, he said, "Eliot, that Warren is an artful man, and will get to windward of us all. He has made a proposition to [a circle of local doctors], that, as there are nearly a dozen pupils studying in town, there should be an incipient medical school instituted for their benefit. . . . After a little maiden coyness, [Warren] agreed to commence a course, as he has many operations and surgical cases in the Continental [Army] Hospital of which he is sole director in every respect; and he can always have command of subjects for dissection, without exciting alarm . . . as most of the inmates of the hospital were foreigners, and no one would scrutinize into the matter. . . . Now, Warren will be able to obtain fees from the pupils who will attend his lectures on Anatomy and Surgery, and turn it to pecuniary advantage. But he will not stop there; he well knows that moneys have been left to the college . . . and he is looking to the [Hersey] professorship."[42]

At about the same time that Warren, Clarke, and others were introducing formal medical instruction in Boston, Jack and several colleagues garnered recognition in a second way—through the establishment of New England's first continuing professional associations for doctors, the Boston Medical Society (1780) and the Massachusetts Medical Society (1781). Open to members by invitation only, the societies quickly began to define professional status and acceptability.

Of the two organizations, the Massachusetts Medical Society was the more widely influential. Edward A. Holyoke, mentor to so many of the revolutionary generation's physicians, served as the state society's first president, and six members of the generation were among its thirty-one founders; for more than a decade two of them were the primary forces behind the institution. Nathaniel Walker Appleton was its recording secretary from 1781 to 1793, and Thomas Welsh was its treasurer from its founding to 1798 and later its corresponding secretary and vice president.[43]

The underlying purpose of the Massachusetts Medical Society was simple enough: to draw a bold line between the practitioners and practices it considered legitimate on one side and quackery on the other.[44] While it tried to improve medical knowledge and the public standing of those it accepted as qualified to practice, it distanced itself from others of whose training and methods it did not approve. Although the organization never enrolled all of the state's traditionally trained physicians and surgeons in its membership, which its act of incorporation initially limited to seventy, election as a fellow of the society was a distinguishing mark. It attested to professional competence and medical orthodoxy. In much the same way that a Harvard undergraduate education set a genteel college alumnus apart from the rest of society, admission to the Massachusetts Medical Society opened the door to an elite professional community, one with the power to define acceptable and unacceptable clinical practices.

Meetings, publications, and state licensing constituted the Massachusetts Medical Society's formal program in the late eighteenth and early nineteenth centuries.[45] Shortly after the society's establishment, Jack Warren, a charter member, drafted a succinct public statement of its purposes: "The design of the ... institution is, 'to promote medical and surgical knowledge, inquiries into the animal economy & the promotion & effects of medicine,' by encouraging a free intercourse with the Gentlemen of the Faculty throughout the United States of America, and a friendly correspondence with the eminent in those professions throughout the world." The society devoted its meetings to medical presentations, and it published many of them in its periodical, *Medical Communications*, which Appleton and Welsh edited. Through a clause in its charter, the society also held the power "to make a just discrimination between such as are duly educated and properly qualified ... and those who may ignorantly and wickedly administer medicine, whereby the health and lives of many valuable individuals may be endangered and perhaps lost to the community."[46] Eventually, eleven members of the revolutionary generation were raised to fellowship in the Massachusetts Medical Society, elected in most cases when they were about thirty years old.[47]

The establishment of a medical school at Harvard and a state medical society were steps in a broader initiative, a movement by doctors coming of age as professionals, including many from the revolutionary generation, to enhance the respect accorded to physicians and surgeons. Although the sequence of events was different, at about the same time New England's attorneys and Congregational clergymen were also taking measures to secure the respectability of their callings—not to mention their own personal professional status with their peers and others.

In each case, young professionals—members of Harvard's revolutionary generation and their contemporaries—moved to institutionalize their vocation and control access to it. By screening out pretenders who lacked appropriate training and the necessary ability, they attempted to ensure the quality of professional services. Such self-regulation had at least two further benefits: a profession that policed its own practitioners was less likely than one that ignored malfeasance and incompetence to face attempts at external control. Moreover, in the case of attorneys, self-regulation allowed local bar associations to restrict the number of recognized practitioners, thus limiting competition for clients and fees.[48]

Professional organizations were the principal regulatory agencies in each instance. Lawyers had tried with indifferent success to establish bar associations in many Massachusetts counties in the 1760s; by the 1780s and 1790s, with members of the revolutionary generation often in the lead, they were able to institute standards for admission to the bar that usually combined a liberal education with a clerkship in the office of an established practitioner.[49] At about the same time, the Congregational clergy of Massachusetts moved to require all ministers in fellowship with them to join one of the established regional ministerial associations and to compel all would-be clergymen to obtain permission from one of these bodies before becoming a candidate for a pulpit.[50]

Unlike in medicine, in the law and in the church formal professional education was not an early step in regularizing the calling but the culmination. The Hollis Professorship of Divinity, which dated from 1721, and a bequest for a professorship of law made in 1781, although the chair went unoccupied until 1815, provided the foundations for a divinity school and a law school, respectively, at Harvard, but neither was established until the 1810s.[51] Legal historians point to Tapping Reeve's Litchfield Law School, established in Connecticut in 1784, as the first institution of its kind in the United States, but Reeve's school had no Massachusetts counterpart until the establishment of Harvard Law School in 1817.[52] By then, New England already had two divinity schools, Andover Theological Seminary, established in 1808 (Eliphalet Pearson was one of its founders), and Harvard Divinity School, instituted in stages over an eight-year period, 1811–1819.[53]

It would be too much to say that every member of the revolutionary generation who lived to maturity burnished the honor of his family and earned the respect of his neighbors through his work. There were a few abject failures (notably Sam Jennison) and others (for example, Onesiphorus Tileston, a modest, unmarried clerk) for whom success by any definition always seemed beyond reach.[54] Every life combined failures with successes, disappointments with triumphs. For most members of Harvard's revolutionary generation, though, middle age brought at a minimum the love of a family and the acceptance of professional colleagues.

On the cold, cloudy evening of January 24, 1791, eight men gathered in the drafty, high-ceilinged parlor of an imposing residence on Boston's Prison Row. The mansion belonged to William Tudor, Fisher Ames's professional mentor and a member of the Harvard class of 1769. In fact, six of the eight men were Harvard graduates in their thirties and forties.[55] The members of this small circle of friends shared an enthusiasm for the study of the past and a concern that the basic sources for historical research—principally manuscript collections and printed works—were being lost owing to neglect. By the end of the evening, the men present had agreed to organize. Their new association, the Massachusetts Historical Society, was the first institution anywhere "to collect, preserve and communicate, materials for a complete history" of the United States.[56]

Of the men who had gathered in Billy Tudor's elegant parlor that evening, John Eliot, age thirty-six, was particularly supportive of the new initiative. His friend and mentor Jeremy Belknap was the moving force behind the plan, but Eliot was Belknap's alter ego, and by the end of the meeting he had undertaken an avocation that would occupy him for more than twenty-two years until his death in 1813.

John Eliot left the Tudor mansion on January 24 with two new titles, librarian and cabinet-keeper of the Massachusetts Historical Society. Every new accession by the society became his responsibility. Books, pamphlets, manuscripts, maps, and paintings as well as scientific specimens were all in his charge. He held his dual roles until 1793. Two years later, in 1795, he resumed the librarianship, which he held until 1798, when he exchanged it for the office of corresponding secretary—in effect, the society's contact with the outside world. He was still serving as corresponding secretary at his death fifteen years later.[57]

The events in Tudor's parlor were part of a much broader development. The institutional ecology of New England changed in a generation's time after the end of the War for Independence. If it is possible to talk about an organizational revolution without descending into oxymorons, then that is what the region was experiencing, the creation piece by piece of an ambitious new network of voluntary associations. Humane societies, dispensaries, orphanages, missionary associations, Bible societies, private subscription libraries, literary guilds, social clubs—they were all innovations as far as New Englanders were concerned in the years after the Revolution, and all belonged to this transformation. Hardly anything of the sort had existed in New England before the war. After the conflict, however, they developed by the hundreds. Across the region, for instance, the number of organized charities increased from 42 in 1772 to more than 1,400 in 1817.[58] Civic, charitable, and cultural institutions—in every case their supporters considered them to be agents for productive change. As far as they were concerned, these organizations served society at large, not the self-interested ends of their members. Yet no one could completely subordinate personal ends to civic benefits, and a clear-eyed analysis of them reveals the potential advantages of membership, which included community influence and public recognition. The institutions themselves set their public-spirited members apart from the rest of society. As middle-aged association men such as Eliot recognized, moreover, they afforded many new opportunities for leadership.

Everywhere the members of Harvard's revolutionary generation looked, they saw new and promising initiatives, and nobody was more involved in this development than they were. Undergraduate societies such as the Speaking Club and the Clitonians had been good preparation for the institutional world of postrevolutionary New England.

In postwar Boston no one had a busier social calendar than John Eliot. Constant social and literary activity compensated for the perceived social shortcomings of his congregation. When Eliot had reluctantly agreed in 1779 to succeed his father in the pulpit of New North, its parishioners' lack of cultivation had bothered him, but he could find no graceful way to decline the church's offer. "Many clergymen may make companions of their parishioners," Eliot confided to Belknap in 1781. "But mine are to be kept at their proper distance. They are poor, & many of them very ignorant."[59] In his friends John wanted more refinement, and he found his closest companions within the organizations he joined, a list that grew as the roster of Boston's cultural and charitable institutions lengthened. Eliot's affiliations included organizations of almost every description. There were social circles, secular philanthropies, missionary agencies, and cultural organizations. In addition to the Massachusetts Historical Society, he joined the American Academy of Arts and Sciences, the Boston Library Society, the Wednesday Evening Club, the Massachusetts Humane Society, the Massachusetts Charitable Fire Society, the Immigrant Aid Society, the Boston Society for the Reli-

gious and Moral Improvement of Seamen, the Massachusetts Congregational Charitable Society, the Freemasons, the Massachusetts Bible Society,
and the Society for Propagating the Gospel among the Indians and Others
in North America. When a circle of his friends decided in 1782 to establish
a literary periodical, the *Boston Magazine*, John was an enthusiastic partici-
pant in its parent organization, the Society for Compiling a Magazine.
Because Eliot was the minister of one of Boston's Congregational churches,
established practice automatically made him a member of Harvard's Board
of Overseers.[60] Then in 1804 the college's self-perpetuating Corporation
chose him to fill a vacancy.

John once commented to Belknap that "I never yet begun a sermon till
the last moment."[61] How could he? Where would he have found the time?

Not only was John Eliot a joiner, he was also a leader. He held office after
office, including trustee of the Library Society, the Bible Society, and the
Charitable Fire Society; secretary of the Congregational Charitable Society;
and grand chaplain of the Freemasons' Massachusetts Grand Lodge.[62] He
had had early reservations about the Massachusetts Humane Society, which
he dismissed in 1786 at its founding as "some vain thing to make some
young physicians important,"[63] but these doubts did not prevent him two
decades later from serving as its treasurer.

No one was more interested in New England's institutional revolution
than Eliot was, but he was unusual only in the extent of his involvement.
All told, Eliot's college contemporaries joined more than fifty organizations. At least sixty-eight individuals affiliated with one or more associations.[64] Twenty-one of them, more than 10 percent of the generation, became Freemasons.[65] Ten veterans of military service joined the Society of
the Cincinnati.[66] Nine men eventually joined the Massachusetts Historical
Society.[67] And like Eliot, many of them were leaders of the institutions in
which they participated: Thomas Edwards, a 1771 graduate, served for
many years as the secretary of the Massachusetts Society of the Cincinnati,[68] and Eliphalet Pearson spent thirteen years, 1789–1802, as the corresponding secretary of the American Academy of Arts and Sciences.[69]

Boston was the hub of New England's institutional revolution, so it is
not surprising that an avid joiner like Eliot turned up many opportunities
to associate with other men of taste and refinement. It is noteworthy, however, that many of his college contemporaries who were more inconven-
iently located but who shared his enthusiasm for clubs and associations also
sought out cultural and charitable liaisons. The Reverend John Bradford of
the Second Church in Roxbury, for instance, no more impressed with the
quality of his own parishioners than Eliot was with that of the congregation
of New North, regularly made the long trip into town along the slender

neck of land that separated Boston from the mainland for the spiritually revitalizing meetings of the Wednesday Evening Club, the Society for Compiling a Magazine, and the Massachusetts Historical Society.[70] Farther from Boston, Clement March, Jeremiah Barnard,[71] and others seized the initiative and brought together community leaders to form cultural organizations such as the Greenland (New Hampshire) Social Library and the Amherst (New Hampshire) Social Library.[72]

In the end, as members and officers of the Pilgrim Society of Plymouth[73] or the Medford Association for Discountenancing Intemperance and Kindred Vices[74] or the Massachusetts Society of the Cincinnati[75] or the Middlesex Musical Society,[76] genteel members of the revolutionary generation set themselves apart from society at large while at the same time offering themselves as its leaders.

As COMMUNITY leaders, John Eliot, Jack Warren, and dozens of Harvard contemporaries were in an enviable position. Their professional and civic activities were making a difference, and public recognition often flowed from their accomplishments. It would be a mistake, however, to overlook another side of their lives. No one succeeded at everything he tried, and for most of them middle age brought its share of disappointments. Eliphalet Pearson, Tilly Merrick, and Tom Coffin embodied the mixture of professional and personal achievements and discouragements that were the lot of most members of the revolutionary generation at middle age.

Eight years after Eliphalet and Sam Phillips established Phillips Academy in Andover, to general applause, Pearson received an offer that attested to his high repute as a teacher and scholar, an invitation to join Harvard's faculty. In the fall of 1785 the Harvard Corporation dismissed Stephen Sewall, the Hancock Professor of Hebrew and Other Oriental Languages, for intemperance. Despite his distinction as an orientalist, Sewall, unable to control his drinking, had become unfit to continue at the college.[77] Before long, the search for a successor led to Andover and to Eliphalet. A strict instructor with a well-deserved reputation for being personally cold to the boys he taught, Pearson was not at all liked by the academy's students. "I have been so long a teacher of boys," he confessed, "that I have spoilt my temper."[78] Competence, however, not popularity, was what the Corporation wanted in a faculty member. Pearson might be personally unpleasant, but of his abilities as an instructor and a scholar there could be no doubt.

By the fall of 1786, Eliphalet was comfortably settled into his new position in Cambridge. Perhaps to compensate consciously for his surly temper at Andover, he tried at first to reach out to the college's undergraduates: "The Professor, is a much more agreeable, and indeed a more polite Man, than I should have suspected, from what I have heard," John Quincy Adams, a Harvard senior at the time, marveled during Pearson's first autumn in Cambridge: "I have not seen any Person belonging to the [college's] Government, so polite to Scholars, or show so few Airs."[79]

Over the course of the next two decades, Pearson was a fixture at Harvard. Honored with a position of great professional prestige and considerable influence, Eliphalet took his duties seriously. Inside the classroom, lacking many students interested in Hebrew and cognate tongues, he devoted most of his efforts to teaching English composition and rhetoric. Consideration toward his students did not come naturally, however, and before long most Harvard undergraduates developed as sour an opinion of him as his Andover pupils had held. Through close attention to detail, Eliphalet shaped the writing styles of a generation of leading New Englanders. "Professor Pearson was an excellent critic," Justice Joseph Story later admitted, "but somewhat severe and exact in his requirements. . . . I think we all greatly profited by his instructions, even when we thought them not delivered in very gentle accents."[80] Outside the classroom, Eliphalet served as an important aide to Joseph Willard, the college president, for whom he often transacted business, including negotiating with the legislature on behalf of the school for state support.[81]

As valued as Pearson was for the services he performed for the college, he nevertheless continued to fall far short in the important area of student relationships. Most of his pupils despised him. In the course of his years at Phillips Academy and at Harvard, Pearson taught more than a thousand students. None of his contemporaries had more opportunities to be a mentor to a boy or a man traversing a critical stage of life. And none of them had a worse record in this regard. Unable to establish a bond of trust, friendship, and affection with most of the boys he taught, Eliphalet inspired harsh and bitter memories among many of his former pupils as an "austere, conceited, & pedantic man."[82] As a role model Pearson was as much of a failure as he was a success as an instructor.

Tilly Merrick, after fourteen years in trade in South Carolina, saw his business success suddenly give way to failure in 1796. Merrick had imprudently countersigned a commercial note for his friend Jonas Wilder, a Charleston merchant, whose bankruptcy resulted in calls from creditors that Tilly could not meet. Wilder's collapse also brought Merrick down, and the following year Tilly left South Carolina for his family home. Here in Concord, Massachusetts, no longer an international merchant and plantation owner, he made a modest living as a small-town shopkeeper trading in spools of thread and glasses of rum, not in cargoes of indigo and rice.[83]

As for Tom Coffin, though divorced from his New England roots, he was

probably the most powerful and influential member of his college generation at midlife. Career success, however, came at a personal cost.

Tom's return at thirty-two to North America in 1786 with his patron,
Guy Carleton, lord Dorchester, opened a path to remarkable accomplishment for a provincial if defined in traditional, imperial terms. Dorchester as
governor-general and commander in chief of the crown's North American
possessions was in a position to advance his favorites. Coffin settled in
Quebec, where he became Dorchester's personal secretary as well as the
commissary and controller of public accounts to the forces in North America. These were the first in a series of offices that placed Coffin in positions
of ever-increasing responsibility and income in Canada between 1786 and
1800, and again between 1802 and 1804.[84]

His ascent through the crown's Canadian establishment began thanks to
Dorchester's favor, but given the opportunity, he impressed his superiors
with his energy, competence, and loyalty. At every turn, he allowed his
official duties to take precedence over his personal affairs. Near the start of

Tilly Merrick. Following his business failure in Charleston, South Carolina, in 1797,
Merrick returned to Concord, Massachusetts, where he sat for this miniature portrait.
(*Tilly Merrick* [early nineteenth century], by an unknown artist. Oil on ivory, 3.5 × 2.75
in. Concord Museum, Concord, Mass. www.concordmuseum.org. Gift of Mrs. Stedman
Buttrick. Pi-101.)

1806, Tom's superiors rewarded him for his dedication with an appointment as commissary general of Great Britain. In this powerful and profitable post, which he held until 1809, his job was to provide food and clothing for the British army throughout England.[85]

The personal price for these achievements was steep, however. Tom never married, although a series of transitory liaisons produced a gaggle of illegitimate children, and his responsibilities separated him from his mother and siblings. Duty forced him repeatedly to postpone planned trips to Boston to visit his mother and sisters. Between 1783 and his death in 1810, Tom returned home to see his family only three times.[86]

Tom Coffin was as successful as any member of the revolutionary generation, at least according to the traditional standards of provincial Massachusetts, but even his accomplishments were compromises. Most of his college contemporaries had not gone as far as Coffin, and in comparison with his, their achievements were distinctly circumscribed.

HARVARD COLLEGE provided New England with more than its share of men of influence and power both before and after the Revolution, but in every college class, by middle age most of the members had settled into a comfortable mediocrity as respected members of their communities but without substantial say in the affairs of the wider society. When the members of Harvard's revolutionary generation grew old enough to play a civic leadership role, many served their communities, but most were not viable candidates for New England's most prominent positions of recognition and responsibility.

Civic leadership took a variety of forms. Across New England, small communities and large turned to men of ability, experience, and judgment as selectmen, moderators of the town meeting, and deacons to govern their polities and guide their churches. The civic leaders whom eighteenth-century New Englanders regarded most highly took on additional roles—in offices in the provincial, state, or federal government.

High public office required a combination of energy and accumulated experience that was more possible at middle age than either before or after. Untested youths rarely possessed either the discretion or the popular acceptance to govern effectively, and the weight of physical and mental stresses and strains eventually told aging officeholders that it was time to give up their responsibilities.

Between the late 1780s and 1800, James Sheafe's political career revealed what was possible for a man of ambition and talent in postrevolutionary New England. As the son of one of colonial Portsmouth's leading lights,

James had been to the manner born. Perhaps he committed an indiscretion through his early loyalism, but Sheafe, unlike Tom Coffin, found a way to recover, a way to come home and thrive. Within a decade after he had fought his way through an angry crowd of patriots to reach the courthouse in Exeter, James married into a wealthy Portsmouth family, fathered his first child, a son, and established himself as a merchant. In the late 1780s, when fifteen of Portsmouth's most prominent citizens organized a club for social purposes and mutual aid, the Federal Fire Society, Sheafe was one of the founders. He had regained the respect of his neighbors and was back on course to become a civic leader. To the port's finest social circle he had been readmitted.[87]

In late 1788, at age thirty-two, James successfully stood for a seat in the New Hampshire state legislature. The voters of Portsmouth added another office to his portfolio in the spring of 1789: selectman. During the 1790s he also served several terms as the port's state senator.[88] Sheafe's public service was now following a predictable path for the son of a prominent merchant. It was almost as if he had never made a false step in the mid-1770s.

Although leadership, even on the local level, was not the lot of every Harvard man, a college education could be a shortcut to a position of responsibility and authority. More than two-thirds of the members of Harvard's revolutionary generation, 145 of them, lived to at least age forty-five—that is to say, to an age when most men who would ever hold a responsible public office had begun their careers in leadership. Twenty-five of those who lived to age forty-five were clergymen and were thus by local custom unlikely ever to achieve a major secular position. Of the 120 laymen who reached the age of forty-five, at some point 44—more than one-third—held a major office either civil or ecclesiastical.[89]

In most cases, the path to positions of state, regional, and national leadership passed through local offices. Although a few members of the revolutionary generation took on important community offices by their late twenties, it was much more common for men to wait for the better part of another decade before assuming any of the most important local positions: selectman, town meeting moderator, or deacon. Members of the revolutionary generation were typically in at least their mid-thirties before they took up such community offices.[90] Anyone who assumed state or federal duties ordinarily stepped into them a few years later, at about age forty.[91]

Until they slowed down, usually at about sixty, New England's leaders drew on their years of service to benefit their neighbors. Leaders in waiting, men who would govern one day, had to stand by until middle age to see if their time would arrive.[92]

IT WAS THE fate of the most ambitious members of Harvard's revolutionary generation to reach the age for taking on society's most important positions of professional, religious, and political honor and responsibility at a time when New Englanders were starting to feel the effects of an extraordinary cultural transformation, one that had significant consequences for their lives and aspirations. At the close of the eighteenth century, New Englanders found themselves on the threshold of an unprecedented era of structured, organized competition. Aspirants to professional leadership struggled with one another for power. Within the church, longstanding but informal sects began to develop into discrete denominations, which institutionalized ecclesiastical strife. Meanwhile, in the government, fluid factions started to assume the more permanent characteristics of political parties.

As young men, the members of the revolutionary generation had prepared themselves to serve their communities, but what were they to make of this new state of affairs? What were its consequences for the ambitions many had nurtured for years? They were ready to take their places in due course as the region's leaders had done by tradition for generations; they were not ready for the changing circumstances they would encounter.

7

PARTY PASSIONS

IN 1798, when James Sheafe was forty-two, New Hampshire voters sent him to the United States House of Representatives. Here he remained for a single two-year term before the state legislature, which filled both of New Hampshire's Senate seats prior to the introduction of direct elections to the chamber, elevated him to the upper house.[1] Not long after this promotion, though, something happened. The small, well-connected circle of politicos who had retained nearly complete control over the state's government since it had engineered the ratification of the federal Constitution there in 1788 began to lose its grip on the levers of power. A portion of the press, unwilling to concede the legitimacy of Sheafe's advancement, attacked him, alleging that he was using his high office to influence the disposition of naval contracts. Under savage fire, Sheafe resigned his place after one year.[2]

By the turn of the nineteenth century, New Hampshire politics had become venomously partisan.[3] For a time, the Republican and Federalist parties were competitive in New Hampshire. The Republicans dominated the state for half a decade after Sheafe's resignation, but then national developments sabotaged them. The Embargo of 1807, followed by war with Great Britain in 1812, undermined Republican prospects across New England, encouraging Sheafe and his Federalist allies. "We expect to succeed in our election, but not with a great majority," he correctly predicted in 1814.[4] After the war ended, though, James found himself involved in a viciously divisive campaign. New Hampshire's Federalist Party turned out to be its chief victim.

As party competition flared in 1816, potential Federalist candidates were unwilling to subject themselves to the rancor of a gubernatorial campaign. Feeling pressure from party power brokers, James reluctantly agreed to stand for election. Relieved Federalists actively promoted his candidacy. "I have been acquainted with Mr. Sheafe for many years," Governor John Taylor Gilman, the retiring incumbent, wrote a friend the month before the election. "He is a Merchant of the first reputation, mild in his manners and strict of integrity." According to Gilman, public spirit, not personal ambition, had persuaded Sheafe to take up the cause: "An ardent desire to promote the public welfare was the sole motive of his compliance with the urgent requests of a large number of persons."[5]

But Sheafe's election was not to be. William Plumer, the Republican standard bearer, defeated him by 2,300 votes after a campaign immersed in invective and charges of loyalism. When the same two candidates faced each other again the following year, once more the victor was Plumer.[6]

James never again offered himself for public office. He was now sixty-one. Electoral defeats and the passing years had exacted their toll. It was time for someone else to have a turn.

COMPETITION per se was nothing new to New England, but as James Sheafe came to know only too well, near the end of the eighteenth century the forms that it took began to change. Institutional development intersected with the career development of the members of the revolutionary generation. For as long as anyone could remember, New England's typical contests had pitted one individual against another. Lawyers fought with one another over clients, merchants competed in the marketplace over sales, doctors even contended quietly for patients. After the war, though, as a result of independence, formal organizations—political parties and religious denominations as well as banks, insurance companies, turnpikes, and even theaters and missionary societies—now wrestled with one another, changing the very nature of competition.[7] For the most ambitious members of the revolutionary generation, the consequences of this development were substantial.

Anyone who aspired to a public career at the highest levels from the late 1790s onward had to come to terms with an unavoidable fact of life: the rise of organized parties, both political and ecclesiastical. Several members of the Harvard classes of 1771 through 1774 actively promoted the institutionalization of competition, and many more were caught up in its consequences. For some of the revolutionary generation's most prominent members, the transformation of competition had substantial personal implications, and everyone recognized that it affected the tone of public life. Just as they were reaching the pinnacle of their careers, Fisher Ames, Levi Lincoln, Eliphalet Pearson, and others discovered that the terms of the contest had changed. In bygone days, New Englanders had deferred to their social betters. No longer. By the turn of the nineteenth century, neither birth nor breeding was enough. There would be more losers than winners as organized parties now snuffed out the aspirations of many of the generation's brightest lights, disappointing many men while at the same time promoting the prospects of others. As for everyone else, they found it increasingly difficult to participate in public life in any meaningful way without taking sides.

From the first, politics and religion had shaped the public discourse in colonial New England. This continued to be the case at the turn of the nineteenth century. Political differences had embroiled the Massachusetts Bay Colony repeatedly since 1634, when John Winthrop, its founding governor, had first lost his office to insurgents led by Thomas Dudley.[8] Meanwhile, theological conflicts had fractured the region's Calvinist majority from time to time since the mid-1630s, when Anne Hutchinson threatened the Massachusetts Bay's spiritual harmony with claims of her ability to discern God's hidden purposes.[9] Discord between the reformed majority and groups outside the Congregationalist establishment or Standing Order—principally Baptists and Anglicans—was also common.[10] Near the close of the eighteenth century, however, there was something novel about the developing storm.

There had been nothing especially stable about the political and religious factions that contested for office and influence within the New England colonies time and again between the 1630s and the Revolution. There were no durable political coalitions of any kind, and the Congregationalists' provincial ministerial conventions impartially welcomed all of their clergymen in good standing without reference to doctrinal positions. In government, informal legislative factions came and went following the dictates of personal advantage. Even within informal Congregationalist combinations— which exhibited considerably more staying power than colonial political factions because, unlike public officials, their members ordinarily coalesced around deeply held beliefs—impermanence was ultimately the order of the day.

Near the close of the eighteenth century, however, in the revolutionary aftermath, recognizably modern political and ecclesiastical connections began to emerge. Absent the need for unity in the face of British power, fragile religious and political coalitions cracked as competing groups claimed the mantle of New England's Puritan and republican heritages. Although they followed different evolutionary courses—political parties grew from the top down out of small legislative factions, while from the outset church parties had more popular roots—once they matured, they were functionally similar, martialing opposing armies of followers. What is more, after the war, ideology began to play a more important role in political life, meaning that in both the civic and the religious arenas the members of opposing parties grew increasingly committed to their causes.

Over a ten-year period between the mid-1790s and the midpoint of the next decade, competing coalitions reached into every corner of New England, attracting widespread support. Political and ecclesiastical parties, which became commonplace by the 1820s and 1830s, were still novelties at the turn of the century, as members of the revolutionary generation took their turn for leadership and power. New though the parties were, they fundamentally changed the pathway to the most influential civic and ecclesiastical offices. The battle order was drawn along institutional lines with the result that many of the revolutionary generation's most successful public figures were not the men anyone would have predicted before the war.

IN POLITICS, organized parties took shape at the top and gradually reached out to individual voters. Before partisan divisions began to disrupt local town meetings, eighteenth-century New England's civic leaders confronted one another as individuals or as small cliques and factions struggling for control of provincial legislatures and postwar state governments. By the time that partisan controversy regularly penetrated the region's towns, many members of Harvard's revolutionary generation were already comfortably entrenched in positions of community influence as selectmen, town moderators, and town clerks.

Political factions, the precursors of formal parties, began to appear in colonial assemblies well before the Revolution. These combinations, legislative alliances without direct connections to the electorate, frequently followed regional lines. When it came to the important issues of the day such as militia expenditures, currency policy, tax policy, and the appointment of civil officeholders, the metropolitan merchants and lawyers who dominated the political life of colonial New England's largest towns often observed different priorities than the pioneers, farmers, and craftsmen who sat on the legislative back benches.[11]

By the 1760s, competing regional interests affected the legislative politics of each of the four New England provinces. In Connecticut and Rhode Island, the major towns contested for preeminence—Hartford versus New Haven, Providence versus Newport.[12] In New Hampshire, merchant worthies in Portsmouth and Exeter dominated the government to the disadvantage of the residents of inland communities.[13] Meanwhile, in Massachusetts, the "River Gods" of the major towns along the Connecticut River allied with the great merchants and well-connected barristers of the province's commercial centers in opposition to the representatives of most of the colony's small towns to control the Great and General Court and the Council.[14]

The factional politics of the late colonial period never reached very deeply into the communities of New England, however, and with a couple of major exceptions, as late as the mid-1780s intramural legislative struggles continued to dominate the region's civic life. In Massachusetts, for instance, without the support of any identifiable party, John Hancock nevertheless drew on his reputation to win the favor of voters, who regularly elected him governor in preference to two other celebrated public figures, Samuel Adams and James Bowdoin, Jemmy's father. It took Hancock's temporary retirement from public life in 1785–86 to clear the way for Bowdoin, who served two one-year terms in the governor's chair.[15] Adams eventually served in the same office from 1793 to 1797.

The first popular challenges to this pattern became apparent in the mid-1780s. A credit crisis that had developed in the agricultural regions of Massachusetts and New Hampshire touched farmers and other men of modest means. Efforts in Massachusetts by commercial interests to ensure the soundness of the local currency collided with widespread rural borrowing. The upshot was Shays's Rebellion, a debtors' protest in central and western Massachusetts against hard money.[16] At about the same time, in New Hampshire rural debtors demonstrated unsuccessfully for an issue of paper money tied to a land bank.[17]

During the 1780s, competing legislative factions never allied themselves with rural demonstrators in either state. Responsible leaders in both Massachusetts and New Hampshire spoke out against politics "out of doors." In retrospect, however, it is clear that energizing rural debtors in the mid-1780s constituted an important step toward politicizing New England's electorate. The adoption of a new constitution in each state (Massachusetts in 1780, New Hampshire in 1776, 1784, and 1792) gave voters increased responsibility and politicians many new opportunities for office.[18] Men who had voted only for local posts and provincial representatives during the colonial period now encountered slates of candidates for offices that included governor and U.S. representative when they ventured to the polls. It was only a matter of time before the factions began to connect with the voters.

Conflict in the late 1780s over the ratification of the proposed federal constitution underscored the regional tensions that were shaping local politics in the years after the Revolution.[19] After their defeat in 1787, the Shaysites continued to clamor for relief from debts, while the more cosmopolitan residents of the seaboard pressed for centralized government to facilitate foreign trade. By the mid-1790s, differences over the French Revolution were producing New England's first stable political parties with real grass roots. When in 1795 American diplomats and representatives of the British government negotiated an accord—the Jay Treaty—citizens who favored a strong Franco-American alliance were incensed. In both Massachusetts and New Hampshire tensions came to a head in 1800. As

Thomas Jefferson was winning the White House, Federalists and Republicans did battle, their causes bolstered by new tools to reach the individual voter such as caucuses, political clubs, and party newspapers.[20]

Political maturity for the members of the revolutionary generation consequently coincided with a period of partisan wrangling and vituperation, a new experience for the young nation. Without a heritage of party politics, and convinced that parties undermined civic harmony, Federalists and Republicans each tried to speak for the nation as a whole, dismissing the opposition as a disruptive splinter group. With David Osgood of Medford, they deplored that "men . . . lose sight of their principles in their blind, yet violent attachment to their respective parties."[21] Each side charged the other with acting in bad faith. Neither acknowledged the sincerity of their differences over the nature of the revolutionary legacy.

At the turn of the nineteenth century, two members of Harvard's revolutionary generation, Fisher Ames speaking for the Federalists and Levi Lincoln as a spokesman for the Republicans, summarized the views of the competing parties. Disturbed by unseemly scrambling for office and power in the United States as well as the bloodshed of the French Revolution, Ames erected three pillars as "principles of federalism": "the Union should be maintained"; a "republican government" was vital to American liberty; and "the particular form of a republican government for the Union ought to be very nearly such as was agreed on in 1788," that is, a representative polity, not a direct democracy on one extreme or a monarchy on the other.[22] In contrast to Ames, whose precepts amounted to a brief for the importance of social and political order, Lincoln focused on the American people as the source of the government's power and the locus of sovereignty. Citing Virginia lawyer George Wythe, Lincoln discovered the roots of freedom in popular constraints on government power. Annual elections, rotation in all offices, nearly universal participation in the militia by men armed for their own security, widespread public education, and personal frugality were the Republicans' ingredients for a stable state devoted to the freedom of the governed.[23]

Think of Ames and Lincoln as epitomizing two different definitions of the revolutionary legacy—the spirit of 1776 and 1787 that had resulted in the Constitution. Ames embodied the Federalists' desire to preserve the social order. In contrast Lincoln, a Republican voice for personal liberties instead of centralized public power, focused on sovereignty and the right to govern, which he traced to the individual. So long as men such as Ames and Lincoln sincerely believed in competing principles, the division within the body politic promised to be long and bitter.

INDEPENDENCE HAD resulted in unprecedented opportunities for ambitious members of the revolutionary generation. It raised the stakes for them by virtue of the creation of dozens of new offices on the federal level at the same time that it made others—especially governorships—more available to American-born contenders than ever before. Because of intensified competition, however, it often turned out to be impossible to take full advantage

Fisher Ames. (*Fisher Ames* [undated], by John Rogers after Gilbert Stuart. Engraving. Massachusetts Historical Society.)

of the opportunities. Attracted by the prospect of important public offices at the state and federal levels, men such as James Sheafe, Fisher Ames, and Levi Lincoln were willing to offer themselves as candidates. Who seemed better suited to public office, after all? In their formative years before the war, they had absorbed colonial New England's traditional approach to civic life. In the seventeenth century, the Reverend Samuel Stone of Cambridge and Hartford had deftly captured the common understanding of the ideal polity: "*a speaking* Aristocracy *in the face of a silent* Democracy."[24] Educated and polished, most of the members of the revolutionary generation had no difficulty identifying themselves with Stone's speaking aristocracy.

The new politics, though, called for a popular touch that genteel colonial officeholders had rarely needed to cultivate. For the members of Harvard's revolutionary generation at the turn of the nineteenth century, there were more competitors for public office than ever before, including many who had never seen the inside of a college classroom. There would be no major political success now without partisan conflict. Increasingly, this meant appealing directly to the electorate. Only a few Harvardians were up to the challenge.

As late as the election of 1798, political success and Federalism were nearly synonymous in New England. In Massachusetts, New Hampshire, and Connecticut, the Federalists ruled as if by natural right throughout the first decade of the new republic. Elsewhere, particularly in the southern states, the Republicans, the party of Thomas Jefferson and James Madison, held sway; but in New England a Federalist coalition of established and wealthy merchants, lawyers, and farmers, men devoted to a strong central government and convinced of their own innate abilities as leaders, held power without a serious threat to their monopoly until the turn of the century.

Of the members of Harvard's revolutionary generation, Fisher Ames, as a congressman from 1789 to 1797, was the greatest beneficiary of the Federalists' extended ascendance.[25] Fisher's modest origins in a Dedham tavern give the lie to the common assumption that leading Federalists invariably inherited their wealth, their politics, and their public station. The younger brother of Dr. Nathaniel Ames, A.B. 1761, an active and highly partisan Republican operative with whom he sometimes squabbled, Fisher learned his conservative values and developed his establishment connections on his own between the late 1770s and the late 1780s.[26]

Fisher had been a precocious Harvard student, the second-youngest member of the class of 1774, and in civic affairs he was equally advanced. Elected to office by his neighbors for the first time at twenty-one in 1779 to represent Dedham at a convention to consider remedies for revolutionary-

era inflation, Ames committed himself early to public service. By the mid-
1780s, still only in his late twenties, he began to write for the press. In two
series published in Boston's *Independent Chronicle*, Fisher deplored the tendency of Shays's Rebellion to destabilize government and society. "Upon
the whole," he wrote, "we may pronounce the rebellion the most radically
wicked in principles and purposes, and the most rapid and audacious in its
progress, that ever disturbed the peace of mankind."[27] Not long after, in
1787 and 1788, as a Massachusetts convention considered whether or not
to ratify the United States Constitution, Ames represented Dedham, which
he served as a strong advocate for federal union. Brief service in the Massachusetts General Court was followed in December 1788 by election at
age thirty to the first federal Congress.[28]

The first enduring American political parties were beginning to emerge
in Congress, and Ames took an active role their development. Supportive
of a powerful central government, property rights, and strong Anglo-
American diplomatic relations, he agreed on most controversial issues with
the men who became the leading voices of Federalism. An engaging orator
and a persuasive writer, he was soon one of the most visible and respected
advocates of his circle's views.

After Ames retired from public office in 1797, the victim of a combination
of bad health and growing Republican opposition in his congressional district, he remained active in Massachusetts politics. Nothing persuaded him
that it was a good idea to open governmental decision making to the "rab-
ble," but the consequences of failing to appeal to the public were too dreadful to contemplate.[29] In caucus with other prominent conservatives at the
turn of the century, he worked to organize sympathetic voters throughout
the commonwealth. Newspapers provided his most important public plat-
form after 1797. During the late 1790s, his essays on public issues appeared
in the most important voice of Massachusetts Federalism, the *Columbian
Centinel*. Then in 1801 Fisher and a group of friends acquired a paper of
their own, the *Massachusetts Mercury*. They renamed it the *New England
Palladium* and attempted to make it the national voice of Federalism.[30]

By the early nineteenth century, partisanship was molding political life
at the state and federal levels. Thanks to the efforts of men such as Fisher
Ames, the parties' messages were reaching the electorate. As late as July
1801, Republican Levi Lincoln could still report optimistically to Thomas
Jefferson that Federalists with whom he had talked at Harvard's commencement, though "opposed to your election . . . would give you their support."[31]
Less than two months later, however, after a bitter statewide campaign,
Lincoln charged the Federalists with "the grossest misrepresentations &
basest acts. Emissaries were sent round . . . to propagate slanders in a way

which could not be detected until it was too late."[32] The following year, in 1802, Ames and Lincoln engaged in an uncompromising war of words through the essay series each wrote for his party newspaper.[33]

Since electoral politics is a zero-sum game, the success of Federalists such as Ames meant failure for Republicans such as Levi Lincoln and vice versa.[34] After his brief military service in April 1775, Levi settled in Worcester and immediately became active in local affairs. Town and county offices came easily to him between the late 1770s and the early 1790s, but when his aspirations reached beyond Worcester, success touched him less often at first. Electoral politics frustrated Massachusetts Jeffersonians before the late 1790s. Lincoln was able to capture only a single term in the state House of Representatives in 1796 and one in the state Senate in 1796–97 before success in a by-election in 1800 to finish an incomplete term in the United States House of Representatives propelled him into the national arena. Months later, Lincoln won reelection to the House, but before he assumed his seat, in March 1801 Thomas Jefferson named him U.S. attorney general, an office he held until the end of 1804.[35]

Lincoln remained politically active after returning to Massachusetts. Elected to the Governor's Council in 1806, he quickly advanced to the lieutenant governorship, an office he held in 1807 and 1808. Meanwhile, as President Jefferson's man in Massachusetts, he was such a partisan adviser on the distribution of patronage that he earned widespread Federalist enmity.[36] The death of Governor James Sullivan in December 1808 briefly made him acting governor, but he occupied the position only until May 1, 1809. After a bitter campaign, he lost to his Federalist rival, Christopher Gore.[37] Lincoln served two more one-year terms on the Governor's Council before retiring from politics at the age of sixty-three in 1812.[38]

By 1823, when William Eustis won election to the governorship of Massachusetts at the age of sixty-nine, partisanship had so infected the political process that thoughtful community leaders were looking for ways to mitigate it.[39] Eustis had tasted both success and failure over a long public career lasting four decades, and he had had his partisan moments.[40] After six years in the Massachusetts House, he had left public service in 1794, disgusted by choreographed confrontations that left him "sick of the whole of this kind of life."[41] He had been unable to stay away, however, and after holding a series of local posts in the late 1790s, he won election to Congress in 1800 and 1802 before losing in an acrimonious campaign in 1804. Service as James Madison's secretary of war and ambassador to The Hague as well as another term in Congress preceded three failed bids for the governorship in 1820, 1821, and 1822. After decades in the thick of partisan politics, Eustis became the compromise choice for governor in 1823 when he ran against arch-Federalist Harrison Gray Otis. Although a Republican, Eustis reached out to each side, making him generally acceptable to power brokers in both parties. As national political leaders attempted to coalesce behind compromise candidates for the White House, in Massachusetts leading figures also attempted to dull the edges of party wrangling through the selection of men who urged bipartisan cooperation.[42]

Eustis died in office in 1825 at seventy-one, the last member of his generation to hold a major public post.[43] For him, as for the rest of his Harvard contemporaries, partisan politics had shaped the mature phase of his public life.

Collectively the generation's members compiled a creditable record in taking advantage of the opportunities that had resulted from independence. At the state level, both Lincoln and Eustis served as governor of Massachusetts, and Winthrop Sargent held the same office in the Mississippi Territory. Lincoln and Sam Phillips were elected lieutenant governor of Massachusetts, and Perez Morton served the commonwealth as attorney general. In New Hampshire, Oliver Peabody's public offices included state senator and state treasurer.[44] On the federal level, in addition to James Sheafe's terms in the House and the Senate, Ames, Samuel Tenney, and Laban Wheaton all served terms in the U.S. House of Representatives. Lincoln (as attorney general) and Eustis (as secretary of war) served in Washington as members of the cabinet. In addition Eustis served as minister to The Hague, and Jemmy Bowdoin was appointed minister to Spain, although poor health on his arrival in Europe prevented him from assuming the post.[45]

And yet seductive opportunities had often proved to be out of reach. At the end of the day the political battlefield was littered with casualties. There were talented men who stood for office and lost: Josiah Smith, an Anti-Federalist and then a Republican in predominantly Federalist Newburyport, offered himself for public office repeatedly but won only a single term as a selectman.[46] There were races that were fought so bitterly that it was hard to know who really won: in Concord in 1810, Federalist Tilly Merrick defeated his Republican opponent for the state legislature 129–124 thanks to a controversial decision by the town's Federalist-dominated board of selectmen concerning the eligibility of eight contested voters. Republican state legislators forced the Massachusetts House of Representatives to review the vote, and while Tilly occupied the seat pending a resolution, a partisan firestorm raged unquenched for a year until the next annual election mooted the issue.[47] For some men electoral politics apparently became so distasteful that they chose not to subject themselves to the fray: Thomas Rindge Rogers, the son of a member of colonial New Hampshire's King's

Council, stood on the sidelines rather than participate in the carnage.[48] And there were some whose civic successes simply fell short of what they might have anticipated achieving in another day: although Jemmy Bowdoin served as a state senator and was appointed American minister to Spain, no one dared to compare his public career with that of his father, the governor.[49]

Indeed, the most striking fact about the generation's leading civic careers is that, except for James Sheafe's and Jemmy Bowdoin's, they belonged to men of decidedly modest origins. Consider the seven men who held federal office: Fisher Ames was born in a tavern, Levi Lincoln's father was a farmer and glazier, a housewright sired William Eustis, Samuel Tenney was the son of a farmer and miller, and Laban Wheaton's father was a doctor but without a college education. Only Jacob Sheafe, a wealthy Portsmouth trader, and Governor James Bowdoin were men of prominence.[50] Instead of Olivers and Sparhawks, Rogerses and Marches, the men who might reasonably have expected to hold high office under the crown, it seemed that voters wanted leaders who spoke their own language. As undergraduates in the late 1760s and early 1770s, the members of the revolutionary generation had aspired to genteel polish, confident that a refined manner would serve them well in later life. By the time they were ready for power, though, the electorate was less interested in well-mannered leaders who governed by virtue of their family background or their elegant style than in office-holders whose origins and interests resembled their own.

Changing voter expectations resulted in bitter campaigns. These were trying times for many men whose background and education might have guaranteed them respect and responsibility in an earlier day.

At the same time that partisanship was infecting New England's politics, an ecclesiastical development had similar consequences for the members of the revolutionary generation. In contrast to political parties, though, church alliances relied from the first on popular support. When more than six decades of acrimony reached their climax in 1805, six men meeting behind closed doors, the members of the Harvard Corporation, confirmed a religious realignment that New Englanders had already been effecting. Members of Harvard's revolutionary generation played central roles in two of the day's critical ecclesiastical events.

New England had never been free from religious conflict. Recall that the men and women who settled the region in the 1630s had felt strongly enough about their faith to uproot themselves and cross a frightening ocean to face an uncertain future on an unexplored continent. Nevertheless, although ecclesiastical party lines began to harden as early as the 1740s, they remained permeable for decades. Before the Revolution, as long as New

Englanders had to pay attention to British ecclesiastical affairs, the threat that the Church of England posed to their independence tempered the urge to split from one another.[51] In the 1790s, most New Englanders could still agree to disagree over many important doctrinal issues. Within a few years, however, partisan church alliances were as apparent as political ones. It was increasingly difficult to remember what it had been like before they existed.

The fissure that reshaped religious life for most members of Harvard's revolutionary generation took place within New England's Congregational Church. Baptists and Episcopalians, who could trace their New England roots to the seventeenth century, and several other small sects that appeared before the mid-1770s were increasingly important factors after the Revolution, but most of the region was a Congregationalist preserve until well after the war. As a predominantly Congregationalist institution, Harvard College was particularly sensitive to turmoil within New England's dominant confession, its Standing Order.

Tensions within the Standing Order erupted periodically throughout the seventeenth and eighteenth centuries, but it took a religious revival, the Great Awakening, which swept New England from one end to the other in the late 1730s and early 1740s, to expose the fault lines along which the establishment was fracturing. In the years following the revival, its supporters took an increasingly rigid approach to matters of religious faith and church organization. Emphasizing God's unquestioned power to separate the saved from the damned, they underscored every sinner's duty to submit to the Lord.

Between the 1740s and the early nineteenth century, New England's Standing Order addressed a constellation of vital theological issues. Ministers and members of the laity alike contested positions on subjects such as original sin, the freedom of the will, justification by faith alone, rationalism, the benevolence of the deity, the Trinity, and the right of private judgment. In the course of more than six decades of theological inquiry, the boundary between Congregational orthodoxy and liberal Christianity—that is, between the progenitors of the Congregationalist and Unitarian denominations—was defined.[52] For some members of Harvard's revolutionary generation, it was occasionally possible to straddle the growing divide between the two claimants to the heritage of the Standing Order, but for most there eventually came a time when declaring a side was unavoidable.

Much as Federalists and Republicans each viewed themselves as the true heirs of the War for Independence, orthodox Congregationalists and liberal Christians alike saw themselves as the rightful successors to the religious legacy of New England's Puritan settlers. Among the leading religious thinkers within Harvard's primary sphere of influence in eastern Massachusetts and coastal New Hampshire, a growing majority inclined toward the liberal, or Arminian, position by the outbreak of the Revolution. In contrast to the orthodox, who emphasized the omnipotence of God and the inability of sinners to affect their prospects for salvation, the Arminians believed that men and women could take active steps to prepare themselves to receive divine grace. By leading pious and moral lives, the liberals believed, Christians might play a pivotal role in their own salvation.[53] Both the orthodox and the liberal positions had undeniable roots in the faith of New England's Puritan founders.[54]

Members of Harvard's revolutionary generation who fixed their career sights on the Congregational ministry could choose either of two spiritual paths in the late 1770s and early 1780s as they settled on a professional course. Each avenue implied a different understanding of God. Was the Lord a God of laws, stern and strict in His dealings with sinners, so incomprehensible to them that it was hard to see how rational inquiries might supplement revealed insights into the ways of the world? The minority of the members of Harvard's revolutionary generation who gravitated toward this understanding of God inclined toward orthodox Congregationalism. Or was God a benevolent father who adhered to rational rules and appreciated the efforts of His sons and daughters to make themselves worthy of salvation? The majority of the generation who accepted this view were drawn almost inexorably to the liberal or Arminian wing of New England Congregationalism.

Although the dispute between Congregationalist orthodoxy and liberal Christianity did not come to a head until after 1800, a controversy in the early 1780s in which a member of the class of 1774 played a prominent role was a major factor in solidifying partisan lines within New England's Standing Order. Like the factional disputes that dominated the political sphere at the same time, this conflict took place within a small circle of leaders. The subject of the moment was universal salvation, and the revolutionary generation's chief controversialist was the Reverend John Clarke, a minister of Boston's First Church.[55]

THE REVEREND John Clarke, no kin to Dr. John Clarke or to the British theologian John Clarke, was the ministerial colleague of Charles Chauncy, the most prominent Arminian clergyman of the day. Chauncy, a 1721 graduate of the college, had been a leader among the liberal Christians since the Great Awakening. During the years immediately following the revival, the Arminian clergy valued discretion for fear that too much candor about their reservations with regard to orthodoxy would stir up opposition, publicly discrediting them and their views. Thus in the early 1750s, when Chauncy began to question the traditional doctrine that God condemned some of His children to eternal damnation, he did so circumspectly. A lengthy treatise that he wrote during the 1750s on universal salvation (referred to by insiders cryptically as "the pudding") remained in manuscript in the early 1780s, passed quietly from one reliable minister to another. Unanticipated developments in 1782, however, forced Chauncy's hand. John Clarke, as the older man's much younger colleague, played a significant part in the unfolding drama.[56]

For Chauncy and Clarke, the problem came out of the north—to be precise, from Gloucester. Here, John Murray, an immigrant Englishman without formal theological training, had begun to serve a small cluster of religious dissenters in 1774. The congregation, which included Winthrop Sargent and his family, held to the radical tenet that every sinner would be saved.[57]

Universal salvation—universalism—was also the inevitable conclusion of Chauncy's unpublished treatise, but to his mind Murray was not the man to promote the doctrine. Murray's lack of formal training was one problem; he did not have the personal gravitas, the professional carriage, of an educated clergyman with a prestigious settlement. He gave universalism a bad name. Even more important, as far as both Chauncy and Clarke were concerned, Murray had arrived at the right result for the wrong reasons. In "the pudding," Chauncy, expanding upon one of the logical consequences of New England Arminianism, had quietly concluded that God was too merciful, too benevolent, to consign any of His sons and daughters to eternal damnation, although He might punish them temporarily for their transgressions. Murray quite publicly followed a different logical path. Drawing on the doctrine of the atonement, Murray reasoned that Jesus had saved all sinners through his sacrifice. For Chauncy and Clarke, this argument posed a problem because of its libertine implications. If everyone were saved as a matter of course, then what was the point in being moral, honest, or compassionate?[58]

A short anonymous pamphlet was the first attempt by Chauncy and Clarke to lay out their doctrine of universal salvation. Stitched together awkwardly by Clarke from generations of writing on the subject by church fathers, *Salvation for All Men* persuaded no one and disappointed many. "From Mr. Clarke's reputation much was expected," John Eliot wrote to a friend after the tract appeared. "Had he enterered into the argument, and treated the subject delicately, he would have obliged his friends, served his cause, and gained a reputation. Instead of this, he threw a weapon into the hands of his opponents, with which they will cease not to maul him."[59] The orthodox rejoinder, *All Men Will Not be Saved Forever*, by Samuel Mather, a 1723 graduate of the college, the "last and least" of the clergy members of a distinguished family of New England ministers, was no more convincing.[60] Chauncy finally published his lengthy tome, *The Mystery Hid from Ages and Generations*, in 1784.[61]

Despite all the ink and paper expended on the doctrine of universalism between 1782 and 1784, neither side won the field of battle. Neither persuaded either the other or the public at large of its position. Nevertheless, the controversy had continuing consequences. As each side stated its case, its friends enlisted on its behalf. The lines dividing the orthodox and the liberals hardened further.

From the struggle over universal salvation in the mid-1780s, many ministers learned important lessons. Burned by the critical failure of *Salvation for All Men*, John Clarke determined to avoid partisan controversy at all costs. Throughout the remaining fourteen years of his ministry, he concentrated on the central doctrines of reformed Christianity, those beliefs about which no one had reservations.[62] Many of his liberal contemporaries, afraid that theological controversy might destroy the influence of the church in New England's affairs both sacred and secular, followed suit. John Eliot remarked to a friend in 1783, "I never drop a word about religion."[63] Decades later, as tempers flamed in 1815, Charles Stearns pleaded for ecclesiastical peace: "Characterizing men by names of division can only tend to create heats, foment party spirit, and bring the most odious passions into operation."[64]

By the early nineteenth century, though, all reasonable hope for avoiding sectarian rifts was gone. Believing that they had little in common with the liberals, orthodox clergymen began to associate only with their own. Institutionally and culturally, the two paths permanently diverged.[65] Missionary, clerical, and tract societies intended to promote divisive issues began to appear in eastern Massachusetts around 1800. First in 1799 came the Massachusetts Missionary Society, a tool of the most conservative faction within New England Congregationalism, the New Divinity or Hopkinsian movement. Then in 1802 orthodox ministers organized a Calvinist ministerial society, the General Association of Massachusetts, followed in 1803 by a Calvinist tract association, the Massachusetts Society for Promoting Christian Knowledge. By the time liberal ministers responded with their own tract organization in 1805, the Massachusetts Society for Promoting Christian Knowledge, Piety, and Charity, the region had already passed the defining moment in its religious history, a crisis that occurred in February at Harvard.[66]

From 1805 onward, there was no turning back. Certain that they preserved the central tenets of New England's Puritan founders, both the orthodox and the liberals increasingly resisted the impulse to compromise their positions.[67] Religious alliances were commonplace, and their emergence had consequences for the careers of many ministers. At various points in the drama's final act, Eliphalet Pearson, John Eliot, and Fisher Ames would all have lines to read.

IT HAD BEEN New England's worst winter in living memory, but February 1, 1805, was a day of blessed respite. After weeks of snows so persistent that the glistening drifts rose to ten feet in some places, after seductively beautiful ice storms that ripped down encrusted tree limbs and made it treacherous to venture outside, after roaring gales that drove oceangoing vessels ashore and capsized a small boat in Marblehead Harbor with the loss of three lives, the first of February was cloudy, drizzly, and a bit warmer than normal for the date. The ice and snow could begin to melt. It was a day for cleaning up.[68]

Snow-choked paths and fallen branches were not the only problems Harvard College faced. The school was cleaning up a quarrel quite as ferocious as the weather of that bitter winter, a battle for its very soul. The immediate issue was the future of the college. Not far beneath the surface, religious partisanship was shaping the outcome.

At a time when factionalism threatened the religious tranquillity of New England, some community leaders still held out hopes for future harmony. Two of the most respected voices for conciliation in eastern Massachusetts had belonged to Harvard faculty members, David Tappan and Joseph Willard. Both were now stilled, however, and on February 1 the college was coping with the consequences of their deaths. Professor Tappan had been the first to die, on August 27, 1803, more than thirty-two years after the graduation of his class in 1771. Then, before the college had agreed on a new Hollis Professor, President Willard passed away on September 25, 1804, some three decades after he had tutored the men of the revolutionary generation. New Englanders attached high symbolism to the presidency of Harvard College even though its practical influence over their day-to-day lives was ordinarily negligible. The search for a successor for Willard consequently became a high-stakes test of the relative power of the orthodox and liberal parties, at least in eastern Massachusetts.[69]

The college Corporation was responsible for filling both vacancies, and no one doubted that the school's religious future hung in the balance. The Corporation ordinarily had seven members, but one of them was the president, so it was up to the surviving six to come to a majority decision over each opening. The fact that the professorship was still unfilled on February

Eliphalet Pearson. Large, overbearing, and with a loud, deep voice, Pearson successfully intimidated generations of students both at Phillips Academy and at Harvard College. (*Eliphalet Pearson*, by James Frothingham after Samuel F. B. Morse. Oil on canvas, 54.93 × 44.45 cm. Harvard University Portrait Collection. Gift of the Massachusetts Historical Society, 1940. Photo credit: Harvard University Art Museums Photographic Services. Image copyright © President and Fellows of Harvard College.)

1, more than seventeen months after Tappan's death, was a measure of their difficulty in agreeing on an acceptable candidate.

In fact, the Corporation itself was divided between the orthodox and the liberals. Among the orthodox, after Willard's death Eliphalet Pearson, a member of the board since 1800, was a powerful, even domineering force. Pearson, fifty-two years old now, had spent about half his life at Harvard as a student and faculty member. He had passed from adolescence to early adulthood here, and then after his return from Andover in his early thirties, he had grown into middle age at the college. No candidate had more relevant experience than Pearson. As everyone suspected, Eliphalet harbored personal ambitions for the college presidency, which he had been filling on an interim basis since Willard passed away. Among the liberals, John Eliot— gentle, judicious, and naturally inclined to compromise—the most recent addition to the Corporation by virtue of his selection the previous year, was a measured voice for rational religion. As Eliot's diary reveals, with each succeeding meeting he was growing increasingly resentful of the orthodox Pearson—large and overbearing in middle age with a deep, booming voice and beetling brow—whom the pudgy, mild-mannered Boston preacher considered a bully.[70]

The Corporation met at the college on February 1, possibly in the Philosophy Room on the second floor of Harvard Hall, a large Persian-carpeted chamber dominated by scientific apparatus and full-length portraits of three of the college's major donors.[71] After fruitlessly reviewing various compromise proposals that would have split the presidency and the professorship between the liberals and the orthodox, maintaining a factional balance within the college community, the members determined to defer the selection of the executive to a later date and to focus for the moment on the choice of the Hollis Professor. When the ballots were counted, the successful candidate was Henry Ware, the minister of the First Church in Hingham, a graduate of the college in the class of 1785 and widely known as a liberal. Because the proffered compromises had not succeeded, Ware's selection was an unequivocal statement that Harvard had gone over to the Arminians. In the religious wars of the day, the liberals had won a momentous victory. In effect, they now controlled the most important educational institution in New England.

Even though the meeting had not settled on a successor for Willard, its decision on the Hollis Professorship contained a bitter message for Pearson. Because the liberals were now in control of the Corporation, his ambitions that harsh winter to save the college for orthodoxy and claim the presidency for himself were moribund. If he wished, he might remain at Harvard, but this much now seemed clear: the college's next president would not be a Calvinist. Indeed, if Eliphalet stayed, he might pass the rest of his Harvard career under an Arminian chief executive. No matter whom the Corporation chose, Pearson would not be happy with the selection.[72]

To all intents and purposes, Eliphalet Pearson's presidential dreams were dead, the victim of sectarian infighting and his own overbearing personality; but he remained in Cambridge, a painful reminder of the division within the college, a member of the faculty and of the Corporation for more than another year. If he still harbored faint hopes that he might reverse the course of the college, they expired in late February 1806.

The previous December the Fellows had offered the presidency to Fisher Ames, the retired congressman, who had declined it citing ill health. Instead of turning to Pearson after receiving Ames's rejection, the Corporation chose another member of the faculty, Samuel Webber, a 1784 graduate and the Hollis Professor of Mathematics since 1789. Webber promptly accepted.[73]

Disappointed, hurt, and frustrated, Pearson angrily resigned both his professorship and his membership in the Corporation on March 8. When the Fellows attempted a reconciliation several weeks later, he curtly rejected their advance: "With best respects Mr. P. returns his thanks to the Corp of H. C. for their polite invitation to dine with them this day, but he is obliged to deny himself that honor."[74] Within weeks Pearson was gone. After two decades on the faculty, he turned his back on Harvard and Cambridge in favor of the more orthodox environment of Andover.

HISTORIANS HAVE sometimes pointed to the struggle to control Harvard in 1805–6 as the first volley in the so-called Unitarian Controversy, which resulted in the fragmentation of New England Congregationalism.[75] By the time the controversy was concluded a generation later, New England had been given over to formal religious denominations. In addition to Unitarians and Congregationalists, there were other confessions—including Baptists, Methodists, Episcopalians, Universalists, and a number of smaller sects—each with its own conventions of clergymen, periodicals, and missionary associations.[76] Denominational bureaucracies were forming, as were seminaries.

Whether or not someone aspired to high office, this much was clear: in both church and state, parties had become the order of the day. They had reshaped public life, transforming in the process the career prospects of many men.

8

The Best and the Brightest

When Eliphalet Pearson offered himself for the presidency of Harvard College, he ran the risk of rejection. James Sheafe took the same gamble when he agreed to be the Federalist Party's candidate for governor of New Hampshire. Both men dared to dream of the honor and influence that would be theirs through high office. In the end, however, there was nothing left to do but admit defeat.

As they aged, Pearson, Sheafe, and the other members of Harvard's revolutionary generation came to terms with their ambition. It was a drive they all possessed, although no two men's purposes in life were identical. Without dreams, after all, both theirs and their parents', none of them would even have gone to college. As boys they had wanted to make places for themselves in society—perhaps to be worth ten thousand pounds, ride in a carriage, command a militia regiment, and sit on the Provincial Council, as John Adams had once wished. Then as men they were the beneficiaries of all the new opportunities that resulted from national independence and led some of them to reassess their objectives. They were the best and the brightest of turn-of-the-century New England—Harvard men, pedigreed men, products of the day's premier education with more advantages than almost any of their contemporaries could boast. With so much going for them, it was natural for them to have big plans. Still, a college degree did not guarantee fame, respect, influence, wealth, or happiness. Sooner or later, almost every member of the generation asked himself whether he had made the best of his opportunities.

Think of life as a suite of relationships joining a man to God, to his family, and through daily life to society at large. The dreams of revolutionary Harvard men encompassed all three sets of connections. At the final accounting, no matter the context, there were two standards for the members of the college's revolutionary generation, gauges of success and of satisfaction. Successful men met the expectations of others; satisfied men met their own. Success brought acclaim, but satisfaction's most important product was even sweeter—peace of mind.

Success and satisfaction were demanding masters. The best and the brightest faced the curse of high expectations. The more others expected of them, and the more they expected of themselves, the more likely it was that their reach would exceed their grasp and the outcome would be disappointment.

THE END WAS near for Joshua Armsby on June 11, 1825, and he knew it. Half a century after stage fright had blocked his plans for a life in the ministry, relegating him to farming, Armsby at eighty-two lay on his death-bed settling the last of his affairs. There was the matter of a parcel of land. Joshua had some real estate to convey. In deeds and wills New Englanders of his day identified themselves by their occupations as well as by their names, and in the past whenever Armsby had bought or sold land he had described himself as a "yeoman" or a "gentleman." Not now. For the first time in his life, on the day before his death, using the customary legal term for a clergyman, on a deed the former divinity student became "Joshua Armsby . . . clerk."[1] After decades of working his fields to make a living, after fifty years of disappointment, he would go out on his own terms. At least in his own mind, now he was what he had always wanted to be—a minister.

Establishing a satisfactory relationship with God was a common ambi-tion for the members of Harvard's revolutionary generation, but as Joshua Armsby knew all too well, nothing was more frustrating. No goal was more glorious, but in view of the Lord's inscrutability, no outcome was more uncertain. Who was rash enough, after all, to feel assured of God's final judgment? Hope and insecurity characterized most relationships with the divine, and it was not a good idea to be very confident about the future.

The religious ambitions of the members of the revolutionary generation took two forms: service and salvation. From their earliest days the men had learned that Christians had a duty to do the Lord's bidding. At the same time that the generation's members attempted to promote the spiritual interests of their neighbors, they yearned for their own salvation. In the last analysis, there was no way to know whether they had achieved either end. Faithful men and women did their best to serve the Lord, but how were they to learn whether they had done enough? Had they glorified God through their service? Only the Lord knew the answer. By the same token, when a man or woman was alive, the Lord in His inscrutability never offered a clue to a sinner's fate. If there were a logic to the divine decision process, it lay beyond mortal ken. All one could do was to conduct the Lord's business and await the day of final judgment.

Most of the members of the generation who became actively involved in serving the Lord were Congregationalist ministers. Only a few Congregationalist laymen performed substantial service of any kind to God. The number of the generation's Episcopalians and Universalists who actively served their faith was also negligible. Among the revolutionary genera-tion's 204 men, there were thirty-five clergymen or would-be clergymen, the majority of whom spent their entire adult lives in the Congregationalist parish ministry.[2] Many of them had long and apparently rewarding settle-ments. Consider Charles Stearns, whose contented tenure in Lincoln lasted more than four decades, or Jabez Chickering, who gently ministered to the Second Church in Dedham from 1776 to 1812. Throughout the Reverend John Clarke's nineteen-year settlement, the congregation of Boston's First Church regularly acclaimed his elegant sermons and genteel manner.[3] Only twenty-seven of the thirty-five aspiring clergymen were ever formally in-stalled over a church, however, and their average tenure—30.7 years—combines settlements of various lengths and different levels of mutual satisfaction.[4] For example, compare the shortest pastorate, that of Daniel Adams, who died of dysentery less than five serene months after the Con-gregational church in Watertown settled him in 1778,[5] with the longest, that of pugnacious Jeremiah Barnard, who endured fifty-four sometimes stormy years in Amherst, New Hampshire, where he battled with the town over pay and other issues.[6]

Where a ministry thrived, a clergyman served God by effectively serving his congregation. Through preaching, prayer, counseling, ritual, and moral instruction a pastor nourished his parishioners' spiritual health. Many of the best settlements left very little actual evidence of their character. In fact, silence—the absence of a written record of conflict—can suggest a healthy congregation. Jonathan French, who served Andover's South Par-ish for thirty-six years, and David Osgood, Medford's preacher for forty-eight years, both seem to have had such ministries.[7]

In contrast, by almost any temporal standard more than one settlement in four did not work out. Problems such as Jeremiah Barnard's marred them. Lassitude, parish tensions, a poor match between a clergyman and a congregation, disputes over compensation, or personal problems undercut them, leaving the spiritual needs of a community unmet and both a pastor and his people unsatisfied. Josiah Badcock's tenure in Andover, New Hamp-shire, ended and he turned to farming when, after twenty-seven years, much of his congregation, nearly anesthetized by his uninspiring preaching, melted away, leaving the residue incapable of supporting him.[8] Joseph Ha-ven stayed on too long in Rochester, New Hampshire; membership rose rapidly almost immediately after the church called a younger and more passionate preacher as a ministerial colleague near the close of his forty-nine-year settlement.[9] Benjamin Thurston squabbled in 1800 with the town

meeting of North Hampton, New Hampshire, over his salary; when it refused him a $100 raise, he quit.[10] In Haverhill, John Shaw, Abigail Adams's
brother-in-law, developed a drinking problem that polluted both his ministry and his family life.[11] Meanwhile, both John Eliot at Boston's New North
Church and John Bradford at the First Church in Roxbury, bored by their
congregations and by the ministry in general, devoted less and less attention to their positions, although neither resigned his office. Having lost
interest in his calling, each man spent more energy on social and cultural
activities than on his church. Belles lettres did not pay enough to be anything more than a hobby, but for both men their literary efforts were their
real passion.[12] Whether explicitly or tacitly, all seven men effectively conceded the failure of their ambition to serve the Lord as well as their ultimate
dissatisfaction with the ministry.

As for the rest of the revolutionary generation's clergymen, none of them
left his reflections on his ministry, so contemporary reports constitute the
best surviving evidence about these pastorates. One observer "found the
grief universal" in Boston after John Clarke died of a seizure while deliver-
ing a sermon on April 1, 1798.[13] The town of Lincoln erected a monument
in grateful memory of Charles Stearns's long ministry there.[14] And Moses
Hale's sudden death in Boxford at thirty-seven in 1786 was "a shocking loss
. . . to his people."[15] Whether or not these men felt satisfied with their ministries, at least their congregations considered them successful.

As difficult as it was to measure the success of service to the Lord, it was
infinitely easier than trying to gauge something even more urgent: the
prospects for salvation. In the reformed Protestant tradition to which the
Congregationalist members of the generation belonged, no ambition was of
greater concern and none was more vexing.

The best evidence of a personal quest for salvation dates from the undergraduate years. Sam Phillips's fragmentary college journal, a rare surviving
example of a student's spiritual diary, reveals his hopes for his relationship
with God. The anguish he felt in March 1770 in the aftermath of the Boston
Massacre as he struggled to come to terms with the sudden deaths of the
five American demonstrators slain by the town's British garrison exposed
the religious yearnings of this sensitive young man. Phillips's parents were
intensely devout, and their faith became his as well. As he took periodic
readings of his spiritual health during his junior and senior years, he hoped
that the "Being who has Power in his Hands would . . . take me Captive at
his Will."[16]

In itself, the mere desire to submit to God was not enough. By June 1770
Sam was worried: "Three long months have elapsed, and not one Word said
of the Case with my Soul. Shocking Reflection. Had my Body been Labour-

ing under any Disorder nothing so dangerous, how would the most prudent Caution, and diligent Care have been exercised for its Safety? And yet the distemper that threatens my Soul are [sic] far more alarming, as they in themselves have a greater Tendency to work it's Ruin; and as it's Ruin would be infinitely more terrible than the fall of the frail Tabernacle." As late as September, at the close of the journal's surviving fragment, Phillips still harbored grave doubts about his fate: "I find in me a great share of unbelief; I have often Scruples and Doubts of Christ's Death & Sufferings; of God's Power & Holiness; I find that my Heart takes no Relish in the Service & Worship of God, but is rather pleased & delighted [by] the sensual Enjoyments."[17] If Sam ever established the kind of relationship with God for which he yearned, it happened after the close of his undergraduate journal.

At about the same time that Sam Phillips was struggling to come to terms with God, Daniel Chaplin began to hope that he and the Lord had arrived at just such an understanding. In March 1769, during his freshman year, Chaplin made a public profession of his faith. A personal covenant, to which he committed himself shortly after graduation in 1772, further nourished his relationship with God. Daniel resolved "to keep one day in every month, when my circumstances will admit of it, as a day of fasting and prayer, more especially to seek unto God for ministerial gifts and graces, for direction and assistance in all spiritual life, and for the enlargement of Christ's kingdom in the world."[18]

Of the entire generation, no one was more certain of the strength of his relationship with God—or more optimistic about his prospects for life after death—than its most spiritually eccentric member, William Scales.[19] A charity scholar from frontier Maine who waited on tables at Commons in order to pay his way through school, Scales as a student developed a passionate antipathy toward his well-heeled classmates, a sentiment he expressed in religious terms: "As soon as I entered college, it seemed to me, that I was in the midst of young devils. Nor could I perceive the least spark of sobriety among the Collegians: Profaneness and obscenity were their chief conversation. . . . Nor is it to be wondered at; for they to whom the care of them was intrusted, were proud and lifted up, in whose minds the grace of GOD could not enter."[20]

After graduation, William returned to Maine, where he allied variously with the Quakers and the Shakers, eventually becoming an impoverished itinerant preacher. He lived on freewill contributions and was at one point an unwelcome squatter on property belonging to classmate Jemmy Bowdoin.[21]

God was within, not in the polished preaching of a settled, salaried clergy, as far as Scales was concerned: "True religion is not known through the excellency of a man's wisdom, but in demonstration of the spirit and power.... They who are the real disciples of CHRIST ... *are sealed with the Holy Spirit of promise*, as Paul hath it: that *they have drunk into that Spirit*: that *they are led by him*, and *the same mind is in them as in* JESUS CHRIST."[22] If such an influence rested in anyone's heart it was, not surprisingly, most apparent to William in his own.

Contemporaries eventually dismissed Scales as a "Crazy Shaker,"[23] a verdict with which he did not take issue. William conceded publicly that he suffered from "insanity, or a fracture in the intellect."[24] His faith and his mental imbalance both revealed themselves during occasional disruptive trips back to Harvard, including commencement in 1794, when he was ejected from the Yard for calling out during the ceremony and trying to address the audience.[25]

Classmates might not covet the particulars of Scales's direct conversation with God, but there could be no doubt that William was persuaded of its validity. In his troubled mind, if in no one else's, he had a genuine relationship with the Lord. Nothing could have mattered more to him. As far as anyone can tell, he was satisfied with this conversation, although it is hard to believe that anyone would have traded places with him.

In the end, there was no way to know whether most men were either successful or satisfied in their service to God. With respect to a man's relationship to the Lord, a Harvard education provided no particular advantage. Like all New Englanders, the members of the revolutionary generation went to their graves unsure of what lay in store for them.

THE HEREAFTER was the ultimate concern of everyone who dreamed of an intimate relationship with God. Wasn't salvation the reward for anyone who truly came to know the Lord? But goals frequently took other forms. For many fathers ambitious for their children, sons and daughters often became the chief source of satisfaction. Most fathers wanted the best for their children, and some men even saw them as their own best chance for a certain form of immortality. As parents they had three goals. Children should bring them credit, avoid discredit, and carry on the family name.

Reflected credit was one reward for the proud parents of accomplished children, one that steered the ambitions of many members of the generation. Sometimes a son followed directly in the footsteps of his father. Jack Warren ensured that his eldest boy, John Collins Warren, would receive the best available medical education. In 1815, when the younger Warren succeeded his late father as Hersey Professor of Anatomy and Surgery at Harvard Medical School, he was literally taking up Jack's burden. John C. Warren held the chair until 1847, thirty-two years after his father's death, perpetu-ating what had already become by then an important medical dynasty.[26]

Sam Jennison, who had abandoned his family, nevertheless took pride in the achievements of his third child, Samuel Jr. Notwithstanding Sam's ab-sence, Samuel Jr., grew up to be one of the leading men of Worcester, Massachusetts. As the cashier, or operational head, of a bank, the younger Jennison personally signed all the notes it circulated. When a Worcester $20 bill reached Thomaston, Maine, where Sam Sr. lived, he proudly claimed the cashier as his son. "It was, at first doubted, that you was a Connexion of mine," Sam wrote his son a few days later. The citizens of Thomaston had difficulty accepting their troubled neighbor as the father of a man of consequence. Sam produced a letter from his son, though, and "a comparison of hands (writing) dispell'd every doubt and procur'd me many complimentary Congratulations."[27]

The opposite of reflected credit was reflected blame. A child's fall from grace might embarrass his father. Thus family ambitions often included the hope that a son or daughter not disappoint.

John Trumbull's only child was an illegitimate son, born in 1792 to a servant of one of his brothers eight years before John's marriage to another woman. Trumbull accepted responsibility, but at the cost of considerable emotional distress when the youth, John Trumbull Ray, acquired an en-sign's commission in the British army. As war threatened between the United States and Great Britain in 1811, the king's army was no place for an American citizen, and certainly not for the son of the leading painter of the American Revolution. "You have chosen, of all times, to enter the British Army at the moment when a war with America is almost inevitable: and when of course your entering the military service of [Great Britain] may be regarded, & perhaps justly as an Act of Treason to your native Country," Trumbull urgently wrote his son. "I should hope that you would not will-ingly expose me to those accusations [that friends of President James Mad-ison's administration] will not fail to ground upon such a step."[28]

The best way to ensure that a son honored both himself and his family was to make certain that he clearly understood what was expected of him. Through a firm set of written instructions, Eliphalet Pearson left his way-ward son, Henry, no room for misunderstanding: " 'Take not the name of the Lord thy God in vain'; indulge no resentment against any one in the [college] government, not even in thought; reverence your superiors, and obey the laws; apply diligently to your College duties . . . daily and deeply humble yourself before God for the pride of your heart, & for your recent heinous offences; [pray] the God of mercy to give you a just sense of all your sins, & to grant you repentance and a humble mind."[29]

For wealthy and well-born Jemmy Bowdoin, success's bar turned out to be set very high. His father posed the original challenge. The family's ambition: to ensure the survival of the Bowdoin lineage.

Before the death of Governor James Bowdoin in 1790, Jemmy made him a solemn promise. Governor Bowdoin was concerned about the future of the family line, and Jemmy, his only son, was childless, although he had been married for nearly ten years. If Jemmy failed to produce a male heir to continue the Bowdoin house, he agreed to pick the son of a relative, "a young man of worth & of good reputation, to bear up his name." Jemmy's designated heir would receive most of his estate, much as James Ivers had inherited his uncle Barlow's property after assuming the surname Trecothick in 1771.[30]

Jemmy took one step to secure the family name in 1794, the year that he gave $1,000 and one thousand acres of Maine land to the school that became Bowdoin College in honor of his father.[31] Through many additional gifts to the school he ensured that the Bowdoins would be recognized long after he was gone. Still, support for the institution did not directly address Governor Bowdoin's concerns. Although Jemmy's munificence perpetuated the Bowdoin name, it did not extend the family lineage.[32]

Not until 1803, when Jemmy and his wife, Sarah, were about fifty, did he take steps to keep the Bowdoin estate within his father's line. Elizabeth Bowdoin, Jemmy's only sibling, had made a good match before the Revolution, and over the years she had borne a surplus of sons—grandsons of the governor. Her husband, Sir John Temple, though an American by birth, had spent his entire career in the British Customs Service, ensuring his loyalty to the crown at the outbreak of the War for Independence. James Bowdoin Temple, Elizabeth's and John's second son and a junior officer in the British army, already carried the family name, though not as a surname. Would he consider reversing the order of his middle and last names? If so, the Bowdoin inheritance would make the change worth his while.

Jemmy wrote to his nephew in 1803 outlining the situation and offering him a deal. The family inheritance came with four conditions: Temple had to give up his British military commission, move to Massachusetts, petition the General Court for permission to adopt the Bowdoin surname, and take an oath of allegiance to the United States. The Bowdoins were a Massachusetts family, and a Massachusetts family they would remain. The estate would not be transferred until after Jemmy's death, but in order to enable his nephew to marry well and begin to sire sons promptly, Bowdoin offered James an immediate annual stipend of $1,000. Temple accepted the proposition readily, and in 1805 the General Court approved his petition for a change of name.[33]

If the future of the Bowdoin name and fortune appeared secure in 1805, however, there were still some unforeseen hurdles to clear. Although Jemmy did not acknowledge them, there were already signs that his prospective heir was struggling with second thoughts about certain conditions of the offer. It turned out that altering his name from James Bowdoin Temple to James Temple Bowdoin also meant dramatically changing his way of life, and it took him awhile to come to grips with the full magnitude of this step. Temple was slow to give up his army commission and even slower to move to Massachusetts.[34]

For a time, Jemmy found it convenient to write to his nephew, still in England, with orders to fill for a small boat or a plow or a length of railing to enclose his fruit yard in Boston with a light iron balustrade. Bowdoin's cheerful and engaging letters to his nephew were filled with plans for updating his house and grounds, property that the young man would eventually inherit. Since young James would occupy the residence one day, Jemmy was solicitous about his nephew's tastes and preferences. Eventually, however, Jemmy began to feel uneasy about the repeated delays. Young James did not marry until the spring of 1808, and the newlyweds did not reach Boston until the fall of the year, more than five years after Jemmy had first extended his offer.[35]

Once the couple arrived, it took no more than a few months for everyone to conclude that there was a serious problem. Neither young James nor his bride was happy with what they found. To them, Boston appeared desperately unrefined, a minor provincial backwater compared with the much larger, trend-setting metropolises of Great Britain. Far from their families, their friends, and their accustomed diversions, the newlyweds were slow to warm to their new surroundings. Before long, James and his wife began to talk of returning to England.[36]

As far as Jemmy was concerned, this would not do at all. On February 27, 1809, in the most determined language he could muster, he laid down the law to his nephew. "My original propositions to you were grounded upon no equivocal duties," he instructed, "nor on your part, did I suppose, that they rested on an equivocal acceptance." Young James would not be permitted "to frustrate my father's wishes & my own expectations!" Jemmy could not imprison his prospective heir. There were no penitentiaries for would-be inheritors with second thoughts. James was free to "pursue that course which upon mature reflection, shall best comport with your future interest & happiness." If he chose to return to England, however, everything would revert "as nearly as possible to the state, as though you had neither changed your name or situation." Then there would be no inheritance for James. Bowdoin would settle it on another heir.[37]

Jemmy could not have been more blunt. The most important responsibilities his father had placed in him, the disposition of his estate and the survival of the Bowdoin name, now hung in the balance. His pledge to his father, his duty to his family, his own ambitions, and the legacy that was entrusted to him were all on the line. Nothing meant more to Jemmy.

Faced with a choice between certain wealth and an uncertain future, the new James Temple Bowdoin and his wife reluctantly opted for the estate.[38] Governor Bowdoin's wishes would be fulfilled. The family name would survive. The property would remain in Massachusetts securely in Bowdoin hands. And Jemmy could breathe a sigh of relief, his obligations met, his ambitions achieved.

In case of another change of heart for James, though, Jemmy took precautions. He designated as additional heirs four more distant relatives on whom he also settled handsome bequests in exchange for adopting the Bowdoin surname. It seemed best not to leave such an important matter to chance.[39]

Governor Bowdoin had set his son a more difficult task than either had imagined in 1790. If Jemmy felt more relieved than satisfied in the spring of 1809, it was understandable. Neither relief nor satisfaction, however, was an apt description of the mood of John Trumbull in 1809, or for that matter at any other time.

IN THE SPRING of 1794, at the age of thirty-seven and at the height of his powers as an artist, John Trumbull set aside his oils and his brushes in favor of concurrent careers as a diplomat and a merchant. For the next half-dozen years, Trumbull had nothing to do with the calling to which he had devoted himself so single-mindedly since childhood. Then in 1800, recommitted to painting he returned to his easel.

The artist, who was among the most celebrated and accomplished members of his college generation, was also among the least satisfied with his own achievements. Cursed with impossible expectations for himself, he struggled with his ambitions more than any of his college contemporaries. If any member of Harvard's revolutionary generation can be said to have experienced a midlife career crisis, it was John Trumbull.

For most members of the revolutionary generation, the recipe for success and satisfaction in daily life called for varying combinations of power, wealth, and recognition. Some men clung to the ambitions they had brought to college. If a man was satisfied with local prominence—perhaps as a selectman or a deacon—then he was as likely to achieve it after the Revolution as he would have been before the war. The opportunities that developed in the 1780s and 1790s inspired many to strive for more, however, and the more ambitious a man became, the more difficult it was to achieve his goals. Like Trumbull, a small number struggled to leave society a permanent legacy as evidence that their lives had made a difference.

The boys who grew up in the most modest circumstances tended to be the most satisfied with their accomplishments. A childhood on a farm or in a craftsman's shop offered a simple standard for comparison. For instance, how could callow Levi Lincoln, who set out from his father's Hingham farm in his early teens intending to become a blacksmith, have envisioned as a boy a life that included a college education, admission to the bar, appointment as attorney general of the United States, and the acting governorship of Massachusetts, as well as an opportunity (which he declined) to sit on the United States Supreme Court?[40] Some of these posts had not even existed when he was charting a course for himself as a youth. In Groton's parsonage, meanwhile, as the autumn of life turned to winter, Daniel Chaplin must have wondered at the developments that had transported him from his father's unassuming Rowley farmstead to the pulpit of a substantial parish, respected and beloved throughout his community.[41] And then there was Jacob Welsh, the son of a Boston jeweler, who satisfied his yearnings for recognition in 1820 by founding a town in Geauga County, Ohio, thirty miles from present-day Cleveland, and naming it Welshfield after himself.[42]

Trumbull's case was quite another matter, however. This was, after all, the man who had angrily resigned his colonel's commission at age twenty when he concluded that Congress had compromised his honor. As the son of a governor and a man born into the highest tier of Connecticut society, he had the loftiest of expectations for himself. He wanted to leave the United States a permanent cultural legacy. His ambition to become the preeminent painter of the American Revolution encompassed two subordinate objectives. On the one hand, he sought to consecrate the pivotal experience of his generation, "to preserve and diffuse the memory of the noblest series of Actions which have ever presented themselves in the History of Man," as he grandly told Thomas Jefferson in 1789.[43] In fact, in the end Trumbull gave the nation a series of visual icons as a personal and enduring legacy.[44] On the other hand, through his paintings he longed to secure his own immortality. By capturing the essence of the glorious cause on canvas, he would go down in history as the great artist whose work best embodied the American spirit.

Men with ambitions as elevated as John Trumbull's are difficult to please. Was there any way for someone like him to feel successful and satisfied short of stellar achievements, the sort that resulted in a timeless reputation?

Trumbull's early accomplishments gave him every reason to believe that his objectives were within reach. In 1785, while still living in London, he painted the first two works in a projected series of thirteen.[45] The first, *The Death of General Warren at the Battle of Bunker's Hill, June 17, 1775*, received an ecstatic response. Caught up in his enthusiasm over the tableau, Benjamin West, Trumbull's mentor, effusively called it the "best picture" ever painted of a modern battle scene.[46] And Abigail Adams, who was in London accompanying her husband, John, the American ambassador to the Court of St. James's, went to see the painting and was stunned by its power: "My whole frame contracted, my Blood Shivered & I felt faintness at my Heart."[47] The second work in the series, *The Death of General Montgomery in the Attack on Quebec, December 31, 1775*, also won plaudits from those who ventured to a London gallery to view it.[48] Trumbull's reception from open-minded British art connoisseurs was all he could have wished.

Yet as John continued his work, the cheers began to fade. In London, the excitement that his first pictures generated waned as his subsequent efforts seemed less and less novel. To his despair, moreover, the American audience on which he depended to make his series a paying proposition proved to have short memories and little interest in his project.

Between 1786 and 1789 Trumbull began three more major paintings. Two of them belonged to his series on the American Revolution: *The Declaration of Independence, July 4, 1776* and *The Surrender of Lord Cornwallis at Yorktown, October 19, 1781*. The third, intended to appeal specifically to a British audience, was a scene from a recent military engagement, *The Sortie Made by the Garrison at Gibraltar*, which depicted a battle in 1781 between redcoats and Spanish troops. John also arranged for engravings of his first two important paintings—of the battles of Bunker Hill and Quebec. Unlike his early efforts, however, his depiction of the action at Gibraltar met with little interest in London when he exhibited it in the spring of 1789.[49] As disturbing as this development was, even worse news awaited at home.

In order to advance his series—and also to secure subscriptions for the engravings of his first two paintings—Trumbull returned to the United States in November 1789. Over the next four years he traveled the Atlantic coast between New Hampshire and South Carolina making studies of the scenes and individuals he planned to portray in subsequent works. Although his progress on the series was substantial, he was stunned by the indifference he encountered. A decade after independence most Americans were no longer interested in their country's origins: "Wherever I went I offered my subscription book, but wretched now was the success, and rapidly decreasing the enthusiasm for my national work."[50]

Trumbull had sunk significant amounts of time and money into his series of Revolutionary War paintings, and now it appeared that it would be difficult to recover either investment. More to the point, he had also wagered his dreams of honor and recognition on the reception he anticipated for his works. If Americans were uninspired by his paintings, then his prospects for artistic immortality were dead.

Shaken by the public's tepid response, John questioned his future as an artist. In the spring of 1794, when John Jay offered him a place as his personal secretary in the American delegation to negotiate an important treaty with the crown, Trumbull seized the moment. Who cared that he was at the peak of his artistic abilities if no one bothered to look at his paintings? Perhaps diplomacy would afford him recognition. As time allowed, on the side he conducted a bit of trade on his own account.[51]

Trumbull's existential crisis ended in 1800, when he returned to his studio.[52] Painting, still a source of personal pleasure, could also make a name for him, he persuaded himself, if he redoubled his efforts. Somehow, he would achieve the immortality he craved.

Like Trumbull, a number of other apparently successful members of the revolutionary generation struggled to find contentment. Fisher Ames was one. Fisher never felt a strong personal commitment to the law, notwithstanding years of success at the bar. The satisfaction that eluded him as an attorney he found in public service.[53] Ames was among the members of the generation whose quest for fulfillment led them eventually to equate satisfaction with a personal legacy; one way or another, they wanted to leave the world a better place. At the turn of the century there were certain widely accepted ways to achieve this end. There were also some controversial ones, as Ames discovered.

Ames, Levi Lincoln, and Jemmy Bowdoin all took up farming in their later years, thinking that society at large might be the ultimate beneficiary. If the agriculture they now pursued had been that of their childhood, then no one but their own families would have been the better for their efforts. It was, however, a new, scientific agriculture—agronomy—that captured their imagination at the turn of the century.[54]

Agricultural improvement efforts were not unique to New England, or even native to the region. Decades before New Englanders took up the cause, many of Britain's great landowners began to experiment with ways to increase the quality and yield of their harvests.[55] With such origins, the movement for scientific agriculture held a double attraction for men such as Ames, Lincoln, and Bowdoin. Cachet combined with practical advantages. At the same time that they were attempting to improve New England's food stocks, they might emulate the great lords of the mother country.

There were as many ways to improve New England's harvests as there were crops. Fisher Ames, whose Dedham farm lay only about ten miles from Boston, focused on garden crops, meat, butter, and other perishables for rapid sale in the capital's markets. In contrast, farther from major population centers, Lincoln in western Worcester County and Bowdoin on Naushon in the Elizabeth Islands both paid special attention to merino sheep, which each man imported and bred in an attempt to develop superior wool-bearing strains. As far as they and New England's other scientific farmers of the day were concerned, the specific crop was less important than the approach to farming. Scientific farmers experimented with seeds, planting schedules, fertilizer, feed, cross-breeding, and a variety of other innovative techniques in order to improve production, then pooled their information with like-minded men. In theory, the most successful innovations would eventually trickle down from the gentlemen farmers responsible for them to the agricultural populace at large and make a contribution to the national well-being.

Agricultural societies were the principal means of communication. The Massachusetts Society for Promoting Agriculture, founded in 1792 on the model of England's Bath and West Society, was the preserve of gentleman farmers interested in agricultural improvement; Jemmy Bowdoin was a founding trustee of the society, on whose board he sat until 1795. Even Tom Coffin, serving the crown in Quebec, was in contact with them; in the late 1790s he shared both information and seeds with the organization.[56] By 1818, when agricultural improvers in central Massachusetts established the Worcester Agricultural Society, Levi Lincoln was generally recognized as his county's most prominent scientific farmer. The new society's members elected Lincoln president, an office he occupied until his death in 1820.[57]

Scientific farming failed to achieve the advances at the turn of the century that its practitioners envisioned for it. For Ames, Lincoln, and Bowdoin, agriculture remained at best a break-even proposition. Notwithstanding their disappointments, they saw in agronomy a genteel opportunity to serve the public good. If their efforts were unsuccessful, at least their contemporaries recognized the public spirit that underlay them. Other efforts to create a public legacy were more controversial.

THE PASSIONS that divided party men, both political and ecclesiastical, in the late eighteenth and early nineteenth centuries drew frequently on personal aspirations, but it would be a mistake to characterize their motivations as entirely self-serving. Many of the most partisan members of the revolutionary generation continued to fight for their causes long after their public careers had ended. Even after the last chance for personal advancement had disappeared, ideals remained. Party objectives were often principled ones, too.

Consider the public career of Fisher Ames. The consumption that compelled Ames to leave Congress in 1797 affected him for the rest of his life, forcing him into semiretirement on his Dedham farm. Fisher's strength waxed and waned, but he was never able to recapture the sustained health and energy that had allowed him to become an influential officeholder and an admired orator. Members of the Governor's Council had undemanding roles, and Fisher held a seat on the body for two years, 1799–1801, but these were his last terms in any public office. Prevented by his lack of strength from taking an active role in government, Ames nevertheless remained the Federalist Party's most articulate public voice through the essays he contributed to sympathetic periodicals as well as through his share in the ownership of the *New England Palladium.*

Ames's Federalist vision for American society—ordered, refined, and commercial—was controversial. Political opponents reviled Fisher and disparaged his objectives. Theirs was a more turbulent and meritocratic image of America's future. Nonetheless, Ames's opinions were an honest expression of his dreams for American society long after he was gone. In 1825 Daniel Chaplin's dreams extended only as far as the Groton town line, but like Fisher Ames, in the face of controversy he tried to secure his vision of the future.

By 1825 it was difficult to see how New England's orthodox Congregationalists and liberal Christians, or Unitarians, would ever be able to cooperate with each other. The differences at Harvard over the appointment of the Hollis Professor of Divinity had escalated and spread, reaching into parishes throughout the region. Seminaries, missionary societies, and ministerial conferences promoted the partisan aims of each bloc. In Dedham's First Parish, meanwhile, a dispute between the two factions in 1819 over calling a minister permanently ruptured the congregation. A similar controversy struck in Groton in 1825.

During the afternoon service in Groton on Sunday, July 10, 1825, Daniel Chaplin fainted in the pulpit. Daniel was eighty-one years old and still a large and imposing man. Some even thought he resembled George Washington. His health was failing, however, and he was going deaf.[58] Parishioners helped their pastor home. He never preached in Groton's meetinghouse again.

In order to meet the needs of his community, Chaplin required help. Under normal circumstances, Congregational churches in such a situation would call a younger man as a colleague in the same way that the church in Rochester, New Hampshire, provided assistance for Joseph Haven. Depending on the older man's health, the two colleagues might share in the pastoral duties at first. Over time, though, the responsibilities would pass to the

younger man. Eventually, the senior minister would die or grow too enfee-
bled to continue, leaving the younger man to carry on alone.

Such gradual transitions worked as long as everyone agreed on what
qualities were desirable in a junior colleague. In Groton in 1825, however,
there was a serious difference of opinion. Although the members of the
congregation continued to love and respect Chaplin personally, the majority
was diverging from him theologically. Chaplin wanted to shape his community's spiritual life even after he was gone. But the orthodox course he
wished to set for Groton ran counter to the liberal wishes of the preponder-
ance of his parishioners.

As the sturdy granite of New England Congregationalism began to
crack in the early nineteenth century, Daniel had made a series of public
choices. He had been a founding member of the Massachusetts Society for
Promoting Christian Knowledge, an orthodox association, as early as 1803,
and in 1825 it was no secret where his sympathies lay. Several weeks after
Chaplin's collapse, John Todd, a recent graduate of the Andover Theological Seminary, appeared in Groton to help him, it seemed, without a formal
invitation. Chaplin and Groton's orthodox minority described Todd's arrival as "providential." To the liberal majority, however, it "was evidently one
of those *prepared* providences, which so often occur in human affairs."[59]

After a brief probationary period, Chaplin and the orthodox faction concluded that Todd was satisfactory in every respect. They attempted to
ordain and install him. Meanwhile, a town meeting dominated by the liberal
majority established a committee to supply the pulpit. Its choice, Charles
Robinson, was a recent Harvard A.B. who had followed his baccalaureate
degree with graduate training at Harvard Divinity School, the Unitarians'
seminary.

Months of meetings failed to produce an acceptable compromise. At one
evening gathering the candles flickered and blew out, turning the room
pitch black. Three volumes of church records disappeared before the light
was restored. Each party called on outside sympathizers, who issued predictable denunciations of the opposition. By late 1826, with no accord in
sight, the division of the congregation in two seemed inevitable. On November 1 the liberal faction ordained and installed Robinson; later the same
month the orthodox side established its own church, which ordained and
installed Todd on January 3, 1827.[60]

Daniel Chaplin had tried to control Groton's religious future by imposing John Todd on the community. Instead of the legacy of religious orthodoxy that was his intention, his bequest to Groton turned out to be division
and bitterness.[61]

There was nothing easy about being one of the best and the brightest. All the advantages in life did not ensure success, to say nothing of satisfaction. Education, contacts, and opportunities encouraged men to dream, but all too often their reach exceeded their grasp, leaving them defeated and frustrated. Think of James Sheafe and Eliphalet Pearson, successful men by most standards but thwarted in their last campaigns for high office. Or think of John Trumbull, Fisher Ames, and Daniel Chaplin, their successes overshadowed in their own minds by their failures.

They were victims of the curse of high expectations. Favored and talented, they had answered every accomplishment with a new wish list. Why did success so often fail to lead to satisfaction?

9

THE LAST GREAT CHANGE

THE SEASON was growing late, and David Stinson, a Harvard College junior, did not yet have all of his heavy clothing with him at school. Sometime around December 1, 1769, Stinson went home to Georgetown, a brawling, timber-shipping town of about 1,400 on the Maine coast at the mouth of the Kennebec River, for the supplies that he needed to carry himself through a snowy Cambridge winter. His plan was to return to college after spending a week with his family. He would travel back to school by means of a small coasting vessel out of the port of Falmouth, now the city of Portland.[1]

Shortly after leaving the dock on the return to Boston, however, while David's craft was still in Falmouth Harbor, it glanced off a submerged rock. The crew went below to inspect for damage; no leaks were apparent, so the coaster continued out toward open water. Suddenly, while it was still in Casco Bay, near enough to be within sight of the shore on a fair day, the weather closed in. A harsh, icy wind rose from the west, quickly beating the waves to a froth, and the pitching vessel started to take on seawater in torrents through an expanding gash where the hull had struck the underwater hazard. Frigid brine gushed through the growing rupture too fast for the vessel's pump to keep pace. The schooner began to list badly. It was going down. "For God's sake," the captain cried, "take to the boat!"

Terrified, Stinson and the crew, five souls in all, found themselves at the mercy of the storm in a leaky, overcrowded open lifeboat. There was no help in sight. It was the dead of night now, and thrashing waves tossed them about wildly, continually pushing them away from the coast. Soon one of their two oars snapped, making it difficult to steer the craft, much less to row for land.

Before the seas calmed and the boat reached safety the next morning after hours in peril, two of its occupants died of exposure, a cabin boy and Stinson. At the time of his death on December 9, David was twenty-five years old.[2]

DAVID STINSON was the first member of Harvard's revolutionary generation to die, the only one while still an undergraduate. He was not the youngest to perish, however, nor was he alone for very long. As one member of the generation later remarked: "Death is the common lot of mankind. There is no discharge in that war."[3] In the eighteenth century, the end often came early, at least by modern standards. It never came by surprise at any stage from infancy to old age. Life was fragile, and if they were honest with themselves, the men of Stinson's college generation admitted that most of them would probably not survive much past sixty to see its winter. The likelihood of lasting to a ripe old age was "so very small," Jack Warren recognized in 1801, when he was forty-seven, that it was a waste of time to worry about it.[4]

Reliable statistics for colonial America are hard to come by, but existing studies paint a consistent picture of adult male mortality. If only those who reached adulthood are taken into account, it appears that during the eighteenth century, on average, American males died at some point in their fifties or early sixties—in some populations, in fact, in their early fifties.[5] Of course, averages can combine very different values: some individuals lived into their seventies, eighties, nineties, and occasionally even beyond one hundred, but many more died in their twenties, thirties, and forties.

Harvardians were as susceptible to the perils of life as less favored men, and throughout the eighteenth century their experiences were not very different from those of their contemporaries. The median member of the Harvard classes of 1721 through 1724 died at the age of 59.5. A quarter of a century later, for the men who attended the college in the classes of 1746 through 1749, the median age at death was 56. The average age at death in each instance was several years below the median—56.9 for the classes of 1721 through 1724, 53.5 for the classes of 1746 through 1749.[6] Education, relative affluence, adequate diets, and (in most cases) occupations that were not particularly hazardous bought many Harvard men several extra years, but these advantages saw relatively few of them very far into old age. About two-thirds of them died before they reached the age of 70. Only one in eight attained the age of 80.[7]

The story was much the same for the members of Harvard's revolutionary generation. The median age at death (62.5) and the average age at death (57.4) reveal that at about the same time many of these men started to relinquish posts of prominence and power and step out of the limelight, their numbers began to dwindle rapidly. Nearly one-fifth of the men died in their sixties and another one-fifth in their seventies. Like their Harvard predecessors, fewer than one in three remained alive by the age of 70, and fewer than one in seven lived to the age of 80.[8] More often than not, death came before a man reached old age, whether one equates that season of life with the feebleness and dependence of the superannuated or with the more gentle decline in energy and abilities that is often apparent at some point in the sixties, at about the age that modern Americans commonly consider appropriate for retirement. As for those few who did survive until senescence, most died after a brief encounter with it.

Despite the most advanced medical care that early-nineteenth-century New England could provide, Jack Warren died of an inflamed lung in 1815 at sixty-one, still vigorous almost until the end.[9] He had been right not to worry about old age. John Eliot passed away in 1813 at fifty-eight, a victim of heart disease. Eliot, whose father and elder brother had died of the same cause at about the same age, accepted death with grace and resignation: "The will of the Lord be done."[10] In John Trumbull's case, an accumulation of ailments combined to take him in 1843 at the advanced age of eighty-seven. To the end, Trumbull was an angry, unhappy man.[11] After years of progressive invalidism, Fisher Ames died of consumption on July 4, 1808. He was not quite three months past his fiftieth birthday.[12]

Some mortal illnesses struck quickly—for instance, heart attacks, strokes, and certain epidemic diseases. Others took a long time to follow their course. Witness Fisher Ames's consumption, which plagued him for the last thirteen years of his life.[13]

Fragmentary surviving records for the late eighteenth and early nineteenth centuries provide an incomplete account of the causes of death among the members of Harvard's revolutionary generation, but David Stinson's case was clearly uncommon in one important respect: accidental and violent deaths were rare. Although recent college graduates, because of their age, were prime candidates for military service beginning in 1775, the Revolution was not a deadly experience for many members of the college's classes of the early 1770s. Notwithstanding the seven service-related deaths that the revolutionary generation suffered, its members were only about as likely to die by the age of thirty as those of the classes of 1721 through 1724, and only half as likely as the members of the classes of 1746 through 1749. Accidental drownings, shipwrecks, and falls (the last typically among the elderly) took only eleven lives.[14] There were also three suicides and a fourth attempt.[15]

When death came in the late eighteenth and early nineteenth centuries, it usually resulted from lingering, often chronic illnesses for which the answers of contemporary medical science were inadequate. To be sure, the revolutionary generation lost men to epidemic threats such as "camp fever" or typhus,[16] dysentery,[17] influenza,[18] malaria,[19] smallpox,[20] and yellow fever.[21] Indeed, the incomplete state of mortality records may conceal other deaths due to epidemics. Consumption (tuberculosis), heart disease, and strokes, however, were almost certainly the most common causes of death.

Jemmy Bowdoin battled bad health, particularly asthma, throughout his adult years. First stricken with serious illness at about the age of eighteen during his senior year of college (his trip to England in 1771 was undertaken in part for his health), he suffered repeatedly from various ailments over the next four decades. Chronic sickness made military service impossible during the Revolution, and it still plagued him thirty years later on his aborted diplomatic mission to Spain. Once he reached fifty, failing eyesight limited his reading to volumes with large, clear type.[22] By the summer of 1811, worn out from years of disease, Bowdoin was obviously in failing health. In June, Jemmy told his wife, Sarah, "that October or November would he expected terminate his course here, that he should acquiesce to having the scene closed, that he did not fear to be dead, that he put his whole trust, and confidence in his God, that whatever he did would be right."[23] On October 11, seated in a Federal-style easy chair in his bedroom at his country home on Naushon in the Elizabeth Islands near Martha's Vineyard, Jemmy peacefully passed away. He was fifty-nine, a few years shy of the median age of death for his college contemporaries.[24] According to the arrangements he had made before his death, the bulk of his estate now passed to his nephew James Temple Bowdoin. Without his benefactor as a monitor, James, who was visiting England at the time, never returned to Massachusetts.[25] It was fortunate that Jemmy had made provisions for additional heirs to carry on the Bowdoin name.

For David Stinson, Fisher Ames, Jemmy Bowdoin, and the majority of their peers, not only did old age never come, but also, in all probability, they honestly did not expect it. Like Jack Warren, they knew that life was full of risks. Many young Harvard men were vigorous and active until the day they died. Given more effective medical care, they might have enjoyed many additional years or even decades. Perhaps all they needed was better luck. Laban Wheaton, at ninety-two the last surviving member of the revolutionary generation and the eldest at the time of his death, attributed imprecisely to "old age," lived nearly seventy-two years longer than the youngest to die, Edward Hill, a member of the class of 1772, who passed away from camp fever one month after his twentieth birthday in 1775.[26] Wheaton's death in 1846 came more than seventy-six years after David Stinson's in 1769. Absent the medical advances of a later day, death—the last great change for the members of the revolutionary generation—came not at a single, predictable stage of life but at any age.

IT IS A TRUISM that on one level, death is an individual experience. Even crowded shoulder to shoulder in a rolling, leaky lifeboat with three other men and a boy, David Stinson met his maker by himself. Most of the time, no one is more interested in a death than the deceased.

Nevertheless, on another plane, death is also a social experience. Every death takes place in many contexts and has many different social implications or meanings. Whether death came at the end of the biblical three score years and ten or decades earlier, cutting a man off before he had a chance to blossom, its social meanings were consequences of the life it concluded. Classmates mourned each passing; their letters to one another conveyed their grief that they would never see their friend again. But death at an early age had different implications than at middle age or at old age. Its repercussions were not the same for someone with a wife and small children as they were for someone who was young and without family responsibilities or aged and dependent on others. Moreover, as a consequence of his passing, a man who had touched many people through public service or commercial activities continued to affect them long after he was gone.

Death meant anguish and loss to survivors when it came before the age of responsibility, but the ripples of its impact usually did not spread very far beyond relatives and friends who were left to wonder what might have been. The passing of Nahum Cutler in his late twenties a couple of years after his graduation, the first member of the class of 1773 to die, stunned Nathaniel Walker Appleton, who only learned of it in 1776, when he saw a telltale star next to his friend's name in the college's triennial list of alumni. "Alas!" Appleton wrote to Eliphalet Pearson, Nahum's former roommate, "our good Friend *Cutler* appears first with an *Asterism* prefix'd to his Name— grant that it may be truly ominous of his being in those *starry* Regions, where there are no *Wars*, nor Rumors of Wars, but where all is *peace*, Harmony, & Happiness."[27] Cutler's classmate Theodore Parsons, lost at sea at twenty-eight when his privateer disappeared without a trace in 1779, left relatives and friends behind who refused to accept that he was dead. How could someone so young, so vibrant, and so promising be gone? For months, letters crossed the Atlantic between Theodore's worried connections, hoping in the face of growing resignation about his death that instead his vessel had been taken captive and that he was languishing somewhere in a British naval prison. More than half a year after Parsons's disappearance, in the spring of 1780 his friends listed him among the incorporators at the founding of the American Academy of Arts and Sciences. Perhaps by some miracle Theodore was still alive.[28]

Cutler and Parsons were bachelors when they died. They were young men with promising futures, but no children depended on them for support, nor had a young bride built her life around either of them. Relatives and friends missed them, even despaired over their deaths. Still, neither had yet taken on an adult's full complement of family, business, and community obligations.

The same was not true of Fisher Ames, Jack Warren, or George Inman. It is probably impossible to compile a complete census of the dependents that middle-aged members of Harvard's revolutionary generation left behind at their passing, but widows and minor children felt the loss the most intimately. In addition to the men who left dependent children at death, about one-quarter of the generation left a widow, in some cases a young mother struggling to provide for small sons and daughters, in other instances an energetic woman with years, even decades, left to live.

When Fisher Ames passed away in 1808, he left Frances, his wife of nearly sixteen years, and seven children ranging in age from fifteen to one.[29] In her grief, Frances had to find a way to provide for a large, young family. Jack and Abby Warren were the parents of nineteen children when he died after more than thirty-seven years of marriage in 1815. Their oldest children were adults by now, but their youngest was only ten years old.[30] George Inman's death from fever in 1789 at thirty-three after a decade of marriage left his wife and four small daughters destitute on the Caribbean island of Grenada. A British army officer, Inman had lived well beyond his means since he received his commission in Boston on the day of the Battle of Bunker Hill in 1775. There was nothing left for Mary Inman, who was reduced to accepting the charity of Hannah Rowe, her husband's wealthy aunt by marriage.[31]

Fisher and Jack also left their community bereft of their contributions. Ames's Federalist Party was already in steep decline at the time of his death, and it seems unlikely that he could have found a way to save it from its eventual demise. Nevertheless, when his pen was stilled, the Federalists lost one of their most articulate controversialists. No one could quite replace him. In contrast, Warren, a founding member of the faculty of the Harvard Medical School, provided a very capable successor in his eldest son, John Collins Warren.[32] Jack's death nevertheless left a void in Boston's medical community, which he had served for decades both as an educator and as an influential member of the Massachusetts Medical Society.

Death at an advanced age was yet another matter. By the time John Trumbull died at eighty-seven in 1843, his most productive period was long past. His wife, Sarah, had been dead for nineteen years, and he had no particularly close living relatives. No longer one of his nation's great painters, he had nevertheless been one for years. At the end of his life, Trumbull single-mindedly devoted his energies to ensuring a place for himself in the annals of American art.

John Trumbull was a difficult, abrasive man, filled with a volatile combination of hauteur and insecurity. Still, his death touched the American art community, which recognized that for all of Trumbull's personal shortcomings, he was nevertheless a pioneer in its world. It would not see his like again. Trumbull's "fame [was] interwoven, not merely with the history of the arts of design, but also with the political history of the country," declared Samuel F. B. Morse.[33] More than most history painters, he had lived his subject. As his friend Philip Hone concluded, Trumbull was "a distinguished man during the whole of his long life, a patriot of the Revolution, a chevalier 'sans peur et sans reproche,' a gallant soldier."[34]

ALTHOUGH PRICKLY John Trumbull had attained old age, whether or not he was fortunate to outlive his wife by nearly two decades and to die practically alone, after most of his contemporaries, is an open question. What is certain is that because so many of members of his generation were gone by their sixties, his experience was comparatively uncommon at the time. Only twenty-five members of the revolutionary generation reached the age of eighty;[35] and only six survived Trumbull.[36] Because in the early nineteenth century the majority of men barely tasted senescence if they reached it at all, as a season in the lives of the members of Harvard's revolutionary generation it reflects the most common experience to consider old age after death, not before it.

In broad outline, John Trumbull's final decades were typical of old age as his long-lived contemporaries experienced it. Over the years, his decline was gradual. There were only a few points of transition, only a few landmarks along the way. In his case, the most important of these were, first, the death of his wife, then a period of partial dependence on others, and the end of his active career as a painter. Vigorous enough to continue to work into his early eighties, Trumbull eventually lost his health and passed away.

Modern scholars sometimes differentiate between the "young-old," still independent and productive (albeit at a reduced rate), and the "old-old," increasingly feeble and dependent on others. In this distinction they echo classifications common to early Americans, who differentiated between a "green old age" and "decrepitude."[37] If one understands that an indistinct borderland, not a sharp boundary, divided the two conditions, then John Trumbull's experience bears out these categories.

Never able to save enough through his art, government service, or trade to secure his old age, Trumbull approached his sixties still forced to work to support himself and his wife. After John returned to his easel sometime around 1800 when he was in his mid-forties, he and Sarah spent time on both sides of the Atlantic looking for commissions. They remained in England until 1804, settled in New York City for the next four years, went back to England in 1808, and then returned to the United States for the final time in September 1815.

John was fifty-nine when he and Sarah made their final Atlantic crossing. He was sufficiently self-critical to recognize that he was no longer the artist he had once been. After his extended sabbatical from the palette between 1794 and 1800, although he was certainly still a capable painter, he never returned to the level of mastery he had previously attained.[38] Nor did he win back the popular acclaim that he had relished in the 1780s, when he was a young man in London bursting into the art world with his first heroic paintings of Revolutionary War scenes.

To make a living—to survive—after he resumed his brush in 1800, he had turned to portraiture, the déclassée expedient that he had disdained before when his history paintings were beginning to cause a stir. Trumbull's heart was not in this facet of his craft, and his renderings often turned out to be dark, dull, and lifeless.[39] Meanwhile, in his excessively abundant free time he began to dabble in landscapes and scenes from the Bible.[40]

Shortly after his last return from England, John turned to his past to provide for his future. The Rotunda in the United States Capitol afforded the opportunity he needed. What better place to install a series of patriotic paintings. This was the ideal setting for the scenes of the American Revolution that he had planned since the mid-1780s. Trumbull had connections, and he lobbied everyone he could think of to promote the project and win a commission for himself. There was room for eight large canvases in the Rotunda, but when the series was authorized, he was asked to do only four of them. Still, he would receive $8,000 per work. For someone who needed a way to support himself, $32,000 was a magnificent sum.[41]

Trumbull completed his commission over the course of half a dozen years, ending in 1824, when he was sixty-eight. There was nothing especially original about his work on the Rotunda series, nor did his artistry match his previous high standards. Two of the paintings he submitted, *The Declaration of Independence, July 4, 1776* and *The Surrender of Lord Cornwallis at Yorktown, October 19, 1781*, were enlarged versions of works he had painted better on a smaller scale in the late 1780s. The other two works, *The Surrender of General Burgoyne at Saratoga, October 16, 1777* and *The Resignation of General Washington, December 30, 1783*, depended on research and sketches that he had prepared in the early 1790s. Hampered by his damaged eyesight, which made painting in perspective very difficult, especially on a large scale, John did as well as he could, but his best in his sixties did not rise to the level of his best in his twenties and thirties. Still, all four paintings were well received, and in 1818 and 1819, when he took *The Declaration of Independence* on a national tour before he turned it over to the federal government, paying crowds thronged to see it. The pictures, especially *The Declaration of Independence*, serve today as the basis of Trumbull's claim to an honored place in the history of American art.[42]

Trumbull in his sixties was a faded talent, still capable of admirable paintings but not of the quality of performance that once was his standard. In fulfilling the Rotunda commission, he drew on past achievements. Throughout the rest of his life, his important artistic accomplishments invariably owed a heavy debt to the successes of a younger man—John Trumbull in his twenties and thirties.

In the same year that Trumbull turned the last of his paintings over to the government, his wife, Sarah, died. They had been married for twenty-four years. The Trumbulls had not had any children together, and John's ties to his illegitimate son were not close.[43] Although he could turn to acquaintances and relatives, he was more alone now in his bereavement than he had been for decades.

As his artistic abilities gradually waned, he retained valuable intellectual capital of two sorts. Versions of many of his most important early paintings remained in his possession, and so did his memories. Pensions were very uncommon in New England in the second third of the nineteenth century, but Trumbull was able to use his early years of productivity to provide himself with a comfortable annuity. In exchange for scores of drawings, sketches, and paintings still in his hands, in 1830 Yale University offered him $1,000 per year for as long as he lived. What peace of mind this arrangement brought him! Not only would he have money to live on, but also, thanks to the college, what he called "the Labor of my Life" would have a permanent home.[44]

Seven years later Trumbull followed his works from New York to New Haven. A niece had married Benjamin Silliman, Yale's noted professor of chemistry. Silliman urged Trumbull to recount the story of his life the way he wanted it told, and he offered the artist a place to stay while he worked on his memoirs. Trumbull could find companionship here while he wrote and a compassionate hand if he became ill. Though never fully dependent on the Sillimans, Trumbull lived with them from 1837 to 1841. His autobiography, published in 1841, was the first work of its kind by an American artist.[45]

John had returned to New York to live out his days by 1843, when he died at eighty-seven. Although he had continued to paint until about 1840,[46]

his Capitol commission was his last important body of work. Still ind
dent enough to get by on his own, he was nevertheless worn out. B
time of his death, he had accomplished all he could.

EVEN THOUGH no two men followed precisely the same path, John Trumbull's course resembled that of most of the members of the revolutionary
generation who lived long enough to know old age. Sooner or later almost
everyone encountered much the same set of experiences. Friends and family
members died, leaving an emotional void. Health deteriorated. Although
retirement was uncommon—perhaps one member in eight of the generation can be said to have retired, and even then bit by bit, not at a generally
accepted time as the faculties declined—eventually most men who lived
long enough gave up some of their independence when they recognized
their need for help and went to stay with relatives.[47] Men differed more in
the age at which they reached certain milestones and the order in which
they came upon them than in the catalogue of major events they experienced. Consider the cases of Eliphalet Pearson and Sam Jennison.

Pearson still had more than twenty years left to him when he quit Harvard in a huff in the spring of 1806 at the age of fifty-three. His declining
years were not as productive as his decades at Phillips Academy and at
Harvard, but throughout most of them he was still a force with which to be
reckoned.

In Andover, where he retreated after leaving Cambridge, Pearson vigorously did all he could to thwart the Unitarians whom he believed to have
stolen the college from him. His first scheme was to establish an orthodox
theological seminary to counteract their liberal influence. As he began to
promote his project among potential supporters, he learned of a similar
initiative also in the planning stage. The Reverend Samuel Spring of Newburyport and the Reverend Leonard Woods of West Newbury were also in
the process of organizing a divinity school.[48] Why not join forces?

It did not take Pearson long to answer this question. Spring and Woods
were disciples of Jonathan Edwards, whose rigid version of Calvinism
turned out to be even less palatable to him than Harvard's Unitarianism.
He taught at the new institution, Andover Theological Seminary, for a year,
1808–9, and then, unhappy with doctrinal compromises that were required
of him, he withdrew from its faculty.[49]

Pearson's resignation at fifty-seven did not end his active life, but he
never held another paid position. His withdrawal coincided with the opening in 1809 of the Park Street Church in Boston, a flagship institution for
evangelical Christianity in New England. Eliphalet had helped to organize

the new congregation, and in 1815, at sixty-three, he was also an organizer of the American Education Society, a voluntary association to raise college scholarship money for men intended for the Calvinist ministry.[50]

As long as he remained in tolerable health, Eliphalet worked strenuously in part-time, volunteer positions on behalf of the two institutions about which he cared most, Phillips Academy and the American Education Society. He had become president of the academy's board in 1802, and he sat at the head of the table for nearly two decades. He was also president of the Education Society, an office that required frequent correspondence as well as occasional travel.[51]

These activities came to a halt when he was in his late sixties. Rheumatism in his back grew increasingly debilitating, and he had to resign both posts in 1821. A trip to the spa at Saratoga Springs, New York, to find relief for his ailments signaled the end of Pearson's productive life. Shortly thereafter, Eliphalet and Sally moved to Harvard, Massachusetts, thirty miles west of Boston. Sally had grown up in the town, and she had inherited property there. To make it even more attractive to the Pearsons, one of their daughters lived there with her husband, the minister of the local church. It would be comforting to be close to her.[52]

Freed from the pressures and responsibilities that had occupied him throughout his adult life, Eliphalet lived quietly in Harvard. He had always been strong-willed, and in his declining years nothing changed. "He is too old to be contradicted," his son Henry wrote in 1824, "too slow for business; and too unbending for rational conduct."[53] Through the spring of 1826 he remained cheerful, but perhaps as the result of a stroke, he had difficulty making himself understood when he spoke.[54] Finally on September 12, while visiting Greenland, New Hampshire, where another of his daughters resided, he died of dysentery. He was seventy-four years old. Ironically, in his last days, put off by the growing influence in orthodox circles of the theological heirs of Jonathan Edwards, he had renounced his Calvinist beliefs in favor of the liberal Christianity against which he had fought for so long.[55]

Pearson's death came two weeks after the passing of another member of the revolutionary generation, Sam Jennison, who had died at sixty-seven on August 31. Like Eliphalet, Sam experienced decline and dependence during his last years. Unlike Eliphalet, Sam was already in trouble as he reached senescence. After struggling as a young veteran, then being unable to find a respected niche for himself in society at middle age, Sam arrived at his declining years a marginal man, a failure in life and a disappointment to everyone who knew him. Nothing about the end of his life altered this harsh verdict. As miserable as his life was, it grew even worse as he reached old age.

Separated by many days' journey from his children, divorced from his wife, Sam had lived an isolated and lonely existence for more than three decades in Thomaston, Maine. For most of this time he had supported himself by farming, teaching school, and bookkeeping, but in 1820 he experienced a crisis. Sam had a drinking problem, and it became so severe that in early 1821, when he was sixty-one, he became a public ward. Based on a report from the selectmen of Thomaston, the Lincoln County Probate Court declared him *non compos mentis* and appointed a local justice of the peace as his guardian. For the next five years, as the court supervised him, he got by on a small veteran's pension.[56]

By the early 1820s, both Pearson and Jennison had withdrawn from the public sphere, Pearson because his health prevented him from being active and Jennison because of his alcoholism. Retirement and death had crept up on each of them as the final steps in a gradual succession.

For Trumbull, Pearson, and Jennison, practical necessity had governed their declining years. They had worked as long as they could, become dependent on others when they had no other choice, suffered personal losses, and struggled with deteriorating health when medical science was unable to help them. In this regard they were following the common course in the early nineteenth century. The small minority of men who were elderly did not ordinarily have very many options. They retired only when they could no longer do their jobs: as late as the age of sixty-three in 1814, Sam Emery taught himself how to bleach wax and started a new business, a candle factory. He might be aging, but he could still support himself and his wife.[57] The elderly went to live with their children, other relatives, or a court-appointed ward when they could no longer take care of themselves: for nearly two decades, John Hastings shuttled from child to child in Medford, Cambridge, Lancaster, and Castine, until he finally returned to Cambridge, where Professor Sidney Willard, an old family friend, became his legal guardian.[58] They made do if they were widowed: when Sam Emery's wife, Polly, died in 1824, he was left to get by on his own without close relatives for fourteen years until his own death.[59] And they did their best to cope with declining health: "the infirmities of age" plagued Thomas Welsh in his seventies as he struggled to provide for his wife and two of his children, each too ill to be self-supporting.[60]

Whether the end came at eighty-seven, seventy-four, or sixty-seven, men who lived as long as John Trumbull, Eliphalet Pearson, and Sam Jennison were clearly the exception, not the rule. Although there was a common pattern to old age—retirement, dependence, surviving a wife—for most of the members of the classes of 1771 through 1774 these were experiences missed.

By five o'clock in the afternoon of July 6, 1808, the procession had begun to form in Boston near Christopher Gore's impressive brick mansion on Park Street. According to a printed broadside, the vanguard included the junior and senior classes at Harvard College, the institution's faculty, local clergy, and a phalanx of other dignitaries. In the rear guard were ranks of Massachusetts officeholders—among them, the governor, the lieutenant governor, members of the Governor's Council, the justices of the Supreme Judicial Court, and various lower court judges—a delegation of members of Congress, another delegation from the local bar, and even one from the Massachusetts Historical Society. The place of honor at the center of the extended line of march belonged to a smaller number of friends and relations. And of course there were the pallbearers, a distinguished group that included Harrison Gray Otis, Theophilus Parsons, Timothy Pickering, and Gore.[61] They were carrying the coffin of Fisher Ames, who had died two days before on Independence Day.

Contemporary estimates placed the number of mourners in the procession at one thousand. Thousands more men, women, and children lined Winter and Marlborough streets, Cornhill, and Court and Tremont streets, the route that the cortege followed to King's Chapel, the site of the funeral. Ames's pastor, the Reverend William Montague, the rector of St. Paul's Church in Dedham, conducted the service with the assistance of the Reverend Samuel Gardiner of King's Chapel. A large choir with organ accompaniment filled the bursting meetinghouse with music, and then Samuel Dexter, persuasive and sociable, a leading Federalist and a fellow member of the Wednesday Evening Club, offered the eulogy, a flowery tribute to a life devoted to public service. At the close of the ceremony a party of mourners conveyed Ames's remains home to Dedham for burial.[62]

Fisher Ames's funeral, which the Federalist leadership of Massachusetts organized as a political statement, was among Boston's largest, most elaborate, and best documented to that date. No member of Harvard's revolutionary generation went to his final resting place with more ceremony or attention. For most, no record even survives to chronicle the occasion. Their funerals were probably unremarkable rites, no different from the mass of others. Size and display have little to do with the fundamental objectives of a funeral, after all. Whether the service attracts a dozen or a thousand, its purposes are the same: to mourn a death and celebrate a life.

Time after time, between David Stinson's passing in 1769 and Laban Wheaton's in 1846, death turned the minds and hearts of friends and loved ones to the spirit, the character, and the accomplishments of members of the revolutionary generation.

Just as death ends a life, it also begins something else, a process of coming to terms with the loss of a lover, spouse, parent, child, friend, acquaintance, colleague, or competitor. Eliphalet Pearson's son, Henry, who lived hundreds of miles from his parents, struggled with the news of his father's passing, which he received by mail. He would "not believe my Father's death until I see the home he rendered dear—until I see his chair vacant—until I listen in vain for his faltering accents—until the awful vacuum convinces me that, he, my Father, my guardian, my pride, is dead."[63]

Ostentatious or plain, the funeral and the rituals surrounding it were important to the process of accepting a death.[64] There were three sets of mortuary rites. The funeral was the most public and visible of these ceremonies, but other traditions preceded and followed it. Not long after death, close members of the departed person's family laid him out. They washed him, combed his hair, and shaved him. Then they dressed him, often in a shroud or winding sheet. For as many as three days, the body remained at home while acquaintances came to view it and pay their respects to the bereaved survivors, who maintained a constant watch. During at least part of the period of vigil, the corpse probably rested in an open coffin, often a hexagonal pine box. This first stage in coming to terms with a death allowed those close to the deceased to gather, confirm the sad news, share memories and a meal, and begin to support one another at a difficult time.

The funeral service itself usually took place in the meetinghouse of the congregation to which the deceased belonged, although it might also take place at home. Most of the members of the revolutionary generation were either Congregationalist or Unitarian, and their funeral services had much in common. The churches of New England's Standing Order were self-consciously simple liturgically, and their funerals were true to their customs. The sermon is the centerpiece of a religious service in the reformed tradition, and funerals usually followed this practice. In place of the eulogy offered at Fisher Ames's rites, a clergyman ordinarily preached on an appropriate topic, using the short concluding passage, the "application," to draw connections between his theme and the departed. Prayers and hymns complemented the sermon.

Following the funeral, the mourners carried the coffin to its final resting place, usually the town graveyard. Before they lowered the box into the ground, a minister might offer a prayer or other suitable remarks. Often, before they filled the grave with dirt, members of the funeral party tossed a branch or a clump of sod on top of the casket in testament to their ties to the departed.

Although the progress from deathbed to graveyard usually followed a common course, no liturgical regulations stood in the way of innovation. The decision to ask a layman to eulogize Fisher Ames in lieu of a sermon was one such change. In 1819 the Reverend Moses Adams instructed before his death that he did not want a sermon at his funeral.[65] John Eliot, maintaining his distance from his congregation to the end, indicated in 1813 that he did not want a funeral at all. Instead, while the members of the New North Church gathered for a memorial service with the Reverend William Ellery Channing, the most prominent Unitarian divine of his generation, relatives and close friends met privately in Eliot's parlor, where the Reverend John Lathrop guided them in prayer.[66]

Because the classes of the revolutionary generation included some of New England's leading citizens, a few of its members went to their graves with almost as much attention as Fisher Ames received. The largest displays took place in and around Boston, the region's cultural, political, and financial focal point. The metropolis's church bells tolling somberly announced the death of Governor William Eustis in 1825; the Independent Corps of Cadets stood watch over his coffin; and on the day he was interred, artillery batteries in Charlestown and Roxbury fired salutes every half hour from sunrise until 1:00 P.M., when the funeral procession commenced.[67] The church bells of Dorchester accompanied Jemmy Bowdoin to the grave.[68] As for the Reverend John Clarke of Boston's First Church, who died of a stroke in 1798, forty members of the clergy led the long procession that escorted his coffin from his home to his congregation's meetinghouse.[69] Smaller towns also recognized the passing of community leaders, though on a lesser scale: when Judge Samuel Fales of Taunton passed away in 1818, fellow members of the board of Bristol Academy attended the final rites en masse and instructed the school's students "to wear suitable mourning badges" for thirty days.[70]

In the end, however, function was more important than form. If bereaved survivors drew comfort and strength from a funeral, then whether simple or elaborate, it was a success. If the service did not help them come to terms with their loss, then however ornate it was, it was irrelevant to their needs.

SOON ENOUGH the bells stopped pealing, the spades were put away, and the mourning badges came off. For the survivors, it was time to get on with life.

One way or another, survivors had to deal with legacies. Of course, there was an estate to divide. It was up to the executor and the courts to see to it that creditors and heirs all received their due. There was property to appraise and bills to pay before each beneficiary received a share of whatever was left. Moreover, some legacies reached beyond the purview of the probate system. For someone who cared about the departed, it was at least as important to think about the life of a loved one. There were comforting recollections. A grandchild of Levi Lincoln "distinctly remember[ed] his erect form as he sat in his old-fashioned, straight-backed chair, by the library fire."[71] And there was time to take stock of his accomplishments. What had he achieved? What had his life meant? Had he made a difference? Beyond his estate, what had he left to his family, friends, and nation? After Eliphalet Pearson's death, his widow drew consolation from the Bible, and his children concluded that he merited a stone monument on the campus of the Andover Theological Seminary.[72]

For the heirs, death often led directly to probate court. Of the 204 members of the revolutionary generation, 157 were married at least for a time, and as a group they sired about eight hundred children. Ninety-eight members left a widow, and hundreds of sons and daughters also survived them.[73] Although many wills provided for bequests outside the nuclear family—usually to friends and more distant relatives, occasionally to institutions such as schools and charities—for the most part, estates went to the widows and children. By custom the widow received one-third of the estate, with the balance divided among the other beneficiaries, ordinarily the children. Sometimes a son received an early bequest, perhaps in the form of college tuition payments, or a daughter received her inheritance in advance as her dowry. To compensate siblings after their father's death, children who had benefited from early inheritances usually received smaller portions.

As educated men the members of the revolutionary generation had been very fortunate. Nevertheless, the advantages of a college education did not always translate into affluence. Death offered an opportunity for a final accounting. Not every executor filed an inventory of the estate with the register of probate; there are no full inventories for some of the wealthiest men of the generation, including James Trecothick and Jemmy Bowdoin, and in some instances early distributions subtracted from an estate before death and probate. Still, the final tallies offer hints of the varied fortunes of Harvard's revolutionary generation.

When James Sheafe battled his way through an angry mob to the courthouse in Exeter, New Hampshire, in 1776, he could not have envisioned the future, but if such prescience had been possible, in contrast to his mixed political success he would have foreseen unparalleled financial prosperity. At his death at age seventy-four in Portsmouth on December 5, 1829,

Sheafe was very wealthy, by some contemporary accounts the richest man in New Hampshire. He had benefited from a head start. Because his father was a prominent Portsmouth merchant, James began his career with both wealth and contacts. Nevertheless, he had parlayed these advantages into much more. A clever trader in the late 1770s, with most of his resources tied up in commerce, by the end of his life he had become an astute, diversified investor with money in almost every kind of asset imaginable in New Hampshire at the time. The inventory of his estate lists bridges, a wharf, a shipyard, a gristmill, houses, stores, seven farms with livestock, thirteen thousand acres of land, and about $200,000 in financial investments such as bank stock, shares in manufacturing companies, and government bonds. All told, he was worth about $1 million.[74]

No other member of the generation for whom a probate inventory survives died as affluent as Sheafe, although both Bowdoin and Trecothick must also have enjoyed extraordinary riches. Still, by the standards of the times, more than a few members of the generation were very wealthy at death. In 1820 Levi Lincoln's agricultural holdings alone, worth about $54,000, included the farms that he had tried to make models of scientific agriculture—five of them.[75] William Eustis's estate was almost as large as Lincoln's. When Eustis died intestate in 1825, his widow's agent went from room to room in the late governor's Roxbury mansion listing and appraising furniture and fittings, made his way to the stable and fields, and then remembered to include investments in two insurance companies and four banks before he arrived at a final figure of $51,619.52.[76] Clement March, who had traveled back to Cambridge with his nephews Clement and Billy Weeks in 1775 to pick up his master's degree, left an estate of $18,661.25, largely a farm with livestock and equipment, when he died of palsy at sixty-seven in Greenland, New Hampshire, in 1818.[77]

In contrast, at least eight men were broke when they died, the product of a combination of imprudence, bad luck, and poor business decisions.[78] Joshua Bailey Osgood, who brought refinement to the backwoods of Maine, did so at an unsustainable cost. In order to pay for the silverware, the jewelry, the fine furnishings, the clothing, and the library with which he surrounded himself in Fryeburg, Osgood depended on Maine's lumber industry to provide for him better than it did. His means were limited, it turned out, and he was living well beyond them. The claims against him totaled £3,382.2.0; his available assets amounted to only £63.8.8.[79]

Somewhere between Sheafe's affluence and Osgood's insolvency it was possible to find the rest of the members of the generation. Consider the contrasting cases of Sam Jennison and Edward Barnard. Thanks to the careful oversight of his guardian, although Jennison was incapable of han-

Levi Lincoln. One of Lincoln's grandchildren "distinctly remember[ed] his erect form as he sat in his old-fashioned, straight-backed chair, by the library fire." (*Levi Lincoln, Sr.,* by James S. Lincoln, in *History of the Lincoln Family,* comp. Waldo Lincoln [Worcester, 1923], opp. p. 157.)

dling his own affairs, he was solvent at death, albeit barely. The military pension that had supported him since 1818 accounted for most of his assets: sundry articles of clothing and a small chest, together worth $13.00, combined with $65.46 due him from his pension, to bring his estate to $78.46, his total financial worth after more than sixty-seven years of sweat and anguish.[80] Dr. Edward Barnard's situation was more typical than Jennison's. Barnard, who had worried at home in Salem over the fate of his sailor son, left approximately $5,200 at his death from kidney disease in 1821, when he was sixty-five. The estate included a house, medical compounds, and shares in insurance, bridge, and turnpike companies,[81] resources sufficient to support a comfortable but not an opulent way of life.

For the most part, the men of the revolutionary generation had lived like Barnard, not like Sheafe or Osgood, and certainly not like Sam Jennison. They had been able to take care of themselves, they had been prudent, and they had done well enough to set some money aside for emergencies and old age if it came. Competent lives produced comfortable estates. Their heirs would benefit from their bequests, but for the most part there would be no opportunity to retire early on the proceeds.

In fact, it was not their estates that constituted the most important legacies of Harvard's revolutionary generation. By accident, not skill or determination, they had been born into interesting times, and as a consequence their lives had followed courses that none of them could have anticipated when they entered college.

The Revolution had sent them off on untested paths, and wherever they followed these tracks, there had been new opportunities. The story had been at once the most trying and the least innovative for Tom Coffin and the small group of men who clung to the crown. Coffin's career in the British military was the generation's most traditional success story. His achievements as an army commissary, impressive as they were, broke no new ground.

Unlike Coffin, whose most daring career decision came through inadvertence when he retained his ties to the monarchy, many of his schoolmates made conscious decisions to test the limits of their society. Whether they were successes or failures, defined financially, in each case an important part of their legacy came from their willingness to try something new. Jacob Welsh's plan to memorialize himself through the town that he founded was sidetracked after his death when the residents of Welshfield, Ohio, renamed their community Troy,[82] but he was still a builder, an agent facilitating the expansion westward. Perhaps Robert Williams ran aground when he attempted to tap the riches of the Near East through commerce, but he was

Samuel Phillips. (*Samuel Phillips*, by an unknown artist after John Johnston.
Engraving. John L. Taylor, *A Memoir of His Honor Samuel Phillips, LL.D.* [Boston,
1856], frontispiece.)

also a builder. It took adventurers like Williams, who were willing to carry
the American flag to new theaters of trade, to open up potential new commercial opportunities. Sam Emery was also an adventurer. When he opened
his candle factory, he became a large-scale manufacturer by the standards
of his times. Men such as Emery had taken the first steps along the road
that eventually led to the nation's industrial development.

And then there were the organization builders. These were men such as
Jack Warren, whose efforts helped to build the Harvard Medical School and
the Massachusetts Medical Society; Jemmy Bowdoin, whose financial con-

Declaration of Independence. John Trumbull died in 1843 convinced that he had failed to make an eternal mark on the annals of Western art, but this image, engraved two years before his death, suggests a different conclusion. There have been many reproductions of Trumbull's iconic painting, including U.S. currency. When the U.S. Mint issued a new $2 bill in 1935, it placed an engraving of Trumbull's painting on the verso. (*Declaration of Independence* [1841], detail from engraving by D. Kimberly after John Trumbull. Massachusetts Historical Society.)

tributions supported the college named after his father; Fisher Ames, whose public service in Congress and in the Federalist Party helped to develop the American polity; Sam Phillips, benefactor of the academy that bore his family name; and Eliphalet Pearson, whose efforts on behalf of Phillips Academy, Harvard College, Andover Theological Seminary, and the American Education Society were his lasting public legacy. Compared with the American colonies at the time when the men of Harvard's revolutionary generation graduated from college, the United States was a strikingly different place by the early nineteenth century.[83] No single individual was the principal agent of these changes, but many of the men we have been following were active contributors to it.

As their community was transformed, some men, understanding the magnitude of these changes, took it upon themselves to record them for posterity. John Trumbull, as the preeminent artist of the American Revolution, and John Eliot, as a founder and officer of the Massachusetts Historical Society, the country's first such institution, became custodians of the national memory. Generations of Americans have benefited from their public legacy.

Finally, there were the fathers. One hundred thirty-six members of the revolutionary generation became fathers, exactly two-thirds of the men in the classes of 1771 through 1774. Their family legacies varied. Not everyone had distinguished children, just as not every member of the revolutionary generation became distinguished in his own right. Not every child heeded the religious and moral teachings that most parents offered. But as parents, these men did their part in fulfilling what is collectively a vital responsibility: producing and raising the next generation. This, too, was an important legacy.

In the years, the decades, since they walked the paths of Harvard Yard, the members of the revolutionary generation had witnessed extraordinary changes. They had been the agents of many of them. Their legacy to family, community, and nation was secure.

EPILOGUE

American Scholars (August 31, 1837)

HARVARD BEGAN the 1836–37 academic year looking backward, reminiscing over the two centuries of its history. At the most memorable moment of the following school year, however, the annual meeting of its chapter of Phi Beta Kappa, the university found itself very much in the present.

Ezra Ripley's step-grandson was not the first choice to address the meeting. The Reverend Jonathan Mayhew Wainwright, an 1812 graduate and an Episcopal clergyman, had received the initial invitation. The committee in charge of arranging the exercises did not contact Ralph Waldo Emerson until Wainwright asked to be excused on June 22, ten weeks before the program on August 31. At least Emerson did not have to provide a topic on short notice; it was the same year after year, no matter who spoke: the American scholar. Every August the speaker, whoever he was, faced the same problem: how to say something—anything—new and interesting on a hackneyed subject.

The ceremonies at the annual meeting of Phi Beta Kappa's Massachusetts Alpha chapter bore more than a passing resemblance to those at the celebration of Harvard's two-hundredth anniversary. The university followed an established formula on public occasions. Three hundred fifty-seven days earlier the bicentennial procession had organized in front of University Hall before marching a few hundred feet to the meetinghouse of the First Parish in Cambridge for a program of odes, poems, and a major address. If the planners of the fraternity's exercises ever considered a different format, no record of their deliberations survives. The Phi Beta Kappa procession organized at noon in front of University Hall and set off in a column of twos for the carpenter Gothic edifice across the street. This time, only 215 black-coated men followed the band that led the way, but when the caravan arrived at its destination, it found the hall well filled in anticipation of the coming performance.

Emerson's talk followed a voluntary by the band and a prayer. As the tall, slender thirty-four-year-old orator rose to speak from the plush-draped pulpit, the meetinghouse must have seemed hot and stuffy; two days later, one newspaper reported that it had been "crowded (almost to suffocation)."[1] The orator spoke for an hour and a quarter on "the topic which not only usage, but the nature of our association, seem to prescribe this day,—the AMERICAN SCHOLAR."[2] Custom dictated his subject, but in his handling of it Emerson combined the traditional with the novel. Defining his topic as "man thinking," he enumerated the influences on the scholar. There were three in his view. Human beings are a part of nature, which imprints every soul. Through books, the past is also inscribed on every heart. Finally, action is also essential; humans learn by experience. None of these lessons was uniquely the speaker's, but the conclusion he drew from them was remarkable in its orientation toward the present.

"The eyes of man are set in his forehead, not his hindhead," Emerson reminded his listeners, and the task at hand was not to venerate the past but to create for the here and now. "Life lies behind us as the quarry from whence we get tiles and copestones for the masonry of to-day." The importance, the usefulness of the past is only as great as the preparation it provides for the present: "Give me insight into to-day, and you may have the antique and future worlds." Emerson lived in revolutionary times, he believed, and if there were "any period one would desire to be born in,—is it not the age of Revolution; when the old and new stand side by side, and admit of being compared ... when the historic glories of the old, can be compensated by the rich possibilities of the new era?"[3]

Here was a philosophy for a time of change, for a people who believed that their differences from their ancestors outweighed their similarities. What could have seemed more natural after the past decades of transformations? For if anything were obvious now, it was that change was the essence of life. More than six decades earlier, the men of Harvard's revolutionary generation had prepared themselves to lead the lives of their fathers. The lesson of their own lives was the importance of the here and now.[4]

ELEVEN MEMBERS of Harvard's revolutionary generation were still alive when the school observed its two hundredth anniversary on September 8, 1836. By August 31, 1837, when Emerson spoke, the number had slipped to ten; it would drop to eight by the end of the year. Samuel Emery, who had led the bicentennial procession of graduates, died on March 8, 1838, the victim of the fragile health that had been apparent eighteen months before. James (Ivers) Trecothick passed away in London on September 11, 1843; he never returned to his native country after he left Boston for England in 1771 and gave up his surname in favor of his uncle Barlow's. Two

Laban Wheaton in early old age. At his death in 1846, Wheaton was the revolutionary generation's last survivor. (*Laban Wheaton [1754–1846]*, by Eunice Makepeace Towle. Oil on canvas, 29.5 × 25 in. Beard and Weil Galleries, Wheaton College, Norton, Mass.)

months later, on November 10, John Trumbull died in New York, an old, tired, and disappointed man.[5]

With the death of Laban Wheaton in 1846, the last of the revolutionary generation passed into history. Its members had lived through momentous changes—they had taken the lead in some of them—and the revolutions of their times had reshaped their world.

Before his passing, Wheaton and his wife, Fanny, ensured in a small way that their generation would not be forgotten. In early 1834, Wheaton's daughter, Eliza, died without issue. Heartbroken, Laban and Fanny determined to find a way to memorialize her. A marble monument was one possibility, but the Wheatons' daughter-in-law suggested as an alternative the establishment of a female training school. The Wheaton Female Seminary opened in Norton, Massachusetts, in 1835; it changed its name to Wheaton College in 1912. There had been no place for women in college when Laban Wheaton was an undergraduate in the early 1770s, but now a Harvard alumnus and his wife were pioneers in women's education.[6]

Wheaton College was the last of the revolutionary generation's bequests to posterity. There had been many others—in education, religion, medicine, government, trade, culture. Thanks in part to the generation's efforts, Harvard itself had grown; at the start of classes in 1836, the school's four faculties—divinity, law, and medicine in addition to the college—taught more than four hundred students.[7] The end had come, however, as it always does. Now it was time for new generations, building on the foundation stones they had been left, to take their turn. The revolutionary generation would rest in peace.

Appendix

Life Structures and Generations: Understanding the Harvard Classes of 1771–1774

*R*evolutionary Generation tells how 204 men, the members of the Harvard College classes of 1771–1774, grew up and then grew old. As a group biography it relies on the assumption that its subjects, though individuals whose lives were in some respects quite dissimilar from one another, experienced enough in common to make a collective account productive. But what were their common experiences? Beyond the fact that the members of the generation were college contemporaries, what features did their lives share?

This appendix offers a brief schematic understanding of the individual lives of Harvard's revolutionary generation intended to underscore those common features. It proposes two points, first, that the "life structures" of most of the generation's members were similar. Comparable in age, most of them, they encountered most of life's major passages at about the same time and on roughly the same schedule. Second, it suggests that an important event, the American Revolution, shaped their lives in similar and critical ways. The Revolution came at a sensitive time for the members of the generation, most of whom were just beginning to plan their future when the shooting started in April 1775.

An eight-stage familial, educational, and occupational model accounts for the principal features of the lives of most of these men:

Stage	Age Range
Youth	
Early Childhood (infancy through breeching)	0–7
Middle Childhood (dame and grammar school student)	5–17
Late Childhood (undergraduate)	15–21

Maturity

Novice Adulthood (apprentice adult)	18–25
Rising Adulthood (journeyman adult)	20–35
Seasoned Adulthood (master adult)	30–65

Old Age

Early Old Age (elder adult)	55–75
Late Old Age (senescent adult)	70–plus

The first three stages (Youth) encompass periods of increasing independence, the next three (Maturity) constitute a time of full independence and responsibility, and the final two (Old Age) phases of decreasing independence. Note that the age ranges overlap and are only approximations. Because of innovations such as universal education, the military draft, mandatory retirement, and Social Security, individual experiences throughout American society began to be much more closely tied to chronology after the middle of the nineteenth century than they were when the men of the revolutionary generation were alive.[1] Consider the age ranges offered here to be guideposts, not rigid categories.

In recent decades, many psychologists, psychoanalysts, sociologists, and historians who have studied human development have followed one of two different approaches: life-cycle investigations and life-course inquiries. Life-cycle and life-course analyses are not inherently contradictory, but they use different sources and methods to arrive at distinctly different outcomes. Life-cycle research has usually been the preserve of psychologists and psychoanalysts, who have drawn their conclusions from interviews with small populations of patients and other subjects. These encounters, which have tended to focus on cognitive and emotional matters, have resulted in multiple-stage theories of human development, each phase concerned with resolving a central issue. For instance, Erik H. Erikson believed that the principal task for adolescents is to arrive at a sense of self—a personal identity.[2] In contrast, through the use of vital records, questionnaires, and other quantifiable sources of data, students of the life course such as Glen H. Elder, Jr., and Tamara Hareven have looked at large populations in search of patterns in major identifiable transition points—for instance, first marriage, the birth of the first child, and death.[3]

Revolutionary Generation follows the cyclical approach in thinking of life as a series of periods, each defined by a characteristic problem or problems. To delineate these stages, however, it often makes use of the transitional events that are so important to life-course research.

The availability of evidence limits almost every historical project, and this book is no exception. Unlike psychologists, psychoanalysts, and sociologists, who can ordinarily question their subjects, most historians depend on the written record. In the absence of substantial evidence about the psychological development of the members of Harvard's revolutionary generation, information crucial to the life-cycle research of social scientists, this study relies on other data, principally accounts of family life, education, and careers.

- Early Childhood: If most of the boys who eventually became members of Harvard's revolutionary generation encountered any unusual developmental experiences in their early years, the evidence for it has not survived. This period, which concluded at six or seven with "breeching"—the exchange of a young child's robe for a man's breeches, shirt, waistcoat, and jacket—encompassed the first stages of socialization, the development of language skills, and the start of religious instruction. For every boy during this stage of life, the primary challenge was to become a functioning member of society. Modern specialists in early development would undoubtedly subdivide this category into many more precise steps, but existing sources do not permit such particularity for the members of the revolutionary generation.[4]
- Middle Childhood: In eighteenth-century New England, most children learned the rudiments of reading, writing, and arithmetic, but by the time a boy reached his teens (and often two or three years before), he and his parents needed to make decisions about his future. Grammar school beckoned to potential collegians, while work (possibly following an apprenticeship in a craft) lay immediately in store for everyone else. Modern Americans sometimes speak disparagingly of educational tracking. Eighteenth-century terminology was different, but the consequences were quite similar as boys and their parents addressed the principal challenge of life's second stage, choosing between skilled or unskilled manual work on the one hand and a liberal education on the other.
- Late Childhood: The baccalaureate years separated a collegian from his contemporaries as effectively as the fence around Harvard Yard marked off the college grounds from the outside world. Classroom studies were only a portion of the four-year agenda for undergraduates, who were expected to emerge from college with both the contacts and the social polish that would serve them for life. Personal refinement was the principal task of the student's college years.
- Novice Adulthood: Many boys who chose not to attend college pursued craft apprenticeships between their early teens and their early twenties,

but a liberal education deferred occupational training until nearly twenty or later. For Harvard graduates, who used these years to make some of life's most enduring choices, Novice Adulthood was a time for crucial decisions. Collegians who followed a profession could expect to spend several years learning the substance and style of their calling and then starting to establish themselves. At the same time, they began to look for a wife, although most did not yet settle down and begin a family.

- Rising Adulthood: Between their early twenties and mid-thirties, young men completed the process of establishing themselves in their careers, communities, and families. At the end of this stage of life, successful men were competent, respected, and accepted in their calling; prepared for community leadership; and married, usually with children.
- Seasoned Adulthood: Men between their early thirties and early sixties provided leadership in almost every aspect of life in late-eighteenth-century and early-nineteenth-century New England. Members of this group held most major town offices, as well as the majority of important state and federal posts. Church deacons assumed office during these years, although many remained in place until Late Old Age or death. Within the professions, most of the mentors who trained apprentice practitioners were in this age range, which also encompassed the most active years of family life.
- Early Old Age: Before twentieth-century developments such as mandatory retirement and Social Security, there were no rules to establish the beginning of Early Old Age, a period of gradually decreasing responsibilities, both public and private. By the time a man reached his late fifties, however, more and more of his contemporaries were passing away, and his own energies were beginning noticeably to wane. Except at the highest levels of government, officeholders usually retired from public service in their late fifties or early sixties. The orderly turnover of responsibility to the next generation constituted the most important duty of this stage of life.
- Late Old Age: Very few men achieved Late Old Age, beginning sometime in their early to mid-seventies. Personal and private considerations predominated, as most seniors permitted younger men to control public affairs day to day.

This familial, educational, and occupational model accounts for most of the members of Harvard's revolutionary generation, but not all of them. A few men who entered college late—for example, Jonathan French and Daniel Chaplin, both of whom had reached their twenties by the start of freshman year—had already decided on a career in the ministry before matriculation. For them, college was a necessary stepping-stone toward a calling on which they had already settled. As for the boys who entered college especially early—for instance, Sam Jennison and Fisher Ames, both pre-teens during their first year—it was necessary to pause after graduation before actively pursuing a career.

Shared structure ensured that the remaining members of Harvard's revolutionary generation would undergo a common series of life experiences at about the same pace. Roughly the same age at matriculation, they followed similar—or at least comparable—paths through life. The greatest event of their moment in history, the American Revolution, further shaped their lives, linking them forever by the challenges and the opportunities it presented them.

For everyone who lived through it, the American Revolution was a defining event. Much as the Civil War, the Great Depression, World War II, the Baby Boom, and the Vietnam War later left their imprints on those who experienced them, the Revolution marked its generation for life. The war affected men and women on several different levels: in contemporary experiences, in opportunities and obstacles, and in myths and recollections.

Soldiers and sailors, especially those who served in combat (including many Harvardians), underwent the most obvious war-related experiences, but in one way or another the conflict touched every almost member of the generation who lived to see it. Combat could be shattering or exhilarating or some combination of the two, but whatever its consequences, it was hard to ignore or forget. The stresses and hardships of life on the home front extended the effects of the Revolution to noncombatants as well.

Because the men of the revolutionary generation, combatants and non-combatants alike, were making decisions that would affect them for life when the war arrived, the conflict posed for them an especially serious problem. Graduates a class or two ahead of them had already settled on careers, wives, and residences. The men of the revolutionary generation, though, would have to defer these decisions to a more peaceful time.

The war continued to mold the lives of the generation's members even after it ended. In many respects it recast American society, foreclosing certain opportunities, particularly for those who had benefited the most from provincial ties to the mother country, but opening many more—in trade, in government, in the professions, and on the frontier—to everyone else. The Revolution came along at a particularly critical juncture for the members of Harvard's revolutionary generation. At the point, in most cases in their early twenties, to make life choices involving career, marriage, and place of residence, they were especially vulnerable to the consequences of major contemporary developments. Events that opened or closed potential paths were of special significance for a generation at a crucial decision point. Men such as Joshua B. Osgood, who found himself on the Maine frontier in the early 1780s, and Tilly Merrick, trading internationally in the Netherlands and in Charleston, South Carolina, at about the same time, were pursuing courses that had been unimaginable before 1775.

Decades later, the war continued to affect the members of the generation. In their old age, men who had spent time under arms might look back in satisfaction or in horror at their military service, but it was hard to be free of its recollection. For many, the objective of postwar politics was to safeguard the revolutionary heritage. Political controversy arose when competing factions, often under the influence of competing myths, were unable to agree on the war's meaning.

For the members of Harvard's revolutionary generation, then, the War for Independence had peculiarly pervasive and enduring consequences. Affected by the timing of the conflict as well as its character, they lived out their days under the influence of an event that had ended while they were still young men but never ceased to shape their lives. Theirs is the story of a generation of men indelibly marked by their times.

TABLES

Table 1. Places of Birth, Classes of 1696–1699

Place	1696	1697	1698	1699	Totals
Massachusetts (incl. Maine)	6	7	12	7	32
New Hampshire	2	0	0	0	2
Connecticut	1	6	2	5	14
Rhode Island	0	0	0	1	1
Middle Atlantic	1	0	1	0	2
Foreign	0	1	0	1	2
Totals	10	14	15	14	53

Source: *Sibley's Harvard Graduates,* vol. 4.

Table 2. Town of Entry, Classes of 1771–1774

Place	1771	1772	1773	1774	Totals
Massachusetts (incl. Maine)	62	45	33	47	187
New Hampshire	0	4	1	4	9
Connecticut	1	0	1	0	2
Rhode Island	1	0	2	1	4
Canada	0	0	1	0	1
Caribbean	0	1	0	0	1
Totals	64	50	38	52	204

Source: *Sibley's Harvard Graduates,* vols. 17–18.

Table 3. Father's Occupation, Classes of 1771–1774

Occupation	1771	1772	1773	1774	Totals
Farmer	4	11	8	11	34
Merchant	5	9	5	10	29
Minister	7	5	4	8	24
Artisan	4	3	4	8	19
Shopkeeper	6	2	4	0	12
Doctor	1	5	1	4	11
Government official	2	3	0	0	5
Sea captain	2	0	0	1	3
College official	1	1	0	0	2
Land speculator	0	0	2	0	2
Lawyer	0	0	1	1	2
Gentleman	0	1	0	0	1
Teacher	0	0	0	1	1
Unknown	32	10	9	8	59
Totals	64	50	38	52	204

Source: *Sibley's Harvard Graduates*, vols. 17, 18.

Table 4. Age at Matriculation, Classes of 1771–1774

Age[a]	1771	1772	1773	1774	Totals
11	0	0	0	1	1
12	3	1	0	1	5
13	1	1	4	3	9
14	10	9	5	7	31
15	18	14	2	10	44
16	8	10	8	7	33
17	8	7	3	4	22
18	7	1	3	5	16
19	3	2	1	6	12
20	0	1	6	0	7
21	0	2	1	4	7
22	3	0	0	1	4
23	0	1	3	3	7
24	0	0	0	0	0
25	2	0	1	0	3
26	0	0	0	0	0
27	1	0	1	0	2
Unknown	0	1	0	0	1
Totals	64	50	38	52	204

Source: *Sibley's Harvard Graduates*, vols. 17, 18.

[a] Age as of August 15 of year class matriculated.

Table 5. Place of Residence, August 1767

| | Harvard Classes of 1698–1767 | | | | | | | |
Place	1698–1707	1708–1717	1718–1727	1728–1737	1738–1747	1748–1757	1758–1767	Totals
Eastern Mass.[a]	10	17	72	88	95	87	183	552
Other Mass.[b]	4	6	32	49	49	56	94	290
Other New England	3	5	27	45	26	42	55	203
Mid-Atlantic	0	1	2	3	4	0	2	12
South	0	0	1	1	0	0	4	6
Caribbean	0	0	0	2	0	2	6	10
Canada	0	0	0	2	3	1	0	6
Europe	0	0	0	2	1	1	4	8
Unknown	0	0	0	1	2	4	39	46
Totals	17	29	134	193	180	193	387	1133

Sources: *Sibley's Harvard Graduates*, vols. 4–16; *Quinquennial Catalogue of Officers and Graduates of Harvard University, 1636–1905* (Cambridge, Mass., 1905).

[a] Eastern Massachusetts includes the modern counties of Essex, Middlesex, Norfolk, and Suffolk.

[b] Other Massachusetts includes Maine.

Note: Table includes only alumni living in August 1767.

Table 6. Occupations, August 1767

| | Harvard Classes of 1698–1767 | | | | | | | |
Occupation	1698–1707	1708–1717	1718–1727	1728–1737	1738–1747	1748–1757	1758–1767	Totals
Minister[a]	8	18	69	90	67	69	104	425
Business[b]	3	3	16	36	41	47	67	213
Teacher	3	2	7	20	10	11	67	120
Doctor[c]	0	1	11	14	18	20	46	110
Lawyer[d]	0	0	6	9	9	17	38	79
Farmer[e]	2	2	6	10	16	11	11	58
Government	0	3	8	4	6	3	4	28
Gentleman	0	0	9	3	7	7	2	28
College Faculty/staff	1	0	2	3	0	1	5	12
Military	0	0	0	1	2	3	1	7
Mariner	0	0	0	2	0	0	2	4
Ill/insane	0	0	0	0	1	0	1	2
Surveyor	0	0	0	0	1	0	1	2
Student	0	0	0	0	0	0	1	1
Unknown	0	0	0	1	2	4	37	44
Totals	17	29	134	193	180	193	387	1133

Sources: *Sibley's Harvard Graduates*, vols. 4–16; *Quinquennial Catalogue of the Officers and Graduates of Harvard University, 1636–1905* (Cambridge, Mass., 1905).

[a] Ministers include pulpit supplies, divinity students, missionaries, and chaplains.

[b] Business includes merchants, traders, chandlers, braziers, shopkeepers, land agents, distillers, shipbuilders, innkeepers, and ironworks owners.

[c] Doctors include medical students and apothecaries.

[d] Lawyers include law students.

[e] Farmers include planters.

Note: Table includes only alumni living in August 1767.

Table 7. Alma Maters of New England Ministers, August 1767

Affiliation	Harvard	Yale	Princeton	Other college	No college	Totals
Congregationalist	313	202	23	9	27	574
Anglican	10	23	0	5	3	41
Baptist	3	0	2	0	55	60
Other	0	3	0	1	17	21
Totals	326	228	25	15	102	696

Sources: *Sibley's Harvard Graduates*, vols. 4–17; Frederic Lewis Weis, *The Colonial Clergy and the Colonial Churches of New England* (Lancaster, Mass., 1936); Harold Field Worthley, "An Inventory of the Particular (Congregational) Churches of Massachusetts Gathered 1620–1805," *Proceedings of the Unitarian Historical Society* 16 (1970).

Table 8. Distribution of Alumni Taxable Wealth, Boston, 1771

Taxable Wealth (£)	Taxpayers in each wealth bracket	Cumulative % of taxpayers	Alumni taxpayers in each wealth bracket	Cumulative % of alumni taxpayers
3–30	78	5.0	0	0.0
31–40	86	10.6	0	0.0
41–50	112	17.9	1	1.8
51–60	74	22.6	1	3.5
61–70	33	24.7	0	3.5
71–80	165	35.4	4	10.6
81–90	24	36.9	0	10.6
91–100	142	46.1	1	12.3
101–110	14	47.1	0	12.3
111–120	149	56.7	2	15.8
121–130	20	58.0	0	15.8
131–140	26	59.7	1	17.6
141–150	20	60.9	0	17.6
151–160	88	66.6	6	28.1
161–170	11	67.4	0	28.1
171–180	18	68.6	0	28.1
181–190	10	69.2	0	28.1
191–200	47	72.2	5	36.8
201–300	126	80.4	7	49.1
301–400	60	84.2	5	57.9
401–500	58	88.0	4	64.9
501–600	14	88.9	1	66.7
601–700	24	90.4	3	71.9
701–800	26	92.2	3	77.2
801–900	20	93.4	0	77.2
901–1,000	16	95.4	1	78.9
1,001–1,500	41	97.1	5	87.7
1,501–5,000	37	99.5	3	93.0
5,001+	7	100.0	4	100.0
	1,546	100.0	57	100.0

Sources: Adapted from James A. Henretta, "Economic Development and Social Structure in Colonial Boston," *William and Mary Quarterly*, 3rd ser., 22 (1965): 82, 84. Other sources: Bettye Hobbs Pruitt, *The Massachusetts Tax Valuation List of 1771* (Boston, 1978), 2–47; *Sibley's Harvard Graduates*, vols. 4–16; *Quinquennial Catalogue of the Officers and Graduates of Harvard University* (Cambridge, Mass., 1905), 109–131.

Note: Annual real estate rental values in the 1771 tax list have been multiplied by six to determine the worth of the property.

Table 9. Years between Graduation and First Marriage

Classes of 1761–1770			
Class		Median	Average
1761	(N = 32)	5	6.1
1762	(N = 33)	5	7.5
1763	(N = 33)	7	8.9
1764	(N = 38)	6	7.2
1765	(N = 41)	6	7.6
1766	(N = 35)	4	5.5
1767	(N = 33)	5	6.2
1768	(N = 36)	6	7.1
1769	(N = 27)	5	5.6
1770	(N = 26)	4	6.1
1761–1770	(N = 334)	5	6.8

Sources: *Sibley's Harvard Graduates*, vols. 15–17
Note: Calculated in full-year increments from July 15 of the year of graduation.

Table 10. Years between Graduation and First Marriage

Classes of 1771–1774			
Class		Median	Average
1771	(N = 44)	7	8.8
1772	(N = 29)	9	10.0
1773	(N = 28)	6	7.8
1774	(N = 36)	6	7.4
1771–1774	(N = 137)	7	8.5

Sources: *Sibley's Harvard Graduates*, vols. 17, 18.
Note: Calculated in full-year increments from July 15 of the year of graduation.

Table 11. Residences, December 1785

Harvard Classes of 1771–1774		
Place		Percentage
Eastern Massachusetts[a]	(N = 69)	41
Other Massachusetts[b]	(N = 41)	24
Other New England	(N = 21)	12
Mid-Atlantic states	(N = 4)	2
Southern states	(N = 2)	1
Caribbean	(N = 2)	1
Europe	(N = 12)	7
Canada	(N = 3)	2
Unknown	(N = 14)	8
Total	(N = 168)	

Source: *Sibley's Harvard Graduates*, vols. 17, 18.

[a] Includes modern counties of Essex, Middlesex, Norfolk, and Suffolk.
[b] Includes Maine.

Note: Table limited to living alumni.

Table 12. Occupations, December 1785

Classes of 1771–1774		
Occupation		Percentage
Business[a]	(N = 38)	23
Medicine[b]	(N = 31)	18
Ministry[c]	(N = 27)	16
Law[d]	(N = 19)	11
Education	(N = 17)	10
Gentleman	(N = 5)	3
Government	(N = 5)	3
Agriculture	(N = 4)	2
Military	(N = 4)	2
Artist	(N = 1)	1
Mariner	(N = 1)	1
Unknown	(N = 16)	10
Total	(N = 168)	

Source: *Sibley's Harvard Graduates*, vols. 17, 18.

[a] Business includes merchants, traders, chandlers, braziers, shopkeepers, land speculators, distillers, shipbuilders, innkeepers, and ironworks owners.
[b] Medicine includes doctors, medical students, and apothecaries.
[c] Ministry includes ordained ministers, pulpit supplies, divinity students, missionaries, and chaplains.
[d] Law includes lawyers and law students.

Note: Table limited to living alumni.

Table 13. Ever Married, December 31, 1785

| | Classes of 1771–1774 | | | |
Class	Yes	No	Unknown	Percentage ever married
1771	38	10	4	73
1772	24	13	4	59
1773	23	5	4	72
1774	29	9	5	67
Totals	114	37	17	68

Source: *Sibley's Harvard Graduates,* vols. 17, 18.
Note: Table limited to living alumni.

Table 14. Ever Married, December 31, 1760

| | Classes of 1746–1749 | | | |
Class	Yes	No	Unknown	Percentage ever married
1746	6	3	1	60
1747	23	2	0	92
1748	14	3	4	67
1749	10	6	2	56
Totals	53	14	7	72

Source: *Sibley's Harvard Graduates,* vol. 12.
Note: Table limited to living alumni.

Table 15. Number of Children

| | Classes of 1746–1749 | | |
Class	Average (all class members)	Average (of those who had children)	Median
1746	4.4	6.3	5.0
1747	4.5	6.7	3.0
1748	4.4	6.7	3.0
1749	3.7	5.2	2.0
Totals	4.2	6.3	3.0

Source: *Sibley's Harvard Graduates,* vol. 12.

Table 16. Number of Children

	Classes of 1771–1774		
Class	Average (all class members)	Average (of all those who had children)	Median
1771	3.5	5.1	2.0
1772	3.9	5.4	4.0
1773	5.6	7.0	6.0
1774	3.7	5.5	3.0
Totals	4.1	5.7	4.0

Source: *Sibley's Harvard Graduates*, vols. 17, 18.

Table 17. Occupations, December 1760

	Classes of 1746–1749	
Occupation		Percentage
Ministry[a]	(N = 22)	30
Business[b]	(N = 21)	28
Medicine[c]	(N = 12)	16
Law[d]	(N = 6)	8
Agriculture	(N = 5)	7
Government	(N = 4)	5
Education	(N = 4)	5
Total	(N = 74)	

Source: *Sibley's Harvard Graduates*, vol. 12.

[a] Ministry includes ordained ministers, pulpit supplies, divinity students, missionaries, and chaplains.
[b] Business includes merchants, traders, chandlers, braziers, shopkeepers, land agents, distillers, shipbuilders, innkeepers, and ironworks owners.
[c] Medicine includes physicians, surgeons, and apothecaries.
[d] Law includes lawyers and law students.

Note: Table limited to living alumni.

Table 18. First Marriage and Birth of First Child, Continental Army Officers

	Classes of 1771–1774	
	Years Since Graduation	
	Marriage	First child
Average	10.5	10.0
Median	9.0	8.5

Source: *Sibley's Harvard Graduates*, vols. 17, 18.

Table 19. Years between Graduation and Marriage, Loyalists

Classes of 1771–1774	
Average	Median
10.2	9.0

Source: *Sibley's Harvard Graduates*, vols. 17, 18.

Table 20. Age at First Marriage and Birth of First Child, Loyalists

Classes of 1771–1774		
	Marriage	First Child
Average	30.5	31.2
Median	28.0	28.5

Source: *Sibley's Harvard Graduates*, vols. 17, 18.

Table 21. Residences, December 1760

Classes of 1746–1749		
Place		Percentage
Eastern Massachusetts[a]	(N = 44)	59
Other Massachusetts[b]	(N = 16)	22
Other New England	(N = 11)	15
Canada	(N = 1)	1
South	(N = 1)	1
Unknown	(N = 1)	1
Total	(N = 74)	

Source: *Sibley's Harvard Graduates*, vol. 12.

[a] Includes the modern counties of Essex, Middlesex, Norfolk, and Suffolk.
[b] Includes Maine.

Table 22. Number of Marriages

Classes of 1771–1774					
Class	0	1	2	3	Unknown
1771	11	39	9	2	3
1772	11	32	4	0	3
1773	5	21	7	1	4
1774	9	31	9	2	1
Totals	36	123	29	5	11

Source: *Sibley's Harvard Graduates*, vols. 17, 18.

Table 23. Middle-Aged Widowers

Class	Class Size	Number ever married	Number of middle-aged widowers	Percentage
		Classes of 1771–1774		
1771	64	50	15	23
1772	50	36	6	12
1773	38	29	6	16
1774	52	42	11	21
Totals	204	157	38	19

Sources: *Sibley's Harvard Graduates*, vols. 17, 18; Sibley Files, Massachusetts Historical Society.
Note: Men who lost their wife between the ages of 32 and 60 are counted as middle-aged widowers. Six men who were younger than 32 had also lost their wives.

Table 24. Length of Marriages

Class		Mean	Median
	Classes of 1771–1774		
1771	(N = 44)	22.7	22.5
1772	(N = 30)	21.9	20.5
1773	(N = 24)	24.6	23.0
1774	(N = 35)	22.8	18.0
Total	(N = 133)	22.9	22.0

Sources: *Sibley's Harvard Graduates*, vols. 17, 18; Sibley Files, Massachusetts Historical Society.

Table 25. Minor Children at Death

Class	Number with children	Number with minor children at death	Percentage
	Classes of 1771–1774		
1771	44	17	39
1772	32	15	47
1773	28	11	39
1774	35	15	43
Total	139	58	42

Source: *Sibley's Harvard Graduates*, vols. 17, 18.
Note: Minor children defined as under age sixteen.

Table 26. Middle-aged Laymen Holding Major Public Office

Classes of 1771–1774			
Class	Middle-aged laymen[a]	Officeholders	Percentage
1771	39	13	33.3
1772	24	10	42.0
1773	25	14	56.0
1774	32	7	21.9
Total	120	44	36.7

Source: *Sibley's Harvard Graduates,* vols. 17, 18.

[a] Middle-aged defined as at least 45 at death.

Note: Major offices include local (deacon, selectman, town clerk, town meeting moderator, treasurer); province or state (governor, lieutenant governor, attorney general, councilor, senator, representative or equivalent); federal (ambassador, cabinet member, senator, representative); British (commissary general).

Table 27. Age at First Election to Major Local Office

Classes of 1771–1774			
Class		Mean	Median
1771	(N = 3)	33.3	36.0
1772	(N = 6)	38.0	35.0
1773	(N = 6)	40.0	39.0
1774	(N = 4)	34.5	33.5
Totals	(N = 19)	37.2	36.0

Source: *Sibley's Harvard Graduates,* vols. 17, 18.

Note: Major local offices included are selectman, town meeting moderator, and deacon.

Table 28. Age at First Election to State or Federal Office

Classes of 1771–1774			
Class		Mean	Median
1771	(N = 9)	36.5	38.0
1772	(N = 6)	40.0	38.5
1773	(N = 8)	43.8	45.5
1774	(N = 7)	35.6	34.0
Totals	(N = 30)	39.0	39.0

Source: *Sibley's Harvard Graduates,* vols. 17, 18.

Note: Offices included are state or provincial representative, state senator, governor, and U.S. representative.

Table 29. Age at Death

Classes of 1721–1724			
Class		Mean	Median
1721	(N = 34)	56.3	58.0
1722	(N = 30)	59.4	63.5
1723	(N = 38)	59.4	67.0
1724	(N = 40)	53.1	50.0
Total	(N = 142)	56.9	59.5

Source: *Sibley's Harvard Graduates*, vols. 6, 7.

Table 30. Age at Death

Classes of 1746–1749			
Class		Mean	Median
1746	(N = 13)	53.3	54.0
1747	(N = 30)	56.0	57.0
1748	(N = 28)	52.1	54.5
1749	(N = 24)	51.9	57.5
Totals	(N = 95)	53.5	56.0

Source: *Sibley's Harvard Graduates*, vol. 12.

Table 31. Age at Death by Decades

Classes of 1721–1724			
Decade		Percentage	Cumulative Percentage
10s	(N = 5)	3.5	3.5
20s	(N = 10)	7.1	10.6
30s	(N = 16)	11.2	21.8
40s	(N = 21)	14.8	36.6
50s	(N = 19)	13.4	50.0
60s	(N = 22)	15.5	65.5
70s	(N = 32)	22.5	88.0
80s	(N = 14)	9.9	97.9
90s	(N = 3)	2.1	100.0
100s	(N = 0)	0.0	100.0
Totals	(N = 141)	100.0	100.0

Source: *Sibley's Harvard Graduates*, vols. 6, 7.

Table 32. Age at Death by Decades

Decade	Classes of 1746–1749	Percentage	Cumulative Percentage
10s	(N = 6)	6.3	6.3
20s	(N = 19)	20.0	26.3
30s	(N = 8)	8.4	34.7
40s	(N = 8)	8.5	43.2
50s	(N = 10)	10.5	53.7
60s	(N = 15)	15.8	69.5
70s	(N = 16)	16.8	86.3
80s	(N = 10)	10.5	96.8
90s	(N = 2)	2.1	98.9
100s	(N = 1)	1.1	100.0
Totals	(N = 95)	100.0	100.0

Source: *Sibley's Harvard Graduates*, vol. 12.

Table 33. Age at Death

Class	Classes of 1771–1774	Mean	Median
1771	(N = 60)	58.0	62.5
1772	(N = 48)	53.6	52.0
1773	(N = 32)	60.7	65.0
1774	(N = 50)	58.1	62.5
Totals	(N = 188)	57.4	62.5

Source: *Sibley's Harvard Graduates*, vols. 17, 18.

Table 34. Age at Death by Decades

Decade	Classes of 1771–1774	Percentage	Cumulative percentage
10s	(N = 0)	0.0	0.0
20s	(N = 22)	11.7	11.7
30s	(N = 21)	11.2	22.9
40s	(N = 23)	12.2	35.1
50s	(N = 26)	13.8	48.9
60s	(N = 34)	18.1	67.0
70s	(N = 37)	19.7	86.7
80s	(N = 21)	11.1	97.8
90s	(N = 4)	2.1	100.0
100s	(N = 0)	0.0	100.0
Totals	(N = 188)	100.0	100.0

Source: *Sibley's Harvard Graduates*, vols. 17, 18.

NOTES

INTRODUCTION

1. Jonathan French (1740–1809), A.B. 1771. John Langdon Sibley et al., *Biographical Sketches of Graduates of Harvard University, In Cambridge, Massachusetts*, 18 vols. to date (Cambridge, Mass., and Boston, 1873–), hereafter cited as *Sibley's Harvard Graduates*, 17:514–520.

2. Samuel Jennison (1759–1826), A.B. 1774. *Sibley's Harvard Graduates*, 18:439–442.

3. Thomas Aston Coffin (1754–1810), A.B. 1772. *Sibley's Harvard Graduates*, 18:35–50.

4. Fisher Ames (1758–1808), A.B. 1774. *Sibley's Harvard Graduates*, 18:367–380.

5. John Trumbull (1756–1843), A.B. 1773. *Sibley's Harvard Graduates*, 18:331–348.

6. Tilly Merrick (1755–1836), A.B. 1773. *Sibley's Harvard Graduates*, 18:254–261.

7. Samuel Emery (1751–1838), A.B. 1774. *Sibley's Harvard Graduates*, 18:419–422.

PROLOGUE

1. John Pierce, Memoirs, 6:461, Massachusetts Historical Society.

2. George Leonard, Diary, September 15, 1836, Massachusetts Historical Society.

3. C. C. Holmes, *Harvard Graduates' Magazine* 32 (1923–24): 604.

4. *The Journals and Miscellaneous Notebooks of Ralph Waldo Emerson*, ed. William H. Gilman et al., 13 vols. (Cambridge, Mass., 1960–1976), 5:193.

5. This account draws on the following sources in addition to those cited in the preceding notes: Jno. Hales, *Plan of Cambridge From a Survey Taken in June 1830* (n.p., 1830); *Christian Examiner* 16 (1834): 267; Corporation Records, 7:397, 414, 418–443, Harvard University Archives; Faculty Records, 11:287, Harvard University Archives; "Plan of the Pews in the Church of the First Parish in Cambridge, 1833," and undated statement of charges for finishing the meetinghouse, First Parish in Cambridge, Records, Andover-Harvard Theological Library, Harvard Divinity School; *Carmen Seculare: In linguâ Latinâ porcellianâ compositum, et in canticum Nov-Anglis pergratum*, YANKEEDOODLEDANDIUM, *accommodatum* (Cambridge, Mass., 1836); *Harvardiana* 3 (1836–37):1–6; Josiah Quincy, *The History of Harvard University*, 2 vols. (Cambridge, Mass., 1840), 1: frontispiece and 2:639–708; *Boston Daily Advertiser*, September 8, 9, 1836; Hamilton Vaughan Bail, "Harvard's Bicentennial," *Harvard Alumni Bulletin* (1935–36): 964–970, 999–1005; Bail, " 'Fair Harvard' and Its Author, Samuel Gilman," *Harvard Alumni Magazine* (1935–36): 1107–11, 1157–62.

For an engraving of the tent in the Yard, see Quincy, *History of Harvard University*, 2: 708. The pagoda metaphor is from Samuel Eliot Morison, *Three Centuries of Harvard, 1636–1936* (Cambridge, Mass., 1936), 269.

1. FAMILY PRIDE

1. Samuel Cooke, Jr. (1752–1795), A.B. 1772. *Sibley's Harvard Graduates*, 18: 51–52.

2. For a photograph of the parsonage, see Charles S. Parker, *Town of Arlington: Past and Present* (Arlington, Mass., 1907), 44.

3. Benjamin and William R. Cutter, *History of the Town of Arlington* (Boston, 1880), 91n.

4. John Warren (1753–1815), A.B. 1771. *Sibley's Harvard Graduates*, 17:655–669. Edward Warren, *The Life of John Warren, M.D.* (Boston, 1874), 3–4.

5. John Eliot (1754–1813), A.B. 1772. *Sibley's Harvard Graduates*, 10:131, 18:55–68.

6. Irma B. Jaffe, *John Trumbull: Patriot–Artist of the American Revolution* (Boston, 1975), 3–5.

7. Frank Smith, *A History of Dedham, Massachusetts* (Dedham, 1936), 166–167; Winfred E. A. Bernhard, *Fisher Ames, Federalist and Statesman, 1758–1808* (Chapel Hill, 1965), 11, 15.

8. John Trumbull of Lebanon and Daniel Tyler of Canterbury.

9. Peter Heyliger (1750–c. 1785), class of 1772. *Sibley's Harvard Graduates*, 18: 97–99.

10. Benjamin Rice (1749–1782), A.B. 1773. *Sibley's Harvard Graduates*, 18:309–310.

11. See tables 1 and 2.

12. Forty-six (23%) of 204 members of the four classes were sons of Harvard men. *Sibley's Harvard Graduates*, 17:466–679; 18: passim.

13. Levi Lincoln (1749–1820), A.B. 1772. *Sibley's Harvard Graduates*, 18:121–128.

14. See table 3.

15. See table 4.

16. William B. Sprague, *Annals of the American Pulpit*, 9 vols. (New York, 1857–1869), 2:42.

17. Daniel Chaplin (1744–1831), A.B. 1772. *Sibley's Harvard Graduates*, 18:25–33.

18. Joshua Armsby (1742–1825), A.B. 1773. *Sibley's Harvard Graduates*, 18:209–210.

19. See table 4.

20. *The Autobiography of Colonel John Trumbull, Patriot–Artist, 1756–1843*, ed. Theodore Sizer (New Haven, 1953), 3–6.

21. Karin Calvert, *Children in the House: The Material Culture of Early Childhood, 1600–1900* (Boston, 1992), 3–94; Philip Greven, *The Protestant Temperament: Patterns of Child-Raising, Religious Experience, and the Self in Early America* (New York, 1977), 178–191; Edmund S. Morgan, *The Puritan Family: Religion and Domestic Relations in Seventeenth–Century New England*, rev. ed. (New York, 1966), 106–108; Catherine M. Scholten, *Childbearing in American Society, 1650–1850* (New York, 1985), 61–62. For the alternative view that the mid-eighteenth century was not a watershed in the history of family emotion, see Lisa Wilson, *Ye Heart of a Man: The Domestic Life of Men in Colonial New England* (New Haven, 1999), 115.

22. Greven, *Protestant Temperament*, chap. 4, esp. 170–177; Scholten, *Childbearing in American Society*, 59–60. If Edward Shorter is correct, similar but even more dramatic changes in child-rearing practices and relations between parents and children were taking place contemporaneously in western Europe; see Shorter, *The Making of the Modern Family* (New York, 1975). Lawrence Stone also finds the rise of more affectionate family relations and child-rearing practices in England by the late seventeenth century; see Stone, *The Family, Sex, and Marriage in England, 1500–1800,* abr. ed. (New York, 1979), esp. chaps. 6–9.

23. Lawrence A. Cremin, *American Education: The Colonial Experience, 1607–1783* (New York, 1970), 500–501; Morgan, *Puritan Family*, 97–98, 101.

24. Calvert, *Children in the House*, 44–46.

25. Kenneth A. Lockridge, *Literacy in Colonial New England: An Enquiry into the Social Context of Literacy in the Early Modern West* (New York, 1974), 19.

26. Cremin, *American Education*, 181.

27. Bernhard, *Fisher Ames*, 18.

28. Cremin, *American Education*, 500–501.

29. John F. Roche, *The Colonial Colleges in the War for American Independence* (Millwood, N.Y., 1986), 1. For an estimate of the population of the American colonies, see Evarts B. Greene and Virginia D. Harrington, *American Population before the Federal Census of 1790* (New York, 1932), 6, which cites a figure of 2.24 million for 1765.

30. For a fascinating investigation of contemporary female academies, many of which afforded girls a very sophisticated, albeit not classical, education, see Mary Kelley, "Empire of Reason: The Making of Learned Women in Nineteenth-Century America," paper presented to the Boston Area Early American History Seminar, November 2, 2000.

31. On childhood paths, see Harvey J. Graff, *Conflicting Paths: Growing Up in America* (Cambridge, Mass., 1995), 26–66, but note that Graff ignores farming and deemphasizes the crafts.

32. On the apprenticeship alternative in the late colonial period, see W. J. Rorabaugh, *The Craft Apprentice: From Franklin to the Machine Age in America* (New York, 1986), 3–15.

33. See table 5.

34. Greene and Harrington, *American Population*, 21.

35. See table 6.

36. See table 7.

37. Colonial Massachusetts depended on public taxes to support religious institutions, but in an act passed in 1760, the province authorized levies only to support college-educated clergy. See Gerard W. Gawalt, *The Promise of Power: The Emergence of the Legal Profession in Massachusetts, 1760–1840* (Westport, Conn., 1979), 19.

38. Overseers' Records, October 6, 1772, 3:55, Harvard University Archives.

39. Of the twenty-two lawyers who did not graduate from Harvard, fourteen attended Yale and the remainder apparently did not go to college. Charles R. McKirdy, "Massachusetts Lawyers on the Eve of the American Revolution: The State of the Profession," *Publications of the Colonial Society of Massachusetts*, 62:330–358. Harvard men also dominated the bar in New Hampshire and Maine. Of the thirteen lawyers in New Hampshire in 1767, nine were Harvard graduates, one attended Princeton, and three did not go to college. Four of six lawyers in the eastern counties of Massachusetts that later became the state of Maine were Harvardians; the other

two did not go to college. See Charles H. Bell, *The Bench and Bar of New Hampshire* (Boston, 1894), passim; Frederic Allen, "The Early Lawyers of Lincoln and Kennebec Counties," *Collections of the Maine Historical Society*, 1st ser., 6 (1869): 44–48; and William Willis, *The History of Portland*, 2nd ed. (Portland, 1865), 616–624.

40. None of the twelve non-Harvard doctors active in Boston in 1767 had attended a college. Philip Cash, "The Professionalization of Boston Medicine, 1760–1803," *Publications of the Colonial Society of Massachusetts*, 57:95–97.

41. On communication within the professions, see Richard D. Brown, *Knowledge Is Power: The Diffusion of Information in Early America, 1700–1865* (New York, 1989), 65–109.

42. On communication among merchants, see Brown, *Knowledge Is Power*, 112–113.

43. Without the constraints that the professions imposed, trade was open to anyone. Although commerce required capital, which was beyond the reach of many, in the eighteenth century the ranks of Boston's merchants and shopkeepers included women and quondam artisans as well as former apprentices to merchants. By the nineteenth century a small but vigorous community of African American merchants had also developed. See Patricia Cleary, " 'Who shall say we have not equal abilitys with the Men when Girls of 18 years of age discover such great capacitys?': Women of Commerce in Boston, 1750–1776," and Lois E. Horton and James Oliver Horton, "Power and Social Responsibility: Entrepreneurs and the Black Community in Antebellum Boston," in *Entrepreneurs: The Boston Business Community, 1700–1850*, ed. Conrad Edick Wright and Katheryn P. Viens (Boston, 1997), 39–61 and 325–341.

44. For a valuable list of merchants active in prerevolutionary Boston, see John W. Tyler, *Smugglers & Patriots: Boston Merchants and the Advent of the American Revolution* (Boston, 1986), 253–277.

45. *Journals of the House of Representatives of Massachusetts*, 55 vols. (Boston, 1919–1989), 44:6.

46. Of 526 men who served in the lower house between 1740 and 1755, based on the frequency of appointment to committees, 101 apparently held leadership positions. The membership of the house during these years included sixty-two Harvard graduates and eight Yale graduates. Thirty-seven Harvard men (60%) and five (62.5%) from Yale ranked among the leaders. Of the non-graduates, only 13 percent ranked among the leadership. Robert M. Zemsky, "Power, Influence, and Status: Leadership Patterns in the Massachusetts Assembly, 1740–1755," *William and Mary Quarterly*, 3rd ser., 26 (1969): 502–520. In the spring of 1767, nearly one-quarter of the men who attended the opening session of the House of Representatives were college graduates—30 of 121. Twenty-five had graduated from Harvard; five were graduates of Yale. *Journals of the House of Representatives of Massachusetts*, 44:4; John A. Schutz, *Legislators of the Massachusetts General Court, 1691–1780: A Biographical Dictionary* (Boston, 1997).

47. Edward M. Cook, Jr., calculates that on average, college graduates who assumed high local office in eighteenth-century New England began their service at age 33.7, while the average age of first service for all who held high office was 42.7; Cook, *Fathers of the Towns: Leadership and Community Structure in Eighteenth-Century New England* (Baltimore, 1976), 111–112.

48. See table 8.

49. John Adams to Thomas Jefferson, November 15, 1813, in *The Adams–Jefferson*

Letters: The Complete Correspondence between Thomas Jefferson and Abigail and John Adams, ed. Lester Cappon, 2 vols. (Chapel Hill, 1959), 2:402, quoted in John Ferling, "Before Fame: Young John Adams and Thomas Jefferson," in *John Adams and the Making of the Republic*, ed. Richard Alan Ryerson, (Boston, 2001), 72.

50. John Adams, "Defense," in *The Life and Works of John Adams*, ed. C. F. Adams 10 vols. (Boston, 1856), 6:186, quoted in John R. Howe, Jr., *The Changing Political Thought of John Adams* (Princeton, 1966), 142.

51. Henry Adams, *The Education of Henry Adams*, ed. Ernest Samuels (Boston, 1973), 54–55.

52. On the Brattle Street Church, see Anthony Gregg Roeber, " 'Her Merchandize . . . Shall Be Holiness to the Lord': The Progress and Decline of Puritan Gentility at the Brattle Street Church, Boston, 1715–1745," *New England Historical and Genealogical Register* 131 (1977): 175–194.

53. Richard L. Bushman, *The Refinement of America: Persons, Houses, Cities* (New York, 1992), 38–46; Margaretta Markle Lovell, "Boston Blockfront Furniture," and May Ellen Hayward Yehia, "Ornamental Carving on Boston Furniture of the Chippendale Style," *Publications of the Colonial Society of Massachusetts*, 48:77–135 and 197–222.

54. On the development of the bar in Boston and other towns, see Brown, *Knowledge Is Power*, 90, 96; John M. Murrin, "The Legal Transformation: The Bench and Bar of Eighteenth-Century Massachusetts," *Colonial America: Essays in Politics and Social Development*, ed. Stanley N. Katz and John M. Murrin, 3rd ed. (New York, 1983), 552–554.

55. *New England Courant*, May 14, 1722.

56. Eliphalet Pearson (1752–1826), A.B. 1773. *Sibley's Harvard Graduates*, 18:283–304.

57. Henry B. Pearson, Memoir, "Tributes, Family Connections," Eliphalet Pearson Papers, Box 2, Archives Department, Phillips Academy, Andover, Mass.; John W. Ragle, *Governor Dummer Academy History, 1763–1963* (South Byfield, 1963).

58. On tuition, see Robert Middlekauff, *Ancients and Axioms: Secondary Education in Eighteenth-Century New England* (New Haven, 1963), 25–26.

59. F. Washington Jarvis, *Schola Illustris: The Roxbury Latin School, 1645–1995* (Boston, 1995), 126, 128.

60. *Catalogue of the Officers and Students of Dummer Academy* (Salem, 1844).

61. Winthrop Sargent (1753–1820), A.B. 1771. *Sibley's Harvard Graduates*, 17:614–626.

62. Joseph Hall (1751–1840), A.B. 1774. *Sibley's Harvard Graduates*, 18:431–433. Bernhard, *Fisher Ames*, 19. David Hall, Diary, December 27, 1766, Massachusetts Historical Society.

63. William Jennison (1757–1843), A.B. 1774. *Sibley's Harvard Graduates*, 18:443–445.

64. Timothy Jones (1751–1814), class of 1774. *Sibley's Harvard Graduates*, 18:445–447.

65. William Lincoln, *History of Worcester, Massachusetts* (Worcester, 1862), 194; Quinquennial File, Harvard University Archives.

66. Henry F. Jenks, "Historical Sketch," in *Catalogue of the Boston Public Latin School* (Boston, 1886), 36; Middlekauff, *Ancients and Axioms*, 78–80.

67. Middlekauff, *Ancients and Axioms*, 92–93.

68. *Sibley's Harvard Graduates,* 12:490–492; Rowland Ricketts, Jr., "The Tisdale School in Lebanon," *Connecticut Historical Society Bulletin* 34 (1969): 101–105.

69. Jenks, "Historical Sketch," 87–92. *Sibley's Harvard Graduates,* 8:441–446.

70. John Bradford (1756–1825), A.B. 1774; *Sibley's Harvard Graduates,* 18:387–391; William Newell, "Notice of the Rev. John Bradford," *Proceedings of the Massachusetts Historical Society* 1 (1791–1835): 382; John Pierce, Memoirs, 1 (n.s.), 179, Massachusetts Historical Society.

71. *Sibley's Harvard Graduates,* 12:50–51.

72. Samuel Phillips (1752–1802), A.B. 1771. *Sibley's Harvard Graduates,* 17:593–605.

73. Samuel Phillips, Jr., to Elizabeth Phillips, April 5, June 29, 1765; Samuel Phillips, Jr., to Samuel Phillips, Sr., and Elizabeth Phillips, October 1765, Phillips Papers, Archives Department, Phillips Academy, Andover, Mass.

74. Elizabeth Phillips to Samuel Phillips, Jr., May 4, 1766, April 10, 1765, Phillips Papers, Archives Department, Phillips Academy, Andover, Mass.

75. Elizabeth Phillips to Samuel Phillips, Jr., October 17, 1765, March 25 [year illegible], Phillips Papers, Archives Department, Phillips Academy, Andover, Mass.

76. Claude M. Fuess, *An Old New England School: A History of Phillips Academy, Andover* (Boston, 1917), 87.

77. On the common practice of leaving home as a teenager, see Morgan, *Puritan Family,* 75–76.

78. *Catalogue of the Boston Public Latin School,* 80–85. The classes are recorded by the year of entry rather than of completion. These figures are for those entering between 1760 and 1763. Of the thirty-five college men in these classes, thirty-three attended Harvard and two went to Princeton.

2. Cambridge College

1. David Tappan (1752–1803), A.B. 1771. *Sibley's Harvard Graduates,* 17:638–645.

2. Stephen Peabody, Diary, July 14, 1767, Massachusetts Historical Society, Boston. On Phillips and Tappan, see *Sibley's Harvard Graduates,* 17:593, 638.

3. "The Laws of Harvard College [1767]," *Publications of the Colonial Society of Massachusetts* 31 (1935): 347.

4. *Boston Post-Boy,* June 22, 1767.

5. Sidney Willard, *Memories of Youth and Manhood,* 2 vols. (Cambridge, Mass., 1855), 1:255–256.

6. Samuel Phillips, Jr., to Samuel and Elizabeth Phillips, June 15, 1767, Phillips Papers, Phillips Academy, Andover, Mass.

7. Peabody, Diary, July 18, 20, 1767.

8. *Sibley's Harvard Graduates,* 17:466–467.

9. Although it takes a different approach than I have, the most valuable study of the relationship between Harvard and Cambridge is John D. Burton, "Puritan Town and Gown: Harvard College and Cambridge, Massachusetts, 1636–1800" (Ph.D. diss., College of William and Mary, 1996). I have also described Harvard on the eve of the Revolution in the introduction to volume 18 of *Sibley's Harvard Graduates,* ix–xxii.

10. For a map of Cambridge in 1638, see Samuel Eliot Morison, *The Founding of Harvard College* (Cambridge, Mass., 1935), between 192–193.

11. Lucius R. Paige, *History of Cambridge, Massachusetts, 1630 to 1877* (Cambridge, Mass., 1877), 3.

12. Rupert Ballou Lillie, *Cambridge in 1775* (Salem, Mass., 1949), 7 and map.

13. Winfred E. A. Bernhard, *Fisher Ames, Federalist and Statesman, 1758–1808* (Chapel Hill, 1965), 20.

14. Lillie, *Cambridge in 1775*, 11–13; Bainbridge Bunting and Robert Nylander, *Survey of Architectural History in Cambridge: Report Four: Old Cambridge* (Cambridge, Mass., 1973), 33; *An Historic Guide to Cambridge* (Cambridge, Mass., 1907), opp. 14.

15. Burton, "Puritan Town and Gown," 18–20.

16. On the economic relationship between Harvard and Cambridge, see Burton, "Puritan Town and Gown," chap. 6, esp. 182–186 for a discussion of Harvard as an employer.

17. Bernhard, *Fisher Ames*, 20.

18. Richard L. Bushman, *The Refinement of America: Persons, Houses, Cities* (New York, 1992), 110–117.

19. *Publications of the Colonial Society of Massachusetts*, 15:c.

20. Faculty Records, Original, 1771–72, Harvard University Archives. At most, allowing for a private room for each of the four tutors plus the librarian, Massachusetts, Hollis, and Stoughton halls could have accommodated 150 undergraduates. When enrollment exceeded this figure, what would happen to the surplus? Some boys lived with their parents or other relatives, while some took rooms in the homes of approved Cambridge families, many of them faculty members. In 1774 the college added space for approximately another twenty students when it bought Wiswell's Den, a house facing the Yard opposite Massachusetts Hall. Wiswell's Den had been the scene of rowdy partying, so the purchase removed a source of temptation at the same time that it added dormitory space. Harvard renamed the building College House. See Faculty Records, Original, September 14, 1772; Josiah Quincy, *The History of Harvard University*, 2 vols. (1840; Boston, 1860), 2:171.

21. Thomas Jay Siegel, "Governance and Curriculum at Harvard College in the 18th Century" (Ph.D. thesis, Harvard University, 1990), 199; "Harvard in 1790," *Harvard Graduates Magazine* 15 (1906–7):775; Samuel Eliot Morison, *Three Centuries of Harvard, 1636–1936* (Cambridge, Mass., 1936), 97.

22. Hamilton Vaughan Bail, *Views of Harvard: A Pictorial History to 1860* (Cambridge, Mass., 1949), 26–33, 49–57; Bainbridge Bunting, *Harvard: An Architectural History* (Cambridge, Mass., 1985), 15–36.

23. "The Harvard Diary of Pitt Clarke, 1786–1791," ed. Ernest John Knapton, *Publications of the Colonial Society of Massachusetts*, 59:238; Burton, "Puritan Town and Gown," 185.

24. Richard Cranch to Abigail Adams, July 5, 1786, Adams Papers, Massachusetts Historical Society.

25. On the process by which the college assembled the land for the Yard, see Bunting, *Harvard: An Architectural History*, 17.

26. Samuel Phillips, Jr., to Samuel and Elizabeth Phillips, December 1, 1767, Phillips Papers, Phillips Academy, Andover, Mass.

27. Clifford K. Shipton, "Ye Mystery of Ye Ages Solved, or, how Placing Worked at Colonial Harvard & Yale," *Harvard Alumni Bulletin*, December 11, 1954, 258–259, 262–263. Yale followed a similar practice until 1766, when it opted to follow the alphabet instead. See Brooks Mather Kelley, *Yale: A History* (New Haven, 1974), 75–

78. Harvard's decision to reorder the class of 1771 after the complaint over rankings by Samuel Phillips, Sr., had the potential for causing discontent and jealousy. As Samuel Sr. wrote to Samuel Jr.: "You are now in the most Difficult Scituation, the Eyes of all Above and below you will be upon you, and I wish if it might be that you could be at home till the talk about the Change was a little over, but this dont Expect. Every word, action & even your Countenance will be watchd perticularly by those who Envy you, and perhaps by those who do not; Therefore keep as much retired as possible, wave all Conversation about it, dont let it appear that you are in the least degree Affected wth the Change. If any difficulties should arise with any of your Classmates, that now fall below you, treat them with all possible tenderness." August 29, 1769, Phillips Papers, Phillips Academy, Andover, Mass. At about the same time that Harvard and Yale gave up their traditional ranking system, many New England towns abandoned a similar practice—the assigning of seats in their meetinghouses based on personal dignity. See David Hackett Fischer, *Growing Old in America*, rev. ed. (New York, 1978), 78–79.

28. These terms were also used at other American colleges; see Melvin Yazawa, *From Colonies to Commonwealth: Familial Ideology and the Beginnings of the American Republic* (Baltimore, 1985), 66.

29. "Laws of Harvard College," 350, 355, 359.

30. "College Customs Anno 1734/4," *Publications of the Colonial Society of Massachusetts*, 31:383–384; Willard, *Memories*, 258–259.

31. Corporation Records, April 9, 1773, 3:385, Harvard University Archives; "Laws of Harvard College," 357.

32. Peabody, Diary, July 14, 1767.

33. *Sibley's Harvard Graduates*, 9:254.

34. Sibley's Harvard Graduates, 15:108, 112–113.

35. *Sibley's Harvard Graduates*, 12:513. See Edward Wigglesworth, *Calculations on American Population* (Boston, 1775), and Benjamin Franklin, *Observations Concerning the Increase of Mankind* (London, 1755).

36. Seymour E. Harris, *Economics of Harvard* (New York, 1970), 39, 139; Siegel, "Governance and Curriculum at Harvard College," 237, 238, 251–252; Morison, *Three Centuries of Harvard*, 80n.

37. "Laws of Harvard College," 377.

38. Harvard's curriculum was quite similar to what one found at the other colonial colleges. See, for example, Kelley, *Yale: A History*, 78–83; Mark A. Noll, *Princeton and the Republic, 1768–1822* (Princeton, 1989), 20–21.

39. Oratorical training led to periodic public exhibitions and, ultimately, to public addresses at commencement. Declamations took two forms: syllogistic, in which an individual speaker logically analyzed a proposition, and forensic, in which two students debated a point at issue. As Harvard was placing increasing emphasis on public speaking, the same reform was taking place at other American colleges, including Yale and Princeton. See Christopher Grasso, *A Speaking Aristocracy: Transforming Public Discourse in Eighteenth-Century Connecticut* (Chapel Hill, 1999); Siegel, "Governance and Curriculum at Harvard College," 265–266; Quincy, *History of Harvard University*, 2:124–128; Louis Leonard Tucker, *Puritan Protagonist: President Thomas Clap of Yale College* (Chapel Hill, 1962), 77; Noll, *Princeton and the Republic*, 35.

40. Burton, "Puritan Town and Gown," 44; Morison, *Three Centuries of Harvard*, 89–90.

41. Quincy, *History of Harvard University*, 2:163.

42. For a late example of this silver, see Kathryn C. Buhler, *American Silver, 1655–1825, in the Museum of Fine Arts, Boston*, 2 vols. (Boston, 1972), 1:365–367. Buhler also lists three other donations of tutorial silver from this era.

43. Between 1767–68 and 1773–74, the average age of the tutors ranged from 24.75 to 30; the average age of the professors was forty in 1767–68; all three professors were still in place six years later in 1773–74.

44. *Sibley's Harvard Graduates*, 4:162–167, 8:137–140. Also see Daniel Munro Wilson, "Tutor Henry Flynt, New England's Earliest Humorist," *New England Magazine* 23 (1900):284–293.

45. Corporation Records, Harvard University Archives, November 10, 1766, April 20, 1767, 3:268–271, 277.

46. Sheldon S. Cohen, "Harvard College on the Eve of the American Revolution," *Publications of the Colonial Society of Massachusetts*, 59:175; "Harvard Diary of Pitt Clarke," 238; Willard, *Memories*, 313; *Sibley's Harvard Graduates*, 15:448–449.

47. Henry Adams, *The Education of Henry Adams* (Boston, 1918), 54–69.

48. *The Autobiography of Colonel John Trumbull, Patriot-Artist, 1756–1843*, ed. Theodore Sizer (New Haven, 1953), 11. Theodore Parsons (1751–1779), A.B. 1773. *Sibley's Harvard Graduates*, 18:273–275.

49. Israel Keith to Zephaniah Keith, September 11, 1767, Keith Papers, Massachusetts Historical Society.

50. William Gallison to Colonel John Gallison, October 27, 1773, C. E. French Papers, 18:427–428, Massachusetts Historical Society.

51. William Gallison to John Gallison, 18:427–428.

52. John Clarke, *Letters to a Student in the University of Cambridge, Massachusetts* (Boston, 1796), 72, 80–92, 97.

53. Clarke, *Letters to a Student*, 47–48.

54. Clarke, *Letters to a Student*, 76.

55. Corporation Records, 2:260, 322, 327, 338; Clement Weeks, Diary, 1768–1796, July 27, 1772, New Hampshire Historical Society, Concord; Barbara Lambert, "Music Masters in Colonial Boston," *Publications of the Colonial Society of Massachusetts*, 54:1110–12. On the social role of the minuet, see Cathleene B. Hellier, "Dance in the Virginia Gentry Household: A Tutor's-Eye View in the 1770s," unpublished paper, Research Department, Colonial Williamsburg Foundation, Williamsburg, Va., esp. 6–7, 12, and Hellier, " 'These Rules and Customs': Gender, Power, and the Rules of Assemblies in Two Novels by Fanny Burney," unpublished paper, Research Department, Colonial Williamsburg Foundation, Williamsburg, Va., esp. 12–14.

56. Bernard Bailyn, *The Ideological Origins of the American Revolution* (Cambridge, Mass., 1967), 23–24.

57. Gary B. Nash, *The Urban Crucible: Social Change, Political Consciousness, and the Origins of the American Revolution* (Cambridge, Mass., 1979), 393; Jackson Turner Main, *The Social Structure of Revolutionary America* (Princeton, 1965), 96.

58. Harris, *Economics of Harvard*, 40; see also 39, 53–55, 67, 77, 83.

59. Clement Weeks (1750–1830), A.B. 1772. *Sibley's Harvard Graduates*, 18:177–182. Robert F. Seybolt, "Student Expenses at Harvard, 1772–1776," *Publications of the Colonial Society of Massachusetts*, 28:301–305; Weeks, Diary. At his graduation in July 1776, Morey calculated that the total cost of his education since he began to prepare for college was £114.3.1½. Weeks recorded his costs in old tenor; to convert

to new tenor, which Morey used, divide Weeks's figures by 7.5. On the cost of a college education in the seventeenth and early eighteenth centuries, see Margery Somers Foster, *"Out of Smalle Beginnings . . .": An Economic History of Harvard College in the Puritan Period* (Cambridge, Mass., 1962), 65–84; and Harris, *Economics of Harvard*, 39–40, 53–55, 67, 77, 83.

60. Corporation Records, 3:285, 293–294, 301–302, 306–307, 317, 326–327, 337–339, 345, 349–350, 356, 364–366, 371–372, 382–383, 390–391, 395, 398–401; Faculty Records, 3:57, 69, 81, 91, 100, 104–105, 141, 157, 195, 218, Harvard University Archives. On scholarships in the late colonial period, see Harris, *Economics of Harvard*, 85–86, 91–92.

61. Peter Heyliger (1750–ca. 1785), class of 1772. *Sibley's Harvard Graduates*, 18: 97–99. Faculty Records, 3:198, Harvard University Archives.

62. James Bowdoin (1752–1811), A.B. 1771. *Sibley's Harvard Graduates*, 17:487–500. James Bowdoin to Lady Elizabeth Bowdoin Temple, October 31, 1793, *Collections of the Massachusetts Historical Society*, 7th ser., 6:207–208.

63. For the courtship of Joseph Pearse Palmer, class of 1771, and Betsy Hunt, which began with a blind date during college, see *Sibley's Harvard Graduates*, 17:584–585.

64. David Foster Estes, *The History of Holden* (Worcester, 1894), 33.

65. For letters using "Sammy," see Elizabeth Phillips to Samuel Phillips, Jr., August 10, 1767, June 19, 1768, November 17, 1769, Phillips Papers, Phillips Academy, Andover, Mass.

66. Joshua Bailey Osgood (1753–1791), A.B. 1772. *Sibley's Harvard Graduates*, 18: 138–140. Isaac Osgood to Stephen Sewall, September 7, 1768, Wigglesworth Family Paper, Massachusetts Historical Society.

67. Samuel Phillips, Sr., to Samuel Phillips, Jr., November 5, 1769, Phillips Papers, Phillips Academy, Andover, Mass.

68. Elizabeth Phillips to Samuel Phillips, Jr., n.d., Phillips Papers, Phillips Academy, Andover, Mass.

69. Samuel Phillips, Diary, Phillips Papers, Phillips Academy, Andover, Mass.

70. Samuel Phillips, Sr., to Samuel Phillips, Jr., November 20, 1769, Phillips Papers, Phillips Academy, Andover, Mass. In the same collection, see also Samuel Phillips, Sr., to Samuel Phillips, Jr., November 5, 1769.

71. Faculty Records, 2:468–469, 504, 3:37, 83, 131–132, 155, 183, 193, 195, 212–213, Harvard University Archives.

72. Fourteen members of the classes of 1771 through 1774 were degraded at some point during their college careers. Only one student in these classes, John Barnard Swett, suffered both punishments. Twenty-seven of 204 students (13%) incurred rustication, degradation, or both. Faculty Records, 3:67, 132, 162–163, 183–184, 195, 198, 201, 209–210, Harvard University Archives.

73. Faculty Records, 3:152–153, Harvard University Archives.

74. Faculty Records, 3:193, 194, 195, 201, 208, Harvard University Archives; Sarah E. Mulkern, ed., "Harvard on the Eve of the Revolution," *Harvard Graduates' Magazine* 10 (1902): 377–378.

75. Faculty Records, 3:194–195, Harvard University Archives.

76. Faculty Records, 3:152–154, Harvard University Archives.

77. Bernard Bailyn et al., *Glimpses of the Harvard Past* (Cambridge, Mass., 1986), 25.

78. For a useful and provocative picture of a similar twentieth-century adolescent culture, see Louis M. Crosier, ed., *Casualties of Privilege: Essays on Prep Schools' Hidden Culture* (Washington, D.C., 1991).

79. Daniel Tyler (1750–1832), A.B. 1771. *Sibley's Harvard Graduates,* 17:651–653.

80. Willard, *Memories,* 260–261; Peabody, Diary, August 20–24, 1767; Morison, *Three Centuries of Harvard,* 130.

81. Francis Foster Apthorp, "Burning Harvard Hall, 1764, and Its Consequences," *Publications of the Colonial Society of Massachusetts,* 14:2–43. This room arrangement, which had its origins in medieval Oxford and Cambridge, was also common in other American colleges; see Kelley, *Yale: A History,* 60; David C. Humphrey, *From King's College to Columbia, 1746–1800* (New York, 1976), 113; Frederick Chase, *A History of Dartmouth College and the Town of Hanover, New Hampshire,* 2 vols. (Cambridge, Mass., 1891), 1:223. Princeton and the College of William and Mary employed variations on this theme; see Thomas Jefferson Wertenbaker, *Princeton, 1746–1896* (Princeton, 1946), 47; Susan H. Godson et al., *The College of William and Mary: A History* (Williamsburg, 1993), 1: fig. 7. For a useful description of Nassau Hall at Princeton, see Wertenbaker, *Princeton, 1746–1896,* 37–40.

82. Faculty Records, Originals, 1771–1772, Harvard University Archives; Peabody, Diary, August 14, 15, 1767.

83. Faculty Records, Originals, 1771–1772, Harvard University Archives.

84. *The Nation* 98 (1914):295; Morison, *Three Centuries of Harvard,* 91–92.

85. Willard, *Memories,* 315–317; Bernhard, *Fisher Ames,* 25.

86. Weeks, Diary, August 1768.

87. Mulkern, "Harvard on the Eve of the Revolution," 529–530.

88. Peabody, Diary, August 21, 26, 1767.

89. Weeks, Diary, June 9, 1772.

90. Siegel, "Governance and Curriculum at Harvard College," 301; William C. Lane, "A Religious Society at Harvard College, 1719," *Publications of the Colonial Society of Massachusetts,* 24:309–313; Albert Matthews, "A Society at Harvard College, 1721–1723," *Publications of the Colonial Society of Massachusetts,* 24:156–159; Morison, *Three Centuries of Harvard,* 61–63; Peabody, Diary, passim.

91. Articles of an Association for the Suppression of Vice, April 7, 1767, Harvard University Archives.

92. Philomusarian Club, Articles, 1728, Harvard University Archives. A group of resident graduates formed an even earlier society, the Spy Club, for discussing philosophical topics, in 1719. Siegel, "Governance and Curriculum at Harvard College," 302–303.

93. Bernhard, *Fisher Ames,* 27.

94. Speaking Club, Minutes and Other Records, Harvard University Archives; Bernhard, *Fisher Ames,* 28.

95. Speaking Club, Minutes and Other Records, Harvard University Archives; Clitonian Society, Diploma, 1773, Massachusetts Historical Society [photostat]; "A List of the Officers of the Martimercurian Company at College, 1771," *Publications of the Colonial Society of Massachusetts,* 24:161–165; Faculty Records, Original, 1771–1772, Harvard University Archives.

96. The full membership of the Spunke Club is now impossible to reconstruct through a few cryptic surviving mentions. For John Warren's membership, see *Sibley's Harvard Graduates,* 17:655.

97. Morison, *Three Centuries of Harvard*, 141; Albert Matthews, "Officers of the Martimercurian Company," 161–165. Harvard was not alone in sponsoring a student militia company. Yale, Brown, and Columbia also had them. See Kelley, *Yale: A History*, 84; John F. Roche, *The Colonial Colleges in the War for American Independence* (Millwood, N.Y., 1986), 61–63.

98. For a full account of this event, see Sheldon S. Cohen, "The Turkish Tyranny," *New England Quarterly* 47 (1974): 564–583.

99. Peabody, Diary, March 22, 1768.

100. Administrative Records of College Disorders, April 1768, Harvard University Archives.

101. Charles M. Andrews, "The Boston Merchants and the Non-Importation Movement," *Publications of the Colonial Society of Massachusetts* 19 (1916–17): 195.

102. Andrew Eliot to Thomas Hollis, December 25, 1769, *Collections of the Massachusetts Historical Society*, 4th ser., 4:447.

103. By the outbreak of the Revolution, most American colleges were politicized. Of them, King's College (Columbia) was strongly loyalist, while both William and Mary and the College of Philadelphia had significant loyalist factions on the faculty. See David W. Robson, *Educating Republicans: The College in the Era of the American Revolution, 1750–1800* (Westport, Conn., 1985), 29–56.

104. On the sensitization of American undergraduates to threats to their liberties, see Louis Leonard Tucker, "Centers of Sedition: Colonial Colleges and the American Revolution," *Proceedings of the Massachusetts Historical Society* 91(1979):16–34; Robson, *Educating Republicans*, 57–102; Roche, *Colonial Colleges in the War for American Independence*, 47–66; Morison, *Three Centuries of Harvard*, 135–136; J. David Hoeveler, *Creating the American Mind: Intellect and Politics in the Colonial Colleges* (London, 2002), esp. 241–345.

105. Morison, *Three Centuries of Harvard*, 138–140.

106. Quoted in Morison, *Three Centuries of Harvard*, 99.

107. *Sibley's Harvard Graduates*, 5:275.

108. Stephen Sewall, "A Funeral Oration, On the Death of the Revd. Edward Holyoke, President of Harvard College," 5, Massachusetts Historical Society.

109. Corporation Records, December 18, 1769, 3:322, Harvard University Archives.

110. *Diary and Autobiography of John Adams*, ed. L. H. Butterfield et al., 4 vols. (Cambridge. Mass., 1963), 3:260.

111. Andrew Eliot to Thomas Hollis, December 25, 1769, *Collections of the Massachusetts Historical Society*, 4th ser., 4:447–448.

112. Faculty Records, 3:146–147, Harvard University Archives.

113. Theodore Chase, "Harvard Student Disorders in 1770," *New England Quarterly* 61 (1988): 25–54.

114. *Sibley's Harvard Graduates*, 13:624; Faculty Records, 3:168–169.

115. *Sibley's Harvard Graduates*, 13:625–626.

116. Weeks, Diary, July 16, 1772.

117. In September, near the start of their final year, the members of the senior class gathered to hold elections. They voted for two commencement orators and four thesis collectors, who drafted the graduation program. These six men were, in effect, the officers of the graduating class. Morison, *Three Centuries of Harvard*, 119; Siegel, "Governance and Curriculum at Harvard College," 325–326.

118. Andrew Croswell, *Brief Remarks on the Satyrical Drollery at Cambridge Last Commencement Day* (Boston, 1771). For a rejoinder accusing Croswell of being too stuffy, probably by the Reverend Thomas Prentice, minister of the Congregational church in Charlestown and a member of the Board of Overseers, see Simon, the Tanner, *A Letter to the Reverend Andrew Croswell* (Boston, 1771).

119. Theodore Parsons (1751–1779), A.B. 1773. *Sibley's Harvard Graduates*, 18: 273–275. [Theodore Parsons and Eliphalet Pearson,] *A Forensic Dispute on the Legality of Enslaving the Africans, Held at the Public Commencement in Cambridge, New-England, July 21st, 1773* (Boston, 1773).

120. William C. Lane, "The Printer of the Harvard Theses of 1771," *Publications of the Colonial Society of Massachusetts*, 26:1–15.

121. *Boston Post-Boy*, July 22, 1771.

122. Burton, "Town and Gown," 159.

123. Peabody, Diary, July 3, 4, 1767.

124. Daniel Murray (1751–1832), A.B. 1771. *Sibley's Harvard Graduates*, 17:562–566. John Rowe, Diary, July 17, 1771, Massachusetts Historical Society.

125. George Inman (1755–1789), A.B. 1772. *Sibley's Harvard Graduates*, 18:108–117. Elizabeth [Murray] Inman to Lady Don, fall 1773 (filed 1774), J. M. Robbins Papers, Massachusetts Historical Society. A published account of this party appeared in the *Boston Gazette*, July 20, 1772. For these citations I am grateful to Patricia Cleary.

126. For an account of Harvard commencement in the late colonial period, see Morison, *Three Centuries of Harvard*, 123–131.

3. APPRENTICING FOR LIFE

1. Nathaniel Walker Appleton (1755–1795), A.B. 1773. *Sibley's Harvard Graduates*, 18:204–209. *Publications of the Colonial Society of Massachusetts*, 8:291.

2. *Sibley's Harvard Graduates*, 17:596.

3. R. D. Burr (?), April 23, 1857, Quinquennial File, Harvard University Archives.

4. Thomas Edwards (1753–1806), A.B. 1771. *Sibley's Harvard Graduates*, 17:507–510. John Adams, *Diary and Autobiography* (Cambridge, Mass., 1961), 2:52.

5. *Sibley's Harvard Graduates*, 18:368.

6. *Sibley's Harvard Graduates*, 18:274.

7. Robert Middlekauff, *Ancients and Axioms: Secondary Education in Eighteenth-Century New England* (New Haven, 1963), 7.

8. Nahum Cutler (1746–ca. 1776), A.B. 1773. *Sibley's Harvard Graduates*, 18:230–231. Nahum Cutler to Eliphalet Pearson, July 14, 1774, Park Family Papers, Manuscripts and Archives, Yale University Library.

9. William B. Sprague, *Annals of the American Pulpit*, 9 vols. (New York, 1857–1869), 8:92–93; Ebenezer Parkman, Diary, November 21, 1774, American Antiquarian Society, Worcester, Mass.; George F. Daniels, *History of the Town of Oxford, Massachusetts* (Oxford, 1892), 560; *Memoirs of the Social Circle in Concord*, 2nd ser. (Cambridge, Mass., 1888), 58–59; Winfred E. A. Bernhard, *Fisher Ames, Federalist and Statesman, 1758–1808* (Chapel Hill, 1965), 33.

10. *Sibley's Harvard Graduates*, 18:181–182.

11. James Bowdoin III to Elizabeth, Lady Temple, October 31, 1793, *Collections of the Massachusetts Historical Society*, 7th ser., 6:207.

12. On the professions in the British Isles and the American colonies, see Samuel Haber, *The Quest for Authority and Honor in the American Professions, 1750–1900* (Chicago, 1991), 3–87; Richard Harrison Shryock, *Medicine and Society in America, 1660–1860* (New York, 1960), 1–43; John M. Murrin, "The Legal Transformation: The Bench and Bar of Eighteenth-Century Massachusetts," in *Colonial America: Essays in Politics and Social Development*, ed. Stanley N. Katz and John M. Murrin, 3rd ed. (Boston, 1983), 540–572; and J. William T. Youngs, Jr., *God's Messengers: Religious Leadership in Colonial New England, 1700–1750* (Baltimore, 1976).

13. Bernhard, *Fisher Ames*, 33, 37.

14. *Sibley's Harvard Graduates*, 18:285.

15. Eric H. Christianson, "The Medical Practitioners of Massachusetts, 1630–1800: Patterns of Change and Continuity," *Publications of the Colonial Society of Massachusetts*, 57:61; Murrin, "Legal Transformation," 561–563; Gerald W. Gawalt, *The Promise of Power: The Legal Profession in Massachusetts, 1760–1840* (Westport, Conn., 1979), 24; Richard Harrison Shryock, *Medical Licensing in America, 1650–1965* (Baltimore, 1967), 3.

16. Christianson, "Medical Practitioners," 61; Murrin, "Legal Transformation," 561–563; Youngs, *God's Messengers*, 17–24.

17. Haber, *Quest for Authority and Honor*, 3–87.

18. Mary Latimer Gambrell, *Ministerial Training in Eighteenth-Century New England* (New York, 1937), 21–28.

19. Samuel Willard, *Brief Directions to a Young Scholar Designing the Ministry* (Boston, 1735), 1, 3.

20. Youngs, *God's Messengers*, 21. On Haven, see *Sibley's Harvard Graduates*, 13:447–453.

21. Gambrell, *Ministerial Training*, 129–130.

22. Henry K. Beecher and Mark D. Altschule, *Medicine at Harvard: The First Three Hundred Years* (Hanover, N.H., 1977), 14–16. In the 1770s there were still many healers without formal training in Massachusetts. Of more than two hundred "doctors" who began their practice in Massachusetts at that time, fewer than half, according to one study, had served any kind of apprenticeship. Thomas Neville Bonner, *Becoming a Physician: Medical Education in Britain, France, Germany, and the United States, 1750–1945* (New York, 1995), 46, citing Eric Christianson, "The Emergence of Medical Communities in Massachusetts, 1790–1794: The Demographic Factors," *Bulletin of the History of Medicine* 54 (1980): 69.

23. Beecher and Altschule, *Medicine at Harvard*, 14–18.

24. Edward Barnard (1755–1821), A.B. 1774. *Sibley's Harvard Graduates*, 18:381–384. For a picture of the Holyoke mansion, see *The Holyoke Diaries, 1709–1856*, ed. George Francis Dow (Salem, 1911), opp. 58.

25. *Sibley's Harvard Graduates*, 12:30–41.

26. Philip Cash, "The Professionalization of Boston Medicine," *Publications of the Colonial Society of Massachusetts*, 57:76–77; Beecher and Altschule, *Medicine at Harvard*, 15.

27. Edward Barnard, Almanac-Diary, March 30, April 18, May 22–June 21, October 18, 1776, Peabody Essex Museum, Salem.

28. Gerald W. Gawalt, "Massachusetts Legal Education in Transition, 1766–1840," *American Journal of Legal History* 17 (1973): 31.

29. Bernhard, *Fisher Ames*, 39–40.

76. Edward M. Cook, *The Fathers of the Towns: Leadership and Community Structure in Eighteenth-Century New England* (Baltimore, 1976), 23–33, 102–109.

77. Michael Zuckerman, *Peaceable Kingdoms: New England Towns in the Eighteenth Century* (New York, 1970), 128–129, 132, 152; Ola Elizabeth Winslow, *Meetinghouse Hill, 1630–1783* (New York, 1952), 118–149.

78. For interesting accounts of the drawing of the revolutionary lines, see Colin Nicolson, "Governor Francis Bernard, the Massachusetts Friends of Government, and the Advent of the Revolution," *Proceedings of the Massachusetts Historical Society* 103 (1991): 24–113, and Nicolson, " 'McIntosh, Otis & Adams are our demagogues': Nathaniel Coffin and the Loyalist Interpretation of the American Revolution," *Proceedings of the Massachusetts Historical Society* 108 (1996) :72–114.

79. Examples of families with divided loyalties include those of Tilly Merrick, whose stepfather, Duncan Ingraham, was Concord's most visible Tory, and Winthrop Sargent, whose Gloucester relatives included loyalists. *Sibley's Harvard Graduates*, 17:614, 18:255.

80. Ebenezer Boltwood (1752–1804), A.B. 1773. *Sibley's Harvard Graduates*, 18: 217–219. *The History of the Town of Amherst, Massachusetts*, comp. Carpenter and Morehouse (Amherst, 1896), 86–93, 101.

81. Nicolson, ' "McIntosh, Otis & Adams are our demagogues,' " 73–114.

82. William Chandler (1752–1793), A.B. 1772. *Sibley's Harvard Graduates*, 18: 217–219. James H. Stark, *The Loyalists of Massachusetts and the Other Side of the American Revolution* (Boston, 1910), 132–133.

83. Samuel Murray (1754–1781), A.B. 1772. *Sibley's Harvard Graduates*, 18:134–138. John Andrews to William Barrell, August 23, 1774, *Proceedings of the Massachusetts Historical Society*, 8:346.

84. George Wingate Chase, *The History of Haverhill, Massachusetts* (Haverhill, 1861), 374.

85. Warren, *Life of John Warren*, 23.

86. Clement March (1750–1818), A.B. 1772. *Sibley's Harvard Graduates*, 18:132–134. M. O. Hall, *Rambles about Greenland in Rhyme* (Boston, 1900), 198; *Sibley's Harvard Graduates*, 18:181.

87. The four classes that graduated before the revolutionary generation, the classes of 1767 through 1770, returned en masse to accept their master's degrees. Of the 157 graduates in these classes, 134 (85%) took their second degrees on schedule three years after the first degree. In contrast, of the 195 graduates of the revolutionary generation, without the lure of a commencement reunion to draw them back, only 114 (58%) took their second degrees three years after the first. Compiled from the *Quinquennial Catalogue of the Officers and Graduates of Harvard University, 1636–1905* (Cambridge, Mass., 1905), 130–134.

88. Albert Matthews, "Harvard Commencement Days, 1642–1916," *Publications of the Colonial Society of Massachusetts*, 18:353–354.

89. Clement Weeks, Diary, July 31, 1775, New Hampshire Historical Society, Concord.

90. Weeks, Diary, July 31, 1775.

4. A Time for Choices

1. Smith was a cousin of Abigail Adams. Six months earlier, after the imposition of the Intolerable Acts, her older sister, Mary Cranch, had warned him that his politics threatened his career prospects in the ministry: "Orthodoxy in Politicks is full as necessary a quallification for Settling a minister at the present Day as orthodoxy in divinity was formerly, and tho you should preach like an angel if the People suppose you unfriendly to the country and constitution and a difender of the unjust, cruil and arbitrary measures that have been taken by the ministry against us, you will be like to do very little good. I hope you do not deserve it but this is the oppinion that manny in this and the neighbouring towns have of you and the very People who a Twelvemonth ago heard you with admiration and talk'd of you with applause, will now leave the meeting-house when you inter it to preach." Mary Smith Cranch to Isaac Smith, Jr., October 15, 1774, *Adams Family Correspondence*, ed. L.H. Butterfield et al., 6 vols. to date (Cambridge, Mass., 1963–), 1:171.

2. On Isaac Smith's directions to the British troops, see Frank Warren Coburn, *The Battle of April 19, 1775* (Lexington, Mass., 1912), 117; David Hackett Fischer, *Paul Revere's Ride* (New York, 1994), 240–241.

3. The seven who died were Isaac Bangs, of unknown causes while in the service; William Vinal, of camp fever while a British prisoner in New York Harbor; Samuel Murray, of unknown causes while serving as a British army doctor; Stephen Crosby, of illness aboard a privateer off the New England coast; Theodore Parsons, lost at sea aboard a privateer; Nathan Morey, of illness aboard a British prison ship at Halifax, Nova Scotia; and Benjamin Muzzy, lost at sea aboard a privateer. *Sibley's Harvard Graduates*, 17:484, 654; 18:138, 230, 274–275, 457, 458.

4. Fischer, *Paul Revere's Ride*, 127, 184. Fischer confuses Samuel Murray with his older brother, Daniel.

5. Martin Herrick (1747–1820), A.B. 1772. *Sibley's Harvard Graduates*, 18:95–97. Fischer, *Paul Revere's Ride*, 140.

6. William Lincoln, *History of Worcester, Massachusetts* (Worcester, 1862), 194.

7. Jacob Bacon (1751–1816), A.B. 1771. *Sibley's Harvard Graduates*, 17:477–478.

8. William Eustis (1753–1825), A.B. 1772. *Sibley's Harvard Graduates*, 18:70–84. Edward Warren, *The Life of John Warren, M.D.* (Boston, 1874), 24.

9. Thomas Rice Willard (1748–1777), A.B. 1774. *Sibley's Harvard Graduates*, 18:535–536. *Journals of Each Provincial Congress of Massachusetts in 1774 and 1775* (Boston, 1838), 664.

10. *Memoirs of the Members of the Social Circle in Concord*, 2nd ser. (Cambridge, Mass., 1888), 58–59.

11. Benjamin Cutter and William R. Cutter, *History of the Town of Arlington* (Boston, 1880), 75, 83.

12. Resolution of the Massachusetts Provincial Congress, April 28, 1775, printed in *The Journals of the Provincial Congress of Massachusetts* (Boston, 1838), 166.

13. For Jennison's military career, see Charles R. Smith, *Marines in the Revolution: A History of the Continental Marines in the American Revolution, 1775–1783* (Washington, D.C., 1975), 343–357.

14. William Lincoln, *History of Worcester, Massachusetts* (Worcester, 1862), 194.

15. Thomas Welsh (1752–1831), A.B. 1772. *Sibley's Harvard Graduates*, 18:183–188. Warren, *Life of John Warren*, 22–24.

16. *General Thomas Gage reported sixty-five British soldiers dead; the Americans lost fifty dead either in action or from wounds. Fischer, Paul Revere's Ride, 320–321.*

17. Lincoln, *History of Worcester*, 194.

18. William Hobart (1751–1801), A.B. 1774. *Sibley's Harvard Graduates*, 18:437–439. *Massachusetts Soldiers and Sailors of the Revolutionary War*, 17 vols. (Boston, 1896–1908), 8:15.

19. Samuel Prentice (1753–1815), A.B. 1771. *Sibley's Harvard Graduates*, 17:606.

20. *Sibley's Harvard Graduates*, 8:722.

21. Army barracks were much less comfortable, at least for enlisted men, than college dormitories were for undergraduates. The army quartered about 1,700 men in Massachusetts, Hollis, and Stoughton halls and Holden Chapel, facilities that ordinarily accommodated only a little over 100 students. Samuel Eliot Morison, *Three Centuries of Harvard, 1636–1936* (Cambridge, Mass., 1936), 148–151.

22. Willard M. Wallace, *Appeal to Arms: A Military History of the American Revolution* (New York, 1951), 35–39.

23. *The Autobiography of Colonel John Trumbull*, ed. Theodore Sizer (New Haven, 1953), 19–21.

24. Wallace, *Appeal to Arms*, 45–46.

25. "William Cheever's Diary, 1775–1776," *Proceedings of the Massachusetts Historical Society*, 60:92.

26. *Sibley's Harvard Graduates*, 17:477; 18:72, 184.

27. *Sibley's Harvard Graduates*, 18:96, 110.

28. Benjamin Lovell (1753–1828), A.B. 1774. *Sibley's Harvard Graduates*, 18:451–456. *Historical Magazine* (June 1868):368.

29. Wallace, *Appeal to Arms*, 45–47.

30. Wallace, *Appeal to Arms*, 58; Mary Beth Norton, *The British-Americans: The Loyalist Exiles in England, 1774–1789* (Boston, 1972), 29.

31. The three were Samuel Sparhawk, William Chandler, and James Putnam, Jr. *Sibley's Harvard Graduates*, 17:631; 18:24, 472.

32. *Sibley's Harvard Graduates*, 17:657.

33. Israel Keith to Theodore Parsons, July 23, 1775, Israel Keith II Papers, Massachusetts Historical Society.

34. *Autobiography of Colonel John Trumbull*, 21–22.

35. John Homans (1753–1800), A.B. 1772. *Sibley's Harvard Graduates*, 18:104–107. *History of the Town of Dorchester* (Boston, 1859), 334–335; William Dana Orcutt, *Good Old Dorchester: A Narrative of the Town, 1630–1893* (Cambridge, Mass., 1893), 132.

36. *Autobiography of Colonel John Trumbull*, 23–24. *Sibley's Harvard Graduates*, 17:615.

37. Wallace, *Appeal to Arms*, 60–65.

38. "Revolutionary Journal of Dr. John Warren," March 21, 1776, John Collins Warren Papers, Massachusetts Historical Society.

39. "Revolutionary Journal of Dr. John Warren," March 21, 1776.

40. Janice Potter, *The Liberty We Seek: Loyalist Ideology in Colonial New York and Massachusetts* (Cambridge, Mass., 1983), vii; Wallace, *Appeal to Arms*, 65.

41. James H. Stark, *The Loyalists of Massachusetts and the Other Side of the American Revolution* (Boston, 1910), 134.

42. In addition to Murray, Chandler, and probably Coffin, loyalists who took part in the evacuation included Samuel Paine, Jonathan Simpson, James Putnam, and Nathaniel Thomas. *Sibley's Harvard Graduates*, 17:582; 18:155, 472, 508.

43. Thomas H. Raddall, *Halifax, Warden of the North* (Toronto, 1948), 75.

44. Peter Oliver, Journal, April 3, 1776, Egerton Manuscripts, British Museum, London, quoted in Norton, *British-Americans*, 31; Raddall, *Halifax, Warden of the North*, 85–86.

45. Norton, *British-Americans*, 31.

46. Colin Nicolson, " 'McIntosh, Otis & Adams are our demagogues': Nathaniel Coffin and the Loyalist Interpretation of the Origins of the American Revolution," *Proceedings of the Massachusetts Historical Society* 108 (1996):72–114.

47. *Sibley's Harvard Graduates*, 17:563–565; 18:136–138.

48. *Sibley's Harvard Graduates*, 18:23.

49. *Sibley's Harvard Graduates*, 18:132, 177.

50. Joseph Haven (1747–1825), A.B. 1774. *Sibley's Harvard Graduates*, 18:433–437. Franklin D. McDuffie, *History of the Town of Rochester, New Hampshire, from 1722 to 1890*, ed. and rev. Silvanus Hayward, 2 vols. (Manchester, N.H., 1892), 1:57, 60–61, 66.

51. Benjamin Loring (1754–1787), A.B. 1772. *Sibley's Harvard Graduates*, 18:129–131.

52. Isaac Bangs (1752–ca. 1781), A.B. 1771. *Sibley's Harvard Graduates*, 17:480–484. Edward Bangs, ed., *Journal of Lieutenant Isaac Bangs, April 1 to July 29, 1776* (Cambridge, Mass., 1890), 43.

53. Warren, *Life of John Warren*, 49.

54. *New England Historical and Genealogical Register* 19 (1865): 44–45.

55. *Sibley's Harvard Graduates*, 17:614.

56. The infantry officers were John Lindall Borland, George Inman, and Thomas Flucker. Near the end of the war, Daniel Murray, who had led a loyalist militia company on several raids between 1777 and 1779, received a commission as a major in the Royal American Dragoons, provided he assemble a regiment of 360 soldiers. Daniel was unable to raise his unit until the end of hostilities, when it became part of the British garrison in Canada. *Sibley's Harvard Graduates*, 17:564–565; 18:15, 110–113, 240–241.

57. George Inman, Journal, [1776], Cambridge Historical Society, on deposit at Houghton Library, Harvard University.

58. Inman, Journal, [1777].

59. John Lindall Borland (1753–1825), A.B. 1772. *Sibley's Harvard Graduates*, 18:14–17. PRO, A.O. 12/105, fol. 5.

60. John Trumbull to John Trumbull Ray, October 26, 1811, John Trumbull Papers, Sterling Library, Yale University, quoted in Irma B. Jaffe, *John Trumbull: Patriot-Artist of the American Revolution* (Boston, 1975), 29.

61. *Autobiography of Colonel John Trumbull*, 36.

62. Jaffe, *John Trumbull*, 30; *Autobiography of Colonel John Trumbull*, 36–43.

63. *Sibley's Harvard Graduates*, 17:615–616.

64. Warham Parks (1752–1801), A.B. 1773. *Sibley's Harvard Graduates*, 18:270–272.

65. *Sibley's Harvard Graduates*, 18:443–444.

66. On the psychological effects of war on revolutionary soldiers, particularly

post–traumatic stress disorder, see John Resch, *Suffering Soldiers: Revolutionary War Veterans, Moral Sentiment, and Political Culture in the Early Republic* (Amherst, 1999), 61–64.

67. Fred Anderson, *A People's Army: Massachusetts Soldiers and Society in the Seven Years' War* (Chapel Hill, 1984), 160–161.

68. Robert K. Wright, *The Continental Army* (Washington, D.C., 1983), 49, 141.

69. George F. Scheer, ed., *Private Yankee Doodle* (Boston, 1962), 34–40.

70. Howard Peckham calculates that the Americans lost 6,824 men killed in action, 10,000 camp deaths, and 8,500 deaths among prisoners held by the British, although he warns that his figures are incomplete and estimates that they may have suffered approximately 1,000 more killed in action. Howard H. Peckham, ed., *The Toll of Independence: Engagements & Battle Casualties of the American Revolution* (Chicago, 1974), 41–43, 52, 130–131.

71. Anderson, *People's Army*, 77; John Keegan, *The Face of Battle* (London, 1976), 175–195.

72. Wright, *Continental Army*, 134.

73. William Bradford (1752–1811), A.B. 1773. *Sibley's Harvard Graduates*, 18:220–224. William Bradford to "Count," October 16, 1776, Miscellaneous Manuscripts Collection, Manuscripts Division, Rhode Island Historical Society, Providence. The Battle of Pell's Point did not take place for two days. At the engagement on October 18, an American force of 750 men lost 8 killed and 13 wounded, while the British landing party lost at least 4 dead and 20 wounded. Peckham, *Toll of Independence*, 24.

74. Israel Keith (1751–1819), A.B. 1771. *Sibley's Harvard Graduates*, 17:549–553. Israel Keith to Cyrus Keith, November 23, 1776, January 4, 1777, Israel Keith II Papers, Massachusetts Historical Society.

75. Charles Royster, *A Revolutionary People at War: The Continental Army and American Character, 1775–1783* (Chapel Hill, 1979), 190–191.

76. In addition to the doctors who were practicing medicine in the service, Dr. Isaac Bangs served as an infantry officer. *Sibley's Harvard Graduates*, 17:480–484.

77. Samuel Tenney to Elihu Greene, January 15, 1778, Nathaniel Greene Papers, American Antiquarian Society, Worcester, Mass. Tenney was describing life at Valley Forge.

78. John Warren, William Eustis, John Homans, and Samuel Tenney all served in the Continental Army from 1776 until at least 1781; over the same period, Benjamin Loring served with the British army. *Sibley's Harvard Graduates*, 17:657–661; 18: 71–73, 106, 167.

79. Walter Hastings (1752–1782), A.B. 1771. *Sibley's Harvard Graduates*, 17:526. Willard, *Appeal to Arms*, 169–170.

80. *Sibley's Harvard Graduates*, 17:657–661.

81. On revolutionary supply and logistics, see E. Wayne Carp, *To Starve the Army at Pleasure: Continental Army Administration and American Political Culture* (Chapel Hill, 1984).

82. *Sibley's Harvard Graduates*, 17:508.

83. William Eustis to John Warren, October 7, 1776, John Warren Papers, Massachusetts Historical Society.

84. James Putnam, Jr. (1756–1838), A.B. 1774. *Sibley's Harvard Graduates*, 18:36–38, 471–476.

85. Thomas Aston Coffin to Mary (Aston) Coffin, January 31, 1777, Thomas Aston Coffin Papers, Massachusetts Historical Society.

86. Jonathan Norwood (1751–1782), A.B. 1771. *Sibley's Harvard Graduates*, 17: 566. Jonathan Norwood to John Warren, June 5, 1775, John Collins Warren Papers, Massachusetts Historical Society.

87. Isaac Bangs to John Warren, August 26, 1775, John Collins Warren Papers, Massachusetts Historical Society.

88. William Eustis to John Warren, June 30, 1777, John Collins Warren Papers, Massachusetts Historical Society.

89. Israel Keith to Joseph Pearse Palmer, November 19, 1776, Israel Keith II Papers, Massachusetts Historical Society.

90. Thomas Aston Coffin Papers, 1775–1783, Massachusetts Historical Society.

91. Israel Keith to Cyrus Keith, November 15, 1776, Israel Keith II Papers, Massachusetts Historical Society.

92. Thomas Aston Coffin to Mary (Aston) Coffin, May 1, 1777, February 6, 1778, October 1, 1779, July 4, 1780, May 10, July 13, 1782, Thomas Aston Coffin Papers.

93. Thomas Aston Coffin to Mary (Aston) Coffin, October 5, 1778, Thomas Aston Coffin Papers.

94. Thomas Aston Coffin to Mary (Aston) Coffin, August 1, 1779, Thomas Aston Coffin Papers.

95. Thomas Aston Coffin to Mary (Aston) Coffin), November 5, 1777, Thomas Aston Coffin Papers.

96. Thomas Aston Coffin to Mary (Aston) Coffin), May 28, 1778, Thomas Aston Coffin Papers.

97. Thomas Aston Coffin to Mary (Aston) Coffin, October 5, 1778, Thomas Aston Coffin Papers.

98. Thomas Aston Coffin to Mary (Aston) Coffin, May 11, 1781, Thomas Aston Coffin Papers.

99. Thomas Aston Coffin to Mary (Aston) Coffin, August 4, 1781, Thomas Aston Coffin Papers.

100. Thomas Aston Coffin to Mary (Aston) Coffin, August 28, 1781, Thomas Aston Coffin Papers.

101. Thomas Aston Coffin to Mary (Aston) Coffin, October 23, 1781, Thomas Aston Coffin Papers.

102. Thomas Aston Coffin to Mary (Aston) Coffin, February 1, 1782, Thomas Aston Coffin Papers.

103. Corporation Records, 2:426–427; Faculty Records, 4:74–75, Harvard University Archives.

104. Morison, *Three Centuries of Harvard*, 149–150; Faculty Records, 4:17, Harvard University Archives; Allen French, *Old Concord* (Boston, 1915), 42; Townsend Scudder, *Concord: American Town* (Boston, 1947), 113–114; Lemuel Shattuck, *A History of the Town of Concord* (Boston, 1835), 206; Ruth R. Wheeler, *Concord: Climate for Freedom* (Concord, 1967), frontispiece and 68.

105. Ephraim Eliot, "Some Account of My Classmates in College Who Graduated in 1780," *Publications of the Colonial Society of Massachusetts*, 19:290–295.

106. Morison, *Three Centuries of Harvard*, 151–155.

107. Abigail Adams to John Adams, September 29, 1778, *Adams Family Corre-*

spondence, ed. L. H. Butterfield and Marc Friedlaender, 6 vols. to date (Cambridge, Mass., 1963–), 3:95.

108. *Sibley's Harvard Graduates,* 18:285–286. Gad Stevens also made saltpeter; see *Sibley's Harvard Graduates,* 17:633.

109. *Sibley's Harvard Graduates,* 18:122.

110. Other officeholders included Nathaniel Dickinson (Amherst), William Fisk (Waltham), Joshua Thomas (Plymouth), Thomas Farrington (Cambridge), Samuel Henshaw (Milton), Abner Morgan (Brimfield), Warham Parks (Westfield), and John Tucker (clerk of state Supreme Judicial Court). See *Sibley's Harvard Graduates,* 17: 503; 18:85, 172, 237, 247, 262, 271–272, 520–521.

111. Like Merrick, John Thaxter also assisted John Adams, in his case as a private secretary in England. *Sibley's Harvard Graduates,* 18:255, 498–502.

112. *Memoirs of the Members of the Social Circle,* 2:59–60.

113. John Thaxter (1755–1791), A.B. 1774. *Sibley's Harvard Graduates,* 18:494–507. John Thaxter, Jr., to John Thaxter, Sr., February 14, 1780, Thaxter Papers, Massachusetts Historical Society.

114. Isaac Smith to William Smith, October 28, 1775, Smith-Townsend Papers, II, Massachusetts Historical Society; *Sibley's Harvard Graduates,* 16:526–527.

115. [Married] "19 Feb. 1777. James Trecothick, Esq: of Addington Place, in Surrey, to Miss Edmonstone, eldest daughter of Sir Arch. Edmonstone, Bart." *Annual Register* 20 (1777): 219.

116. Samuel Hirst Sparhawk (1752–1789), A.B. 1771. *Sibley's Harvard Graduates,* 17:631–632.

117. *Sibley's Harvard Graduates,* 18:453–454.

118. Jonathan Simpson (1753–1834), A.B. 1772. *Sibley's Harvard Graduates,* 18: 154–158.

119. Jere R. Daniell, *Experiment in Republicanism: New Hampshire Politics and the American Revolution, 1741–1794* (Cambridge, Mass., 1970), 137; Robert A. Gross, *The Minutemen and Their World* (New York, 1976), 137–138; *Sibley's Harvard Graduates,* 18:218; Richard Buel, Jr., *Dear Liberty: Connecticut's Mobilization for the Revolutionary War* (Middletown, Conn., 1980), 94.

120. Solomon Willard (1747–1812), A.B. 1773. *Sibley's Harvard Graduates,* 18: 351–354. Petition of Solomon Willard, October 19, 1785, *Documents Relating to the Province [Towns and State] of New Hampshire,* 39 vols. (Concord, N.H., 1867–1941), 13:690–691.

121. Daniel Rogers (1749–1804), A.B. 1771. *Sibley's Harvard Graduates,* 17:609–610.

122. John Eliot to Jeremy Belknap, May 20, 1777, *Collections of the Massachusetts Historical Society,* 51:116; Henry N. Blake, "Harvard Soldiers and Sailors in the American Revolution," *Harvard Graduates' Magazine* 28 (1919): 254.

123. *The History of the Town of Amherst, Massachusetts,* comp. Carpenter and Morehouse (Amherst, 1896), 86–93; *Massachusetts Soldiers and Sailors,* 2:253.

124. *Documents Relating to . . . New Hampshire,* 8:269–270, 564, 569; Charles W. Brewster, *Rambles about Portsmouth,* 2nd ser. (Portsmouth, N.H., 1869), 132; Sheafe Family Papers, New Hampshire Historical Society, Box 1, Folder 6; *New Hampshire Genealogical Record* 5 (1908) :166.

125. Thomas Rindge Rogers (1755–1807), A.B. 1774. *Sibley's Harvard Graduates,* 18:482–483.

126. *Sibley's Harvard Graduates,* 18:482–483.

127. Thomas Aston Coffin to Mary Aston Coffin, September 18, 1783, Thomas Aston Coffin Papers.

128. Thomas Aston Coffin to Mary Aston Coffin, June 17, 1783, Thomas Aston Coffin Papers.

129. *Sibley's Harvard Graduates,* 17:371.

130. "Ward Chipman's Diary: A Loyalist's Return to New England in 1783," ed. Joseph B. Berry, *Essex Institute Historical Collections* 87 (1951): 223–224.

131. "Ward Chipman's Diary," 223, 224.

132. "Ward Chipman's Diary," 217.

133. "Ward Chipman's Diary," 217–218.

134. "Ward Chipman's Diary," 219.

135. "Ward Chipman's Diary," 220–221.

136. "Ward Chipman's Diary," 228.

137. Located near Harvard Square, the Blue Anchor served Cambridge patrons for nearly a century. George H. Hanford, *"For the Entertainment of Strangers": The Inns & Pubs of Cambridge* (Cambridge, Mass., 1997), 6.

138. "Ward Chipman's Diary," 229.

139. "Ward Chipman's Diary," 230.

140. "Ward Chipman's Diary," 231.

141. "Ward Chipman's Diary," 235.

5. REVOLUTIONARY CHANGES

1. *Magazine of American History* 2, pt. 2 (1878): 754; 3, pt. 1 (1879): 57.

2. George Daniels, *History of the Town of Oxford, Massachusetts* (Oxford, 1892), 560.

3. John Adams Vinton, *The Giles Memorial* (Boston, 1864), 262–263.

4. Lincoln County Registry of Deeds, 19:134. On Thomaston, see Cyrus Eaton, *History of Thomaston, Rockland, and South Thomaston, Maine* (Hallowell, Me., 1865), 2: 78.

5. William Bentley, *Diary of William Bentley,* 4 vols. (Salem, 1905–1914), 1:135; Lincoln County Registry of Deeds, 27:118.

6. Undated biographical note on Sally (Fiske) Jennison, Belcher-Jennison-Weiss Papers, Box 1, "undated" file, Massachusetts Historical Society. On divorce in eighteenth-century New England, see Anne S. Lombard, *Making Manhood: Growing Up Male in Colonial New England* (Cambridge, Mass., 2003), 103–105.

7. For different ways of looking at the social consequences of the American Revolution, see, for example, Benjamin Woods Labaree, *Patriots and Partisans: The Merchants of Newburyport, 1764–1815* (Cambridge, Mass., 1962); Jackson Turner Main, *The Social Structure of Revolutionary America* (Princeton, 1965); and Jean Butenhoff Lee, *The Price of Nationhood: The American Revolution in Charles County* (New York, 1994).

8. Interesting examples include Peter Charles Hoffer, *Revolution & Regeneration: Life Cycle and the Historical Vision of the Generation of 1776* (Athens, Ga., 1983); and Eric T. Dean, Jr., *Shook Over Hell: Post-Traumatic Stress, Vietnam, and the Civil War* (Cambridge, Mass., 1997).

9. *Sibley's Harvard Graduates,* 17:616.

10. Benjamin Brown Plaisted (1754–ca. 1783), A.B. 1774. *Sibley's Harvard Graduates*, 18:467–468. Suffolk County Probate File no. 16560.

11. Francis B. Heitman, *Historical Register of Officers of the Continental Army* (Baltimore, 1982), 319.

12. Dedham Alarm List, Miscellaneous [1775], Massachusetts Historical Society.

13. Heitman, *Historical Register*, 481.

14. "Letters of Nathaniel Walker Appleton, 1773–1784," ed. William C. Lane, *Publications of the Colonial Society of Massachusetts*, 8:313n. A file of correspondence and notes of experiments in the Pearson Papers at Phillips Academy records his search for the formula for gunpowder. See "Papers on Making Salt-petre," Box 1.

15. Charles Royster, *A Revolutionary People at War: The Continental Army and American Character, 1775–1783* (Chapel Hill, 1979), 25–80.

16. John Alford Mason (1750–1831), A.B. 1771. *Sibley's Harvard Graduates*, 17: 554–555.

17. Onesiphorus Tileston (1755–1809), A.B. 1774. *Sibley's Harvard Graduates*, 18: 516–518. *New England Historical and Genealogical Register* 55 (1901): 388–389.

18. Nathan Morey (1747–ca. 1778), A.B. 1774. *Sibley's Harvard Graduates*, 18: 457–458; Bristol County Probate File no. 25:153.

19. Benjamin Muzzy (1752–1777), A.B. 1774. *Sibley's Harvard Graduates*, 18:458. Charles Hudson, *History of the Town of Lexington*, 2 vols. (Boston, 1913), 2:481.

20. Caleb Butler, *History of the Town of Groton* (Boston, 1848), 182–184.

21. *Groton Historical Series*, 2:432–433.

22. Henry N. Blake, "Harvard Soldiers and Sailors in the American Revolution," *Harvard Graduates' Magazine* 28 (1919): 254.

23. On Eliot, see Joseph McKean, "Memoir," *Collections of the Massachusetts Historical Society*, 2nd ser., 1:211–248; and *Sibley's Harvard Graduates*, 18:55–68.

24. McKean, "Memoir," 215.

25. Andrew Eliot, Jr., to Andrew Eliot, Sr., October 10, 1777, Houghton Library, Harvard University.

26. John Eliot to Jeremy Belknap, September 11, 1779, *Collections of the Massachusetts Historical Society*, 54:150.

27. *Historical Notices of the New North Religious Society* (Boston, 1822), 31–32; Andrew Eliot, *A Sermon Preached at the Ordination of the Reverend John Eliot* (Boston, 1780).

28. *New England Historical and Genealogical Register* 12 (1858): 341.

29. *Sibley's Harvard Graduates*, 18:285–288.

30. Jonathan Williams (1753–1780), A.B. 1772. *Sibley's Harvard Graduates*, 18: 193–196. Gerald W. Gawalt, *The Promise of Power: The Emergence of the Legal Profession in Massachusetts, 1760–1840* (Westport, Conn., 1979), 36.

31. John Tracy (1753–1815), A.B. 1771. *Sibley's Harvard Graduates*, 17:646–649. *Essex Journal*, January 5, 1776.

32. *Sibley's Harvard Graduates*, 17:646–647.

33. Other members of the revolutionary generation who had extensive military service led successful civilian lives before exhibiting such problems. See, for example, Phineas Bowman (1750–ca. 1815), A.B. 1772, whose six years as an infantry officer preceded a successful career as a lawyer and New York State legislator, but who succumbed to intemperance *Sibley's Harvard Graduates*, 18:18–20.

34. Philip Cash, "The Professionalization of Boston Medicine, 1760–1803," *Publications of the Colonial Society of Massachusetts*, 57:82–83.

35. *Sibley's Harvard Graduates*, 17:614–626.

36. Daniel Parker (1756–1796), A.B. 1774. *Sibley's Harvard Graduates*, 18:464–465. *Massachusetts Soldiers and Sailors of the Revolutionary War*, 17 vols. (Boston, 1896–1908), 11:844.

37. *Boston Evening Post*, October 9, 1779; *Bostonian Society Publications*, 9:25; *Report of the Record Commissioners of the City of Boston*, 39 vols. (Boston, 1876–1909), 25:155.

38. Clement Biddle, *The Philadelphia Directory* (Philadelphia, 1791), 98; James Hardie, *The Philadelphia Directory and Register* (Philadelphia, 1793), 110; *The Papers of John Marshall*, ed., 11 vols. to date Herbert A. Johnson et al. (Chapel Hill, 1974–), 5:215–227.

39. Jacob Welsh (1755–1822), A.B. 1774. *Sibley's Harvard Graduates*, 18:523–526. Heitman, *Historical Register*, 581.

40. Jacob Welsh to George Washington, November 17, 1791, *The Papers of George Washington: Presidential Series*, ed. Mark A. Mastromarino and Jack D. Warren, 9 vols. to date (Charlottesville, 1987–), 9:195–197.

41. Samuel Tenney (1748–1816), A.B. 1772; John Sprague (1752–1800), A.B. 1772. *Sibley's Harvard Graduates*, 18:166–169, 161–163.

42. John Hastings (1754–1839), A.B. 1772. *Sibley's Harvard Graduates*, 18:87–89.

43. Thomas Flucker (1756–1784), A.B. 1773; Brinley Sylvester Oliver (1755–1828), A.B. 1774. *Sibley's Harvard Graduates*, 17:632, 18:239–244, 459–463.

44. *Sibley's Harvard Graduates*, 18:35–50, 483–488.

45. Isaac Smith to Elizabeth (Storer) Smith, [1780?], Smith-Carter Papers, Massachusetts Historical Society.

46. *Sibley's Harvard Graduates*, 16:527–528.

47. See table 5.

48. See table 11.

49. See table 6.

50. See table 12.

51. See table 13.

52. See table 14.

53. See tables 15, 16.

54. See tables 12, 17.

55. See table 9.

56. See tables 9, 10.

57. See tables 9, 18.

58. See table 18. On Eustis, see *Sibley's Harvard Graduates*, 18:78.

59. See table 19.

60. See table 20.

61. See table 21.

62. See table 11.

63. On the transformative effects of the Revolution, see Gordon S. Wood, *The Radicalism of the American Revolution* (New York, 1992).

64. John Thaxter, Jr., to Francis Dana, July 13, 1783, Dana Papers, Massachusetts Historical Society.

65. Evarts B. Greene and Virginia D. Harrington, *American Population before the Federal Census of 1790* (New York, 1932), 32, 41.

66. James Duncan Phillips, "Folks in Haverhill in 1783," *Essex Institute Historical Collections* 82 (1946): 146–147.

67. *Vital Records of Haverhill, Massachusetts, to the End of the Year 1849*, 2 vols. (Topsfield, 1910–1911), 2:95; *Diary of John Quincy Adams*, ed. David Grayson Allen et al., 2 vols. (Cambridge, Mass., 1981–), 1:335.

68. Greene and Harrington, *American Population*, 21, 27, 29, 30, 73–79, 87.

69. York County Probate, 16:26–28, 498–502.

70. Bowdoin's business dealings are revealed in detail in his letterbooks. See the Bowdoin Collection, George J. Mitchell Department of Special Collections & Archives, Bowdoin College Library, especially Letterbook 1, 1791–1805.

71. Isaac Course to Tilly Merrick, June 2, 1783, Tilly Merrick Papers, Concord Free Public Library, Concord, Mass.

72. *Sibley's Harvard Graduates*, 18:255–258. Merrick's correspondence provides insight into his business dealings. See the Tilly Merrick Papers, Concord Free Public Library.

73. Robert Williams (1753–1834), A.B. 1773. *Sibley's Harvard Graduates*, 18:354–356. *New Hampshire Journal: or Farmer's Museum*, May 9, 16, August 9, 1793; Francis S. Drake, *Memorials of the Society of Cincinnati of Massachusetts* (Boston, 1873), 512–513; Daniel Saunders, Jr., *A Journal of the Travels and Suffering of Daniel Saunders, Jr.* (Salem, 1794); Alexander Williams, Jr., "A History of Our Descent from Robert and Marjary Williams of Boston," typescript, New England Historical and Genealogical Society, Boston.

74. *Sibley's Harvard Graduates*, 18:420–421.

75. Perez Morton (1751–1837), A.B. 1771. *Sibley's Harvard Graduates*, 17:555–561.

76. Samuel Eliot Morison, *Three Centuries of Harvard, 1636–1936* (Cambridge, Mass., 1936), 151–155. On class size, see *Quinquennial Catalogue of the Officers and Graduates of Harvard University, 1636–1905* (Cambridge, Mass., 1905), 132–138; and "Tentative Lists of Temporary Students at Harvard College, 1639–1800," *Publications of the Colonial Society of Massachusetts*, 17:277.

77. Henry K. Beecher and Mark D. Altschule, *Medicine at Harvard: The First Three Hundred Years* (Hanover, 1977), 29–35, 40–45, 47–49.

78. Perez Morton, *An Oration Delivered at the King's-Chapel in Boston, April 8, 1776* (Boston, 1776), 11, 13.

79. John Warren, *An Oration, Delivered July 4th, 1783* (Boston, 1783), 22–23.

80. Joseph Avery, *An Oration, Delivered at Holden, July 4, 1806* (Boston, 1806), 5–6.

81. Carrie Rebora et al., *John Singleton Copley in America* (New York, 1995), 47.

82. *The Autobiography of Colonel John Trumbull: Patriot-Artist, 1756–1843*, ed. Theodore Sizer (New Haven, 1953), 44–45.

83. Trumbull, *Autobiography*, 45. Eustis studied medicine and eventually served as governor of Massachusetts. King, class of 1777, later became a United States senator and the American minister to the Court of St. James's. Gore, class of 1776, later became governor of Massachusetts and a United States senator. Tyler, class of 1776, a lawyer and playwright, served as chief justice of the Supreme Court of Vermont and as a professor of law at the University of Vermont. Dawes, class of 1777, became a judge. Dexter, class of 1776, became a doctor and professor of materia medica at Harvard Medical School.

84. Trumbull, *Autobiography*, 56.

85. On the importance of European training for American artists, see Neil Harris, *The Artist in American Society: The Formative Years, 1790–1860* (New York, 1966), chap. 1.

86. Trumbull, *Autobiography*, 52.

87. Trumbull, *Autobiography*, 58–59.

88. Trumbull, *Autobiography*, 63–72. Some students of Trumbull have concluded that he was on a secret mission for the United States government, although they have not discovered any details. See Irma B. Jaffe, *John Trumbull: Patriot-Artist of the American Revolution* (Boston, 1975), 44–50.

89. John Trumbull to David Trumbull, April 17, 1784, John Trumbull Papers, Connecticut Historical Society.

90. John Trumbull to Jonathan Trumbull, Sr., July 18, 1784, John Trumbull Papers, Connecticut Historical Society.

91. John Trumbull to Thomas Jefferson, June 11, 1784, Charles Allen Munn Collection, Fordham University.

6. THE AGE OF RESPONSIBILITY

1. On the age of officeholders, see Carole Haber, *Beyond Sixty-Five: The Dilemma of Old Age in America's Past* (Cambridge, 1983), 16.

2. It is not easy to study social maturation in colonial New England systematically, but the government and church service of community leaders in the eighteenth century provides useful measures. The typical civil servant began his public career in a minor post, for example, constable or fence viewer. More substantial positions, such as selectman and moderator, were tacitly reserved for men of middle age. A young man proved himself in minor offices in his twenties and thirties. Properly seasoned, having earned the respect and confidence of others, he was ready for greater responsibility sometime between his mid-thirties and his early forties. College men received credit for their education—in the towns that Edward M. Cook, Jr., studied, the average college graduate was 33.7 at his first election to selectman—but in most other cases a man had to reach his early forties before his neighbors were ready to entrust him with the leadership of their community. As a result of low turnover, there were fewer opportunities for lay leadership within the region's churches than in its government. Deacons, the lay leaders of a church, tended to serve for long periods, and when they first assumed office they were as old as or older than selectmen. Cook determined that 54 percent in the towns he surveyed were between the ages of forty and fifty-four, 22 percent were under forty, and 24 percent were fifty-five or older. Edward M. Cook, Jr., *The Fathers of the Towns: Leadership and Community Structure in Eighteenth-Century New England* (Baltimore, 1976), 102–116, 228n. 16.

3. Charles Stearns (1753–1826), A.B. 1773. *Sibley's Harvard Graduates*, 18:321–327. Edward G. Porter, *A Sermon Commemorative of One Hundred Fifty Years of the First Church in Lincoln* (Cambridge, Mass., 1899), 18.

4. William B. Sprague, *Annals of the American Pulpit*, 9 vols. (New York, 1857–1869), 8:96.

5. Zedekiah Sanger (1748–1820), A.B. 1771. *Sibley's Harvard Graduates*, 17:611–613. The Worcester Art Museum owns a miniature on ivory of Keith; Harvard

University has a portrait of Sanger. For photographs of these images, see *Sibley's Harvard Graduates*, 17: betw. 358–359.

6. Jack Larkin, *The Reshaping of Everyday Life, 1790–1840* (New York, 1988), 183.

7. Laban Wheaton (1754–1846), A.B. 1774. *Sibley's Harvard Graduates*, 18:526–534. For an engraving of a portrait of Warren by Rembrandt Peale, see John C. Warren, *Genealogy of Warren* (Boston, 1854), opp. 48, reproduced in *Sibley's Harvard Graduates*, 17: betw. 358–359. The Concord Museum owns a small painting on ivory of Merrick, which appears in *Sibley's Harvard Graduates*, 18: betw. 254–255. Wheaton College, Norton, Mass., owns an oil portrait by Eunice Makepeace Towle of Laban Wheaton.

8. Henry B. Pearson, Memoir, Box 2, Eliphalet Pearson Papers, Phillips Academy, Andover.

9. Winfred E. A. Bernhard, *Fisher Ames, Federalist and Statesman,1758–1808* (Chapel Hill, 1965).

10. Richard H. Saunders, "James Bowdoin III (1752–1811)," in *The Legacy of James Bowdoin III* (Brunswick, Me., 1994), 1–25.

11. *Sibley's Harvard Graduates*, 18:288.

12. See tables 22, 23, 24.

13. *Genealogy of the Waldo Family*, 2 vols. (Worcester, 1902), 1:158–163, 272–279. Gloria L. Main also notes that parenting often continued into one's sixties in *Peoples of a Spacious Land: Families and Cultures in Colonial New England* (Cambridge, Mass., 2001), 167.

14. See table 25.

15. Bernhard, *Fisher Ames*, 219, 276, 303–304.

16. Fisher Ames to Theodore Dwight, February 29, 1804, Fisher Ames Papers, Dedham Historical Society.

17. On the role of New England fathers, see Lisa Wilson, *Ye Heart of a Man: The Domestic Life of Men in Colonial New England* (New Haven, 1999), 115–139.

18. Samuel Phillips to John Phillips, January 24, 1795, Phillips Papers, Phillips Academy, Andover.

19. Henry B. Pearson to Eliphalet Pearson, May 2, 1816, Eliphalet Pearson Papers, Harvard University Archives.

20. John Warren to John Collins Warren, March 15, 1801, Warren Papers, Massachusetts Historical Society. In the end, John C. Warren passed up a degree at Edinburgh because he believed it would take too much time.

21. Fisher Ames to Theodore Dwight, February 29, 1804, Fisher Ames Papers, Dedham Historical Society.

22. Fisher Ames to J. Worthington Ames, February 15, 1808, Fisher Ames Papers, Dedham Historical Society.

23. Fisher Ames to Theodore Dwight, June 10, 1808, Fisher Ames Papers, Dedham Historical Society.

24. Calculated from *Sibley's Harvard Graduates*, vols. 17 and 18.

25. *Sibley's Harvard Graduates*, 18:68.

26. Eliphalet Pearson to Henry B. Pearson, February 3, 1812, Bromfield Family Papers, Manuscripts and Archives, Yale University Library.

27. Edward Barnard, Almanac-Diary, 1802, October 8, 1802, Peabody Essex Museum, Salem, Mass.

28. Samuel Phillips to John Phillips, October 17, 1797, Phillips Papers, Phillips Academy, Andover.

29. Mary Holyoke Pearson to Ephraim Abbott, October 25, 1812, December 20, 1813, Ephraim Abbott Papers, American Antiquarian Society, Worcester, Mass., quoted in Ellen K. Rothman, *Hands and Hearts: A History of Courtship in America* (New York, 1984), 22, 21.

30. Charles H. Bell, *The Bench and Bar of New Hampshire* (Boston, 1894), 519.

31. Gerald W. Gawalt, *The Promise of Power: The Emergence of the Legal Profession in Massachusetts, 1760–1840* (Westport, Conn., 1979), 41.

32. David Osgood (1748–1822), A.B. 1771. *Sibley's Harvard Graduates*, 17:570–580. Sprague, *Annals of the American Pulpit*, 8:247.

33. John Barnard Swett (1752–1796), A.B. 1771. *Sibley's Harvard Graduates*, 17:635–638. James Thacher, *American Medical Biography*, 2 vols. (Boston, 1828), 1:358. Thacher erroneously gives Swett's first name as Jonathan.

34. Thomas Neville Bonner, *Becoming a Physician: Medical Education in Great Britain, France, Germany, and the United States, 1750–1945* (New York, 1995), 42–43.

35. William Frederick Norwood, *Medical Education in the United States before the Civil War* (Philadelphia, 1944), 168.

36. Samuel Eliot Morison, *Three Centuries of Harvard, 1636–1936* (Cambridge, Mass., 1936), 99–100.

37. *Sibley's Harvard Graduates*, 17:664.

38. John Clarke (1753–1788), A.B. 1772. *Sibley's Harvard Graduates*, 18:33–35.

39. Morison, *Three Centuries of Harvard*, 169.

40. *Quinquennial Catalogue of the Officers and Graduates of Harvard University, 1636–1905* (Cambridge, Mass., 1905), 349–351. At first Harvard gave out an M.B., but changed to accord with the practices at other schools.

41. Thomas Francis Harrington, *The Harvard Medical School: A History, Narrative and Documentary*, 3 vols. (New York, 1905), 1:81–82.

42. Harrington, *Harvard Medical School*, 1:78.

43. Walter L. Burrage, *A History of the Massachusetts Medical Society* (Norwood, 1923), 33–35.

44. Richard Harrison Shryock, *Medicine and Society in America, 1760–1860* (New York, 1960), 31–34.

45. Burrage, *History of the Massachusetts Medical Society*, 37–67, 302–316, 350–365.

46. Burrage, *History of the Massachusetts Medical Society*, 38, 350–351.

47. Benjamin Curtis, Samuel Nye, John Barnard Swett, and John Warren, all class of 1771; Joshua Barker, William Eustis, John Homans, Samuel Tenney, and Thomas Welsh, all 1772; Nathaniel Appleton, 1773; and Abijah Richardson, ex-1774. *Fellows of the Massachusetts Medical Society, 1781–1870* (Boston, 1870).

48. Gerald W. Gawalt, "Massachusetts Legal Education in Transition, 1766–1840," *American Journal of Legal History* 17 (1973): 27–50.

49. Gawalt, *Promise of Power*, 131.

50. Gawalt, *Promise of Power*, 93.

51. Conrad Wright, "The Early Period (1811–1840)," in *The Harvard Divinity School: Its Place in Harvard University and in American Culture*, ed. George Huntston

Williams (Boston, 1954), 21–28; Arthur E. Sutherland, *The Law at Harvard: A History of Ideas and Men, 1817–1967* (Cambridge, Mass., 1967), 32–42.

52. Gawalt, *Promise of Power*, 132; Robert Stevens, *Law School: Legal Education in America from the 1850s to the 1980s* (Chapel Hill, 1983), 3–4.

53. Wright, "The Early Period (1811–1840)," 21–28.

54. *Sibley's Harvard Graduates*, 18:439–442, 516–518.

55. In addition to the eight men present, two others were invited but unable to attend. Those present were Jeremy Belknap, class of 1762; John Eliot, 1772; William Tudor, 1769; Peter Thacher, 1769; James Winthrop, 1769 (the former college librarian); James Freeman, 1777; James Sullivan; and Thomas Wallcutt. William Baylies, 1760, was out of town, and George Richards Minot, 1776, was unable to attend owing to illness, but the society has traditionally listed both among its founders. Louis Leonard Tucker, *Clio's Consort: Jeremy Belknap and the Founding of the Massachusetts Historical Society* (Boston, 1990), 87–95.

56. *Circular Letter, of the Historical Society* (Boston, 1791), 1.

57. *Sibley's Harvard Graduates*, 18:63.

58. Conrad Edick Wright, *The Transformation of Charity in Postrevolutionary New England* (Boston, 1992), 63. Following contemporary usage, I include among charitable institutions mutual benefit groups (notably the Freemasons), humanitarian organizations (including dispensaries and orphanages), missionary societies (also encompassing Bible, tract, and ministerial education initiatives), and reform associations (temperance, antislavery, and others).

59. John Eliot to Jeremy Belknap, July 31, 1781, *Collections of the Massachusetts Historical Society*, 54:213.

60. *Sibley's Harvard Graduates*, 18:61–62. *Quinquennial Catalogue of Harvard University*, 14. Between 1642 and 1697, and again between 1707 and 1780, the members of the Board of Overseers were "the Governor and Deputy Governor for the time being, and all the magistrates of this jurisdiction, together with the teaching elders of the six next adjoining towns, viz. Cambridge, Watertown, Charlestown, Boston, Roxbury, and Dorchester, and the President of the College." Chap. 5, sec. 1, art. 3 of the 1780 constitution of the Commonwealth of Massachusetts provided for several new categories of overseers: "The Governor, Lieutenant-Governor, Council, and Senate of the Commonwealth, with the President of the College, for the time being, and the Ministers of the Congregational Churches in the towns of Cambridge, Watertown, Charlestown, Boston, Roxbury, and Dorchester."

61. John Eliot to Jeremy Belknap, January 24, 1786, *Collections of the Massachusetts Historical Society*, 54:304.

62. *Sibley's Harvard Graduates*, 18:62.

63. John Eliot to Jeremy Belknap, January 24, 1786, *Collections of the Massachusetts Historical Society*, 54:307.

64. Calculated from *Sibley's Harvard Graduates*, 17:468–679 and 18 passim.

65. Thomas Edwards, Israel Keith, Perez Morton, Winthrop Sargent, John Barnard Swett, John Tracy, John Warren, and Amos Windship, all class of 1771; Thomas Burnham, John Eliot, William Eustis, Martin Herrick, and John Homans, all 1772; Ebenezer Boltwood, William Caldwell, Thomas Farrington, Thomas Prince, and Nathan Rice, all 1773; and Richard Roswell Eliot, William Hobart, and Abijah Richardson, all 1774. *Sibley's Harvard Graduates*, vols. 17, 18.

66. Thomas Edwards, Crocker Sampson, and William Sargent, all class of 1771; William Eustis, John Hastings, and John Homans, all 1772; Nathan Rice and Robert Williams, both 1773; and Joseph Crocker and Abijah Richardson, both 1774. *Sibley's Harvard Graduates*, vols. 17, 18.

67. Michael Joy and Winthrop Sargent, both class of 1771; John Eliot, William Fisk, Samuel Tenney, and Joshua Thomas, all 1772; Eliphalet Pearson, 1773; and John Bradford and John Clarke, both 1774. *Sibley's Harvard Graduates*, vols. 17, 18.

68. *Sibley's Harvard Graduates*, 17:508.

69. *Memoirs of the American Academy of Arts and Sciences, New Series*, 24 vols. (Boston, 1833–1957), 11, pt. 1:64.

70. *Sibley's Harvard Graduates*, 18:388, 390.

71. Jeremiah Barnard (1750–1835), A.B. 1773. *Sibley's Harvard Graduates*, 18:210–215.

72. *Laws of New Hampshire*, 10 vols. (Manchester, Concord, and Bristol, N.H., 1904–1922), 6:596; Daniel F. Secomb, *History of the Town of Amherst, Hillsborough County, New Hampshire* (Concord, N.H., 1883), 321.

73. *Sibley's Harvard Graduates*, 18:94, 176.

74. *Sibley's Harvard Graduates*, 17:579.

75. *Sibley's Harvard Graduates*, 17:508, 610, 616; 18:74, 88–89, 106, 312, 356, 407, 481.

76. *Sibley's Harvard Graduates*, 18:29.

77. *Sibley's Harvard Graduates*, 15:112–113.

78. Claude M. Fuess, *An Old New England School: A History of Phillips Academy, Andover* (Boston, 1917), 90.

79. *Diary of John Quincy Adams*, ed. David Grayson Allen et al., 2 vols. (Cambridge, Mass., 1981), 2:96.

80. *The Life and Letters of Joseph Story*, ed. William W. Story, 2 vols. (Boston, 1851), 1:49–50.

81. *Sibley's Harvard Graduates*, 18:291–292.

82. John Pierce, Memoirs, Massachusetts Historical Society, 7:308.

83. *Sibley's Harvard Graduates*, 18:259.

84. *Sibley's Harvard Graduates*, 18:42–46.

85. *Sibley's Harvard Graduates*, 18:46–48.

86. *Sibley's Harvard Graduates*, 18:44–46.

87. *Sibley's Harvard Graduates*, 18:486.

88. *Sibley's Harvard Graduates*, 18:486.

89. See table 26.

90. See table 27.

91. See table 28.

92. Robert Zemsky, *Merchants, Farmers, and River Gods: An Essay on Eighteenth-Century American Politics* (Boston, 1971).

7. PARTY PASSIONS

1. Lynn Warren Turner, *The Ninth State: New Hampshire's Formative Years* (Chapel Hill, 1983), 182.

2. For Republican accusations, see *Aurora*, April 29, July 1, 1802. For Federalist

refutations, see *New-England Palladium,* July 16, 1802, and *Columbian Centinel,* July 17, 1802.

3. Donald B. Cole, *Jacksonian Democracy in New Hampshire, 1800–1851* (Cambridge, Mass., 1970), 19–22.

4. James Sheafe to Jeremiah Mason, February 22, 1814, Jeremiah Mason Papers, New Hampshire Historical Society, Concord.

5. John T. Gilman to John Smith, February 3, 1816, John T. Gilman Papers, New Hampshire Historical Society, Concord.

6. Cole, *Jacksonian Democracy in New Hampshire,* 30; Turner, *Ninth State,* 328.

7. Joyce Appleby, *Inheriting the Revolution: The First Generation of Americans* (Cambridge, Mass., 2000), 56–89, provides a useful summary of the period's economic developments. On theaters, see Heather Shawn Nathans, "A Democracy of Glee: The Post-Revolutionary Theater in Boston and Philadelphia" (Ph.D. diss., Tufts University, 1999); and T. A. Milford, "Boston's Theater Controversy and Liberal Notions of Advantage," *New England Quarterly* 72 (1999): 61–88.

8. Richard S. Dunn, *Puritans and Yankees: The Winthrop Dynasty of New England, 1630–1717* (Princeton, 1962), 15–17.

9. Emery J. Battis, *Saints and Sectaries: Anne Hutchinson and the Antinomians in the Massachusetts Bay Colony* (Chapel Hill, 1962).

10. William G. McLoughlin, *New England Dissent: The Baptists and the Separation of Church and State, 1630–1833* (Cambridge, Mass., 1971); Joseph J. Ellis, *The New England Mind in Transition: Samuel Johnson of Connecticut, 1696–1772* (New Haven, 1973).

11. For important insights on Massachusetts politics, see Robert Zemsky, *Merchants, Farmers, and River Gods: An Essay on Eighteenth-Century American Politics* (Boston, 1971). Also see John J. Waters, Jr., *The Otis Family in Provincial and Revolutionary Massachusetts* (Chapel Hill, 1968), 132–161.

12. Urban competitions often involved claims for government favors such as the location of a college. On the battle over Yale between New Haven and Hartford, see Richard L. Bushman, *From Puritan to Yankee: Character and the Social Order in Connecticut, 1690–1765* (Cambridge, Mass., 1967), 140–142. On Rhode Island, see Sydney V. James, *Colonial Rhode Island: A History* (New York, 1975), 294–313.

13. Turner, *Ninth State,* 3–11.

14. Zemsky, *Merchants, Farmers, and River Gods;* Stephen E. Patterson, *Political Parties in Revolutionary Massachusetts* (Madison, 1973), 3–62.

15. Van Beck Hall, *Politics without Parties: Massachusetts, 1780–1791* (Pittsburgh, 1972); William M. Fowler, Jr., *The Baron of Beacon Hill: A Biography of John Hancock* (Boston, 1980), 203–281, and *Samuel Adams: Radical Puritan* (New York, 1997), 161–177; Paul Lewis, *The Grand Incendiary: A Biography of Samuel Adams* (New York, 1973), 328–391; Gordon E. Kershaw, *James Bowdoin II: Patriot and Man of the Enlightenment* (Lanham, Md., 1991), 207–301.

16. Hall, *Politics without Parties,* 166–226; David P. Szatmary, *Shays' Rebellion: The Making of an Agrarian Insurrection* (Amherst, 1980).

17. Turner, *Ninth State,* 48–57.

18. Patterson, *Political Parties,* 218–247; Jere R. Daniell, *Experiment in Republicanism: New Hampshire Politics and the American Revolution, 1741–1794* (Cambridge, Mass., 1970).

19. Hall, *Politics without Parties,* 256–320.

20. James M. Banner, Jr., *To the Hartford Convention: The Federalists and the Origins of Party Politics in Massachusetts, 1789–1815* (New York, 1969); David Hackett Fischer, *The Revolution of American Conservatism: The Federalist Party in the Era of Jeffersonian Democracy* (New York, 1965); Paul Goodman, *The Democratic-Republicans of Massachusetts: Politics in a Young Republic* (Cambridge, Mass., 1964). For more recent discussions of partisan politics in the street, see Simon P. Newman, *Parades and the Politics of the Street: Festive Culture in the Early American Republic* (Philadelphia, 1997); Len Travers, *Celebrating the Fourth: Independence Day and the Rites of Nationalism in the Early Republic* (Amherst, 1997); David Waldstreicher, *In the Midst of Perpetual Fetes: The Making of American Nationalism, 1776–1820* (Chapel Hill, 1997).

21. David Osgood, quoted in Ronald P. Formisano, *The Transformation of Political Culture, Massachusetts Parties, 1790–1840* (New York, 1983), 94.

22. *Works of Fisher Ames*, ed. Seth Ames, 2 vols. (1854; Indianapolis, 1983), 1:231, 233, 234.

23. A Farmer [Levi Lincoln], *Letters to the People* (Salem, 1802), 90–91.

24. Samuel Stone, quoted in Cotton Mather, *Magnalia Christi Americana* (Hartford, 1820), 1:395, quoted in Fischer, *Revolution of American Conservatism*, 4.

25. This discussion of Fisher Ames relies heavily on Winfred E. A. Bernhard, *Fisher Ames: Federalist and Statesman, 1758–1808* (Chapel Hill, 1965).

26. On the political differences between Nathaniel and Fisher Ames, see Samuel Eliot Morison, "Squire Ames and Doctor Ames," *New England Quarterly* 1 (1928): 5–31; Bernhard, *Fisher Ames*, 255–256, 298, 305, 322–323.

27. *Works of Fisher Ames*, 1:47.

28. Bernhard, *Fisher Ames*, 55–94.

29. Bernhard, *Fisher Ames*, 236.

30. Bernhard, *Fisher Ames*, 288–334.

31. Levi Lincoln to Thomas Jefferson, July 28, 1801, Box 1, Folder 4, Lincoln Family Papers, American Antiquarian Society, Worcester, Mass.

32. Levi Lincoln to Thomas Jefferson, September, 16, 1801, Box 1, Folder 4, Lincoln Family Papers.

33. *Sibley's Harvard Graduates*, 18:125.

34. This discussion of Lincoln is drawn from *Sibley's Harvard Graduates*, 18:121–128.

35. *Sibley's Harvard Graduates*, 18:122–126.

36. Formisano, *Transformation of Political Culture*, 77–78.

37. Helen R. Pinkney, *Christopher Gore, Federalist of Massachusetts, 1758–1827* (Waltham, Mass., 1969), 115–116.

38. *Sibley's Harvard Graduates*, 18:126–128.

39. See Harlow W. Sheidley, *Sectional Nationalism: Massachusetts Conservative Leaders and the Transformation of America, 1815–1836* (Boston, 1998).

40. Formisano, *Transformation of Political Culture*, 79–81, 103.

41. William Eustis to David Cobb, November 16, 1794, David Cobb Papers, Massachusetts Historical Society.

42. *Sibley's Harvard Graduates*, 18:70–84.

43. *Sibley's Harvard Graduates*, 18:83.

44. Oliver Peabody (1752–1831), A.B. 1773. *Sibley's Harvard Graduates*, 18:275–283.

45. *Sibley's Harvard Graduates*, 17:490, 492, 493–498, 561, 604, 622; 18:77–79, 81–83, 123–128, 168, 278–279, 371–375, 486–487, 526–534.

46. Josiah Smith (1749–1828), A.B. 1774. *Sibley's Harvard Graduates*, 18:489–492; Benjamin W. Labaree, *Patriots and Partisans: The Merchants of Newburyport, 1764–1815* (Cambridge, Mass., 1962), 140–141.

47. *Memoirs of Members of the Social Circle in Concord*, 2nd ser. (Cambridge, Mass., 1888), 61; Luther S. Cushing, *Reports of Controversial Elections in the House of Representatives, of the Commonwealth of Massachusetts, from 1780 to 1852* (Boston, 1853), 85–90.

48. *Sibley's Harvard Graduates*, 18:482–483.

49. Richard H. Saunders III, "James Bowdoin III (1752–1811)," *The Legacy of James Bowdoin III* (Brunswick, Me., 1994), 13–20; *Sibley's Harvard Graduates*, 17:487–500.

50. *Sibley's Harvard Graduates*, 17:487; 18:70, 121, 166, 367, 483, 526.

51. Carl Bridenbaugh, *Mitre & Sceptre: Transatlantic Faiths, Ideas, Personalities, and Politics, 1689–1775* (New York, 1962).

52. Conrad Wright, *The Beginnings of Unitarianism in America* (Boston, 1955), 59–240.

53. Wright, *Beginnings of Unitarianism*.

54. For the seventeenth-century argument over the role of human agency in salvation, see Norman Pettit, *The Heart Prepared: Grace and Conversion in Puritan Spiritual Life* (New Haven, 1966).

55. John Clarke (1755–1798), A.B. 1774. *Sibley's Harvard Graduates*, 18:395–405.

56. Wright, *Beginnings of Unitarianism*, 191–192.

57. Wright, *Beginnings of Unitarianism*, 189–190; Russell E. Miller, *The Larger Hope: The First Century of the Universalist Church in America, 1770–1870* (Boston, 1979), 3–49.

58. Wright, *Beginnings of Unitarianism*, 189–191.

59. John Eliot to Jeremy Belknap, December 7, 1782, *Collections of the Massachusetts Historical Society*, 54:238–239.

60. *Sibley's Harvard Graduates*, 7:216.

61. Wright, *Beginnings of Unitarianism*, 187–199.

62. *Sibley's Harvard Graduates*, 18:400.

63. John Eliot to Jeremy Belknap, October 22, 1783, *Collections of the Massachusetts Historical Society*, 54:264.

64. Charles Stearns, *A Sermon, Delivered before the Convention of Congregational Ministers in Massachusetts* (Boston, 1815), 24.

65. On the disintegration of the Congregationalist synthesis, see Peter S. Field, *The Crisis of the Standing Order: Clerical Intellectuals and Cultural Authority in Massachusetts, 1780–1833* (Amherst, 1998); Joseph W. Phillips, *Jedidiah Morse and New England Congregationalism* (New Brunswick, N.J., 1983); and Richard J. Moss, *The Life of Jedidiah Morse: A Station of Peculiar Exposure* (Knoxville, 1995), esp. 81–115.

66. On the establishment of these organizations, see Conrad Edick Wright, *The Transformation of Charity in Postrevolutionary New England* (Boston, 1992), 77–90.

67. Conrad Wright, "Institutional Reconstruction in the Unitarian Controversy," and Lilian Handlin, "*Babylon est delenda*: The Young Andrews Norton," in *American Unitarianism, 1805–1865*, ed. Conrad Edick Wright (Boston, 1989), 3–29, 53–85.

68. *The Diary of William Bentley, D.D.*, 4 vols. (Salem, 1905–1914), 3:138–139; Annotated Almanacs, February 1, 1805, John Eliot Papers, Massachusetts Historical

Society. Eliot records that the temperature in Boston on February 1 varied from 30 to 33 degrees, the wind shifted from the southeast to the northwest, and the skies were cloudy and rainy.

69. Wright, *Beginnings of Unitarianism*, 252–280.

70. Conrad Wright, "The Election of Henry Ware: Two Contemporary Accounts Edited with Commentary," *Harvard Library Bulletin* 17 (1969): 261–264.

71. Corporation Records, 4:35–37. If the Corporation did not meet in the Philosophy Room, it may possibly have met in the library or the College commons, both also in Harvard Hall, or at the president's house.

72. *Sibley's Harvard Graduates*, 18:293–297.

73. Bernhard, *Fisher Ames*, 342–343; *Sibley's Harvard Graduates*, 18:297–299.

74. Pearson informed the Corporation of his resignation on February 28, indicating that he knew Webber's election was imminent, although it did not formally occur until March 3. Pearson's resignation did not take effect until March 8. Corporation Records, 4:82–83; Eliphalet Pearson to the Harvard Corporation (draft), March 28, 1806, "Letters to 1803–1806," Eliphalet Pearson Papers, Harvard University Archives.

75. Wright, *Beginnings of Unitarianism*, 252–280.

76. McLoughlin, *New England Dissent*; Stephen A. Marini, *Radical Sects of Revolutionary New England* (Cambridge, Mass., 1982).

8. THE BEST AND THE BRIGHTEST

1. Worcester County Deeds, 245:197. For earlier instances when he called himself a "yeoman" or a "gentleman," see Worcester County Deeds, 128:294; 147:555; 156:162.

2. This number includes the ordained ministers, pulpit supplies, divinity students, missionaries, and chaplains in 1785 tallied in table 12. It also includes Eliphalet Pearson, who was ordained during the opening ceremonies of Andover Theological Seminary in 1808; William Scales, an itinerant never ordained; Samuel Wheeler, who preached in Topsfield for a year but left under a cloud before ordination; Ebenezer Allen, who was not ordained until 1792; and four who had died by 1785: Joseph Crosby, Daniel Adams, Nathaniel Morey, and Benjamin Muzzy. It does not include Joshua Armsby. Thirty–four were Congregationalists. One man, Benjamin Lovell, was ordained by the Church of England. *Sibley's Harvard Graduates*, 18:451–456.

3. Jabez Chickering (1753–1812), A.B. 1774. *Sibley's Harvard Graduates*, 18:321–327, 392–394, 395–405.

4. Calculated from *Sibley's Harvard Graduates*, vols. 17 and 18. Zedekiah Sanger, class of 1771, served two Massachusetts churches—Duxbury, which he left for health reasons after nine years, and Bridgewater, which he took up after recuperating for three years and served for another thirty. This tally considers Sanger's two settlements separately. It does not include Benjamin Lovell's placements in the Church of England, which were numerous and of uncertain length.

5. Daniel Adams (1747–1777), A.B. 1774. *Sibley's Harvard Graduates*, 18:360–361.

6. *Sibley's Harvard Graduates*, 18:360–361, 210–215.

7. *Sibley's Harvard Graduates*, 17:514–520, 570–580.

8. Josiah Badcock (1752–1831), A.B. 1772. *Sibley's Harvard Graduates*, 18:5–8.

John R. Eastman, *History of the Town of Andover, New Hampshire, 1751–1906* (Concord, N.H., 1910), 76.

9. Franklin McDuffee, *History of the Town of Rochester, New Hampshire, from 1722 to 1890*, ed. and rev. Silvanus Hayward, 2 vols. (Manchester, N.H., 1892), 1:243.

10. Benjamin Thurston (1750–1804?), A.B. 1774. *Sibley's Harvard Graduates*, 18:511–516. Jonathan French, *Reminiscences of a Fifty-Years Pastorate: A Half-Century Discourse* (Portsmouth, N.H., 1852), 13–14.

11. Paul C. Nagel, *The Adams Women: Abigail & Louisa Adams, Their Sisters and Daughters* (New York, 1987), 60, 63.

12. *Sibley's Harvard Graduates*, 18:61–65, 389–390; John Pierce, Memoirs, 4:185–186, Massachusetts Historical Society.

13. *Diary of William Bentley, D.D.*, 4 vols. (Salem, 1905–1914), 2:264.

14. William B. Sprague, *Annals of the American Pulpit*, 9 vols. (New York, 1857–1869), 8:148.

15. Moses Hale (1749–1786), A.B. 1771. *Sibley's Harvard Graduates*, 17:523–524. Stephen Peabody, Diary, May 26, 1786, American Antiquarian Society, Worcester, Mass.

16. Samuel Phillips, Diary, Box 5, Folder 4, Phillips Papers, Phillips Academy, Andover, Mass.

17. Samuel Phillips, Diary.

18. Sprague, *Annals of the American Pulpit*, 2:148–149.

19. William Scales (1741–1807), A.B. 1771. *Sibley's Harvard Graduates*, 17:627–630.

20. William Scales, *Priestcraft Exposed from Its Foundations* (Danvers, Mass., 1781), 15.

21. *Sibley's Harvard Graduates*, 17:628; Alan Taylor, *Liberty Men and Great Proprietors: The Revolutionary Settlement on the Maine Frontier, 1760–1820* (Chapel Hill, 1990), 148–151.

22. William Scales, *The Confusion of Babel Discovered* (n.p., 1780), 46–47, 63, v, quoted in Taylor, *Liberty Men and Great Proprietors*, 149.

23. *Diary of William Bentley*, 1:146.

24. *Collections of the Maine Historical Society*, 2nd ser., 22:393.

25. Stephen Peabody, Diary, April 15, 1794, American Antiquarian Society, Worcester, Mass.

26. On the Warren family, see Rhoda Truax, *The Doctors Warren of Boston: First Family of Surgery* (Boston, 1968).

27. Samuel Jennison, Sr., to Samuel Jennison, Jr., April 19, 1813, Belcher-Jennison-Weiss Papers, Massachusetts Historical Society. On the role of the cashier in early-nineteenth-century banks, see Naomi R. Lamoreaux, *Insider Lending: Banks, Personal Connections, and Economic Development in Industrial New England* (Cambridge, 1994), 3–4.

28. John Trumbull to John Trumbull Ray, July 10, 1811, quoted in *The Autobiography of Colonel John Trumbull: Patriot-Artist, 1756–1843*, ed. Theodore Sizer (New Haven, 1953), 341.

29. Eliphalet Pearson to Henry B. Pearson, March 8, 1813, Henry Bromfield Pearson Papers, Manuscripts and Archives, Yale University Library.

30. James Bowdoin to James Bowdoin Temple, September 11, 1803, James Bowdoin III Letterbook 1, Bowdoin Family Papers, George J. Mitchell Department of Special Collections & Archives, Bowdoin College Library.

31. Charles C. Calhoun, *A Small College in Maine: Two Hundred Years of Bowdoin College* (Brunswick, Me., 1993), 18.

32. James Bowdoin to Bowdoin College Overseers, June 27, 1794, *Collections of the Massachusetts Historical Society*, 7th ser., 6:210–212.

33. James Bowdoin to James Bowdoin Temple, September 11, 1803, and Bowdoin to James Temple Bowdoin, September 17, 1805, James Bowdoin III Letterbook 1, Bowdoin Family Papers.

34. James Bowdoin to James Bowdoin Temple, May 19, 1804, James Bowdoin III Letterbook 1; Bowdoin to Thomas Dickason, November 8, 1808, James Bowdoin III Letterbook II, Bowdoin Family Papers.

35. James Bowdoin to James Temple Bowdoin, May 11, July 3, 1808, James Bowdoin III Letterbook II, Bowdoin Family Papers.

36. James Bowdoin to James Temple Bowdoin, February 27, 1809, James Bowdoin III Letterbook II, Bowdoin Family Papers.

37. James Bowdoin to James Temple Bowdoin, February 27, 1809, James Bowdoin III Letterbook II, Bowdoin Family Papers.

38. Linda J. Docherty, "Preserving Our Ancestors: The Bowdoin Portrait Collection," in *The Legacy of James Bowdoin III* (Brunswick, Me., 1994), 72–73.

39. Docherty, "Preserving Our Ancestors," 73.

40. *Sibley's Harvard Graduates,* 18:123–127.

41. *Sibley's Harvard Graduates,* 18:27–33.

42. *Pioneer and General History of Geauga County* (Burton, Ohio, 1880), 604–607.

43. John Trumbull to Thomas Jefferson, June 11, 1789, Charles Allen Munn Collection, Fordham University Library, Bronx, New York.

44. See Holly Heinzer, "Virtue, Heroism, and Character: The Military Paintings of John Trumbull and Nation Formation in the Early Republic," seminar paper, Yale University, 1998.

45. Jules David Prown, "John Trumbull as History Painter," in *John Trumbull: The Hand and Spirit of a Painter,* ed. Helen A. Cooper (New Haven, 1982), 31–38.

46. John Trumbull to David Trumbull, January 31, 1786, John Trumbull Papers, Connecticut Historical Society, Hartford, quoted in Cooper, *John Trumbull,* 8.

47. Abigail Adams to Elizabeth Smith Shaw, March 4, 1786, Adams Papers, Massachusetts Historical Society.

48. Irma Jaffe, *John Trumbull: Patriot–Artist of the American Revolution* (Boston, 1975), 91.

49. Jaffe, *John Trumbull,* 123–139.

50. *Autobiography of Colonel John Trumbull,* 171–172.

51. *Sibley's Harvard Graduates,* 18:342.

52. *Sibley's Harvard Graduates,* 18:343.

53. *Sibley's Harvard Graduates,* 18:368, 375.

54. *Sibley's Harvard Graduates,* 18:378, 128, 17:499.

55. Tamara Plakins Thornton, *Cultivating Gentlemen: The Meaning of Country Life among the Boston Elite, 1785–1860* (New Haven, 1989), 24–26.

56. Thornton, *Cultivating Gentlemen,* 215–216, 63n.

57. Levi Lincoln, Jr., *Address, Delivered Before the Worcester Agricultural Society, October 7, 1819* (Worcester, 1819), 4.

58. Sarah Pearson to Ephraim Abbot, April 10, 1826, Bromfield Family Papers, Manuscripts and Archives, Yale University Library.

59. [Lyman Beecher,] *The Rights of the Congregational Churches of Massachusetts* (Boston, 1827), 4; [John Lowell,] *The Rights of the Congregational Parishes of Massachusetts* (Boston, 1827), 7.

60. *Sibley's Harvard Graduates*, 18:30–32.

61. *Sibley's Harvard Graduates*, 18:30–32.

9. The Last Great Change

1. David Stinson (1744–1769), class of 1771. *Sibley's Harvard Graduates*, 17:634–635. The population of Georgetown was 1,329 in 1765. It grew to 1,700 by the start of the Revolution. Evarts B. Greene and Virginia D. Harrington, *American Population before the Federal Census of 1790* (New York, 1932), 27; James S. Leamon, *Revolution Downeast: The War for American Independence in Maine* (Amherst, 1993), 9.

2. *Massachusetts Gazette and Boston News-Letter*, March 29, 1770.

3. Jonathan Allen, *A Sermon Delivered December 31st, 1794, at the Funeral of Mrs Mehitabel Dutch* (Haverhill, 1795), 3.

4. John Warren to John C. Warren, January 21, 1801, John C. Warren Papers, Massachusetts Historical Society.

5. David Hackett Fischer estimates the average age of death for American men in 1750 at about 52 and in 1800 at about 56; see *Growing Old in America* (1977; Oxford, 1978), 279. In Andover, more than half the men born between 1700 and 1729 died before the age of 60. The average age at death for men born in the town's fourth generation—in most instances between 1730 and 1759—was 59.8. See Philip J. Greven, Jr., *Four Generations: Population, Land, and Family in Colonial Andover, Massachusetts* (Ithaca, 1970), 192–194. The age at death for men in New England may have declined from the healthier seventeenth century. Gloria L. Main finds that in the late seventeenth century the average age was 63 or 64; see *Peoples of a Spacious Land: Families and Cultures in Colonial New England* (Cambridge, Mass., 2001), 168–169. Clayne L. Pope calculates, however, that for those born between 1750 and 1759, men at age twenty could expect to live an additional 44.3 years; see his "Adult Mortality in America before 1900: A View from Family Histories," in *Strategic Factors in Nineteenth-Century American Economic History: A Volume to Honor Robert W. Fogel* (Chicago, 1992), 277. Also see Herbert S. Klein, *A Population History of the United States* (Cambridge, 2004), 55–56, 99–103.

6. See tables 29, 30.

7. See tables 31, 32.

8. See tables 33, 34.

9. *Sibley's Harvard Graduates*, 17:669.

10. *Collections of the Massachusetts Historical Society*, 2nd ser., 1:247–248; John Lathrop, *The Gracious Appointment of God, a Sound Foundation of Comfort and Hope* (Boston, 1813), 16. John Eliot echoed his father, Andrew, who had faced death in 1778 saying, "I have finished my course with joy.... [God's] will be done." John Eliot to Jeremy Belknap, October 5, 1778, *Collections of the Massachusetts Historical Society*, 54:131.

11. *Sibley's Harvard Graduates*, 18:348.

12. Winfred E. A. Bernhard, *Fisher Ames: Federalist and Statesman, 1758–1808* (Chapel Hill, 1965), 348.

13. Bernhard, *Fisher Ames*, 255–329.

14. John Alford Mason (run over by milk cart), Jonathan Norwood (drowning), Joseph Pearse Palmer (fall), David Stinson (exposure), Edward Kitchen Turner (lost at sea), Phillips White (lost at sea), Theodore Parsons (lost at sea), William Jennison (fall), Benjamin Muzzy (lost at sea), Onesiphorus Tileston (drowning), and Bela Whipple (lost at sea). See *Sibley's Harvard Graduates*, 17:555, 566, 590, 634–635, 650; 18:188–189, 274–275, 445, 458, 518, 535.

15. The suicides were Samuel Ruddock, Thomas Sanders, and Martin Leavitt. William Caldwell, who tried to kill himself, was not successful but so weakened himself that his wounds may have led to his death a short time later. The number of suicides was extraordinarily high, although the proximate causes, to the extent that they can be determined, show no clear pattern. The toll of successful attempts approached a rate equivalent to 1,500 per 100,000. By comparison with the revolutionary generation's suicide record, the suicide rate in Massachusetts in 1998 was 8.2 per 100,000. For modern statistics from the American Association of Suicidology, see *Boston Globe*, January 2, 2001, A9. For Ruddock, Sanders, Leavitt, and Caldwell, see *Sibley's Harvard Graduates*, 18:145, 148, 229, 251.

16. William Vinal and Edward Hill. *Sibley's Harvard Graduates*, 17:654–655, 18: 102.

17. Daniel Adams. *Sibley's Harvard Graduates*, 18:361.

18. Clement Weeks. *Sibley's Harvard Graduates*, 18:182.

19. Nathaniel Walker Appleton. *Sibley's Harvard Graduates*, 18:208.

20. Thomas Rice Willard. *Sibley's Harvard Graduates*, 18:536.

21. John Barnard Swett, Isaiah Doane. *Sibley's Harvard Graduates*, 17:637–638, 18:411.

22. James Bowdoin to Jesse Putnam, March 12, 1803, quoted in Kenneth E. Carpenter, "James Bowdoin III as Library Builder," in Katherine J. Watson et al., *The Legacy of James Bowdoin III* (Brunswick, Me., 1994), 103.

23. Robert L. Volz, *Governor Bowdoin and His Family* (Brunswick, Me., 1969), 83–84.

24. Richard H. Saunders III, "James Bowdoin III," *Legacy of James Bowdoin III*, 25; *Sibley's Harvard Graduates*, 17:499–500.

25. Patricia McGraw Anderson, *The Architecture of Bowdoin College* (Brunswick, Me., 1988), 25.

26. Edward Hill (1755–1775), A.B. 1772. *Sibley's Harvard Graduates*, 18:100–102, 533.

27. *Publications of the Colonial Society of Massachusetts*, 8:316.

28. *Publications of the Cambridge Historical Society* 3 (1908): 66, 75; *Continental Journal*, May 18, 1780.

29. Bernhard, *Fisher Ames*, 219, 302–304.

30. John C. Warren, *Genealogy of Warren* (Boston, 1854), 51.

31. *Sibley's Harvard Graduates*, 18:108–117.

32. John Collins Warren was adjunct professor of surgery from 1809 to 1815, Hersey Professor of Anatomy and Surgery from 1815 to 1847, and Hersey Professor Emeritus from 1847 until his death in 1856. He served as dean of Harvard Medical School from 1816 to 1819. *Quinquennial Catalogue of the Officers and Graduates of Harvard University, 1636–1905* (Cambridge, Mass., 1905), 33, 94, 146.

33. Quoted in Helen A. Cooper, *John Trumbull: The Hand and Spirit of a Painter* (New Haven, 1982), 19.

34. Bayard Tuckerman, ed., *The Diary of Philip Hone* (New York, 1889), 2:200–201.

35. See table 34.

36. The six were: Samuel Nye (88) and William Vassall (90), both class of 1771; Abner Morgan (91) and James (Ivers) Trecothick (89), both 1773; and Joseph Hall (88) and Laban Wheaton (92), both 1774. *Sibley's Harvard Graduates*, 17:568, 653–654; 18:261–264, 328–331, 431–433, 526–534.

37. See W. Andrew Achenbaum, *Old Age in the New Land: The American Experience since 1790* (Baltimore, 1978), 2–3.

38. Oswald Rodriguez Roque, "Trumbull's Portraits," in Cooper, *John Trumbull*, 103. Trumbull was well aware that his skills had deteriorated. See Irma B. Jaffe, *John Trumbull: Patriot-Artist of the American Revolution* (Boston, 1975), 198.

39. Roque, "Trumbull's Portraits," 103.

40. See Patricia Mullan Burnham, "Trumbull's Religious Paintings: Themes and Variations," in Cooper, *John Trumbull*, 180–204.

41. Jaffe, *John Trumbull*, 234–263.

42. Jaffe, *John Trumbull*, 234–263.

43. Jaffe, *John Trumbull*, 224–226, 246–248.

44. John Trumbull to Benjamin Silliman, November 30, 1831, John Trumbull Papers, Manuscripts and Archives, Yale University Library.

45. Jaffe, *John Trumbull*, 285–286.

46. Trumbull's last works include *Christ Crowned with Thorns*, a copy after Titian completed about 1840. See Theodore Sizer, *The Works of Colonel John Trumbull: Artist of the American Revolution*, rev. ed. (New Haven, 1967), 110. Jaffe, *John Trumbull*, 286, reports that by 1841, Trumbull "seems to have given up painting and drawing completely, conserving the strength of his good eye to correct the proofs of his book."

47. Since most New Englanders were self-employed and their occupational activities are not well recorded, it is difficult to determine when they typically stopped working. Of the members of the revolutionary generation who received a salary, the majority were clergymen. Most ministers occupied their pulpits until they died, although in their sixties and seventies a few shared their duties with younger colleagues. Two ministers, Joseph Avery of Holden and Zedekiah Sanger of Bridgewater, formally retired, both at seventy. Most who held town offices gave them up in their fifties or sixties, although William Eustis assumed the governorship of Massachusetts at age sixty-nine. Others who may have retired in addition to Trumbull, Avery, and Sanger include John Frothingham, David Osgood, Samuel Phillips, John Tracy, John Lindall Borland, Daniel Chaplin, Thomas Aston Coffin, John Hastings, Levi Lincoln, Samuel Smith, Clement Weeks, Thomas Welsh, Jeremiah Barnard, Daniel Parker (1773), Eliphalet Pearson, James (Ivers) Trecothick, Jonathan Allen, Joseph Allen, Fisher Ames, Samuel Jennison, William Jennison, Robert Junkins, John Rice, and John Tucker. *Sibley's Harvard Graduates*, 17:521, 579, 603–604, 649; 18:17, 32, 48–49, 88–89, 127–128, 160, 182, 187–188, 214–215, 269, 301–302, 330–331, 365, 366, 377–379, 442, 444–445, 449, 478, 522. On retirement, see Carole Haber, *Beyond Sixty-Five: The Dilemma of Old Age in America's Past* (Cambridge, 1983), 18–20; and Main, *Peoples of a Spacious Land*, 167. On Avery and Sanger, see *Sibley's Harvard Graduates*, 17:476, 613.

48. Leonard Woods, *History of Andover Theological Seminary* (Boston, 1885).

49. Despite Pearson's resignation from the seminary's faculty, he remained chair-

man of the board of Phillips Academy. Since the academy's board also oversaw the seminary, Pearson remained involved with the institution until his resignation in 1821.

50. *Sibley's Harvard Graduates*, 18:301–302.

51. *Sibley's Harvard Graduates*, 18:301–302.

52. *Sibley's Harvard Graduates*, 18:302.

53. Henry B. Pearson to Ephraim Abbot, January 8, 1824, Bromfield Family Papers, Manuscripts and Archives, Yale University Library.

54. Sarah Pearson to Ephraim Abbot, April 10, 1826, Bromfield Family Papers, Manuscripts and Archives, Yale University Library.

55. *Sibley's Harvard Graduates*, 18:302–303.

56. Lincoln County Probate Records, 23:93–94, 221; 21:316, 519; 24:362, 663; 28:64–65.

57. *Philadelphia Directory* (1814, 1830); John Pierce, Memoirs, 7:230, Massachusetts Historical Society; will, February 12, 1838, microfilm copy, Historical Society of Pennsylvania, Philadelphia.

58. *Sibley's Harvard Graduates*, 18:89.

59. Rufus Emery, comp., *Genealogical Records of Descendants of John and Anthony Emery, of Newbury, Mass.* (Salem, 1890), 20.

60. Revolutionary War Pension File no. S3502, National Archives, Washington, D.C.

61. Bernhard, *Fisher Ames*, 349; Helen R. Pinkney, *Christopher Gore, Federalist of Massachusetts, 1758–1827* (Waltham, 1969), 89.

62. For an account of the procession and service, see Bernhard, *Fisher Ames*, 348–351.

63. Henry B. Pearson to Ephraim Abbot, September 29, 1826, Bromfield Family Papers, Manuscripts and Archives, Yale University Library.

64. This discussion of funerals and the rites surrounding them depends heavily on Gary Laderman, *The Sacred Remains: American Attitudes toward Death, 1799–1883* (New Haven, 1996), esp. 29–38. See also Jack Larkin, *The Reshaping of Everyday Life, 1790–1840* (New York, 1988), 98–104; and Main, *Peoples of a Spacious Land*, 184–185.

65. Moses Adams (1749–1819), A.B. 1771. *Sibley's Harvard Graduates*, 17:468–471.

66. *Columbian Centinel*, February 17, 1813; William B. Sprague, *Annals of the American Pulpit*, 9 vols. (New York, 1857–1869), 8:95.

67. *Columbian Centinel*, February 9, 12, 1825.

68. *Sibley's Harvard Graduates*, 17:500.

69. *Diary of William Bentley, D.D.*, 4 vols. (Salem, 1905–1914), 2:264.

70. Samuel Fales (1750–1818), A.B. 1773. *Sibley's Harvard Graduates*, 18:233–236. Samuel Hopkins Emery, *History of Taunton, Massachusetts* (Syracuse, N.Y., 1893), 301.

71. Worcester Historical Society Publications, n.s., 1 (1928–29):152.

72. *Sibley's Harvard Graduates*, 18:304. On Sally Pearson's reliance on the Bible, see Sarah Pearson to Ephraim Abbot, September 21, 1826, Bromfield Family Papers, Manuscripts and Archives, Yale University Library.

73. Tabulated from the entries in *Sibley's Harvard Graduates*, vols. 17 and 18. Figures for children of the class of 1771 take into account the genealogical sources included in the footnotes.

74. Box 1, Folder 7, Sheafe Family Papers, New Hampshire Historical Society, Concord; *Biographical and Historical Sketches of the Sheafe, Wentworth, Fisher, Bache, Satterwhite, and Rutgers Families of America* (n.p., 1923), 59.

75. Richard B. Lyman, Jr., " 'What Is Done in My Absence?': Levi Lincoln's Oakham, Massachusetts, Farm Workers, 1807–20," *Proceedings of the American Antiquarian Society* 99 (1989): 159.

76. Norfolk County Probate File no. 6297.

77. Rockingham County Probate File no. 9809 o.s.

78. Estates for the classes of 1772, 1773, and 1774 have been systematically pursued. Insolvent members included Thomas Burnham and Joshua Bailey Osgood, both class of 1772; William Caldwell, Oliver Peabody, Joshua Plummer, and Abel Whitney, all 1773; and Joseph Emerson and John Tucker, 1774. *Sibley's Harvard Graduates*, 18:22, 140, 229, 283, 306, 350, 419, 522.

79. York County Probate File no. 16:498–502.

80. Lincoln County Probate Records, 23:93–94, 221; 21:316, 519; 24:362, 663; 28:64–65.

81. Essex County Probate File no. 1737.

82. *Pioneer and General History of Geauga County* (Burton, Ohio, 1880), 604–606.

83. For an interesting account of the postrevolutionary changes in American life, see Joyce Appleby, *Inheriting the Revolution: The First Generation of Americans* (Cambridge, Mass., 2000).

EPILOGUE

1. *Boston Courier*, September 2, 1837.

2. Ralph Waldo Emerson, "The American Scholar," in *The Collected Works of Ralph Waldo Emerson*, ed. Robert E. Spiller and Albert R. Ferguson, 6 vols. to date (Cambridge, Mass., 1971–), 1:52.

3. Emerson, "American Scholar," 57, 61, 67.

4. In addition to the sources cited above, this account draws on the following: John Pierce, Memoirs, Massachusetts Historical Society, 7:155–156; Bliss Perry, *The Praise of Folly and Other Papers* (Boston, 1923), 81–113; Henry Nash Smith, "Emerson's Problem of Vocation: A Note on the 'American Scholar,'" *New England Quarterly* 12 (1939): 52–67; John McAleer, *Ralph Waldo Emerson: Days of Encounter* (Boston, 1984), 234–239; Robert D. Richardson, Jr., *Emerson: The Mind on Fire* (Berkeley, 1995), 262–265.

5. *Sibley's Harvard Graduates*, vols. 17, 18.

6. *Sibley's Harvard Graduates*, 18:532–533. On the early history of Wheaton College, see Paul C. Helmreich, *Wheaton College, 1834–1957: A Massachusetts Family Affair* (New York, 2002), chaps. 1–3.

7. *A Catalogue of the Officers and Students of Harvard University for the Academical Year 1836–7* (Cambridge, Mass., 1836), 22.

APPENDIX

1. See Howard P. Chudacoff, *How Old Are You?: Age Consciousness in American Culture* (Princeton, 1989); Carole Haber, *Beyond Sixty-Five: The Dilemma of Old Age in America's Past* (Cambridge, 1983), 4–5.

2. Erik H. Erikson, *Childhood and Society*, 2nd ed., rev. and enl. (New York, 1963), 247–274. For another example of the life-cycle approach, one that has influenced this book at many junctures, see Daniel J. Levinson, *The Seasons of a Man's Life* (New York, 1978).

3. Interesting and influential examples of research into the life course include George Alter, *Family and the Female Life Course: The Women of Verviers, Belgium, 1849–1880* (Madison, 1988); Glen H. Elder, Jr., *Children of the Great Depression* (Chicago, 1974); and Tamara K. Hareven, *Family Time and Industrial Time: The Relationship between the Family and Work in a New England Industrial Community* (Cambridge, 1982).

4. Gloria L. Main recognizes a series of physiological steps that must inevitably have taken place, including weaning, teething, and the maturing of the digestive tract and the immune system; see *Peoples of a Spacious Land: Families and Cultures in Colonial New England* (Cambridge, Mass., 2001), 118.

INDEX

Page references given in *italics* indicate illustrations or information contained in their captions.

Abbott, Ephraim, 141
Adams, Abigail, 74, 103, 258n1
Adams, Charles, 104
Adams, Daniel, 179, 276n2
Adams, Henry, 23, 41, 55, 60–61
Adams, John: early ambitions of, 22, 177; on gentlemen, 23; as legal mentor, 119, 142; marriage of, 74; wartime diplomatic missions of, 104, 126
Adams, John Quincy, 104, 126, 152
Adams, Moses, 208
Adams, Samuel, 161
African Americans, as merchants, 244n40
agricultural societies, 190
agriculture, 69, 189–90
Albany (N.Y.), 92
Allen, Ebenezer, 276n2
Allen, Jonathan, 281n47
Allen, Joseph, 281n47
All Men Will Not Be Saved Forever (Mather), 172
American Academy of Arts and Sciences, 149, 150, 198
American Education Society, 204, 215
American Revolution: American casualties during, 95, 261n70; artistic portrayals of, 134–35, 188, 201–2; battle experience during, 93–95; economic changes following, 113; economic hardships during, 102–3, 115, 118; end of, 107; Harvard during, 84–85, 101–2, 259n21; military service during, 91–93; noncombatant military service during, 91–92, 96–98, 103–4; nonpartisanship impossible during, 106–7; partisan decisions at outbreak of, 80–84, 89–91; political tensions preceding, 53–54, 75–78; postrevolutionary apathy about, 188–89; promotion of, 103–4; revolutionary gener-

ation deaths during, 258n3. *See also specific battles*
American Revolution, impact of, 4–6, 81, 114–15, 134–35, 221; on age patterns, 124–25; on career choices, 126–35; career disruptions, 69, 112–13, 115–19, 123–24, 267n83; on civic leadership opportunities, 137; on families, 98–101, 108, 115, 123–26, 257n79; job vacancies, 103–4, 129; on legacies, 212–15; on loyalists, 5, 98–101, 104–6, 121–23, 125, 257n79; on marriage, 124–26, 225; on ministry/clergymen, 98, 103, 116–18; on partisan politics, 103–4, 162, 226, 263n110; on residential patterns, 225–26; on soldiers, 4–5, 114–15, 125, 225, 265n33
Ames, Fisher, *163*; age of matriculation, 14, 225; agronomic disappointments of, 189–90, 193; career of, 5–6, 66, 68, 104; death of, 196, 197, 199, 206; early education of, 17, 26; family background of, 12, 168; as father, 139, 140; as Federalist, 162; funeral of, 206, 208; as Harvard president, 173, 176; health problems of, 138, 191; impact of Revolution on, 104; legacies of, 215; legal studies of, 62, 66; marriage of, 139; military service of, 114; political career of, 164–66, 167, 191; postgraduation occupation of, 61; religious partisanship of, 173; retirement of, 281n47; student activities of, 50, 51
Ames, Frances Worthington, 139, 199
Ames, Nathaniel, 164
Ames, William, 63
Ames, Worthington, 140
Amherst (N.H.) Social Library, 151
Andover (Mass.), 279n5, as cultural backwater, 46–47

CONRAD EDICK WRIGHT was born in Boston and raised in Cambridge, Massachusetts. He received an A.B. magna cum laude in history from Harvard College and earned A.M. and Ph.D. degrees in history from Brown University. He has taught at Brown University and the College of William and Mary. Wright has worked at the Institute of Early American History and Culture at Williamsburg, Virginia, and the New-York Historical Society. Since 1985 he has been on the staff of the Massachusetts Historical Society, where he is currently its Ford Editor of Publications. Wright has edited or co-edited seven volumes of essays and was the editor of the *Proceedings of the Massachusetts Historical Society* for fourteen years. He has also edited documentary material for the Society, including the forthcoming *Pedagogues and Protesters: The Student Diary of Stephen Peabody, 1767–1768*, and was the principal scholar for volume 18 of *Sibley's Harvard Graduates*. He is the author, in addition to *Revolutionary Generation*, of *The Transformation of Charity in Postrevolutionary New England* and a number of scholarly articles. Conrad Edick Wright lives in Medford, Massachusetts, with his wife, Mary, and two daughters.